EARTH

AN ALIEN ENTERPRISE

EARTH

AN ALIEN ENTERPRISE

THE SHOCKING TRUTH BEHIND
THE GREATEST COVER-UP IN HUMAN HISTORY

TIMOTHY GOOD

WITH A FOREWORD BY JONATHAN CAPLAN QC

PEGASUS BOOKS

NEW YORK LONDON

EARTH: AN ALIEN ENTERPRISE

Pegasus Books LLC
80 Broad Street, 5th Floor
New York, NY 10004

First Pegasus Books cloth edition November 2013
First Pegasus Books trade paperback edition November 2014

Interior design by Maria Fernandez

Library of Congress Cataloging-in-Publication Data is available.

ISBN: 978-1-60598-638-8

10 9 8 7 6 5 4 3 2

Printed in the United States of America
Distributed by W. W. Norton & Company

For Professor Stefano Breccia
(1945–2012)

CONTENTS

EARTH

AN ALIEN ENTERPRISE

FOREWORD

by Jonathan Caplan, QC

I n any democratic society, a process for the proper evaluation of evidence is essential, usually within the context of criminal or civil proceedings or of public or governmental inquiries. We are used to assessing the credibility and reliability of witnesses and of seeking corroborative evidence where possible. We know that even honest witnesses may be mistaken, and many people have been sentenced to life imprisonment or even the death penalty on the strength of a single uncorroborated witness.

The history of the UFO phenomenon, going back to Biblical times, is essentially a record of human testimony of lights, objects, or events that cover the spectrum from the unusual to the high strangeness of close encounters. No doubt the same can be said of paranormal phenomena. This record has its share of charlatans, those who are mistaken, and perhaps those who have been deceived by others—or even by themselves. But the fascinating feature of ufology is the core of honest, intelligent people in different eras and from different cultures all over the world, including many who are scientifically or aeronautically trained, who describe very similar objects or similar experiences of high strangeness which on any basis cannot be the product of a "black" research program. In many cases there are multiple witnesses or there is corroborative evidence in the form of photographic images, radar readings, or physical traces. For the lawyer, who too often has to make bricks out of straw, such a body of material represents a refreshingly strong case, particularly if examined in the same way in which we examine evidence in other contexts.

We cannot, of course, though, accept these accounts at face value. In the world we inhabit, all is often not what it seems, so how much more so in the world of ufology where our reference points, let alone our vocabulary, are wholly inadequate? This was the hard lesson of Shakespeare's Macbeth who, having interpreted literally the predictions of the three ethereal witches that strongly implied his future safety, was left dejectedly to ponder that the "instruments of darkness" often "win us to our harm" by half-truths and "with honest trifles."

And so to the question asked as long ago as 1955 by Captain Edward Ruppelt (the former head of the U.S. Air Force Project Bluebook): "What constitutes proof? Does a UFO have to land at the River Entrance to the Pentagon, near the Joint Chiefs of Staff offices?" The answer is no easier to provide after more than fifty years of further reports and investigations, despite the advent of the digital camera. UFOs seem to be a phenomenon that coexists with us and which is as baffling to an Israelite in the Sinai desert, or a medieval monk, or a modern fighter pilot or astronaut. That we are not alone is no longer in doubt. But at present that still remains an inference rather than a proven fact.

There are many powerful institutions that would balk at recognizing such proof even if a landing did occur at the Pentagon on prime-time television. The risk of destabilizing organized government and religion would be too great, and the risk of advanced technology falling into the wrong hands would be greater. In that event, who is to call the shots on whether proof exists or not, especially if key evidence is to be concealed or confuted? If we cannot expect official and honest recognition, then maybe only the people can decide on the basis of the "evidence" that is placed before them. Maybe the much-criticized "new age" culture is the only way to combat the clandestine secrecy that certainly surrounds this subject.

We owe the few reliable researchers like Timothy Good a huge acknowledgment because they keep the record of this phenomenon, which may be all that we can do, and they get it into the public consciousness.

I greatly admire the quality of his books and his perseverance. And I strongly suspect that the real value of his work will only be fully appreciated in years to come.

———

JONATHAN CAPLAN is a well-known lawyer practicing in London and has acted in many high-profile cases. He was appointed a Queen's Counsel in recognition of his standing in the profession. He has been interested in ufology for over forty years.

INTRODUCTION

A liens "have landed on Earth, infiltrated British and American nuclear missile sites and sabotaged weapons, according to U.S. Air Force officers," declared *The Daily Telegraph* in 2010, citing an extraordinary press conference held at the National Press Club in Washington, D.C. "Six retired officers and one former non-commissioned officer claim to have gathered witness testimonies from more than 120 military personnel revealing the infiltration of nuclear sites by aliens as recently as 2003. In some cases, nuclear missiles supposedly malfunctioned while a disc-shaped object hovered nearby."[1]

"We saw this thing—it was coming right at us and was as low as the car and huge," reported Bruce and Priscilla Wetherill in January 2012, two years after an incident which had occurred between Gainford and Barnard Castle, in the Teesdale area of England's Northern Pennines. "It was very frightening," admitted Priscilla. "Bruce kept driving but we both ducked down, expecting it to hit us. I thought, 'This is it. We've had it.'"

Described as saucer-shaped, dark on top but glowing underneath and soundless, the object also had "steel-like tentacles hanging down." At the last moment, it lifted up and narrowly missed the car before disappearing into the sky. The couple expected the car roof to have scratches, but none could be seen. "I'm a realist, but I know what I saw and it was unbelievable," said Mr. Wetherill. "If I lived to two hundred I would never see anything like it again." The couple came forward two years after the event, following a spate of sightings in Teesdale.[2]

Roy Shaw did not believe in aliens, ghosts, flying saucers—or anything he could not touch or explain. That is, until 2010—around the same period as the Wetherills' experience. At about 21:30 on February 6th, he encountered a large craft of unknown origin while walking his dog in Phear Park, Exmouth, Devon.

"The object was round in shape and about thirty feet in diameter and a hundred feet long, with blue and red flashing lights on its perimeter, and it appeared to land at the top end of the park by the bowling green," he described to local reporter Becca Gliddon. "My dog started to growl when what I can only describe as a white shape came toward us. It was about four feet high and seemed to be translucent, and moved very slowly toward us. I was transfixed because it made a droning sound. . . . I didn't know where the sound was coming from but it was coming straight toward me. I immediately ran back down through the park."

Mr. Shaw said the UFO seemed to hover over the hedge of the bowling green, then flew horizontally from left to right before immediately shooting off at high speed back to the left, at a 45-degree angle. It had "appeared from nowhere"—he did not see it actually land or fly overhead. His normally placid border collie dog ran away from it after baring its teeth at the approaching object. "I twisted my ankle when I ran like hell. My dog Syd kept whimpering and looking out of the bedroom window toward the park until at least two in the morning.

"I still can't believe what I saw and I am still in a state of shock. Syd doesn't like going back up there. Something put him off. Everybody thinks you are a crank when you report something like this. I am an engineer. I like to touch and feel things. If I can touch it, it exists, but there's no way I can explain this."[3]

Another dog-walker told Roy Shaw the following morning that he had also witnessed the incident.[4]

In August 2010, the Ministry of Defence released another of its voluminous (if often innocuous) files on reported UFO sightings and related correspondence. True to form, *The Times* remains behind the times—at least from an editorial standpoint—debunking the subject in its tendentious commentary on leading articles:

"In reality, there is exactly no evidence that Earth has ever been visited by spacecraft from other worlds, but reports of UFO sightings do form a pattern. They manifest the boundlessness of human credulity, which takes shifting forms in different ages but has a stubborn irrationalism at its core. . . . A culture of pseudoscience impoverishes the condition of the masses as well as the life of the mind."[5]

In late December 1980, an extraordinary series of incidents occurred in Rendlesham Forest, adjoining the twin U.S. Air Forces Europe NATO bases of Bentwaters and Woodbridge (81st Tactical Fighter Wing), near Ipswich, Suffolk. This well-known case—now dubbed "Britain's Roswell"—was first revealed in a front-page story in 1983.[6] On several nights, security patrolmen observed small, remotely controlled probes, which at one stage beamed rays of light at the Bentwaters nuclear weapons storage area (where at the time more nuclear weapons were stored than anywhere else in Europe). Lieutenant Colonel Charles I. Halt, a deputy base commander at the time, witnessed a number of these events. Most dramatically, an elongated triangular-shaped craft (associated with the smaller probes) landed in the forest in full view of a couple of security personnel, Staff Sergeant Jim Penniston and Airman First Class John Burroughs.[7] In response to Col. Halt's official memorandum to the Ministry of Defence at the time, detailing some of these events, the MoD has gone on the record stating repeatedly that the incidents were of "no defence significance." At the Washington conference cited earlier, Halt hit back:

"The security services of both the United States and the United Kingdom have attempted, both then and now, to subvert the significance of what occurred at RAF Bentwaters by the use of well-practiced methods of disinformation. The UFOs I saw were structured machines moving under intelligent control and operating beyond the realm of anything I have ever seen before or since. I believe the objects I saw were extra-terrestrial in origin."[8]

As admitted in Ministry of Defence documents released in early 2011, certain intelligence papers relating to the Rendlesham Forest incident have gone missing. "The files reveal the MoD received a request for its own records of the incident in 2000, but when officials looked they discovered a 'huge' gap where defence intelligence files relating to it should be," reported Neil Henderson of BBC News. "The hunt generated a series of notes, with one official speculating that 'it could be interpreted to mean that a deliberate attempt had been made to eradicate the records covering this incident.'"[9]

In 2011, U.S. Air Force Colonel Theodore "Ted" Conrad, base commander of Bentwaters and Woodbridge at the time of the multiple Rendlesham Forest incidents, provided David Clarke, a skeptic and adviser on UFO matters to the National Archives, with a series of statements condemning Halt's testimony. "We saw nothing that resembled Lt. Col. Halt's descriptions either in the sky or on the ground," he claimed. "We had people in position to validate Halt's narrative, but none of them could." There was no "hard evidence" of anything suspicious, he continued, adding that the Geiger counter radiation readings at the landing site were later found to indicate "normal" levels of radiation. All of which is strongly disputed by the witnesses and by Nick Pope, a former MoD UFO investigator who later requisitioned the relevant data proving otherwise.

Halt "should be ashamed and embarrassed by his allegation that his country and England both conspired to deceive their citizens over this issue," Conrad's diatribe—revealed in *The Sunday Telegraph*—continued. He also disputed the subsequent testimony of Penniston, a security policeman who was in the woods on the first night of the sightings and has since claimed he touched the alien spacecraft. "Although he cannot explain the subsequent accounts of his subordinates," reported Jasper Copping, "Col. Conrad said he thought the incident may have been a hoax."

"I don't think anyone, least of all Conrad, doubts that Halt and his men saw 'something,'" said Clarke. "They had an extraordinary experience [which] would remain extraordinary regardless of whether ultimately it was a lighthouse or poachers' lanterns—which has also been suggested. But Col. Conrad is responsible for the only proper investigation of this incident. He went to look and if there was anything to be seen, I cannot see how he could not have seen it."[10]

I have remained in contact with Col. Charles "Chuck" Halt periodically since the Rendlesham case was first revealed in 1983. "The fact is, [Conrad] never investigated," he told me when the article was published:

"I took Penniston, Burroughs and the others to him and then took him out into the forest (with his whole family). He didn't even know where the site was but now claims he was out there the day before. . . . Up until now he denied being in contact with me on that night and now he says he was, and was out in the yard. I guess he fails to remember telling me on the radio he could see something. He also doesn't know U.S. and U.K. radar picked up an object and the Bentwaters Tower Operators saw the object streak by and go down into the forest. My memo was typed in our office and he reviewed it and showed it to [Colonel Gordon] Williams before it was given to [Squadron Leader] Don Moreland. He and Williams wanted to stay at a distance. . . ."[11]

"Ted Conrad is either having memory problems, has his head in the sand, or continuing the cover-up," wrote Halt (in part) to Jasper Copping. "When I talked with Gordon Williams, neither he nor Conrad wanted their name mentioned with the incident. Thus, I was directed to get with Don Moreland (RAF) and see what he wanted as it was to become a British affair. I did so and he asked for a memo. I wrote it and it was typed by Conrad's Secretary. Conrad read it, showed it to Williams, and both approved. It was never meant for public dissemination. . . . I suppose having to look for details or the truth is less important than the 'story.' It's sad, but I've come to understand how the mainstream press works. Truth gives way to the 'Story.' Prove me wrong."[12] The letter was not published.

"I've heard many people say that it's time for the government to appoint an agency to investigate," said Halt during a conference on the subject at the National Atomic Testing Museum, New Mexico, in association with the Smithsonian Institution, in September 2012. "Folks, there *is* an agency, a very close-held, compartmentalized agency that's been investigating this for years, and there's a very active role played by many of our intelligence agencies that probably don't even know the details of what happens once they collect the data and forward it. . . . In the last couple of years, the British have released a ton of information, but has anybody ever seen what their conclusions were or heard anything about Bentwaters officially? When the documents were released, the timeframe when I was involved in the incident is missing. Nothing else is missing. . . ."[13]

In September 2010, a major airport in China was reportedly forced to close down following an intrusion by a UFO. The "flat and tubular" object hovered two miles from Bootee in Inner Mongolia. "Astonished officials say it then zoomed in to circle the airport before suddenly vanishing," reported *The Sun*. "Three flights from Beijing and Shanghai were diverted to nearby airports. It is the third mysterious UFO sighting this year to have resulted in Chinese airfields being closed. Xiaoshan, in Zhejiang province, shut for a few days in July after an 'oddly-shaped, twinkling bright light' was seen nearby. Another scare was reported in the summer at Hong Kong.

"The latest UFO was spotted by air traffic controllers in Inner Mongolia's capital Hoot on radar screens. But they could not make radio contact with it and immediately warned Bootee. A spokeswoman said: 'Aircraft had to land at secondary airports to avoid a collision.' The airport was closed for around an hour last month. The Chinese authorities have refused to comment but some experts believe the three sightings could be evidence of a new Chinese military aircraft."

Asked for a comment, Nick Pope declared: "Whatever you think about UFOs, there are serious national security and air safety issues involved."[14]

On August 3, 2011, Mike Sewell, a sports journalist for BBC Radio 5 Live, described his encounter with a flying craft while driving through the village of Cottered, near Buntingford, Hertfordshire, at 04:15 that morning. "There was this big bright light in the sky descending toward the road," he reported to Radio 5 Live presenter Nicky Campbell via his cell phone shortly afterwards. "It was certainly a kind of—and I dread saying this—disc shape. As it got closer, it then banked to the left [and] went across the countryside and just sat or circled a certain area above the field. I could see underneath it. It wasn't an aeroplane, and it wasn't a helicopter. . . . It had several lights flashing all around it." Underneath could be seen at least two large, soft white panel lights. A driver in front also observed the craft.[15, 16] A few hours later, I was interviewed by Nicky and offered my opinion that the craft might have been "one of ours."

On June 16, 2012, two glowing unidentified objects were reported to have buzzed the Shenzhou-9 spacecraft a few minutes after its launch in the Gobi Desert. The objects were recorded by an infrared video camera monitoring the launch and spotted on a screen at a control center in Beijing about four minutes after the Long March-2F rocket had blasted off from the Jiuquan Satellite Launch Centre in northwest China's Gansu Province.

According to Wang Sichao, an astronomer and UFO expert at Nanjing Purple Mountain Observatory of the Chinese Academy of Sciences, the objects "couldn't be planes, meteors, birds or separated parts from the rocket." The Shenzhou-9's crew of three included China's first female astronaut, Liu Yang.[17]

In November 2012, several international news outlets reported numerous sightings of UFOs by Indian Army troops in the Ladakh region of Jammu and Kashmir. And between August 1 and October 15 that year, an Indo-Tibetan border police force unit deployed in Thakung, near the Pangong Tso Lake, reported over a hundred sightings of "unidentified luminous objects" (ULOs). Apparently neither the Indian Army, the Indian Space Research Organization, the Defence Research Development Organization, nor the National Technical Research Organization were able to identify these objects. By day and night, the "yellow spheres" were seen to rise up on the horizon from the Chinese side of the border, gliding across the skies for three to four hours before disappearing. "Something is clearly wrong if our combined scientific resources can't explain the phenomena," said a senior Army official in Delhi. "These objects may be a crude psychological operation put forth by the Chinese or sophisticated probes to gauge India's defense preparedness in Ladakh." However, unmanned aerial vehicles (UAVs) and Chinese drones, at least, were ruled out.[18] To me, the most likely explanation could be the ubiquitous "Chinese lanterns," though their candle-powered flight duration is normally a great deal shorter than is described in the above report.

According to *Pravda* (Правда—"Truth"), half of the entire Chinese population believes in UFOs.[19] And hundreds, possibly thousands, of Chinese scientists are involved in research. Sun Shili, a former foreign minister official and chairman of the Beijing UFO Research Society, firmly believes extraterrestrials are living among us.[20] I share that view. In common with thousands of people around the world, I have had personal experiences, described herein.

In 2011, Nick Pope openly admitted to having been part of an official U.K. policy to ridicule UFO reports, in commenting on the release by the MoD in August of yet another huge batch of previously classified (mostly at a low grade) UFO-related reports, typically from members of the public, totaling about nine thousand pages covering the period from 1985 to 2007. During that period (1991–94), Nick was in charge of the official MoD unit. "What's abundantly clear from these files is that while in public we were desperately pushing the line that this was of no defense interest," he told the *Huffington Post*, "we couldn't say 'There's something in our air space; pilots see them; they're tracked on radar; sometimes we scramble jets to chase these things, but we can't catch them.' This would be an admission that we'd lost control of our own air space, and such an admission would be untenable. . . .

"To really achieve our policy of downplaying the UFO phenomenon, we would use a combination of 'spin and dirty tricks.' We used terms like 'UFO buffs' and 'UFO spotters'—terms that mean these people are nut-jobs. In other words, we were implying that this is just a very somewhat quaint hobby that people have, as opposed to a serious research interest. . . . Another trick would be deliberately using phrases like 'little green men.' We were trying to do two things: either to kill any media story on the subject, or, if a media story ran, ensure that it ran in such a way that it would make the subject seem ridiculous and that it would make people who were interested in this seem ridiculous."

Nick Pope further admits that he may have been the one who drafted actual MoD statements contributing to the ridicule policy. "If it was my words, then I apologize, I'm very sorry for that," he confessed. "I believe in open government and freedom of information. I believe that the UFO phenomenon does raise important defence, national security, and air safety issues, and if I helped kill any initiative on that, I'm deeply sorry. . . ."[21]

As Stephen Bassett, director of Paradigm Research Group, quips: "It's not just about lights in the sky: it's about lies on the ground."

In recent years, by way of demeaning the subject, the media frequently belittles those involved in UFO research as "conspiracy theorists." But conspiracies there are, and researchers are justified in theorizing thereon.

In 2012, Nick Pope commented publicly on an extraordinary photo of a UFO received at the MoD. "The saga began on 4 August 1990 when two members of the public out walking in the vicinity of Calvine, near Pit-lochry, in Scotland, sighted a massive, diamond-shaped, metallic UFO. The UFO was virtually stationary and hovered silently for what the witnesses believe was several minutes, before accelerating away vertically at massive speed. During the sighting, a military aircraft, believed to be a Harrier, was seen, but it wasn't clear if it was escorting the craft, attempting to intercept it, or whether the pilot was ever aware of it at all.

"A number of color photographs were taken and passed to the *Scottish Daily Record*, who in turn contacted the MoD, probably because they were seeking a comment for the story. It's not clear what happened next, because I didn't join the MoD's UFO project until 1991 and this investigation was handled by my predecessor. It seems that, somehow, MoD managed to persuade the reporter to part with not just the photos, but the negatives.

"The photos were then sent to the Defence Intelligence Staff (DIS) who then sent them on to imagery analysis at JARIC (Joint Air Reconnaissance Intelligence Centre). Yet at the time, MoD hadn't even publicly acknowledged that there was any intelligence interest in UFOs at all. The whole situation was positively Orwellian. On the one hand, our line to Parliament, the media, and the public was that UFOs were of 'no defence significance.' We implied and sometimes stated that we didn't 'investigate' UFOs, but merely 'examined sightings to see if anything reported was of any defence interest'—as if the two were somehow different!

"So why the MoD interest and secrecy? Though we'd never say so publicly, the bottom line was that we wanted the technology. . . . I first came across this story in 1991, when I joined the UFO project. A poster-sized enlargement of the best photo was prominently displayed on the office wall [and] I asked my DIS opposite number about the image. I was told that the official assessment was that the photos were real and the craft had a diameter of around 25 meters (over 80 feet). At one particularly surreal briefing on the UFO phenomenon, my DIS opposite number indicated the photo and pointed his finger to the right: 'It's not the Americans,' he said before pointing to the left and saying 'and it's not the Russians.' There was a pause, before he concluded 'and that only leaves. . . .'—his voice trailed off and he didn't complete the sentence, but his finger was pointing directly upwards. . . .

"What happened next? The suspicion was that someone had shredded the photo, but whatever the truth of the matter, it was never seen again. . . . Despite the various media interviews that I did on this story, and associated public appeals, the witnesses have never come forward. Neither has anyone at the *Scottish Daily Record* (or any other Scottish newspaper) come forward to say that they worked on this story back in 1990. . . . In their desperation to acquire the photos/negatives (and maybe kill the story), maybe DIS staff somehow tricked the journalist into handing over all the material and never gave it back. If the journalist hadn't briefed the editor, he may have stayed silent out of embarrassment. Similarly, maybe the witnesses were told that it would be better if they didn't discuss what they'd seen and took this as a threat. . . .

"I don't know if the photos or negatives will ever turn up, but I certainly hope they do. Because whatever people's views on UFOs, these are the photos that changed the minds of numerous skeptical civil servants, military personnel, and intelligence specialists. I should know. I was one of them."[22]

The Ministry of Defence claims that it no longer investigates UFO reports.

Interestingly, on November 5, 2012, a "diamond-shaped" UFO in Pitlochry was filmed several times on video and mobile phone by Adrian Musat, a Romanian chef. At 07:30, while looking out of the window of his flat, he spotted the object hovering above Clunie Wood. "I saw this light pulsing about a mile away," he told a reporter. "It wasn't on the ground but floating above the trees and moving left to right, [then forty minutes later] just disappeared, as if it 'switched off.'"

Later that day, at around 17:00, Musat saw the object again. "For about twenty-five minutes I saw a small red cloud above the object. All the other clouds were moving across the sky, but this one stayed above the object all the time. It stayed until after 6 P.M. It didn't make any noise." He described the craft as being around five meters wide and changing color.

"I'm a little skeptical on this one," commented Nick Pope. "Many diamond-shaped UFOs turn out to be caused by a camera effect. When people zoom in on a bright light source, the iris opening creates a diamond-shaped image which is effectively superimposed on to the light."[23] Correct—in some cases. But the fact remains that an unknown craft was seen on two occasions that day by several witnesses. And some of the images clearly reveal a structured craft.

"Belief in the alien phenomenon is now more widespread than ever, with many wondering how we and our governments would react to the news that aliens existed," declared Nick in October 2012, during his promotion of a new video game. He also maintains that figures show that twenty percent of the U.K. believe UFOs have landed.[24]

It is unfortunate that the acronym "UFO" has become synonymous with "alien spacecraft." Hence, the commonly asked question "Do you believe in UFOs?" is redundant in this context. A UFO is an "unidentified flying object" per se. It *may* be an alien craft, but in the vast majority of cases—90% or more—it turns out to be nothing of the sort. Conventional aircraft (and/or their landing lights), balloons, planets (such as Venus), stars and satellites, the International Space Station, and so on account for many observations. And in recent years, a proliferation of "Chinese lanterns" is responsible for the large percentage of sightings appearing in the local and national newspaper reports I regularly receive from my press-cutting agency and other sources. I should also mention here the presence of "USOs"—unidentified submergible objects—which continue to be reported in our seas.[25]

This book examines in-depth claims that the United States in particular, and some other countries, including the U.K., have developed advanced spacecraft, thanks partly to the recovery of a number of crashed alien vehicles and, more comprehensively, an alien liaison program. I also feature numerous reports of encounters and contacts with aliens of varying types, many of them published here for the first time. As will become evident, some of these aliens have our best interests at heart. Others do not. We are not the only ones with a vested interest in Earth.

Earth: An Alien Enterprise is dedicated to Professor Stefano Breccia, who sadly died prematurely in March 2012. One of the most remarkable men I have ever met, Stefano magnanimously provided me with an abundance of information relating to the "Amicizia" group of aliens and those humans collaborating with them, described herein. His extraordinary acumen has widened my horizons, as no other, to the complex panoramas of this multi-faceted subject. . . .

PART ONE

CHAPTER ONE
ENVIRONMENTAL SURVEY

I t was a late afternoon in the summer of 1932. A mile and a half east of Killdeer, North Dakota, two farm boys, twelve-year-old Leo Dworshak and his younger brother Mike, had finished their chores for the day and were exploring a grassy hilltop near the farm. It was little Mike who first spotted a strange object in the valley below.

"It was a huge, round thing," Leo recounts in his remarkable book, *UFOs Are With Us—Take My Word*.[1] "We just stood there gaping at it and began excitedly discussing what it was doing down there and trying our best to understand just what we were seeing. It was silvery, and although it was probably more than half a mile away, we could tell it was certainly as big as our barn, maybe even bigger. It appeared to be perfectly round [and] I counted many different colors of light on it that came from a band around the edge.

"I thought it must be a machine because it was rotating in a complicated way. The flashing colored lights formed an outer shell, like a band or belt that went completely around it at the widest point and was turning one way. The inner shell seemed to be standing still or perhaps turning the other way. . . . It was totally silent and produced no cloud of exhaust fumes or smoke.

"We stood there on the hilltop for some time, just watching that incredible machine. . . . Then we decided to try to get closer for a better look. As we began to walk downhill toward the machine, we were still more amazed to find our way blocked by an invisible force that would not let us get any closer. It was as if we were bumping up against an invisible fence or wall. We encountered that invisible 'something' again and again, sliding to one side and the other against its unyielding surface. Finally we gave up our efforts to approach it and just sat on the hillside next to the barrier, watching the machine and debating the situation. . . ."

The boys renewed their efforts to penetrate the invisible barrier by approaching it from different directions. To no avail. "Finally we just sat back down and watched," Leo continued.

"Before too long, we saw the curious rotation slow and eventually stop, and the colorful lights stopped blinking at the edge of the machine. We also noticed that the outer shell now had an opening [that] had somehow opened up in the side of the machine. Out of it came three people who walked down a sort of ramp that, just as miraculously, sprouted out of the side of the machine. They stood in the dry weeds beside their enormous, silvery machine. . . .

"We watched the distant figures very closely and saw that they were all wearing the same type and color of suit or coverall. These people walked only a short distance from the machine and moved around near it. . . . They finally returned to the machine and closed the door, and the ramp just went away again."

The boys were anxious to return to their farmhouse near Killdeer, a long walk away, in time for dinner. They refrained from telling the rest of the family what had happened. The next day, they hiked directly back to the hillside, but the huge machine was nowhere to be seen, nor did they see it again until two weeks later.

"It was mid-afternoon as we stood in the same valley, looking at the ground, and puzzling about how there was no sign that anyone had even walked here," wrote Leo. "I cannot explain why, but our senses somehow told us to look up. There, high in the sky and almost straight above us, we saw the machine. It was flying! It was an airship! We quickly moved back up the hillside and out of the way behind some bushes. The airship we had spotted was now slowly nearing the valley floor. It was clearly coming in for a landing.

"We could sense a strange stillness that grew about us. This stillness gave us the first hint I can remember of a feeling that these people could stop all movement around them at any given time. . . . I am certain we were the only witnesses to the ship's landing. The appearance of the ship was the same as we remembered from our first sighting—a mirror-like exterior with a central rotating band that emitted colored lights. When the ship came to rest, the rotating band slowed to a stop, and the lights went out as before."

Once the craft had landed—on four legs with pads at the end of each—the boys were again prevented by the mysterious invisible force from approaching. "We noticed nothing was moving, not a blade of grass or the branches on the bushes," Leo continued. "While we sat by the barrier and watched this huge machine, the strange door started to open again. . . .

"A total of six men emerged from the door and walked down the ramp. They were dressed in a different kind of uniform than when we first saw them, but we were somehow certain they were the same men as we saw before. We were close enough to see that they now wore a shirt-slack type of clothing that looked quite comfortable. We wished we had such fine clothes, instead of our ragged overalls and patched cotton shirts.

"The men began doing something that looked peculiar. We couldn't figure out what they were up to. All six men would repeatedly reach down to the ground and apparently pick up something from the earth. Whether or not they took it with them, we could not tell. I don't know why, but I was convinced they could see us. . . ."

The boys stayed for an hour or so but, as before, needed to return home for supper. "Mike and I were not happy about leaving, but the length of the shadows and the position of the sun told us our time that day was up. . . ."

Leo and Mike decided to tell their parents. "Mom and Dad listened patiently to our excited story," explained Leo. "They agreed with us that something like this machine, this airship, could exist, but advised us just to forget about everything we had told them. We were very, very disappointed at their response to what was for us the most exciting experience of our lives."

The next day, Leo and Mike went into Killdeer, anxious to discuss the matter with their friend Mr. Brooks (described for me by Leo's friend Barry

Potter as "an educated, well-traveled man—Killdeer's cosmopolitan intellectual"), who operated the grain elevator and who they thought might be able to explain what they'd seen. "One of our theories about the machine," said Leo, "was that it was a new government plan for killing the hordes of grasshoppers that were eating our crops. We thought these people might be part of a government project to spray the countryside with DDT, a new chemical that was supposed to kill troublesome insects like grasshoppers and mosquitoes." (DDT, per se, was not introduced until 1939. However, as Barry explained to me, Leo had described spray units driving through Killdeer around this time, fogging the neighborhoods with what he referred to as DDT.)

"Boys, I don't think you are crazy," said Mr. Brooks. "I saw one of those things flying through the air without a sound. It was definitely some kind of airship. What I saw fits right in with what you have seen." He was mystified, however, that the machine made no sound, such as produced by Zeppelins, for example.

"In those days, people did not even mention things like what we had seen," Leo explained. "The talk was about the drought and the depression and the government and local doings. Many families went broke in those times and gave up, auctioning the farm to pay the bills and then leaving town. That is part of the reason Mike and I were not afraid when we first saw the ship and the men. I felt that they would do us no harm and might, in some way, help us out. I don't know why I felt like that, but I was convinced we were safe with them. . . ."

Although the boys visited the site repeatedly, it was weeks before they had another encounter. "One afternoon," Leo recounted, "our persistence was rewarded and we again watched the ship come in for a landing. This time, we were about 800 feet from the spaceship when we encountered their invisible wall, the closest we had been to them yet. I still figured there must be some way we could get closer, and somehow get to talk to these men. We waved and hollered, but to no avail."

Many return trips proved uneventful, though others brought insights about the strangers. The boys would check the actual landing area for signs of the landed machine, but found no markings of any kind. "The earth was completely undisturbed," observed Leo. "I thought it was mighty strange that there was no sign of any heavy object having landed there [and that] surely those four mighty prongs beneath the ship would have left some holes in the ground."

One afternoon the boys watched a jackrabbit bounce off the invisible "force field." "The rabbit [then] nuzzled up against the 'wall' with what must have been a sore nose, moved along it one way and the other, and then just hopped off. . . .

"We got a peaceful feeling from [the men]. Their movements near the ship were peaceful and purposeful. I got the feeling they probably were making a survey of some kind. We always thought of them as men, people, humans like us. . . . Neither of us could quite accept the fact that these people might be from a very distant planet, yet both of us were able to sit there and think about the possibility."

Leo describes the departure of the spaceship. "There was no sound, but we could distinctly feel the earth vibrating," he explained. "This vibration continued for long moments until we wondered what was going to happen. Then we heard a slight hum, and the vibration ended. It was the first time I ever heard anything like a mechanical sound associated with the ship. The outer shell of the ship started turning, rotating faster and faster with perfect smoothness. Then it suddenly started rising. . . .

"Those four tremendous prongs, which were maybe four feet by eight feet, began receding into the body of this flying machine. Again the earth started vibrating and we heard this slight hum. It was not loud enough to draw attention for any distance at all. Then the ship started lifting higher, going straight up. A tremendous amount of colored light flashed out from the ship. It kept going straight up. The speed was so great that when it got about ten or fifteen feet off the ground, it completely vanished. . . ."

"It is significant," Barry pointed out to me, "that although the ship was literally as big as a barn, it did not exert enough force on the earth to leave 'footprints.' The four-foot × eight-foot prongs would imply four contact points with earth, each the size of two coffins side by side. Perhaps the prongs served an electrical grounding function rather than providing mainly structural support. Vibration ended when the prongs left the earth."[2]

Leo wished they could have taken photographs, but the cost of a camera, films, and processing was beyond most adults in those difficult times. Leo also expressed doubt that the unusual men would want any photographs taken. Attempts to obtain proof were further stalled when the boys failed to persuade some of their playmates to accompany them on their trips.

Another landing occurred toward the end of August 1932. On this occasion the brothers were a little closer than before. "As the ship approached the ground, we found ourselves immersed in the invisible field of force. It came over us like a flood of water that got thicker and thicker as the ship dropped lower and lower until we could not move. Always before, we couldn't get any closer. Now we couldn't get out. We were caught inside the shell of force and were unable to free ourselves, no matter how hard we tried. . . .

"We were just sitting on the ground and watched the door open and the men appear again. The door was so different from any doors we had ever seen, and it opened in such a very unusual way, I have no words to describe it. Anything capable of traveling at such a great speed, I reasoned, would have to be very complex. . . . We thought if we could get close enough to them, we might be able to talk with them. I knew this wouldn't be easy and I was a little scared to try it . . . but they held us in their forces. We could not get any closer to them [so] we just sat there keeping an eye on that ship. They had come here for some other reason than just advertising.

"Here we were, trapped maybe two or three hundred feet from the ship, fighting our feelings of panic. I wish I could adequately convey the way we were rapidly alternating from feelings of fear to safety, from doubt to curiosity, from wonderment to speculation. The great intensity of the experience is very memorable to this day. . . . They gave us the feeling that they were very interested in what was happening with the plants and creatures in the countryside. These impressions were entering our minds just like our own thoughts."

Three days later, on August 28, at around eight in the evening, the craft returned to the valley. "As we approached the ship, moving carefully down the brushy, uneven hillside, we could see them moving about, strangely illuminated in the growing shadows. We again found ourselves blocked by that invisible force, but we were now far closer than we'd ever been. By this time, we had concluded the barrier was like a magnetic force that affected people and animals instead of iron and steel. . . .

"Six men were outside the craft, all about the same build and size, between five and six feet tall, wearing a similar light coverall or jumpsuit. They appeared to be smooth-faced, with no sign of a beard or moustache. The men near the ship often bent down and touched the ground. From a distance of no more than forty feet, Mike began waving and yelling at them and shaking the bushes to attract their attention, which resulted in the invisible force-field preventing any further approach."

Although convinced the craft was an airship of some kind, at no point did Leo and Mike think the operators were from another planet. "I had to agree with Mike that I didn't think they were Americans," said Leo. "Maybe they were Canadians, though most of the Canadians we had seen looked like ordinary North Dakota Americans to us." However, once the ship had taken off with the familiar spectacular display of brilliant colored lights, and the boys were walking home under the stars, having been released from the force-field, they began to wonder what place the travelers called home.

The boys revisited the landing site the following day at dawn, hoping for another encounter, but nothing happened. They went home, returning to the site in the early afternoon. Again, nothing. But following a hunch, Leo told Mike that they should wait for a while. "After we spent only a short time on the hilltop, our ship approached," said Leo. "We could not understand how, but we felt they had some way they could land the ship and depart again without being seen. We had experienced this before. When we watched them take off, the minute they got a few feet above the ground, we lost sight of them. They were just gone. The feeling was growing in us that they were instantly moving so fast that they were just invisible to us [and] if they could move out that quickly, they could certainly slow their ship just as quickly."

As the boys tried to approach the ship, they were blocked as usual by the force-field—but this time while they were still very near the hilltop. Mike worried that the men might have lost some confidence because of the way he'd acted the previous night. "They did not want us any closer," said Leo, "but again we finally managed to draw their attention. They raised their hands and then mostly ignored us. As we stood watching and speculating about them, we could feel them looking us over, examining us in some way I could not quite define. We felt they were definitely interested in us in a friendly way. . . .

"Whatever it was they were doing, they were very busy about it, coming and going from the ship with small parcels and odd gadgets we couldn't quite see. There could have been dozens of them inside, but we never saw more than six of them outside at one time. As before, they all wore similar clothing, the coveralls I admired. There were no visible buttons or even a seam in front that might be hiding the buttons. . . .

"After a time, the activity near the ship died down until only one of them remained outside, wandering here and there with no pattern. He came quite close to us, maybe ten or twelve feet away. Whatever was holding us seemed to have no effect upon him. He looked directly at us and smiled in a peaceful and friendly way, raising his hand with the palm open toward us. Then he turned and walked directly back to the ramp and entered the ship. Although the ramp retracted into the ship and the strange door closed, nothing else happened."

After the door closed, the boys were released from the force-field. Though tempted to approach the ship, they decided it would be unwise.

On arriving back at the farm—this time late for supper—so engrossed were the boys with the day's encounter that they were unable to eat. "There was no thought of mentioning what happened to us that night," explained Leo. "Our parents still thought we were imagining all these things and Mom was unhappy and worried because we did not eat. . . .

"When I think back now, I know their huge ship was the key to our interest in them. As individuals, they were not all that much different from ordinary people. If you dressed them in ordinary clothing, you would pass one of them in a strange town without blinking an eye. We were quite convinced that if they could build and fly this amazing airship, they could do many other exciting things we could only imagine. By now, we had begun to suspect they could somehow control the weather,[3] because the conditions were always calm and clear each time they landed . . . I knew that one day we would come into closer contact with them, but did not know if we would ever be allowed to enter that spaceship."

One day, worried about becoming involved in some kind of serious situation with the men in the airship, the brothers felt compelled once more to tell their parents. "I am sure they noticed how we had developed knowledge they could not account for," said Leo. "They listened to our excited words, but watching them, I don't think they quite believed us."

FIRST CONTACT

Early one evening, following numerous unsuccessful trips to the site, the boys had another close encounter with the mysterious men and their flying machine. "As we started down the hill," said Leo, "we found ourselves in quite a different situation than before. The magnetic force they used to keep us at a distance was behind us and we were free to walk cautiously up toward the landing site. . . .

"As we approached the ship, these people were outside with smiles on their faces. They were very calm [and] just went about their exercises and made us feel welcome, like we weren't in the way. We stopped our approach at maybe eight or ten feet from the nearest of them, and just stood there watching. . . . We could hear no sounds in the strange stillness so near the tremendous ship.[4] This close, we were nearly overwhelmed by its huge dimensions. . . .

"These men were so ordinary looking in one way and so exotic in another. I noticed that they had light brown hair that was cut much the same as Mom cut ours. Their complexion was very light beige, resembling a good tan. Their eyes were blue with a dark pupil. I would guess their weight to be about 140 pounds, since they were a little taller and more heavily built than my father. . . . All of them looked to me to weigh about the same and be about the same size and build. Their hands and feet were shaped like ours, but their shoes were totally unlike our own, without laces or soles.

"The fabric of their clothing was very unusual, with a subtle pattern visible only when the light was just right. The color and cut of the uniform was the same from a distance, but that subtle pattern was different from one to another of them. Their otherwise identical uniforms looked like they were neatly pressed, but did not have badges or any other insignia that might show rank, like our soldiers did. These men were as alike as peas in a pod.

"Now that we were up close to it, we found the color of the ship to be a light blue that blended smoothly into the color of the sky. When viewed against the sky, the ship was strangely difficult to detect, either close up or from a distance. There was sort of a haze to it. We just stood there and looked back and forth from the ship to the men. They occasionally looked at us and smiled, then continued with their exercises. I was able to talk German probably better than English at that time, although our tongues were tied and we just couldn't speak.

"There were three of them, and they stood there and looked at us. They appeared to be very relaxed with that unusual smile on their faces. Their smile was like ours [and] maybe more gentle than any smile I have ever seen."

When Mike tried talking (in a mixture of English and German) to the closest man, they all merely continued with their "exercises." Two of the men walked back into the ship and another came out, walked over to the boys and said, in German, "I can speak your language," and then, in English, "We speak all languages of all people on your planet."

"We asked them some questions, not very deep questions, because we felt curiously tongue-tied," explained Leo. "We had meant to ask a million questions, but in the end we asked very few. The conversation with him lasted for only a few minutes."

Leo now noticed that the men were wearing thin, light-colored gloves. No women were on board. I asked Leo why this was so.

"There are women," he responded, "but I never met them."[5]

The brothers were hoping to be invited on board. But it was not to be. Finally, one of the men approached the boys and addressed them, in perfect German:

"You have had quite an experience with us [and] shown great determination in coming to visit us again and again. You have seen much, you have learned much, and you know more about us than most people in your world. No one will believe you when you tell them about us," and, addressing Leo, "not until you are an old man. . . . In your own minds, you will always know the truth about what you have experienced and felt." The man repeated this in English, then continued in German:

"We are very real and we are from another galaxy. We have traveled to your planet for over five thousand years. We are from a place far beyond your world by millions of years in time. We continue traveling to your planet because it is part of our responsibility. We are showing you a small part of what you can expect in the future. You cannot learn everything at one time without rest. You will see us again before long. . . ."

"Leo used the term 'galaxy' very loosely," Barry advised me. "I got the impression that, in his mind, the term would apply to the planetary system of another star or perhaps to a different dimension or time as easily as to another star cluster beyond the Milky Way. He often called the visitors 'time-travelers.'"[6]

"I did not ask them any more questions and we did not get into the spaceship," Leo continued. "When we wanted to know something, it was clear we had to be able to ask the right questions before we could get any answers. He stood before us for a few seconds more with that gentle smile on his face, then turned and joined the others. . . .

"I was now certain that they were far older than anyone we had ever met before," explained Leo. "They had very old, wise eyes in bodies that appeared to be young and fit. I decided that they must have far better methods to protect their health and must live in a much better environment than we do. They glowed with perfect health. I also knew they deeply respected our Earth. . . . This was why they didn't leave rubbish about, why their area was always clean.

"I was now firmly convinced that these travelers from the spaceship could definitely read our minds. They responded to the questions, thoughts, and desires in our minds, and in turn were able to place their own thoughts, intentions and beliefs in our minds without using words. . . ."

When viewed close up, the craft appeared to be constructed of one single piece of material without individual component parts. The ramp and supports beneath the ship appeared to join to the main body of the ship with no visible seams.

Another encounter occurred in the same valley, late in the day on September 19. Again, the boys were not prevented from approaching the craft. "I do not know why, but I had the impression that the force-field was still there, but they 'tuned' it somehow to allow us to pass through," Leo asserts.

The craft did not reflect light like ordinary objects; rather, it seemed to absorb the light around it and produce its own subtle light of any color or pattern of shades. "Sounds did not echo off it like the wall of a barn or the face of a cliff. You could stand right next to it and not even notice it was there. . . . It was more like a living thing that watched and reacted to its surroundings, than a machine or building. Maybe they were putting on a show for us, because the appearance of the ship began doing the most amazing things.

"One moment it would blend into the sunset, matching every color and pattern. Then it would go like oily water and abruptly change to a polished mirror or a dark, non-reflective surface like a hillside. It took many minutes for us to work our way to the clearing near the ship. . . ."

At first, the boys did not notice anyone near the ship as they walked up to it, nor the silent lowering of the ramp. But they became aware of a man standing next to one of the huge legs that supported the ship. The man made eye contact with the boys and had started to speak before they suddenly realized there were two men.

"The one who had started to speak to us continued, turning to the other as he spoke [in flawless German]. 'These boys would like to touch our ship. Make sure it is well grounded, for we probably have developed some [electrostatic charge] in our travels.' There was no greeting. I think he simply picked the top item off the jumbled pile of our thoughts and responded to it. Then we were given the opportunity to touch something from another galaxy for the first time. The feeling of touching the ship, which definitely sent a chill up my spine, is also very difficult to explain.

"I expected it to be hard and metallic, but to this day, I find it hard to believe the feeling I had touching something that was so smooth and exchanged no heat with my hand. It was neither warm nor cold, and was definitely smoother than glass or polished metal, which will stick to your hand. It was like trying to press one magnet against the same pole of another, like I was not really touching anything at all. . . .

"The colors were somehow projected from inside it, or emanated from it, instead of reflecting as from a painted surface or a mirror. At that particular moment, the colors seemed to match the sky and even the clouds. . . . The ship was made in such a way, or of such a material, that once it rose several hundred feet in the air, it looked just like the sky. . . .

"We accomplished our next goal in short order when we found ourselves shaking the hand of one of the visitors. It was his actual hand, not through a glove like I had often seen them wear. . . . The hand was soft and warm, the grip firm. Although I was right in the middle of what was probably the biggest thrill I ever had, I found myself thinking, 'Sure would like to get into that ship.' . . .

"I think that can be arranged," came the reply to Leo's unspoken thought. "But first, you will have to go through a 'process' to enter the ship. There is nothing to be afraid of [and] you will have to go through the process again to leave the ship."

The man explained that this process was controlled by what today might be termed an invisible energy beam or field of radiation, comparing it with the energy field that prevented approaching the ship. "I understood that it was a modified form of the invisible shield," said Leo.

"I finally began to recognize that they were giving us information in some way other than by just what they had told us [and that] they were communicating with us, not so much by what they were saying and we were hearing, but more by what we were feeling." As Leo explained to me: "They can open up areas of the brain that we don't use. And they made it clear that we have twelve senses, not five.[7]

"They seemed to realize that our world was in trouble, and understood about the depression and the drought as we talked about failed crops and the grasshoppers that were invading our country. They [also] gave us the indication that Man would soon bring terrible wars and suffering upon himself. . . ."

INSIDE THE SPACESHIP

Finally, the boys were invited aboard the spaceship. "The huge ramp descended silently [and] almost before we knew it, we were escorted up the ramp by the man we had been speaking directly with and at last found ourselves entering the ship.

"There was an inner and an outer door. When one door opened, the other door closed. Some kind of mist would go across the door. We asked him what it was. He told us that [it] was a 'disinfectant,' as we would call it. . . . One moment there was a wall, the next it was an open door. I could see no hinges or handle, not even a joint where the door met. . . .

"After we had entered the compartment and the door had closed behind us, our guide told us we had to remove our clothes so the disinfecting process would be effective. Mike and I were both a little nervous about taking off our clothes in front of these people, but felt a little better about it when we saw that we would get to wear some of their clothing.[8] I was glad we had both taken baths the night before. . . .

"I was looking around for light bulbs or fixtures or switches, but there was nothing on the walls or ceiling. There weren't any shadows, either. The light just seemed to come from everywhere at once. After we had dressed in their clothing, which opened at the back like one of those hospital gowns, we passed into another compartment which contained some kind of haze that went over our entire bodies.

"They had given us some light jackets to put on that, compared to any clothing we had ever seen, were just beautiful. They were made from a material of a very slick texture [and] when the edges of the fabric were brought together, they attached themselves without buttons. . . . When the inner door eventually slid open, we came into what must have been their main compartment. The first thing I noticed was their chairs. They were wonderful, just out of this world.

"Our host invited us to sit in these great chairs [which] were completely adjustable, though the travelers were all so similar to each other, I am certain one size of chair would fit them all . . . like the ship itself, they didn't seem to have any individual parts. A force of some kind made them move toward you when you were about to sit without anyone appearing to touch them [and] Mike had a great time trying to outwit the chairs, to the great amusement of our friendly hosts. When I sat, the chair subtly and automatically adjusted to fit and support my body from my heels to my head."

A screen measuring about five by four feet appeared, showing pictures of "a place or process" that the boys simply could not fathom. Opposite the screen were other types of machine, described as "magnetic sensors."

"Their meals and the cooking thereof are impossible to explain, although they were very nice about trying to explain it to us. We saw what I would call sleeping compartments with unusual beds, but we asked no questions about their sleeping customs. The toilet facilities were fully automatic; things like towels and toilet tissue were not there. It all seemed to be operating by the 'magnetic' force, or maybe some chemical reaction. . . .

"The largest room we saw was their laboratory or workshop. I saw many different things I could not even begin to grasp [though] I tried to ask some questions about these machines." The men replied that, no matter how they explained it, it would be impossible for the boys to understand any of it.

"Why do you keep coming to our valley?" asked Mike.

"We study the life patterns," came the simple reply.

Although the inside of the craft couldn't be seen from outside, from the inside everything was visible. "We could see clearly through to the outside and observe clouds in the darkening sky," Leo explained. "We called it glass, but they informed us it was some other type of material which they did not explain to us."

Also, images of real-time scenes could be projected from anywhere on to a screen—evidently imagery being fed in from their sensor systems.

When I interviewed Leo at his home in Helena, Montana, in 2004, he revealed more. "There's a screen on that panel that shows the entire world, like a map, but it's different," he said. "As they travel, the information keeps changing. No buttons are used—it's done by brain waves, via the eyes, for example."[9]

"Another of their abilities that we experienced inside that spaceship is just as baffling," Leo reports in his book.

"I sat in one of those wonderful chairs watching the sun go down over the mountains outside and listening to one of our hosts trying to explain something about how far away their galaxy is. . . . Next thing I knew we are walking on the hillside and he was showing us how the grasshoppers lay their eggs under the dirt. Just like that. I blinked my eyes and there we were, back with the galaxy lecture. Blink again and he was showing us how the magnetic 'laser' beam worked.

"They could [also] stop a bird in flight and hold it motionless in mid-air. Now I saw this done, but I am not sure how. They could catch a rabbit in his jump and stop him in midair [and] they could hold these animals like this for minutes or hours. Then, suddenly, they could just release them. In other words, from the understanding we gained, they had the ability to stop any moving object at any range they desired. Our military men should take note. . . .

"These people who we met and talked to in the year 1932 came right out and told us they had traveled to this planet for over five thousand years. They will continue coming to this planet because it is their responsibility. It is important for us to understand that they said the Earth is their responsibility, rather than mankind's. We were told that they will continue traveling to our planet, to this very spot, and to many other places as our world gets deeper into trouble. . . .

"One of the reasons for their great intelligence is their ability to use twelve senses. And they told us that twelve people from their galaxy live full-time on our planet Earth. These people live among us, but we cannot tell that they are different from us. We were also informed that these twelve people have often offered to help our world and were rejected every time. . . ."

Leo related to me some amusing anecdotal information he acquired that year from a Native Indian chief. "They come from the heavens," declared the chief. "They're white, and they dress funny. We got down on our knees to them. They taught us how to plant things. My granddad told me all these things, which he'd learned from his father. They came by season. Then, when the white men came, we originally mistook them for the people who had come from the heavens!"[10]

FURTHER CONTACTS

Further landings and contacts took place occasionally over the years. "I saw the spaceship off and on after that first year, and even saw it land several times," wrote Leo. Mike was not present at these events. "In 1933, I had the pleasure of seeing it landing about two miles south and a mile and a half east of Dunn Center, North Dakota. It continued landing at that location from 1933 to 1934. . . .

"In August of 1936, about the end of the month, around 9:45 in the evening, I again saw their ship land at the location near Dunn Center and decided to walk up to them. As I approached the ship, I was allowed to enter through their magnetic forces. The ship didn't look any different from the ship I'd seen in 1932. I was welcomed by three people and was certain they were the same people I had met back in 1932 [and] I did not have to ask to enter their spaceship.

"They said the world would have many problems, but they would not interfere [and] re-affirmed that this planet was their concern, that Man has his own mind, and that he must learn to take care of his planet if he wants to keep his home. [He] assured me our planet would continue to exist. But I was not assured that Man would continue to exist on it, if he did not learn to take better care of his most valuable possession. . . ."

In October 1936, Leo enrolled as a laborer with the Civilian Conservation Corps (CCC)—a public work-relief program for unemployed youth during the Great Depression—receiving an honorable discharge in March 1937.[11]

There were no further contacts until 1938, at Watford City, North Dakota, close to the Missouri River bridge. Then, on the evening of September 15, 1939 at around 21:30, as he was en route to Watford City, a spaceship landed about three hundred feet off the side road. Two men—identical to those from the previous encounters—alighted and greeted Leo. Expressing their pleasure at seeing him again, they added that he had changed a lot since 1932. Leo said he was bemused that they, on the contrary, had not changed at all.

"We are several thousand years ahead of your time. We are germ-free and our life expectancy is quite different from yours. At this time, it would be impossible for us to explain to you how we have accomplished all this in our lives. . . . But we can assure you, if your scientists would devote their time to increasing your life span, people on Earth would be capable of living in good health much longer than you do now."

In *You're Looking Very Well: The Surprising Nature of Getting Old* (Faber, 2010), author Lewis Wolpert states his belief that one day human beings may have a lifespan of six hundred years.

Leo was puzzled to note that, although it was now about ten o'clock at night, the area around the spaceship was not dark. "Some type of glow kept shadowless light in the area," he observed. As Barry Potter pointed out succinctly to me: "The alien light is *always* described as 'shadowless,' which is directly contrary to our understanding of light as a radiant effect, i.e. proceeding in a straight line from source to a reflecting surface."[12] I concur. Additional evidence for this technology is provided later, particularly relating to the Amicizia saga (Chapter 13).

Asking if they were worried about people noticing the glow, Leo received an interesting reply:

". . . We have stopped all movement for three miles around us. There is no way that anything can move within that area. No person can approach the ship unless we allow them entrance. It will be some time, well in the future, before people will be able to understand and do much, if any, of what we are capable of doing now. This new understanding will make a tremendous change on your planet Earth."

Leo was invited aboard, involving the same "disinfection" process and change of clothes as before. Six men, seated in the main compartment, were watching an image on the large TV-like screen, which Leo learned was of their galaxy. Again, he marveled at the lack of any visible light fittings in the ship, and inquired how the light was generated. "Our lighting system is in our metal," he was told. "The power for our machines is also generated in our metal. This is all we can tell you, for it would be impossible for you to understand how our energy system works."

By around 23:30 Leo felt it was time to leave. "The first man put his hand on my shoulder. After hesitating for a moment, I put my hand on his shoulder. In turn, I did this with all six men. After I entered the outer compartment, I removed the jacket and handed it inside to them. The door closed and again the mist covered my entire body . . . as I finished dressing, the unusual door opened and I stepped out of the spaceship."

Heading back to the car, Leo was astonished to find his way illuminated in some way by the same shadowless light all the way to his car.

In 1941, Leo was called to service with the U.S. Navy and eventually participated in the invasions of Okinawa and Iwo Jima. Most of this period was spent with the Amphibious Unit in the South Pacific, serving, for example, in the minesweeper USS *Skirmish* (AM-303). He also served in the USS *Missouri*, witnessing the surrender of Japan to General Douglas MacArthur on that ship. I surmise that he probably served with either the Office of Naval Intelligence or Office of Strategic Services—though he never confirmed as much—as he was involved, for example, with the occupation force in Japan, interrogating prisoners, and also served in Africa,[13] mostly related to counter-intelligence.

Following the war, Leo moved to Bozeman, Montana, working as a salesman, returning to Killdeer in 1948. In 1950, he saw a spaceship landing in the high hills along the highway between Norris and Sappington Junction (some thirty miles from Bozeman). He planned his business trips so as to pass through that area regularly, in the evenings, and observed the craft on a number of occasions. "Because the ship was usually well back from the highway in very difficult terrain," he explained, "I had no real chance to make a personal contact with them."

Leo does not provide dates of these events, but it is worth noting here that on the late afternoon of April 12, 1950, in Helena—some sixty-five miles from the landing site described by Leo—a Mrs. Ida Welch reported an object that looked like "two soup plates put together," larger than a bomber, flying so close to the ground that "anyone could have shot it down with a rifle." Three months later, five Helena residents in different locations reported an object, described variously as cigar-shaped, a flaming disc, or wing-shaped.[14]

Sadly, Leo's younger brother Mike was reported killed in action in 1950, during the Korean War.

In 1962, while driving with his three young daughters and two of their friends at Sappington Junction, Montana, Leo saw a spaceship moving through the evening skies. Perhaps this was an ideal opportunity to secure supportive evidence.

"It was difficult to pick my way over the dark mountain roads, but finally I drove my car within about two hundred feet of the spaceship. It was hovering about twenty feet off the ground, producing all the colors I had witnessed before. . . . It was very hard to contain my disappointment when I saw [that the girls] were all frightened. There was no way to convince them no one would hurt us. We watched the ship for only about half an hour. Several times, I flashed my headlights at them, certain they knew the girls were with me and were scared. . . . I was convinced it was the same spaceship I had seen back in 1932 and again in 1939, and had no doubt that the same people were aboard."

In 2010, Leo's only surviving daughter, Frances Dworshak Hankinson, provided a testimonial to this event for me:

"The only experience that I have had with UFOs is when Dad took me, my two sisters, and two of their friends over to Sappington Junction. It was late evening. He told us there was something he wanted us to see. He parked out in the middle of nowhere, and had us watch the sky for lights. It was getting late and darker and we wanted to go home. When we spotted lights in the sky—to the best of my recollection the lights were auburn, green, and yellow—the lights were flashing but stationary. Dad flicked the headlights in their direction, and they repeated the same pattern back at him. He did this several times, then it was gone. I have never seen anything like it since."[15]

One summer's evening in 1963, Leo was driving from Ennis to Sappington Junction when he spotted a craft in the process of landing in the foothills about six or seven miles off the main highway. He stopped the car to watch. Another car drew up and a couple got out and confirmed what Leo was seeing. He then asked the man to follow him, planning to drive as close as they could, then walk the remaining distance to the ship. The man refused, explaining that he'd experienced a close encounter with a craft in California which had alarmed him.

While driving through the same area on the evening of October 21, 1963, Leo decided to try to initiate another contact. At around 20:15, he parked his car and set off on what he guessed would be a very long walk to the landing site. Arriving in the vicinity, he could see the ship, parked down a rugged slope. "When I was about halfway down, I noticed the area around the spaceship was lit up with the soft, indirect light I remembered so well. I could see about six people moving about on the ground. As I came closer, I saw two of them were moving my way. . . ."

The men greeted Leo enthusiastically in the same manner as before. They confirmed that they had monitored him, for instance, during his experience with the couple in the car. "You should have known, after all these years," they said, "that most people will not believe you. But this time was different. This man knew of our existence. He had seen us before [but] had allowed his fear to convince him that we are a threat. . . ."

On board the craft, sitting in the extraordinary chairs, a lengthy discussion ensued. Part of the information on board referred to attempts by our military to capture one of the aliens' ships.

"Your science and technology have advanced enough to pose a threat to our ships, as well as to the entire planet. If your military leaders continue their efforts to damage our ships, we will be forced to defend ourselves. . . . Our actions to protect and defend ourselves are governed by a simple principle: Anything that is thrown at us will be thrown back to its source."

In this connection, Leo related to me that when he owned some petrol stations in 1974, a man was filling up his car when another customer asked him about UFOs. Leo joined in the ensuing conversation, relating some of his own experiences. The customer—a recently retired Army colonel—revealed an incident that had occurred in the U.S. Southwest. "We had 240 guys out in the desert and we tried to shoot down a craft," he said. "But they returned every shell back into the guns."

"This man had just retired," Leo told me. "He would not talk dates." The colonel advised Leo not to reveal what he had said.[16]

Barry Potter independently confirmed this story, adding that "the rounds fired reversed direction in flight and returned to the guns they were fired from, where apparently they exploded, killing troops on the ground."[17] Those soldiers had no choice; they were simply obeying orders. If true—and assuming this was the same group which contacted Leo—such an egregious retaliation would seem contrary to their declared ethics. Barry, however, emphasized that this was not quite the case. "Leo always maintained that the aliens' concern was with protecting and preserving the planet Earth, *not* mankind," he told me. "He often hinted darkly that the aliens would not hesitate to sacrifice human life to defend their activities or to assure the survival of life on Earth."[18]

I should mention here that since the 1940s, a number of craft—evidently of different origin from those encountered by Leo—have successfully been shot down, resulting in the destruction of a large number of our aircraft by alien craft, as reported in my previous book.[19] "After we left the ship," Leo continues in his book, "we sat on the ground for a while, all seven of us, looking up at the stars [and] talking about different things for perhaps another two hours."

"I hope we will see you again," said one of the men, as they bade Leo farewell. "It will be quite a while, though, because we are traveling back to our own galaxy. There will be another one of our spaceships traveling about your world, but they will make far fewer landings than we have. They will be more interested in what man is doing in outer space. . . ."

"We separated then with very deep feelings," wrote Leo, "and I started back for my car. Light was provided for me all the way back. I was about half a mile from the ship when I began to notice how warm the area around me seemed to be, although it had grown quite cold out. As I approached my car, I heard the motor running. I never understood how or why they had started my car [but] it was nice and warm as I climbed into it. . . ."

———

Leo Dworshak died in April 2007, aged eighty-six years.

In my meetings with him in Helena, Montana, and in subsequent communications, Leo came across as genuine—a "no-nonsense" man. I also learned that he was very well connected.

In his business dealings, Leo proved to be a formidable opponent, Barry Potter told me. "I consider being a rough opponent a positive character trait. His competitors saw this primarily in his behavior while estimating, bidding, and completing jobs, for which he often served as what we call a general contractor, overseeing several sub-contractors involved in the overall job. Leo did no advertising, relying upon word-of-mouth recommendations from his customers . . . his philosophy was to do many jobs with a lower profit margin rather than fewer jobs with a high margin, as was common among his competitors."[20]

There is a wealth of additional information in Leo Dworshak's book. To conclude this chapter, the following is excerpted from the last two pages:

"If their intent is to eliminate humanity, I have no doubt the easiest course would be to step back and allow us to destroy ourselves. Yet they continue to return, year after year, century after century, and work very hard while they are here. We never saw them in the winter months when insects and plant life are dormant. . . . I think part of their work here was related to the study of how we were poisoning the environment in those times. I think they were analyzing the grasshoppers, which eat a large amount of foliage, for chemical poisons in our environment.

"I know they are very concerned about our nuclear and chemical weapons and our warlike nature. What a problem we must be for them, always threatening the health and safety of this beautiful planet, which is their responsibility to protect. The picture that comes to mind is a crowd of unruly children fighting and playing in a carefully tended garden with no regard for the problems they are causing for the gardener. . . ."

CHAPTER TWO
GALACTIC GUARDIANS

Nineteen-year-old Pierre Monnet lived in Orange (Vaucluse), France, at the time of his first encounter with extraterrestrials. This occurred in the small hours one night in July 1951 while cycling home after a visit to his fiancée, who lived in the little village of Courthézon, eight kilometers from Orange—a fifteen- to twenty-minute journey he made twice a week, on the same days.

Monnet had the habit of checking the town clocks before leaving and on arrival, to compare his journey time. "That night was no exception," he pointed out, "and after the normal check I got on my bike." It was 01:30. But this time, something different happened—something that was to become increasingly common in abduction scenarios reported years later.

"I was astonished to find myself instantly transported five kilometers further on, at the entrance of a large, deep pit of sand and gravel, 10–15 meters from the side of the road. Between the road and the pit were a thick hedge, high undergrowth, and bushes.

"My mind felt blank. I was dazed. Then, like an automaton and as though I was being directed by an irresistible force, I followed the large gravel slope which led down to the right and further into the pit. I don't know why, but I got off my bike and continued on foot. I felt very tired and had the impression that my feet weren't touching the ground; but that was only an impression. I was very calm and relaxed. Little by little, a kind of peace came over me.

"The further I went on, the more I had the feeling that one has when getting into water for the first time, up to one's shoulders; a gentle pressure on the lungs . . . and I was short of breath. Then, at a bend in the pit where I moved as though I knew exactly where I was going, I saw a luminescent light about sixty meters in front of me, behind a mound of earth.

"I kept on and then saw in front of me, fifteen meters away, floating between fifty and eighty centimeters above the ground, a disc fifteen to twenty meters in diameter, topped with a central bulge in the form of a dome. From top to bottom the machine must have been about three meters high. The disc pulsated with a white-silver-blueish light, clearly illuminating the walls of the pit ten meters away. This radiation seemed to radiate from the 'soul' of the 'metal' of which this strange machine was made, with a fascinating beauty [and] the metal seemed at the same time to be both material and ethereal, with constant inner movement—almost alive.

"As I came closer, I noticed that the surrounding noises had dimmed. When I was about six meters from the disc, I could no longer hear the noise of traffic [even at that time of night, there was still traffic, owing to the Festival]. As I approached, total silence fell. I could no longer hear the crickets or even the sound of my footsteps on the gravel. It was impressive. I felt great, amazed at what I was seeing. . . ."

I should point out at this juncture that Monnet had no recourse to the Dworshak brothers' experiences, which were not published until 2003.

THE FOUR EXTRATERRESTRIALS

"Probably because I was so fascinated by the machine," Monnet continued, "I had not noticed, in front of it and a little to the side as it still hovered above the ground, four extraterrestrial human beings in tight-fitting catsuits of shiny silver-gray metal which lit up an area of five meters around them. I was no more than a few meters away from them and I went calmly toward them. I was no longer aware of my body.

"Arriving three meters in front of these beings, I stopped and looked at them. They were barefoot. They were tall; they must have measured at least 1.85 meters [over six feet]. They were perfectly proportioned and identical in build. Their hair was blond-white and reached almost to their shoulders. Their faces were beautiful and very refined. They had a light, frank, and gentle expression which I have never seen in Earth people. They were so beautiful, but at that moment I was not sure if they were men or women, since they did not have breasts. But after a brief while there was no doubt—they were certainly men. They gave an impression of great strength and they were built like athletes. Despite that, they were smiling and radiated calmness, gentleness, and goodness. . . .

"They then raised their arms in my direction, almost horizontally, the palms of their hands turned upwards. They made this movement almost in unison, and in silence. I made a gentle movement backward: I wanted to escape, and shivered from head to toe. They made themselves clear to me without opening their mouths: I heard their thoughts very clearly in my head. It was extraordinarily precise and clear. Moreover, while admitting that in our language we have precise words capable of translating perfectly what was said during this contact—which I now describe as telepathic—the quantity of what was said to me in such a short time (I estimated about half an hour) could not be expressed in our language if we were to speak for eight hours a day for a year or two. . . ."

THE MESSAGE

"Given to me were not words but coded thoughts in the form of impulses, for which I could find no words of translation at the time, apart from a few isolated phrases that I could translate instantly," claimed Monnet. "The realization of the concepts which were given to me that night did not become apparent to me until two years after my contact. Here are a few scattered phrases that I could understand immediately as they were 'pronounced.'

"'We want the best for all living beings, especially if they are not aggressive. . . . Do not come any closer to our vehicle. It is dangerous for human beings not in tune with its wavelength: the vibrations it emits would destroy the cells of your body.

"'This meeting will cause you troubles which will affect your health; you will have nervous problems for a certain time, then that will pass. Later, our conversation will become clear and you will be able to let the people of your planet know what we have told you . . . but take care not to allow your own concepts to interfere. . . .

"'You are not the only person on your planet to have spoken with us. Unfortunately, most people do not want to speak about us and the others are not believed. . . . Your life would not be long enough: for this reason, we propose to regenerate the cells of your body so that you will live the value of 120 human years. . . . We will carry out this regeneration inside our vehicle after our meeting, and forgive us that we think it necessary for you not to remember the operation.'

"Then," said Monnet, "the beings stopped emitting their thoughts. I was so intent on receiving these that I hadn't noticed that an opening had appeared in front of the dome, wide enough to allow two men to enter. Inside was a white-orange light almost unbearable to look at. The four beings were there. Then—silence.

"Without saying good-bye, I turned, picked up my bike, and wheeled it back up the slope to the main road. Instantly, I was transported to the outskirts of Orange. I looked at my watch and was amazed to see that it was still 1.30 A.M. I went to compare the time with the town hall clock, which read 1.35 A.M. My watch also read 1.35 A.M. For me, it was incredible. But what was more, I could not remember the journey of eight kilometers [five miles]: it seemed as if I had not traveled at all. Also, unusually, I was not tired or out of breath because of the journey. I hadn't noticed anything; not the headlights of passing cars, nor the passing countryside. . . ."

MISSING TIME

"I had to rationalize it. *Time could not have passed*. Time had stopped during the journey and the meeting—which I thought had lasted about twenty minutes. If you take into account that normally I took twenty minutes to cover the whole distance, theoretically that made forty minutes unaccounted for. The thing seemed so fantastic that during the long days and sleepless nights that followed, I tried to work out what had really happened and posed myself all sorts of questions and proceeded to check it out from the beginning.

"First, checking the time of the two clocks and my watch, I made another return journey between Orange and Courthézon. I noticed that the time on the three was exactly the same—the clock at Orange, the clock at Courthézon, and my watch. Not one of the three had stopped, gained, or lost time.

"Objectively, I thought that all this could have been a particularly vivid dream. To be certain that I did not dream again, that night I woke up my mother, inventing some excuse, in the hope that she would reprimand me. The following morning I was reprimanded. Now I had the proof that I had not been dreaming. In any case, I know the difference between a dream and reality. . . ."

Monnet also rejected the hypotheses that he may have fallen asleep at some stage of the bicycle journey, or suffered from amnesia. Was his experience entirely subjective? Had the four aliens actually been there, in an objective sense? "To this question, I always reply that the four beings were certainly there in front of me, as large as life," he insisted. "But on reflection, taking into account the fantastic scientific lead I know they have, my contact could have been only a perfect three-dimensional projection. This hypothesis is frightening and must bring home to us the psychic and scientific potential which they possess. . . .

"Although I don't exactly remember exactly getting into the craft . . . after they had performed their 'cellular regeneration' on me I did not feel at all different. Only this one thing raises a shadow of a doubt. But despite the fantastic aspect of this regenerating operation, certain details lead me to think they told the truth. For example, at the start of the telepathic contact, the craft had no opening; however, at the end of the contact, a large opening was there, on the right of the dome. While I was 'listening' to their thoughts, I was perfectly aware of what I could see around me. I didn't see this opening appear, though through it shone a whitish-orange light which was unbearable to look at. Not one of the four extraterrestrials was absent during the contact . . . but the telepathic contact had stopped.

"Logically, all this would imply that I had momentarily lost conscious- ness; the opening appeared; I was transported inside and protected by some method or other against the deadly vibrations of the machine; the regeneration was carried out, and I regained consciousness in the same place where I had been before losing consciousness. . . ."[1]

According to investigator Jean-Pierre Troadec, a few years after this encounter a man claimed to have seen the same, or a similar, craft, a few kilometers away. He did not know Monnet—who also told no one about his experience until 1962.[2]

Monnet provided further information from the communications received during this initial contact. The aliens said they had the technology to travel faster than light in both galactic and intergalactic space. Their declared agenda: "To profit from the scientific discoveries they had made, with a view to perfecting their knowledge; to look after and protect those civilizations which had lost all wisdom and in so doing had released on their respective planets processes that are sometimes irreversible and which impact on other extraterrestrial civilizations; to educate developing worlds and assist them technologically."[3]

SUBSEQUENT CLAIMS

After this adventure, Monnet went on to claim further experiences, including the sighting of a flying disc during his military service in Indo-China. And in France in June 1974, while paying for gas at a service station, he recognized two men filling their car (a new, metallic gray Renault 16) as either his original contacts or their doubles. The men imbued him with a sense of "exceptional well-being," radiating "tranquility, power, peace, and love"—identical to that recounted by those involved in the Amicizia saga (Chapter 13). They gave him a penetrating look, transmitted a telepathic message, then departed.[4]

As with "follow-up" experiences asserted by many contactees, we run into apparent absurdities and contradictions. To his credit, however, Monnet acknowledged as much himself, and sought explanations.

While I was performing with the Philharmonia Orchestra at the Orange Festival in July 1978, I interviewed Monnet at his home in Sorgues, together with my friend Ben Cruft (also a violinist with the orchestra). Monnet spoke with conviction about his earlier contact experience. A manuscript with which he presented me—subsequently incorporated into his first book—provides some interesting information.

Monnet claimed that the group that contacted him originated from "the star you call Vega [which] has fourteen planets, of which nine are inhabited." He was informed that they had numerous bases within our solar system—on Mars, our moon, on one of Jupiter's and on one of Saturn's moons—and a number of bases on Earth.

While my skepticism regarding much of the information later provided to Monnet endures, I am including the following, supposedly transmitted telepathically to him in July 1977, against the possibility that some important data may be contained therein. We must bear in mind that Monnet, a factory worker with but a scant knowledge of scientific matters, may well have misinterpreted some of the technical data:

"The surface bases we have introduced on your planet are protected from sight by a powerful magnetic field acting on the molecules of a layer of surrounding air covering the places where the bases are constructed. The principle of this magnetic process is based on bending the molecules of air and taking the form of prisms to avoid the source of light. This process renders invisible every object which isn't naturally compatible with the place, and renders it invisible in the range of this magnetic field. In parallel with that, we give out a wavelength acting on a precise part of the brain of the occasional person who approaches our installations. Our bases on your planet cannot be seen even from a height, remaining unnoticed by your aerial photographers. . . ."[5]

Pierre Monnet passed away in January 2009 at a hospital in Tarascon (Bouche-du-Rhône), aged seventy-eight—well short of the 120-year lifespan predicted for him by his alien contacts. Perhaps he became disillusioned toward the end—perhaps not.

"I could not find then, neither can I find today, a single doubt in my mind as to the reality of my physical contact in 1951," he emphasized in 1978. "For me, it has been the most extraordinary and also the most beautiful experience of my life. The story's resemblance to science fiction does not make it any less true or real. It constitutes and perhaps shows the way to a marvelous future for mankind."[6]

———

"Since the initial appearance of these craft, the entire world's defence chiefs have hidden the truth," wrote Monnet in 1974. "From the outset, civil and military pilots, qualified personnel attached to aerial detection units, as well as astronauts, were sworn to secrecy if they spoke of what they had seen in the sky, on radar screens, or the signals coming in from the various artificial satellites revolving around the Moon, Venus, and from modules sited on Mars. . . .

"The phenomenon generates considerable anxiety among the world's governments, who have only one method of holding back the moment of truth—to maintain the conspiracy. What the public should know is that all over the world, many contacts have been made and continue to be made between the average Earth person and the extraterrestrial representatives of a galactic civilisation which is scientifically, socially, and philosophically very much in advance of our own. . . ."[7]

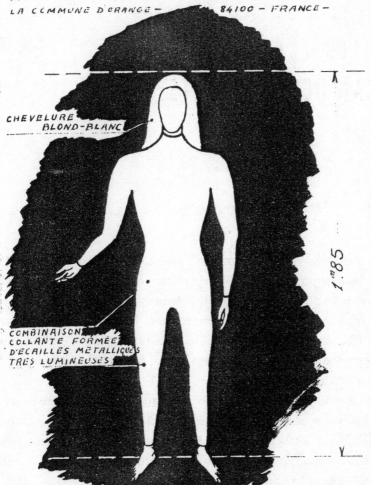

FORMES ET DESCRIPTION EXACTES DES QUATRE ETRES
EXTRA·TERRESTRES RENCONTRÉS EN JUILLET 1951 DANS
LA COMMUNE D'ORANGE — 84100 — FRANCE —

CHEVELURE
BLOND-BLANC

1m85

COMBINAISON
COLLANTE FORMÉE
D'ECAILLES MÉTALLIQUES
TRES LUMINEUSES

CET ETRE HUMAIN ETAIT PIEDS NUS ET MAINS NUES.
VISAGE TRES BEAU, SYMPATHIQUE ET TRES AMICAL. TEINT BLANC.
DANS L'ENSEMBLE, ON NE POUVAIT DETERMINER S'ILS APPARTENAIENT
AU SEXE FEMININ OU MASCULIN, POURTANT, UNE GRANDE FORCE
EMANAIT D'EUX. ILS ETAIENT QUATRE.

A sketch by Pierre Monnet of one of the alien beings he encountered near
Orange, France, in July 1951.

CHAPTER THREE
ITALIAN DEVELOPMENTS

T he proverbial "little green men" have long been associated with aliens, despite the fact that very few encounters relate to such beings. In stark contrast to the Dworshak and Monnet cases is the one reported by Professor Rapuzzi Luizi Johannis, a well-known Italian author and painter in his time. Johannis experienced only one encounter—and it involved little green men. The following is for me the most convincing of such cases.

On the morning of August 14, 1947, Johannis—a keen geologist—was making his way up a short valley called the Chiarsò, near Villa Santina, Carnia (Fruili) in northeast Italy. He had been following a path along the stream, which wound up through clumps of fir trees and deposits of alluvial rubble,[1] when his adventure began.

"As I emerged from one of these clumps of fir," he wrote in his richly detailed report, "I noticed, at a distance of about fifty meters from me, a large lenticular object of a vivid red color. When I had arrived at a spot a few steps from the 'thing,' I was able to establish the fact that it was a disc—seemingly of varnished metal [and] having the shape of a lens and a low central cupola with no apertures. At its tip a sort of shining metallic antenna, of telescopic form, was protruding. . . .

"The object, some ten meters wide, was embedded, to the extent of about a quarter of its length, in a great transverse cleft in the friable rock of the mountain side, and was at a height of about six meters above the bed of the stream. I decided that I would climb up there and see what it was. . . . I looked round to see whether there was anybody about who—should the need arise—could help me. It was then that I perceived, at a distance of fifty meters or so from me, two 'boys.' At any rate, that is what they seemed to be, at first. I shouted to them and pointed to their disc. And then I started toward them. When I had halved the distance between them and myself, I stopped, petrified.

"The two 'boys' were dwarves, the likes of which I had never seen nor even imagined. They were coming toward me slowly, with tiny strides, their hands at their sides and their heads motionless. When they had come to a few paces from me, they halted. I had no strength left. I seemed to be paralyzed, or to be dreaming. But I was able to observe them in every detail. And those details have remained impressed upon me. However, I must confess that the dominating sentiment in me then was one of enormous astonishment combined with fear. . . .

"They were no more than 90 centimeters in height, and were wearing dark blue-colored overalls made of some material that I would not know how to describe. 'Translucent' is the only term for it. They had collars and rather deep belts, all of a vivid red color. Even the cuffs and the shins of the legs ended in 'collars' of the same type. Their heads were bigger than the head of a normal man, and gave them a caricaturish aspect. But I think the sight of their 'faces' would have put an end to anybody's desire to laugh.

"At this point, I am obliged to explain that the terms I have used in this description are purely indications, and are of a purely anthropomorphic nature, because I don't know, today, whether those things that I have defined as nose, mouth, eyes, and hands were like that. . . .

"They had no signs of hair, but in place of it they were wearing a sort of dark brown tight-fitting cap, like an Alpinist's bonnet. The 'skin' of their faces was an earthly green. The only colour that comes close to it is the plasticine commonly used by sculptors, or of clay dipped in water. The 'nose' was straight, geometrically cut, and very long. Beneath it was a mere slit, shaped like a circumflex accent, opening and closing again at intervals, very much like the mouth of a fish.

"The 'eyes' were enormous, protruding, and round. Their appearance and color were like two well-ripened yellow-green plums. In the center of the eyes I noticed a kind of vertical 'pupil.' I saw no traces of eyebrows or eyelashes, and what I would have called the eyelids consisted of a ring, midway between green and yellow, which surrounded the base of those hemispherical eyes, just like the frame of a pair of spectacles.

"I remained there in astonishment, for what seemed an interminably long time, gazing at the two extraordinary creatures. I think the silent confrontation lasted no more than two or three minutes. Then I raised my arm with the [geologist's] pick and waved it in their direction and then in the direction of the disc and, in an agitated voice, I shouted and asked who they were, where they came from, and if I could be of any help. They wheeled round very quickly and I can't remember what I said after that, for things began to happen fast. I now believe that the two beings had interpreted my precipitate gestures as being threatening. . . .

"One of them raised his right hand to his belt, and from the center of the belt there came something that seemed as though it might be a thin puff of smoke. I now think it was a ray or something of the sort. Anyway, before I had time to move or do anything, I found myself laid out full length on the ground. My pick shot out of my hand, as though snatched by an invisible force. Only once in my life have I had the experience of a violent electric shock [and] as soon as I was struck by that ray, I felt a similar sensation. Moreover I felt myself deprived of all strength and all my efforts to raise myself meant an expenditure of energy that was beyond me.

"Meanwhile, the two midgets were coming toward me, and they halted at a spot two meters from me, where my pick had fallen. I managed to roll over on to one side and saw one of them bend over and pick up the tool, which was longer than he was. And this is how I was able to see his green 'hand' quite distinctly. It had eight fingers, four of them opposable to the others! It wasn't a hand: it was a claw, and the fingers were without joints. I also noticed the chests of the two beings were quivering; like a dog's chest when it pants after a long run."

Johannis finally was able to manage a sitting position. "Meanwhile, the two entities had arrived beneath the disc. I saw them climb up, slowly but surely, to the cleft in the rock and disappear into the disc itself, which was embedded almost vertically in the rock. A few more minutes elapsed, and then the strange object shot straight out from the rock and rose into the air. A cascade of stones and earth fell down on to the bed of the river. . . .

"The disc remained there stationary in the sky, like an enormous suspended gong. I could distinctly see its sharply cut flange four or five meters from me, and for a moment I was seized with terror that it was going to come down and cut me in half. . . . I think I shouted at the top of my voice. At any rate, I am certain that I made every effort to get up and escape. The result was that I kept falling back again, supine and racked with pain. Meanwhile, the disc had tipped slightly away from its vertical position, then tilted slightly. Then it suddenly grew smaller,[2] and vanished.

"Immediately afterward, I was struck by a tremendous blast of wind which rolled me over and over on the ground and filled my eyes with dust. I ended up against the stones in the river-bed and remained there for I don't know how long. Finally I managed to get into a sitting position again, and it was then that I looked at my wrist watch. It was 09:14. But it was only at about midday that I was in a fit state to get back home. In the meantime, I even slept for an hour. All my bones felt as if they were broken and my legs were weak and trembling. . . .

"I looked in my rucksack for my thermos flask of coffee and was not surprised to find it shattered to pieces, but what did surprise me was not being able to find any trace of its metal casing. Also gone were my aluminum fork and an aluminum can that had contained my cold lunch. I had to be content with bread soaked in coffee and throw away the salami and all the rest. Finally, I should add that I searched in vain for my pick, which would have been very useful to me at that point as a walking stick."

AFTERMATH

Johannis reached Raveo at 14:00 and promptly went to bed, explaining to the proprietress at the inn where he was staying that he'd fallen from a rock. The following morning, armed with another pick—and a revolver—he returned to the spot.

"Naturally, there was nobody there," he said. "I climbed right up to the cleft in the rock since I thought the two creatures might have thrown my old pick—to which I was very attached—in there, but I found nothing."

Later, he made inquiries in Raveo as to whether anyone had noticed any kind of "aeroplane" in the sky. Two people told him, independently, that they had: in one case at 08:30 and in the other at approximately 10:00. One of the witnesses said he noticed a "red globe being carried aloft by the wind" behind the mountain on the slope on which the village lies.

"At that time," wrote Johannis, "I tried to explain my strange adventure in many different ways, but none of them having anything whatever to do with flying saucers or other craft of extraterrestrial origin. At first I thought the 'saucer' was an experimental machine of the Allied Forces which were then in occupation of the Campoformido aerodrome in the Fruili area. My next thought was of some device of Russian origin. Finally, I wondered about some unknown civilization still hidden away in some unexplored regions of the world like the Matto Grosso of Brazil. The most absurd hypotheses could be adapted to fit my extraordinary adventure. But not one of them was satisfactory, since not one of them could account for the presence of the two men."

Although pilot Kenneth Arnold's famous sighting of what were dubbed "flying saucers" by the press in the United States—which occurred in the state of Washington on June 24, 1947—had been reported worldwide, flying saucers generally were not known about in Italy in the summer of 1947. Johannis decided therefore to tell no one of his experience. It was not until two months later, when he sailed for the United States, that he heard about the Arnold sighting. During a subsequent five-year stay in America, he read everything he could about the subject and in 1950 decided to relate his experience to two trusted friends, whose names and addresses were given to the Italian group which published this account. In 1952, on returning to Italy, he decided to approach a newspaper office.

"I went to Milan and called upon the director of *L'Europeo*. There I was told that the subject was an interesting one but that, in order that it could be published, authenticated, it was necessary for me to furnish 'proofs' of its authenticity. I replied that, if on that morning in August 1947 I had imagined that I was going to encounter creatures from another world, I would certainly not have hesitated for one moment to take along a whole troop of journalists, cinematographers and (why not?) a company of soldiers too. . . ."[3]

In a letter in 1964 to Gianni Settimo, director and founder of the Centri Studi Clipeologici in Turin, Johannis enclosed sketches he had made to illustrate his report, published for the first time in their journal,[4] adding some relevant remarks:

". . . As I told you, at such a distance in time, many of my recollections—exact enough at the time—have weakened and have consequently become a little confused. I refer particularly to the exact appearance of the 'bodies' of the two 'beings' met by me, as well as the shape of the eyes, since I am no longer certain whether they were vertical or horizontal slits or whether there weren't any pupils at all.

"When I sent my account of the episode from America to the Italian weekly *L'Europeo,* I sent it with a sketch of the 'pilots,' but when I came back to Europe that sketch was not returned to me because their editorial office had lost it. That sketch was done by me two months after the encounter, and consequently was much more faithful a reproduction than the ones done by me now.

"However, generally speaking, the front view of the 'head' can be taken (apart from the pupils) as corresponding to the absence or not of ears or something similar that I can't recall absolutely. The sketches of the complete figures are to be considered as rough and approximate outlines and consequently of purely general value. . . ."[5]

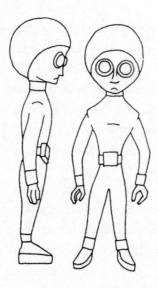

In assessing Professor Johannis's report, we have to take into consideration the fact that, in addition to being well known as a painter, he was a prolific author who wrote at least fifteen books of science fiction. Of course, he could have invented the story. Though to what end? As far as I am aware, the story was never marketed separately nor incorporated into any of his books, and it did not appear in print until 1964, in a relatively obscure Italian UFO magazine.

"I am at present inclined to believe that the two pilots were nothing more than two robots, whereas in 1947 I was convinced that I had met real and actual extraterrestrial beings," wrote Johannis in 1964. "I believe that old pick of mine is now in a museum on some other planet. And I hope that somebody up there is trying to decipher the marks cut in the handle. . . ."[6]

A FLYING SAUCER LANDS IN THE ITALIAN ALPS

As Britain's distinguished researcher Gordon Creighton pointed out in his accompanying notes to this report, there are striking resemblances—disc shape, low central cupola, and shiny metallic antenna—to the disputed photographs of a flying disc and its humanoid occupant taken in 1952 by the thirty-year-old Italian engineer Giampiero Monguzzi, in the presence of his wife, on the Alps (see photo section).

Many researchers have arbitrarily confuted the photos, insisting that models were used. Having a particular prejudice to antennae sticking out of flying saucers and aliens wearing Apollo-type spacesuits (if long before such were used), I initially thought the same. But later, as an experienced photographer, I noted that the depth of field and everything else in the pictures appear proportionately correct in comparison with his written report. And in addition to parallels with the Johannis case, there are others.

Monguzzi's pictures are widely known among students of the subject. His actual report, however, is not.

On the morning of July 31, 1952—a few days after a second wave of flying saucer sightings was reported that month and tracked over Washington, D.C.—Monguzzi and his wife were on a climbing trip near the Cherchen glacier on the Italian side of the Bernina massif, a little to the south of St. Moritz.

"Suddenly, I felt something uncanny around us," begins his account. "A cold wind had been blowing all the time from the summits, and we had just remarked that it sounded like a music chord, similar to that heard in the sails of a boat. But quite suddenly, this noise had stopped completely although we could still see the wind blowing up snow on the mountain rims. And then we noticed that we couldn't even hear our own heavy footsteps on the gravel and icy ground, and we could no longer hear our voices, though we were quite near each other. I saw my wife's mouth move but failed to detect a sound. It was an uncanny, compact silence which surrounded us, a strange kind of vacuum.[7]

"Suddenly, my wife grasped my arm with a frightened look in her eyes, and I also got a real shock, because no farther than 200 meters from where we stood, an enormous object had settled on the rim of the glacier, silently. It appeared to have come from below, from the valley beneath the glacier—certainly not from above. My first guess was that of a plane trying to land, but the object had no wings. Looking at it, I grew more and more uneasy. The ice around us reflected the light, blinding me, as did the sun's rays coming from my right. I turned away, trying not to look at the object again. We both hid ourselves behind a rock. The uncanny silence around still prevailed. I did not even try to talk again—I wouldn't have dared to open my mouth.

"After some moments I gathered enough courage to cast a glimpse over the rock. The strange craft was still there. I now dared to approach it and slithered down on the gravel for about 50 meters. I couldn't go any farther without losing my foothold on the ice.

"I now recognized clearly that it was a round silvery disc with a diameter of approximately ten meters and a height of about three meters. As usual, I had my camera[8] over my shoulder and, becoming bolder, looked through the viewfinder and shot my first picture. But as I failed to hear the usual click, I felt uncertain and shot a second one. For a few more moments the disc lay there in front of me without showing any sign of life.

"But then suddenly I noticed a man beside the craft, wearing a kind of diving-bell which reflected the sun's rays like metal. The figure seemed to move toward me. Instinctively, I shot another picture, although my legs felt as though glued to the ground, as if paralyzed.

"The man seemed not to notice me. He now changed direction and started walking slowly around his disc, as if inspecting it. After every two or three steps he stopped, looking upward to the perimeter of the vehicle. His movements seemed to be hindered somewhat by his dress. In his hand he held an instrument like a flashlight. The figure was not clearly outlined and gave the impression that his dress was of a furry material.

"I fail to remember how long this procedure took, but I would estimate that no more than five minutes had elapsed since the landing of the craft. From the spot where I stood, I was unable to see the whole object; rather, I was seeing its lower part. Nonetheless, I could observe an antenna coming out on the top, and there seemed to be another antenna on the man's 'rucksack.' The pilot, having finished his inspection, showed up once more on the other side of the disc. I presumed that there was an entrance on the side hidden from me. I shot some more pictures.

"After a while, I noticed that part of the completely smooth-surfaced hull seemed to be turning around: the movement might have involved a third of the hull. And suddenly, the craft shot up in the air, noiselessly, hovering a few seconds at a height of approximately ten meters. Then, like a lift, it shot upward toward the summits of the Bernina massif. I had had enough time, however, to note that the antenna had retracted and that the upper part of the craft seemed to have a number of portholes or hatches. I managed to shoot another two pictures of the departing disc, and while the distance grew, I felt life coming back to my legs. My voice also returned.

"I looked at my watch. It was exactly 09:27. Still very confused, and with shaking knees, I went to the rock where my wife was hiding. She had followed everything with her own eyes and was still pale and disconcerted. After a while we went to the landing spot, looking for traces or tracks on the ground, but found none. The snow was absolutely icy. For a while I wondered, however, why the disc, with quite a weight of its own, had left no imprints, but then I remembered that it had hovered at a height of ten meters, and I realized it could also have done this at ten centimeters off the ground. Our own shoes left no marks either, by the way. . . ."[9]

In 1958, my Swiss friend Louise ("Lou") Zinsstag, a distinguished researcher, sent a letter to the Swiss military airfields administration, enclosing a copy of an article which included one of the Monguzzi photos. She received a reply from the operations unit a few days later:

"It is with great interest that we read the article. . . . Above all, we are astonished and surprised by the revealing photographic material, especially the picture taken by the Italian engineer Monguzzi in the Bernina massif which shows a landed flying machine with a human figure beside it.

"As we were looking at that photo we asked ourselves if engineer Monguzzi was able to witness the take-off of this flying saucer. Do we know whether he might have had the opportunity to locate some other witnesses who observed the machine before it took off?

"We must strongly emphasize that our question implies no doubt about the genuineness of the object photographed; it arises from a sincere and intense interest in all the questions it raises, and we would be very grateful if you could reply to us.

"We look forward immensely to your reply and thank you for your trouble. . . ."[10]

A copy of the original letter in German appears on p. 44. Unfortunately, I do not recall the outcome of this correspondence, but I am sure that Lou sent the administration copies of all seven photos, together with a copy of the article written for *Epoca*, which would have resolved their questions.

Feeling certain of having taken the pictures of the year and planning to sell them at a good price, Monguzzi and his wife went to Milan. The engineer—a member of the Edison Society of Italy—showed them to his friends, to his manager, and to some newspaper reporters. But nobody believed him: all were certain that they were clever fakes. A heated controversy arose in the Edison Society with the result that Monguzzi lost his membership—and later his job.[11]

Would a hoaxer have gone that far?

Direktion der Militärflugplätze
Direction des aérodromes militaires
Direzione degli aerodromi militari
Betriebs-Gr. Buochs/Ennetbürgen
STANS Postfach

Buochs , den 28. Juni 1958.

In der Antwort anzugeben
A rappeler dans la réponse

No. ▮

Ihr Zeichen
Votre référence

Frau

Lou Z i n s s t a g ,

Nadelberg 31,

B a s e l .

Sehr geehrte Frau Zinsstag,

Mit sehr grossem Interesse haben wir den Artikel in der " TAT "
vom 25. Juni " Im Sekretariat der Fliegenden Untertassen "
gelesen und sind vor allem über das aufschlussreiche Bildmaterial
erstaunt und überrascht. Ganz besonders trifft das auf jene Auf-
nahme zu, die der italienische Ingenieur Monguzzi im Berninamassiv
gemacht hat und einen gelandeten fliegenden Körper mit daneben-
stehender menschlicher Figur zeigt.

Beim Betrachten dieses Bildes haben wir uns die Frage vorgelegt,
ob Ingenieur Monguzzi auch den Abflug dieser Untertasse verfolgen
konnte. Weiss man, ob ihm die Möglichkeit fehlte, Zeugen zu mobili-
sieren, die die Flugmaschine bis zu ihrem Start hätten überwachen
können?

Wir dürfen ausdrücklich betonen, dass unsere Frage keinen Zweifel
an der Wirklichkeit des aufgenommenen Objektes birgt; sie entspringt
einem tatsächlichen regen Interesse am ganzen Fragenkomplex und wir
wären Ihnen sehr zu Dank verpflichtet, wenn Sie sie uns beantworten
könnten.

Wir sehen Ihrer Nachricht mit Spannung entgegen, danken Ihnen für
Ihre Mühe und grüssen Sie

mit vorzüglicher Hochachtung

DIREKTION DER MILITAERFLUGPLAETZE
Betriebsgruppe Buochs-Ennetbürgen

*A letter from the Swiss Directorate of Military Aerodromes to
researcher Louise Zinsstag confirming their conviction as to the
authenticity of one of the series of photographs taken by engineer
Giampiero Monguzzi in the Italian Alps in July 1952.*

CHAPTER FOUR
EISENHOWER AND THE EXTRATERRESTRIALS

Why don't aliens contact our leaders? My reply to this frequently asked question is that they have done so on a number of occasions, as attested by witnesses. Several such meetings involved President Dwight D. ("Ike") Eisenhower and others in the mid-1950s, such as at Edwards/Muroc Air Force Base in February 1954, discussed later. There is also lesser-known related evidence supplied by Antonio Ribera, a distinguished Spanish researcher, citing an earlier visit to a base by Eisenhower—at that time U.S. Army Chief of Staff.

In Mexico in 1970, the publisher Guillermo Mendizábal Elizalde told Ribera that while attending a gathering during which a title was presented to Miguel Alemán Valdés, President of Mexico (1946–1952), the subject of flying saucers came up. Alemán listened in silence. But on being asked for his opinion, he revealed that when General Eisenhower had visited Mexico shortly before becoming president, he told Alemán that he had once been taken to an air base in the Southwest United States, where he had been shown "a flying disc and the cadavers of several of its crew members."[1]

This report was confirmed by Leonard Stringfield, a former U.S. Air Force intelligence officer, who learned from Dr. Robert S. Carr, a University of South Florida professor, that in 1948 General Eisenhower had been taken to see a craft and bodies captured at Aztec, New Mexico in March 1948, and it was on his command that the secrecy lid was clamped down on the subject, and rigidly enforced.[2] Since another crashed disc had reportedly been recovered that same year just across the Mexican border from Laredo, Texas, it is likely, in my view, that this might have prompted Eisenhower's revelation to Alemán.

Until several years ago, I remained unaware of another incident involving Eisenhower and extraterrestrials, reported to have occurred in February 1955. The noted researcher Art Campbell has been responsible for my education regarding what I now regard as compelling new testimony.

Campbell served his country during the Korean War at naval shore installations and with a fleet electronics unit aboard the aircraft carrier USS *Boxer* (CV-21). After leaving the Navy in the mid-1950s, he became active in UFO investigations, working with Major Donald E. Keyhoe's National Investigations Committee on Aerial Phenomena (NICAP). Campbell is the author of an illuminating book on the recovery of a crashed disc on the Plains of San Augustin, New Mexico, in July 1947, in addition to several books on northwest pioneer history.

More recently, Campbell has uncovered a great deal of evidence that in 1955, President Eisenhower had another meeting with extraterrestrials, which took place at Holloman Air Force Base, New Mexico (currently home of the 49th Fighter Wing, Air Combat Command). The following is summarized from Campbell's investigation reports,[3] as well as voluminous additional material which he has kindly furnished me over a lengthy period.

QUAIL HUNTING

On February 9, 1955, Eisenhower announced to the press that he was going to Georgia for a few days' quail hunting, staying with the Secretary of the Treasury, George H. Humphrey, a millionaire industrialist who owned a plantation near Thomasville, Georgia. Others included in the trip were Humphrey's wife, the First Lady and her mother, and Clifford Roberts, a Wall Street banker.

The party left Andrews Air Force Base, Maryland, on February 10 at 13:00 in Eisenhower's Air Force One, *Columbine III*, a new Lockheed VC-121E four-engined Super Constellation, with a crew of fourteen, piloted by

Major William "Bill" Draper, who also had been Eisenhower's pilot during World War II. Preceding the flight by about thirty minutes, a chartered plane-load of journalists from all the major networks flew to Spence Field, Moultrie, Georgia, some twenty-five miles north of Thomasville. *Columbine III* landed there two and a half hours later.

With its two thousand acres of prime bird-hunting land, Milestone Plantation suited Eisenhower's requirements for privacy. With the exception of a previously arranged photo op, none of the media was allowed on the grounds. "The plantation was so secure," Art told me, "that Ike was able to go there four times in the 1950s. This was his second trip. The press was housed some eight miles away at Scott Hotel in Thomasville. James Hagerty, Ike's press secretary, gave daily international news and briefings in the hotel lounge."

Many commentators wondered why the president had taken a few days' hunting trip at a time when international tensions were mounting. Fear of a nuclear exchange with the Soviet Union was paramount—and a very real threat. As the British journalist and historian Sir Max Hastings succinctly puts it: "A younger generation finds it hard to believe that it was plausible that America and the Soviet Union would come to nuclear blows. Armies and navies, together with fleets of bombers and batteries of missiles capable of destroying civilization many times over, confronted each other at instant readiness. . . ."[4]

The hunting party reached the lodgings at Milestone, changed quickly, and reached the hunting area at about 17:30. Media attendees included well-known journalists Ed Darby of *Time*, John Edwards of ABC, and William Lawrence of *The New York Times*. Why all the prestigious press for a quail shoot? Perhaps the reason lay in the fact that a week earlier, Josef Stalin's replacement leader, Georgi Malenkov, had been forced to resign and was replaced by Marshal Nikolai Bulganin. "A famous military leader taking over an aggressive Cold War government gave the world a severe case of the jitters," Campbell believes.

ARTHUR GODFREY

Campbell questions the presence of Arthur Godfrey on the trip. A famous television personality at the time, Godfrey's shows were watched by millions and helped define the first decade of 1950s television and radio. "What was the one and only indomitable Arthur Godfrey doing on the president's plane?" asks Campbell. "He was not seated with Ike or his social guests in the main passenger section, but in the forward crew compartment with about a dozen others, including the flight crew and some Secret Service agents."

According to news sources years later—including Ted Gup of *Time* magazine—Godfrey and Ed Murrow were part of a huge civil defense effort to assist the government in making pre-recorded taped messages to be transmitted on television and radio in the event of a nuclear attack. Campbell continues:

"Gup said in his article that a number of newsmen had taken oaths of secrecy and had agreed to accompany the president to the relocation site of his choosing, to lend their familiar names and voices to help calm the surviving audience. Recalling the separate press plane that accompanied Eisenhower to Spence air base and Thomasville, one wonders if any of these spokesmen were also along on this strange trip. Was this trip a true potential national emergency? Or another trial run of apparently many in those days?

"There were a number of facilities in the mid-1950s where government could relocate to in the event of a national emergency. One was an underground bunker named Mount Weather, near Godfrey's home in Berryville, Virginia, and another was a facility named Raven Rock, near Gettysburg, Pennsylvania, where Eisenhower and his cabinet convened on a number of 'practice occasions.'"

Of incidental interest, Godfrey had flown for the Air Force and Navy in World War II. In 1965 he reported on his own show that he had been buzzed by a UFO while flying a light plane.[5]

THE WITNESSES
On the day following the arrival at Thomasville, James Hagerty reported that Eisenhower had come down with "the sniffles" and would be staying in for a while. He was not seen again for some thirty-six hours, having secretly been taken to Spence Field and flown in Air Force One to Holloman Air Force Base, New Mexico, together with a team of Secret Service aides and supervisors.

One of the many witnesses to the presence of Air Force One was Airman 2nd Class Manuel W. Kirklin, stationed at Holloman and assigned to the base hospital under the Flight Surgeon, Captain/Dr. Robert N. Reiner. Kirklin held clearance to Secret material at that time.

"In late February 1955," relates Kirklin, "we heard that the president was coming to Holloman. I knew there was going to be an honor parade for him, scheduled for early in the morning. The day before it was due to take place, it was called off. Not only that, but I heard through the grapevine that the base commander [Colonel Frank D. Sharp] had requested leave covering the time the president was visiting. I thought this was unusual—I would have stayed on the base if I was the commanding officer and the president was visiting." (Kirklin later realized that going on leave would allow Col. Sharp to give Eisenhower his undivided attention.)

Later, at the hospital, Dorsey E. Moore, the enlisted men's leading airman, asked Kirklin if he had seen a disc hovering over the flight line. Kirklin replied in the negative. "I'm thinking, a disc that you can throw," he reports, "but the only thing that I knew that hovered was a helicopter and the Navy's hovercraft." He asked what it was made of. "Metal," said Dorsey, "like polished aluminum or stainless steel."

"How big is it?"

"Twenty to thirty feet in diameter. Do you want to see it? Go out to the front of the hospital and look down at the flight line."

"With my luck it wouldn't be there."

"I took my wife to the commissary and it was there thirty minutes later. Go out to the front of the hospital and take a look."

Concerned at leaving his post without permission, Kirklin asked the head nurse if he could go. She consulted the doctor, but permission was refused. Later, the airman happened to be walking behind two pilots and overheard their conversation regarding the event. One of the men, an Officer of the Day, was responding to questions from the other pilot relating to Eisenhower's visit. Kirklin asserts that the officer explained that after Air Force One landed, it had turned around and remained on the active runway. The base radar had then been turned off, after which two discs had approached the base at low altitude via the White Sands National Monument.

"One hovered overhead like it was protecting the other one," explained the officer. "The other one landed on the active runway in front of [Eisenhower's] plane. He got out of his plane and went toward it. A door opened, and he went inside for forty or forty-five minutes." Asked by the other pilot whether he had seen the aliens, the officer replied that he had not: they stayed inside. Eisenhower then returned to his plane.

Later, at about 11:15, Kirklin went to pick up the mail, where he encountered a new 2nd Lieutenant supply officer who asked him if he had seen anything on the flight line. Kirklin replied in the negative.

"After work [about 16:30–16:45], I was in my barracks room when I was called out to see Air Force One fly overhead. It flew over the residential area of the base. This is a no-flying zone for all military aircraft—only the president could get away with it."

After supper, Kirklin noticed that the lights were still on in the Flight Surgeon's office and went over to turn them off. There he saw and heard Dr. Reiner talking to a lieutenant colonel, who mentioned that the Commander-in-Chief (Eisenhower) had addressed 225 men, on two consecutive sessions, in the supply hangar and/or the base theater. Eisenhower spoke only for a few minutes on each occasion.

Asked by Reiner what had been discussed, the lieutenant colonel replied that the subject matter was classified "higher than Secret." I share Art Campbell's opinion that since Eisenhower was supposed to be hunting in Georgia, base personnel were ordered not to mention his presence at Holloman. The actual purpose of the visit would obviously never have been disclosed to so many "uncleared" personnel.

Three months later, while serving in Japan, Kirklin was talking to some airmen, one of whom confirmed that he had heard Eisenhower talk at the base theater. The subject matter was not discussed. Kirklin also said that a mutual acquaintance had learned from a man who had been stationed at Holloman that people were still talking about Eisenhower's visit two years later.

Captain Joseph W. Kittinger, Jr. (retired), who was well acquainted with Kirklin at Holloman, is best known for his daredevil leaps from high-altitude helium balloons as part of research into high-altitude bailout, known as Project Excelsior, culminating in August 1960 when he jumped from *Excelsior III* at 102,800 feet (31,300 meters). In freefall in his pressure suit for four and a half minutes, he reached Mach 0.9—almost the speed of sound. He served three combat tours in the Vietnam War, during which he commanded the F-4 Phantom 555th Tactical Fighter Squadron and vice-commanded the 432nd Tactical Reconnaissance Wing. He was shot down by a MiG fighter in 1972 and spent eleven months as a prisoner-of-war in the notorious "Hanoi Hilton."[6]

What is much less known about Kittinger's background, as I discovered, is his extensive professional contact with Dr. J. Allen Hynek, a scientific consultant on UFOs to both the Air Force's Project Bluebook and the CIA's Office of Scientific Intelligence (OSI).[7] I noted that part of their professional relationship involved, in 1962, Project Stargazer, a balloon-borne project to carry out astronomical studies at high altitude, Kittinger as balloon pilot and Hynek as astronomical adviser. In *The Roswell Report: Case Closed*—the Air Force's second book attempting to deny the July 1947 incident—Kittinger's sworn testimony states as follows:

"I worked very closely with Dr. Hynek over a period of five years from 1958 to 1963. Dr. Hynek would typically spend a half day working on Stargazer and then the rest of the day participating as one of the consultants on the UFO study, Project Bluebook, that was also conducted at Wright-Patterson AFB. [He] was very familiar with the techniques and capabilities of the Air Force high altitude balloon program [and] once approached me and we discussed at length the possibility that Air Force high altitude balloons were responsible for many UFO sightings. . . . I was therefore 'flabbergasted' when Dr. Hynek appeared to believe that some of these sightings were of extraterrestrial origin."[8]

During this period at Wright-Patterson, Captain Kittinger also worked at the U.S. Air Force Aerospace Medical Research Laboratory in connection with Project Excelsior, mentioned earlier. In 1959 and 1960, the laboratory collaborated with the Holloman Balloon Branch for Excelsior, the culmination of high-altitude free-fall studies that began in 1953 using anthropomorphic dummies[9]—the same dummies cited in *The Roswell Report* as probably being responsible for the alien bodies reported by witnesses to the Roswell events in 1947!

Interestingly, according to June Crain, who worked in the Rocketry Section Lab at Wright-Patterson with top-secret clearance at the time, the deceased alien bodies were brought to the Aero Med Lab (as it was widely known). "They had been flown in to the base during the night and were in a freezer locker in one of the hangars and Aero Med had charge of them for examination," she told investigator James E. Clarkson. "The people doing the telling seemed to know what they were talking about. . . ."[10]

In 2007 Kirklin wrote to Colonel Kittinger—who had been transferred to the Air Force Missile Development Center at Holloman in 1954—asking if he recalled the Eisenhower visit, avoiding specifics. "First of all," replied Kittinger, "I remember you and the flight that we made in the Beaver [a bush plane] looking for the downed balloon equipment which we found on the rancher's field. I remember that you were one of the only ones that didn't get air-sick. . . . I do not remember President Eisenhower visiting Holloman but it may have been after I left in 1958 when I transferred to the Aero Med Lab at Wright-Patterson AFB, Dayton, Ohio. . . ."[11]

So, no confirmation from Kittinger. We can surmise, however, that, though well aware of the Eisenhower visit, he remains loath to violate his security oaths. Other witnesses, however, have been forthcoming.

In 2007, Art Campbell interviewed retired Master Sergeant Robert Boord, one of the former security guards who served on *Columbine III*, who said that although the usual complement of Secret Service agents was five or six, if they were flying to somewhere the president had not visited before, two agents would go ahead but five or six were usually on the plane. He learned from Master Sergeant Leo Borega, a colleague and friend, that one trip down to South Georgia had involved "a dozen or so going to this tiny little town [Thomasville]" and that at about 03:00 hours the following day (February 11), the crew received word that the president would be leaving in about an hour (from Spence Field). "We were always ready for this kind of thing," said Borega, "and sure enough, the plane left one hour later." He added that about half an hour before the plane left, two Air Force cars pulled up and six more agents went on board to accompany the flight "to somewhere out West."

Art found another witness to Eisenhower's arrival at Holloman, Albert D. Wykoff (pseudonym), whose military background included assignment as a tail-gunner to a B-29 bomber squadron with the 20th Air Force in the Pacific during World War II. As a staff sergeant on a U.S. Air Force cargo plane that flew into Holloman in February 1955 (he does not recall the exact date), he and the other crew members watched as Ike's Constellation landed. They had no idea that the president was in it until the following morning.

As Wykoff and the rest of the crew were preparing to leave, an officer approached and told them to stay where they were. "But we have to leave," Wykoff protested. "Well, President Eisenhower is here and you can't leave the field until he's gone," retorted the officer. Wykoff and his colleagues were therefore required to kill time at Holloman until they had clearance to leave.

"While in the sergeants' mess at lunchtime," Art recounted to me, "a general invitation was given by an officer to hear the president speak at a nearby hangar. When Wykoff and several of his crew went there, they were denied entry as they did not have a proper Holloman badge. An officer overheard the badge discussion and was able to get them in to hear Ike at another presentation given at the base theater."

Campbell also cites testimony he received from a lady whose father (pseudonym Bill Larson) had been a civilian electrician at Holloman. Larson and his crew worked from a pickup truck that had a Bell Telephone bed and many compartments for electrical gear, including a large spool of wire. From time to time, her father had discussed the day Eisenhower came to Holloman with his family and others. Here follows part of a letter he sent to his daughter a few months before his death:

". . . Sometime after Christmas 1954 we were told President Eisenhower was coming, so George, our boss, went to a meeting to find out more. He would not be inspecting anything, they said, and [we should] just carry on as usual. 'If you see the president, don't gawk, wave or anything—just carry on.'

"So the day the president came, we went out in the truck to a job where we were replacing some wire down the flight line. It was really old stuff, put there in the Second World War. We heard the president's plane in the morning line up for an approach, and watched it land on the far runway. We waited for it to taxi over to the flight line so we could see him. But we didn't hear it anymore, and it had shut down somewhere out there. We went ahead and pulled wire for a while, and one of the men—I believe it was Charlie—said he could 'see out there from that pole over there, so why doesn't one of us go up the pole and see where the plane is?'

"Well, I had my climbers on and I started to unbuckle them and was waiting to give them to the first volunteer when someone said I should do it, as people were used to seeing me up the poles anyway. So, I started up, with my back to the sun—a safety measure—which also put my back to the runway where I thought his Connie [Constellation] was. As I started up, some of the guys reminded me not to gawk, and I heard them laugh. A few minutes later, I heard someone shouting, and some guys tarring the hangar roof nearby started to run, pointing out to the runway. Then I heard our truck start up and some of the crew jumped in, with one or two running after it, and they were pointing out to the flight line. And so I decided to turn around on the pole to see what the ruckus was about—and I could not believe what I saw.

"There was this pie-tin-like thing coming at me about 150 feet away. I thought it was remote-controlled or something, twenty-five to thirty feet across. And I started down the pole as fast as I could go. I was up about forty feet, and I threw my climbing rope out, gave it slack and only touched the spike on each side of the pole three or four times even before I got to the bottom. While I was running toward the big hangar, I looked back and it had stopped, and was just sitting there.

"Well, when we all got back to the shop, and we had a good laugh, one of the guys that saw me come down said, 'He got down that pole a whole lot faster than a fireman!' Apparently, soon after this incident, the saucer just stopped and hovered about three hundred feet over the flight line while the meeting took place on the far runway, near the UFO.

"Dad said that once the people there got over the initial shock, many just stood and watched it. He said it was a beautiful sight. It had an occasional wobble. He recalled that later that day many neon lights needed replacing. . . ." (Art Campbell believes this was apparently the saucer that hovered over the flight line, which Dorsey Moore and his wife saw around 08:45-09:00.) "They all thought it was one of our secret aircraft that the president had come to see. Dad said he never considered it was anything but ours until years later when [the subject] got publicized more—in the 1960s or so. It was only then that he understood what was so secret. . . ."

COLLATERAL EVIDENCE

There is, of course, no official evidence that Air Force One ever left Spence Field, Moultrie—or returned there from anywhere else—during Eisenhower's trip to Holloman, as stated in the official "trip narrative" (see p. 62). Art believes nonetheless that at least one diversionary tactic was employed. For instance, on February 13, the *Thomasville Times-Enterprise* reported on a special dinner for the president's entourage and numerous other guests, held at the Glen Arven Country Club on the evening of February 11, by invitation of Secretary George Humphrey. "About 30 visiting newspapermen, photographers and movie men were on hand for the delicious dinner," noted the paper. "Entertainment [included] several amusing pantomime selections at the conclusion of the dinner."

Art told me that in 2008 he had tracked down a bartender who had been in attendance that evening. "He said it seemed that every divorcee in the county had been invited to meet the lonely reporters: eight to ten had been invited, but sixteen showed up. The pantomime did not go over nearly as well as the southern belles in their strapless cocktail dresses. . . . We believe that Ike and Air Force One slipped into Moultrie at about 20:30 while the party was in full swing. This was the trip that no one knew about—and the party that everyone remembered!"

In May 2010, retiring New Hampshire State Representative Henry W. McElroy, Jr., revealed in a speech that President Eisenhower had been briefed about the presence of extraterrestrial intelligent beings on Earth. McElroy also stated that the document he viewed made reference to the opportunity for Eisenhower to meet the alien visitors. Here follow extracts from the transcript of his speech:

". . . When I was in the New Hampshire State Legislature, I served on the State Federal Relations and Veterans' Affairs Committee. It was, apparently, important that as a Representative of the Sovereign People who had elected me to this honorable office, that I be updated on a large number of topics . . . some of those ongoing topics had been categorized as Federal, State, Local development, and security matters.

"The document I saw was an official brief to President Eisenhower. To the best of my memory, this brief was pervaded with a sense of hope, and it informed President Eisenhower of the continued presence of extraterrestrial beings here in the United States of America. The brief seemed to indicate that a meeting between the president and some of these visitors could be arranged as appropriate and if desired.

"The tone of the brief indicated to me that there was no need for concern, since these visitors were in no way causing any harm, or had any intentions whatsoever in causing any disruption then, or in the future.

"While I can't verify the times or places, or that any meetings occurred directly between Eisenhower and these visitors, because of his optimism in his farewell address in 1961 I personally believe that Eisenhower did indeed meet with these extraterrestrial, off-world astronauts. . . ."[12]

There is some confusion regarding the dates of the prearranged meeting/meetings between Eisenhower and aliens at Edwards/Muroc in 1954. Former Royal Air Force fighter-pilot and author Desmond Leslie (who co-authored *Flying Saucers Have Landed* with George Adamski) learned from a U.S. Air Force officer that "on a certain day" a 100-foot-diameter disc landed on the runway and was housed under guard in Hangar 27. Eisenhower was taken to see it.[13] Gabriel Green, another researcher, spoke to a military officer who claimed to have witnessed the arrival over the base of five UFOs, on February 20. A general ordered all anti-aircraft batteries to open fire—which they did, but with no effect. The men then held their fire and watched as one of the craft landed close to one of the base's large hangars. Two other witnesses, Don Johnson and Paul Umbrello, also claim to have seen one of the discs near the base on the same day.[14]

A retired USAF test pilot reported to the Earl of Clancarty (better known as the author Brinsley Le Poer Trench) that three saucer-shaped and two cigar-shaped craft landed at the base (presumably on the same day). "The aliens looked human-like, but not exactly," he said, adding that they had the same proportions as humans and were able to breathe our atmosphere. They did not say where they came from. In English, they explained to the bemused president that they would like to start an "educational program" for the people of Earth in order to make mankind more aware of their presence here.[15]

Unnerved, Eisenhower responded that he didn't think the world was ready for such a revelation. The aliens seemed to appreciate this, though they indicated that they would continue making further isolated contact with humans. They then demonstrated their ability to overcome gravity and to make their craft invisible. "This disturbed the president greatly," said the test pilot, "because now none of us could see them, although we knew they were there."[16]

But it seems that another, related event took place. In a letter sent in April 1954 to N. Meade Layne, director of a quasi-occult group called the Borderland Sciences Research Associates (BSRA)—photocopy reproduced on p. 63—associate Gerald Light revealed details of events which—if true—must have occurred that month.

"My dear friend," begins the first part of the letter, dated April 16, "I have just returned from Muroc. The report is true—devastatingly true! I made the journey in company with Franklin Allen of the Hearst papers and Edwin Nourse of Brookings Institute (Truman's erstwhile financial adviser) and Bishop McIntyre of L.A. (confidential names, for the present, please).

"When we were allowed to enter the restricted section, (after about six hours in which we were checked on every possible item, event, incident and aspect of our personal and public lives) I had the distinct feeling that the world had come to an end with fantastic realism. For I have never seen so many human beings in a state of complete collapse and confusion as they realized that their own world had indeed ended with such finality as to beggar description. . . .

"During my two days visit I saw five separate and distinct types of air-craft being studied and handled by our airforce officials—with assistance and permission of The Etherians! [a term used by BSRA]. . . . It has finally happened. It is now a matter of history.

"President Eisenhower, as you may already know, was spirited over to Muroc one night during his visit to Palm Springs recently. And it is my conviction that he will ignore the terrific conflict between the various 'authorities' and go directly to the people via radio and television—if the impasse continues much longer. From what I could gather, an official statement to the country is being prepared for delivery about the middle of May.

"I will leave it to your own excellent powers of deduction to construct a fitting picture of the mental and emotional pandemonium that is now shattering the consciousness of hundreds of our scientific 'authorities' and all the pundits of the various specialized knowledges [sic] that make up our current physics. In some instances I could not stifle a wave of pity that arose in my own being as I watched the pathetic bewilderment of rather brilliant brains struggling to make some sort of rational explanation which would enable them to retain their familiar theories and concepts. . . . I shall never forget those forty-eight hours at Muroc!"[17]

Gerald Light makes no reference to the presence of Eisenhower at this meeting, though he makes the statement about "spiriting" Ike to Muroc just above. It is a matter of record that on the evening of February 20, 1954, while on a golfing vacation during which he stayed with his friend Paul Roy Helms at his ranch in Palm Springs, the president went "missing." Nobody seemed to know where he was, and the press corps was left to speculate. United Press suggested there had been a medical emergency, while Associated Press wired that Eisenhower was dead. At a near-hysterical press conference, the "truth" was finally revealed: the president had simply knocked a cap off a tooth chewing on a chicken leg and had been taken by Helms to a local dentist. Officially, there is no record of such a visit.[18]

A handwritten note from Meade Layne on Gerald Light's letter references both Miramar and Gillespie airfields, with an asterisk on the third paragraph seemingly indicating where the intensive security checks had been carried out prior to the Edwards/Muroc visit. The airfields are currently known as Marine Corps Air Station Miramar (San Diego) and Gillespie Field, El Cajon, California.

In Need to Know, I allude to information revealed to me that sometime after one of the Eisenhower encounters, two scientists were taken by jeep to a meeting with aliens "somewhere in the desert." A friend of the source rode "shotgun" in the jeep, together with his buddy in the military. At the rendezvous point was a landed disc, and the scientists went aboard, where a "transfer of technology" ensued for a couple of hours. The source's friend, who held "Alpha" clearance at the time, later became a CIA officer.

In April 2012, Henry W. McElroy, the retired New Hampshire State Representative cited earlier, posted an update on the Internet, part of which relates to the foregoing meetings. "My research and observation of the records," he writes, "suggest that perhaps the information that Eisenhower and possibly others may have received in such alleged meeting(s) with the Off World Astronauts is what motivated President Eisenhower and his administration in 1958 to convert NACA (National Advisory Committee for Aeronautics) to NASA (National Aeronautics and SPACE Administration) which enabled us earth-based Humans to speed up our learning in order to better develop and utilize 'Outer Space Exploration Technologies.' Enlightenment on these Space Technologies may have been given us by the Extraterrestrials for the purposes of more effectively moving into Outer Space on a more timely basis via the Moon, the Space Stations and Mars. . . ."[19]

Art Campbell describes his correspondence with a man who claimed to have had access to highly secret archives of the U.K. Security Service—commonly known as MI5—who asserted that Eisenhower had had meetings with two or three separate groups of aliens during his presidency. "In the 1953–1955 timeline," wrote the source, "the ET visitors had landed at several places and asked for a meeting with the leader of the most powerful country on Earth. The top item on the meeting agendas was continued nuclear research and testing with more and more powerful weapons."

Regarding the nuclear agenda, Campbell's MI5 source alluded to a Russian nuclear weapon test in 1951 (September 24) that was almost double the size of the first weapon in 1949 (August 29), adding that the visitors showed particular concern about the first hydrogen bomb in 1952. (On October 31, 1952, U.S. Operation *Ivy* began with the detonation of *Mike*, the world's first high-yield two-stage thermonuclear device, at the Enewetak Atoll [formerly spelled Eniwetok] in the Pacific. At 10.4 megatons, the experimental liquid deuterium device exceeded the explosive power of all ordnance detonated in World Wars I and II combined.)[20] The MI5 source indicated that there was considerable pressure on Eisenhower to exert influence over his government's accelerated nuclear testing programs.

If President Eisenhower had managed to exert any influence on his military commanders regarding the arms race, there's no evidence of it. And ironically, a few days after the Holloman event, Operation *Teapot* commenced at the Nevada Test Site on February 18, 1955, with a total of fourteen tests conducted to further the development of intercontinental ballistic missiles (ICBMs) with thermonuclear warheads.

George Adamski, who features in several later chapters, was among the first to claim regular contacts with aliens. He was also closely associated with certain high-ranking military and political personnel. According to a friend of mine, the late Madeleine Rodeffer, sometime in 1959–60 Adamski was taken by military limo to a base in California for a meeting with Eisenhower.[21] No further details are available.

"Apparently," writes Art Campbell, "those in government who knew of the alien concerns decided to form a committee to advise the president concerning these matters. My source believes this group was initially called the 'Alternative Committee.' Might this have been the beginnings of the group that, today, is believed to be the extremely powerful worldwide special interest entity which exerts considerable influence on UFO secrecy?

"It is obvious to me that our government is not merely covering up whether UFOs exist, but also that we have had contact with ETs and that they have objected strenuously to our nuclear testing and stockpiling. . . ."[22]

PASSENGER MANIFEST—NONREVENUE					1. NAME OF CARRIER 53-7885			
2. MANIFEST NO.		3. MANIFEST DESTINATION			4. CABIN ATTENDANT (If assigned) Hughes & Woodward			
5.				MANIFEST				
U. S. ARMED FORCES PASSENGERS (Name, grade, and service No.) U. S. CIVILIANS AND FOREIGN NATIONALS (Name, title, nationality, age, sex, passport No.) A		DESTINATION AIRPORT B	STOWED BAGGAGE		PASSENGER WEIGHT PLUS CABIN BAGGAGE E	BAGGAGE CHECK NOS. F	PRIORITY IDENTIFICATION G
			PIECES C	WEIGHT D			

A			B	C	D	E	F	G
Washington, D. C. to Spence Fld, Moultrie, Ga. 10 February 1955 – Leg #1								
1. The President of the United States								
2. Mrs Mamie D. Eisenhower						7. Miss Mary Caffrey		
3. Mrs E. Doud						8. Sgt John Moaney		
4. Hon. George M. Humphrey						9. Mr Clifford Roberts		
5. Mrs. George M. Humphrey						10. Hon. James C. Hagerty		
6. Miss Rose Woods						11. Mr. Jock Whitney		
7. Sgt John Moaney						12. Mrs. Jock Whitney		
8. Mr. Clifford Roberts						13. Jim Rowley		
9. Hon. James C. Hagerty						14. John Campion		
10. Miss Mary Caffrey						15. Agent Walters		
11. Jim Rowley						16. Agent Chavrins		
12. Stewart Stout						17. Agent Kellerman		
13. Gerald Behn						18. Stewart Stout		
14. Dick Flohr				•		19. Gerald Behn		
15. William F. Shields						20. Dick Flohr		
16. Arnold Lau						21. Joe Giordano		
17. Arthur Godfrey								
18. Robert Lennon								
Moultrie, Ga to Washington, D.C. – 13 February 1955 – Leg #2								
1. The President of the United States								
2. Mrs Mamie D. Eisenhower								
3. Mrs E. Doud								
4. Hon. George M. Humphrey								
5. Mrs George M. Humphrey								
6. Miss Rose Woods								
TOTAL						TOTAL WEIGHT PASSENGERS AND ALL BAGGAGE		

6. PREPARING INSTALLATION	7. PLANE NO.	8. TRIP NO.	9.	ROUTE OF PLANE	
			A. FROM	B. TO	C. VIA

The official Air Force One Passenger Manifest for the flight from Andrews Air Force Base, Washington, D.C., to Spence Field, Moultrie, Georgia, on February 10, 1955. (The Dwight D. Eisenhower Library)

HEADQUARTERS
1254TH AIR TRANSPORT GROUP (SPECIAL MISSIONS) MAT:
MILITARY AIR TRANSPORT SERVICE
WASHINGTON 25, D.C.

TRIP NARRATIVE

CONFIDENTIAL _____
OTHER _____

MISSION NBR 59 ACFT TYPE VC-121E FLD NBR_____ ACFT NBR 53-7885

Departed DCA 10Feb55 Returned DCA 13Feb55 Flight Time _____ 5:15
BOF   BOF

Departed U.S._____ Arrived U.S._____
Using Agency_____ Senior Passenger_____

Aircraft Cmdr Lt Col William G. Draper   Engineer M/Sgt John J. Higgins - Mr Sale
1st Pilot Major William W. Thomas   Engineer M/Sgt John R. McLane
2nd Pilot _____   Flight Attendant M/Sgt Robert E. Hughes
Navigator Major Vincent Puglisi   Flight Attendant M/Sgt Jack M. Woodward
Radio Operator M/Sgt Russell F. Ellis   Extra Crew Member Sgts Borega, Campbell, Price
                                          & Markovic - CMs

DATE	POINT OF DEPARTURE	POINT OF ARRIVAL	FLIGHT TIME	NBR OFF. PASS.	NBR OTHER PASS.	STATUTE MILES FLOWN	OFF. PASS. MILES	OTHER PASS. MILES	LEG NBR
10 Feb 55	Wash, D.C.	Spence Fld Moultrie, Ga.	2:45	18		655	11790		1
13 Feb 55	Spence Fld Moultrie, Ga.	Wash, D.C.	2:30	21		655	13753		2
		TOTAL:	5:15	39		1310	25545		

The official Air Force One Trip Narrative for the flights on February
10/13, 1955. (The Dwight D. Eisenhower Library)

GERALD LIGHT
10545, SCENARIO LANE
LOS ANGELES 24, CALIFORNIA
4/16/54

[Letter Received:]
4-16-54

Mr. Meade Layne.
San Diego, California

My dear Friend: I have just returned from Muroc. The report is true---
devastatingly true!

I made the journey in company with Franklin Allen of the Hearst papers and
Edwin Nourse of Brookings Institute (Truman's erstwhile financial adviser)
and Bishop MacIntyre of L.A. (confidential names, for the present, please.)

When we were allowed to enter the restricted section,(after about six hours
in which we were checked on every possible item, event, incident and aspect
of our personal and public lives) I had the distinct feeling that the world
had come to an end with fantastic realism. For I have never seen so many
human beings in a state of complete collapse and confusion as they realized
that their own world had indeed ended with such finality as to beggar description. The reality of "otherplane" aeroforms is now and forever removed from
the realms of speculation and made a rather painful part of the consciousness
of every responsible scientific and political group.

During my two days visit I saw five separate and distinct types of aircraft
being studied and handled by our airforce officials---with the assistance and
permission of The Etherians! I have no words to express my reactions.

It has finally happened. It is now a matter of history.

President Eisenhower, as you may already know, was spirited over to Muroc one
night during his visit to Palm Springs recently. And it is my conviction that
he will ignore the terrific conflict between the various "authorities" and go
directly to the people via radio and television---if the impasse continues
much longer. From what I could gather, an official statement to the country
is being prepared for delivery about the middle of May.

I will leave it to your own excellent powers of deduction to construct a fitting
picture of the mental and emotional pandemonium that is now shattering the consciousness of hundreds of our scientific "authorities" and all the pundits of
the various specialized knowledges that make up our current physics. In some
instances I could not stifle a wave of pity that arose in my own being as I
wtached the pathetic bewilderment of rather brilliant brains struggling to make
some sort of rational explanation which would enable them to retain their familiar theories and concepts. And I thanked my own destiny for having long ago
pushed me into the metaphysical woods and compelled me to find my way out. To
wtach strong minds cringe before totally irreconcilable aspects of "science" is
not a pleasant thing. I had forgotten how commonplace such things as the demat-
erialization of "solid" objects had become to my own mind. The coming and going
of an etheric, or spirit, body has been so familiar to me these many years I had
just forgotten that such a manifestation could snap the mental balance of a man
not so conditioned. I shall never forget those forty-eight hours at Muroc!

*A facsimile of the letter from Gerald Light to Meade Layne describing
the events surrounding the former's visit to Edwards/Muroc AFB in
April 1954.*

63

CHAPTER FIVE
PUBLIC LANDINGS

In mid-July 1955, England suffered a heat wave for a week, with temperatures in some areas soaring to 100°F (38°C) or more. Toward midday on Sunday, July 17, Margaret Fry was at home in Bexleyheath, Kent—part of the London Borough of Bexley—with three of her four children and her sister. Her husband, who worked in Middlesex, was away at the time. Shaun, the eldest child, had a high temperature, so Margaret walked down the road to call her general practitioner (GP) from a public phone box, as relatively few families had telephones in those days.

"My GP was on holiday, but his relief was a young Indian, Dr. Thukarta," her account continues. "He examined my eldest and said we should go to the surgery immediately to get him medication, as he had sunstroke. I arranged with my sister to take care of the children and brought my second son Steve [eight and a half years old] with us, as he used to be rather naughty. He sat in the back of the doctor's brand-new Austin car, and we set off." It was now midday.

"The road I lived on, Hythe Avenue, was quite a long one, and from the outset the car was spluttering and stopping. After a while we became aware of a heavy shadow over the car. The rest of the sky was bright blue and cloudless, the sun blazing to the left of us. We kept peering through the windscreen, wondering what was causing the shadow engulfing the car. Eventually I asked the doctor if we could stop. 'No fear,' he said, 'I'm no mechanic!'

"We turned right onto Ashbourne Avenue and then right into Chessington Avenue, and amazingly this shadow turned at right angles with us. By now we definitely knew something was above the car, which then spluttered and stopped. 'Can we get out now?' Once out of the car, we looked up and were horrified to see a concentrated mass of gray cloud-like material barely eighteen feet above our heads.

"As we watched, this oval mass started spinning. It then slowly solidified, and we saw three ball-bearing-like 'wheels' come down from what I thought was a smooth underside. I did think it was landing and would squash us, but we were so shocked, we did not think to move away from under it. However, the 'wheels' retracted, and it continued to spin and hum like a top, combined with a slight whooshing sound like the sea. There was absolutely no down-draft, as would be under a helicopter. It then flipped on its side, then righted itself again, then flopped down at the crossroads ahead of us. 'My God,' we exclaimed, 'it's one of those flying saucer things!'"

Margaret told me that the craft had landed by the corner house on Chessington/Ashbourne avenues, which now has a garage, but then had only a wooden fence along the Chessington Avenue side.

"In 1955, few working-class people had cars, so road traffic on a Sunday in a suburb was nil. The few cars that people had were parked on the road, and children were playing hopscotch on the pavement. They were around eight to ten years of age. I yelled out to them and they all came and stood around the craft with their mouths open. I then realized it was in fact maybe four or five feet off the ground: maybe it had risen. It seemed huge, although when we measured the spot years later we found it must have been just less than thirty-five feet in diameter.

"It was a typical bell-shaped craft. The surface seemed like pewter; dull, yet at times it shone as well. It could have been described as silver, gray, blue, metallic, yet not really quite like any of these hues. In fact, it looked literally just out of this world. We all knew instinctively what it was. We were aghast. Steve had his face pressed to the car window, watching. The craft had indents or moldings, that I thought must have been portholes, around the center, and below this was a wide ledge, and above, a rounded dome which had further moldings—for a door? What impressed itself in my memory was that the lower circular part was in sections—or so it seemed—with distinct seams and what appeared to be rivets." [A sketch by Margaret is reproduced here.]

"After five or six minutes of being absolutely still near to the road, it then tilted toward us slightly, and in that position went up. It wobbled from side to side, then at about a hundred feet it stood still and a porthole opened up. For the first time, I felt real fear, thinking there had to be people in it: when it was near to the ground and we were standing at arm's length, we were so utterly amazed at the craft itself that we did not think of aliens or anyone being in it.

"It then 'swished' upwards to about thirty thousand feet, which took about seven minutes (for some reason we timed it with our watches). We got back into the doctor's car, still dazed. All the way to the surgery, the doctor kept repeating that he did not believe in flying saucers. He was sure it was a secret American prototype aircraft. 'What sort of secret aircraft would come down in the middle of the day in a built-up suburb?' I replied. We did not even notice that the car was now running perfectly. After getting the medication, the doctor dropped us off at my house.

"I do recall every small detail of this, as does my son Steve. Although I related every detail in a letter to my aunt the next day and wrote notes and drew sketches into a diary one year later, I always refer back to these."[1]

Years later, Margaret gave me a copy of Steve's official report sent to Contact UK, a UFO research group, from which I cite:

". . . It was a small, two-door car, and right away it seemed to be starting and stopping. We turned on to another road and then it stopped. I remember the doctor and my mother got out and were looking in the sky, so I looked through the side window. I could see a silver or metallic craft which had an inner circle of light which was rotating and appeared to me to be flashing orange and red lights. There were some children about my age playing on the pavement and my mother shouted to them to look up at 'the flying saucer.' They all did. The doctor was shaken up [and] it took him ages getting medicine for my brother. I still remember that he was upset. . . . The whole thing has stayed very clear in my memory."[2]

"When we got home," Margaret continues, "both Steve and I were excited in telling our family about the flying saucer. 'What use was that?' said my sister. 'Why didn't they come out?' Shaun was aggrieved, complaining he was feeling so ill, and we were talking rubbish, whereupon Steve wanted to punch him, insisting we had seen a flying saucer."

At the time, Margaret's father was working as a scientist with the Atomic Weapons Establishment at Aldermaston, Berkshire, and lived nearby with his wife. "When they came to visit me the following weekend at Bexleyheath, Dad informed me rather kindly that I had been mistaken; the object I had seen was only the sun! 'Yes, of course,' I said patiently, 'but this thing had come down in front of us while the sun was to the back of us.' Mother promptly went to purchase the *Erith Observer & Kentish Times*, to see if anyone else had reported the object. She returned in triumph, waving the newspaper before Dad. . . . An Erith policeman and several others, it transpired, had also seen this craft fairly low to the ground, just after it left us at midday on 17 July 1955."[3]

Margaret Fry is now a well-known UFO researcher, living in North Wales. We first met at her Bexleyheath house in 1972 and have kept in regular contact ever since. I can vouch for her total integrity and dedication to the subject. Thanks mostly to John Hanson, a retired police constable and UFO researcher, further information has come to light that not only seems to vindicate Margaret's account, but also indicates that *another*, similar event occurred a short distance away, in the same week, involving numerous witnesses.

In 2002, in an attempt to track down further witnesses, John, together with his partner Dawn Holloway, began making inquiries in the Bexleyheath area, first at newspaper offices. This led to an article about the event, including two sketches by Margaret of the craft, appealing for additional witnesses, which appeared in the *News Shopper*, a local newspaper.[4] Two weeks later, an article in the same newspaper published testimony from Rodney Maynard, 62, a former serviceman. Fifteen at the time, Maynard had been working as a labourer on a building site in nearby Streamway.

"We were on our lunch break when we heard something was happening in King Harold's Way, so we went up there to have a look," Maynard told the *News Shopper* following the appeal. "This thing had landed in the roadway. It took up the whole width of the road and overlapped onto the pavements. It wasn't on the ground. It had about eight massive suckers [underneath]. The center was still, but the outer rim was spinning slowly and it had white lights flashing, like a camera flash," he recalled. (Evidently, this craft was different from the one reported by Margaret and others and, as it transpired, the landing had occurred several days earlier.)

"There were about thirty of us staring at it. We could hear it humming. It had what looked like windows but the glass was concave and molded together so you couldn't see in. A couple of us went forward to try and touch it and it began to spin faster. Then the craft lifted slowly off the ground and hovered above our heads, tilting slightly." The craft moved slowly until it was over Bedonwell Primary School, where it stayed for about a minute, then shot up into the sky.

Maynard, whose sixteen-year-old brother was also present, described the craft as "black, sleek and streamlined with a surface like polished metal. It was beautiful. . . . I have never forgotten it. . . . We used to talk about it among ourselves but our mums kept telling us we hadn't seen anything." Maynard also listed several other pals who were present: Ron Deadman, Tony Savin, Vic Clarke, and Tommy Staggs.[5]

Margaret told me that this craft had landed close to the junction of King Harold's Way with Orchard Avenue. Maynard provided further information to John and Dawn. He said that the event had occurred "one hot summer's day in July 1955" when he and his mates and about thirty other youths—all aged between fifteen and seventeen years—were working on a culvert to carry stream water underground, at the base of King Harold's Way. When they heard a commotion up the hill, they had run up the road with other people to see what was happening.[6] Maynard's description given to Ron and Dawn is at variance in several respects with that given earlier to the *News Shopper*—in particular the length of time the craft hovered above Bedonwell School:

"It just lay there on the ground, making no noise, surrounded by at least sixty people, including many children. We stood there watching as it flashed with light, at one-second intervals—so bright, it hurt to look for too long. On top of the object was this oval-shaped protrusion that reminded me of a nipple. I decided to get closer to the structure, which looked like beaten silver, with tiny dots all over it [and] with these massive 'suckers' underneath. I shouted out to my brother.

"We were so close to it, we could have touched it. The object began to wobble from side to side, the suckers drawing in slightly. People started to shout, now alarmed. In the blur of movement, too fast for the eye to catch, it left, leaving an image on the retina, which lasted for a few seconds. I looked across the sky and saw it tilt before coming to a halt in mid-air, over Bedonwell School, where it stayed for about two hours."

Maynard said that, some weeks after the incident, he received a call from the local police constable, warning him not to discuss it with anybody. He says he complied for nearly a half century, until reading the 2002 local newspaper appeal, at which point he reported his own experience. As for the witnesses he names, despite publicity and their own research through electoral rolls, John and Dawn were unable to find them.

Another witness who came forward was David Philips, a retired postman. "I was living on a council house estate in Bexleyheath during July 1955, about a mile away from your publicized incident in King Harold's Way," he told John and Dawn. "It was a beautiful hot summer's day, with patchy cloud, when I noticed a disc or saucer-shaped object hovering a few hundred feet above the ground, about a mile away. Suddenly it tilted, revealing what looked like three ball-bearing-shaped lumps set into its underside. I was so excited I ran to the house, shouting for my mother and father. As they came running out, whatever it was shot off across the sky, like a black streak of lightning, toward the London area, and was gone."[7]

Since this craft is described as having "three ball-bearing-shaped lumps" set into its underside, as opposed to the "eight massive suckers" described by Maynard, it is a fair assumption to suggest that it was the same, or similar, craft as that seen by Margaret and the other witnesses on July 17. The craft reported by Maynard and others is evidently related to another event which occurred a few days earlier.

On the afternoon of Thursday, July 14, as Doris Jacques glanced out of the open French windows at the back of her house in Hythe Avenue, Bexleyheath, she observed a glowing orange half-moon-shaped object in the sky, just above the roof of the house behind her back garden. On the underside of this craft could be seen small gray oval-shaped objects (one of Doris's sketches appears below). These flew off in all directions, returning shortly afterward to the larger craft, which then headed toward Bedonwell Primary School, where it hovered over the playground.[8]

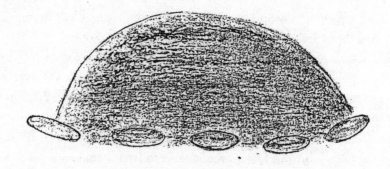

Doris Jacques's daughter Pamela—then a pupil at that school, behind Brabourne Crescent—arrived home, excited, at 15:30. "Mummy, did you see the flying saucers?" she asked.[9]

"We were all in the playground, which is right close to Hythe Avenue, and we were all looking up," Pamela Rossiter told me. "What I saw were lots of little cigar- or oval-shaped objects, like bright lights—and there were so many of them. They were very high up, and they were there for quite a long time. And then they all disappeared into one much larger one, and it was gone. I remember how we were all so excited. And then I went home and told my mum—and she said she'd seen this as well."[10]

In 2005, Margaret Fry received an anonymous letter with an Erith, Kent, postmark:

". . . I was one of a group of children playing in the bottom end of Bedonwell Road when we became aware of a commotion on King Harold's Way, involving lots of people. I ran to see what was going on and had to push my way between a man and a woman. The man said, 'Stay back, we don't know what it is.' I looked and saw on the ground an object in shape similar to a soldier's tin hat, but the dome part more streamlined. It was on the ground I don't know how long, but then the rim started to slowly spin. You couldn't see the join between the rim and the dome. It appeared as one whole thing. . . .

"Its appearance seemed to be fluid, a translucent, silver color. The sun that day was blazing so [that] could have caused the glare from the object, distorting its color. It then rose about a foot off the [ground]. A few seconds later, it rose twelve or fifteen feet. Underneath the craft were nodules. They could have been lights, but [were] the same color as the UFO. All of a sudden, it sped off and hovered over Bedonwell School, but quite high up—then suddenly it sped silently away, but I remember feeling a low hum vibration. There were grown-ups taking children's details, so all us kids took off at this point. . . ."

Through a helpful source at one of the police stations he visited, John Hanson met a retired officer, Jim Streek, a young police constable at the time who had heard about the King Harold's Way incident:

"I was on duty and assisting in the return of some property to some women when I overheard [their] conversation about a 'flying saucer' that had landed in King Harold's Way. I told the Station Sergeant what I had heard. He laughed at me [but] my curiosity was aroused and, after completing my shift, I changed into 'civvies' and went to have a look, as the women had seemed serious.

"When I arrived in King Harold's Way, after cycling there, I noticed a small group of children talking to two smartly dressed men, one of whom had a clipboard with him, standing next to a large black car. They looked like officials from a government department. I decided not to announce myself and left. It was only after all those years later, when I read the article in the newspaper, [that] I realized the connection."[11]

Streek assumed these men to be Air Ministry officials from the Royal Arsenal, Woolwich. "This made me wonder how long after the event the Air Ministry officials arrived at King Harold's Way, to take statements from any people still standing on the pavement," Margaret Fry ponders. "Of course, the Air Ministry officials would not have knocked on people's doors, thereby adding to the significance of the event, which as always Officialdom wants kept secret."[12]

Following the incident, Margaret had an attack of paralysis affecting her lower limbs. "I could not move and was very frightened," she recalls. "My sister came home from work about 6 P.M., fed the children, and sent for our GP, Dr. Lobo, who thought I had polio. These symptoms lasted only a short while and I recovered."

Had being in close proximity to an alien craft had an adverse affect? Dr. Thukarta, the young Indian doctor who together with Margaret and her son witnessed the landing, died young of a brain tumor a few years later.[13]

"Some years later, when I decided to investigate this, our own astonishing sighting, my GP, Dr. Lobo, told me that Dr. Thukarta had reported the incident to the British Medical Board. How much notice did they take, I wonder: they did not bother to interview me nor those children. I have in fact tried to contact them over the years, periodically, without success, as I no longer live in North Kent.[14]

"I calculate that, with the ninety residents of King Harold's Way, plus the thirty teenagers, then the ten or twelve children on Ashbourne Avenue plus Dr. Thukarta, Steve, and myself, approximately 130 people had witnessed these amazing events," Margaret told me. This estimate may be unreliable, bearing in mind that so many could not be traced—or chose not to come forward. Nonetheless, numerous witnesses were present at these events. Close encounters with landed craft reported by large groups are rare. The Bexleyheath incidents, for me, are the most convincing.

And yet, apart from the report in a local newspaper, why did such a momentous story not appear in the national press? "In 1955," Margaret explains, "we were not a publicity-conscious nation of people. I do not suppose that it occurred to any one of those people to contact a [national] newspaper. In addition, the remaining witnesses still on King Harold's Way when the Air Ministry officials had arrived must have been told not to talk about the incident; no doubt later they also informed their neighbors."[15]

And why were no photographs taken? Cameras were not that common in 1955, and it is likely that those who possessed them did not have them to hand when the incidents occurred. In the unlikely event that any photos had been taken, it is also feasible that they would have been confiscated by the Air Ministry officials.

How did Margaret feel in the ensuing weeks after her encounter? "Well, firstly an elation that we are not alone in this vast, vast universe," she explains. "I think almost every human being who has the ability to think must yearn to feel that at least some of the myriad upon myriad of stars we see in the night sky, which represent suns with perhaps planets revolving around them, such as in our solar system, are also teeming with life as we know it. So, I was elated. I felt as though I had my feet striding two worlds—wherever that other world may be. And the link had been that strange object. However, with these feelings of elation came loneliness. My son was too young to share these sentiments with, and it isolated me from the rest of my family. . . ."[16]

AUSTRALIA

The Bexleyheath event is not an isolated case. In 1966, for instance, several hundred Australian witnesses, including students, teachers, and residents in Clayton South—a Melbourne, Victoria, suburb—witnessed an astonishing series of events. The following synopsis is based on an article in an educational magazine by Tina Luton, who interviewed researcher Shane Ryan, an English lecturer at the University of Canberra who has spent five years investigating the case, interviewing hundreds of residents as well as former staff and pupils from three schools in the area to complete his documentary, *Westall '66: A Suburban UFO Mystery*, which aired on SBS television in late 2010.

At about 10:15 on the morning of April 6, a group of Westall High School students were completing a sports session when a silvery gray saucer-shaped craft, about twice the size of a family car, overflew the school and descended behind some trees on the Grange Reserve in front of Westall State School. One girl, Terry Peck, was playing cricket when the craft approached. She chased after it into the reserve. Two other girls were already on the scene. "One was terribly upset, and they were pale, really ghostly white," Terry recalls. "They said they had passed out. One was taken to hospital in an ambulance."

Other staff and students, alerted by cries of astonishment, rushed outside to see what all the commotion was about. "There are flying saucers in the sky!" said one boy as he came in and interrupted a Year 8 science lesson. "We all burst out laughing, but the teacher said, 'Let's go and have a look,'" Joy Clarke recollects. "It took a minute or two to sink in what I was looking at. There were three of them, flying saucers like you see in comic books."

Suzanne Savage, another pupil, was present with Joy and their teacher, Andrew Greenwood, as they observed the objects. One, seemingly larger than the others, disappeared behind some trees and then reappeared, hovering a while before banking on its side and disappearing in seconds.[17]

At one point, five light aircraft, presumed to have come from Moorabbin Airport, arrived on the scene. "They flew low, down toward the flying saucer, as if trying to get closer to it," Shane Ryan reports. "And every time they seemed to edge toward the strange craft, it just flitted away, as if playing a game with them of cat-and-mouse. . . .

"By this stage, about 300 of the high school's 485 students had amassed on and around the oval, many climbing the high wooden fence on the school's western boundary, and the wire fence at the foot of the huge high-tension electric power pylon that stood on the school's southwestern corner." Two such pylons were located at either end of the boundaries of the school property. "The flying saucer had lifted off and over these power lines as it ascended into the sky from the school and moved south toward the Grange [reserve]. At the sight of the flying saucer disappearing behind the pine trees, a huge chunk of kids who had been watching did what they all knew to be clearly against school rules [and] jumped the low wire fence that separated the school from the drainage ditch [and then] ran toward the Grange."[18]

The craft, apparently, had landed. Pauline Kelly, in Year 9 at the time, currently the school's bursar, did not see the craft, but she and two friends saw where it had landed. "There was a perfect circle burned into the grass," she confirms.

Unlike Bexleyheath, the Westall event made the front page of the local *Dandenong Journal* for two weeks running, as well as Channel Nine evening news. But there were repercussions. "The film canister from this coverage was recently found empty," Suzanne Savage reported. And following the incident, she also noted the presence of people in uniforms, including police. "The next morning the principal, Mr. Frank Samblebe, called a special assembly and said he never wanted us to speak of it again . . . and that there was no such thing as flying saucers." Science teacher Andrew Greenwood and others, including students, were warned against speaking about the matter by officials who visited them either at their homes or in the principal's office.

Jacqueline Argent, then in Year 9, was one of the first students over the fence, looking for where the larger saucer had landed. The following day she was called into the principal's office and interrogated by three men. "They had good quality suits and were well-spoken. 'I suppose you saw little green men?' they said."[19]

Although a number of parents—such as those who viewed the circle in the grass—believed their offspring, others did not. "To this day," says Shane Ryan, "after forty-five long years have passed, many are still hurt that their own parents and siblings refused to believe them, or at least were reluctant to. . . ."[20]

CHAPTER SIX
TALES FROM THE VIENNA WOODS

I n *Alien Base*, I cited at some length the remarkable encounter with aliens in the Vienna Woods in October 1962, reported to me by Bobby, a Filipino pianist then studying at the Vienna Akademie. Bobby had been "guided" to a certain area, where he noted a sudden "strange, sinister stillness" (as in the Monguzzi case). "I looked up and saw the leaves and branches of the trees shaking, disturbed by the sudden rush of air coming from a strange object," he reported. "I could hear the whistling sound the object made as it glided smoothly and nearer to where I stood."

The craft landed on three legs about a hundred feet from him. Three humanoid occupants, with lean, strong-looking bodies, dressed in tight-fitting black-brown suits extending from their shoes to their head, alighted. Around their faces—which appeared human—they wore a glass visor with two tube-like devices attached from under their chins to their back, ending in what looked like an oxygen tank.

"Someone said something that seemed like a question, but I couldn't understand a word," said Bobby. One of the group—presumed to be the leader—then pressed something on a small box he was carrying and a beam of red light fell upon Bobby's eyes, inducing a soothing effect. The box also acted in part as a translating device, since the leader asked Bobby a question in English, with a slight accent, similar to that of Germans. The device also was able to detect Bobby's eyeglasses, before he took them out of his pocket.

Asked by the leader if he would like to be with them or visit their place, Bobby declined. There followed a lengthy discourse on the iniquities of mankind, and a number of dire warnings, such as the following:

"Observe carefully the great mass of humanity killing each other through centuries of war and strife. . . . There are thousands of good people on your planet, but the mean and selfish humanity outnumbers the good by millions and millions. . . . Some day you will all be wiped out by your own greediness, and *if* a few good people live through that, then they will propagate and breed an unselfish humanity and no longer will there be continuous strife. . . . There is a great and possible danger, too, that your humanity's intense desire to conquer, eventually seeking power and domination over the other planets, will mean only a complete massacre for Earthmen, because other planets will retaliate with terrifying power and force. . . . This is our message. Transmit it and let humanity beware."[1]

Assuming substance to this story, as I do, since Bobby was a friend at the time, one can only wonder at the apparent lack of discrimination shown by these extraterrestrials regarding their choice of contact. Though deeply affected by this encounter, and other related experiences which ensued, Bobby was reluctant to tell even a few people about it, much less humanity at large. And even if he had transmitted the message to all and sundry, would it have made the slightest difference?

Bobby believed that most people who have had similar encounters suffer from depression and other sequelae, owing to the futility of proving their experiences to others. But at least the story was published.

A REVERSAL OF ROLES

Josef Wanderka must be the only person on this planet who claimed not only to have ridden a motorbike into a flying saucer but—in a refreshing reversal of roles—lectured its occupants on the iniquities of humankind. Born in Vienna in 1929, he became an active member of an anti-fascist sabotage group in 1944, until Austria's liberation from the Nazis the following year. A jeweler by trade, Wanderka's first sighting of an unknown flying craft occurred in 1954. The following is extracted from an account he wrote in 1975,[2] from my interview with him in Vienna,[3] and ensuing correspondence.

Wanderka had bought a Fuchs FM40S 1.5hp single-cylinder engine to attach to the left side of the rear wheel of his bicycle, the better to enjoy recreational trips in the forests surroundings Vienna. On a late summer night in 1954, he was riding his roadster on high ground near Hördl forest in Vienna's 13th district, admiring a magnificent view of Vienna, when suddenly he noticed a cigar-shaped silver object hovering over the city, moving from north to south:

"Its metallic, shining outer skin was so bright that I thought it was reflecting an anti-aircraft defense searchlight, which I recalled from wartime. But I could see no sign of any such searchlight. The distance between me and the craft must have been at least five miles, which made it seem the size of a medium-sized modern airliner, moving at about the speed of a sports plane."

Wanderka dumped his roadster in a ditch and dashed to a nearby field that afforded a better view. There he encountered some Soviet Army soldiers who had a base nearby (part of Austria was under Soviet occupation at the time). They too had been observing the craft, and one joked that it might be a secret Soviet weapon. But Wanderka's definitive close encounter—in late August or early September of 1955—had a much greater impact. It was to change him forever.

On this occasion, he was riding in woodland about fifteen miles from the city, toward Arbesthal. It was between 14:00 and 15:00. "Suddenly, I saw a dull metallic silver light shining through the shrubs. I rode toward the shrubs to find a gap where I could get through [and] when I did, I found myself in a glade.

"On the grass stood a metallic, disc-shaped object of about 2.5 meters height and 10–12 meters width, with a group of people in front of it [see photo section]. I couldn't see any windows, portholes, or lights on its even and arched surface. Neither could I make out any wheels or undercarriage, but there was a ramp of about four meters in length and two meters width [extending from] a roughly rectangular opening [with] half-moon-shaped frames to each side of the opening. The distance between me and the disc was about twenty meters. I decided to enter the disc. . . ."

"What on earth persuaded you to take such a dare-devil risk?" I asked him, when we finally met in Vienna.

"At that time, I didn't care so much what would happen to me," he explained. "I was tired of life, and also had private problems with my girlfriend. I wasn't even that concerned about dying. I already thought the disc was from another planet, and that perhaps they'd come to rescue me!"

His report continues: "The inside of the disc-shaped object was illuminated by an indirect yellow light. It resembled the ideal illumination for an 'intimate' living-room atmosphere, which we try to achieve today. The short, arched walls seemed to continue infinitely in the background. I could see neither levers, instrument boards nor panels, seats, or beds for the passengers.

"The inside of the disc was illuminated in an inviting way, giving me no reason to be afraid. I switched my engine off and freewheeled onto the ascending ramp and into the disc. When I stopped, I found myself in front of a group of five or six beings, about 1.80 meters tall [with] unblemished, beautiful faces that one can only find with children between the age of six and ten.

"Their clothes consisted of overalls of a grayish color without any signs of seams, pockets, or any openings. The shoes were incorporated into this clothing and didn't show any outline of toes. The hands were covered with mitts, also incorporated in their overalls. Since these overalls were loosely covering their slim figures, I couldn't make out the sexes, for example contours of breasts. Their necks came out of a sort of silk frill. Their hair was mid-length and blond, and they wore a close-fitting cap on the back of their heads."

Remaining seated on his bike, Wanderka introduced himself, saying where he lived and apologizing for having intruded in such a fashion. The aliens said they came from "the highest part of the Cassiopeia constellation, from Earth's perspective." Asked how they could speak German, they replied simply that they'd learned it. Their voices were similar to those of female adult humans, with a high pitch. "They pronounced the individual syllables similar to the accent of English people speaking German. Although I didn't know much about astronomy at that time, the distance between our Earth and Cassiopeia sounded enormous to me. However, it seemed more important to ask them what type of society they lived in."

Wanderka—a committed and evidently fanatical socialist at the time—went on to explain Earth's various types of societies and the iniquities of mankind. As leading researcher Gordon Creighton noted wryly in his résumé of the case: "Herr Wanderka [delivered] a summary account of the conditions prevailing upon our planet, delivering himself of a splendid and heated left-wing harangue well larded with all the usual clichés, and directed primarily against inequalities and privileges. Maybe the visitors found this a trifle boring, for after a while their attention seemed to rivet onto the odor of warm oil coming from his little motor."[4]

"Oil was dripping out of the valve near the cylinder, which was also covered with an oily skin and now smelled owing to the heat," Wanderka's report continues. "I changed the subject and explained how my little engine worked—which evidently met with great interest.

"During my explanation of the types of terrestrial societies, the crew appeared to be very open-minded and interested. They told me their system no longer had different classes and that they knew all about the old-fashioned social structure on Earth. This I took as an opportunity to point out the miseries, diseases, and famine which kill millions of people. The surprising reply by the crew was that I myself should lead some attempt to overcome these problems; that I would be the best to understand how to start such a reformation on Earth. I abruptly refused this idea, telling them about the huge number of government officials who only serve a privileged class instead of the whole nation."

Wanderka told the extraterrestrials that they themselves should initiate a type of society on Earth in which everyone is equal, because (he assumed) interplanetary beings were not corrupted by the temptations of Earth and had an overwhelming technological advantage. Such was the strength of his passionate delivery that the crew apparently was moved to tears!

"I therefore decided it was time to leave the spaceship as informally as I had entered it about twenty minutes earlier. I briefly waved my hand and wished them a pleasant day, whereupon they bowed, in a far-eastern style. I turned my roadster, upon which I had been sitting all the time, through 180 degrees, managing it as easily as if on a smooth icy surface, then rolled down the ramp and out onto the grass in front of the spaceship."

Wanderka was puzzled by the ease with which he turned the bike. "The pattern of the floor looked like a Belgian waffle, which normally has grooves—though I can't say there were any," he recalled for me.

"The only way I can explain my being able to turn around so easily—bearing in mind the weight of my bike (30 kg) and myself (80 kg)—is that I was under the influence of the same energy which propelled the craft. This was the most impressive part of my encounter. I was rather disappointed with the rest, since I'd expected the crew to be more helpful. They didn't tell me how to overcome the social problems on Earth, and I didn't feel up to taking a leading part in a revolution. For this reason, I didn't even look back to see the craft taking off, but took the nearest way home . . . also I didn't want to be questioned by any possible witnesses."

Wanderka told no one about his experience for many years.

INSIDE THE CRAFT

"The inside of the flying disc corresponded basically with its outer form, whereby the edge of the inner disc didn't seem to be as curved as the outside, which was probably due to a cavity. When I entered the object, I noticed thick half-moon-shaped corners on both sides of the entrance opening. The ceiling inside seemed to be highly arched at the top—like the outer surface. Because of this, the ceiling and walls gave the optical illusion of blending into each other.

"From my seated position, I was unable to see any instruments—they might have been covered by the crew standing in front of them. Due to the diffused illumination, I couldn't see anything to sit or lie on. It might have been that seats or beds were installed in the walls or floor, or that they were hovering inside the disc during flights.

"I reckoned that the propulsion and guidance instruments were located underneath the floor and between the gaps of the inside and outside walls. As far as I remember from the crew's explanation, they operate by manipulating gravity and antigravity." At that time, Wanderka didn't understand the meaning behind all the technical terms they gave him, but later worked out that they somehow shrank space and time. As he explained to me:

"They told me that a 'cyclotronic aggregate' caused a rotating energy field which puts the whole craft into a 'self-gravitating field.' This form of energy is known to us as gravity and antigravity energy. The direction of flight could be determined by an oscillating frequency. Due to the motive power, it was possible to overcome the distance of light years, which is beyond our terrestrial physical concept of time and space. In nuclear science on Earth, the cyclotronic aggregate creates heavy matter by making atomic particles heavier than their original weight so that they subsequently rotate."

— —

I asked Josef Wanderka for his overall impression of the visitors. "They had a child-like appearance," he replied, "and I got the impression they didn't want to come too close to us. They see us perhaps as we see primitive savages."

"How do you feel now, more than forty years after this extraordinary encounter?" I inquired.

"It was a mental elation for me, and it led me to study technical terms, for example. The whole experience still lurks in my subconscious. It's always there, and it replaces for me what others call religion."

Was he aware that some encounters with extraterrestrials had been less than benevolent?

"There's been a lot said about them being bad," he answered, "but I don't see it that way—at least, not from my own experience. In any case, I don't think there's a civilization anywhere that's as bad as ours. I can hardly imagine them organizing a holocaust like the Nazis did. . . ."

CHAPTER SEVEN
INFILTRATION

A ccording to Harold T. Wilkins, a pre-eminent British author and researcher at the time, an unnamed friend of his who served as a pilot in the U.S. Air Force reported to Wilkins in the summer of 1953 that he had heard sensational rumors purporting that the chiefs of the U.S. Air Force had secret information that "mysterious individuals in the U.S. were known to have had contacts with some of the entities on one type of flying saucer. These individuals were alleged to be meeting flying saucer entities in remote places, in regions of the U.S. that are still unmapped, had taken orders from them, and were going round in parts of the west and middle west on some secret purpose connected with these mysterious objects. Nor, said my friend, did the U.S. Air Force believe that any foreign power was concerned in the matter. . . ."[1]

Reports of flying saucer sightings in California's Mojave Desert were rife in early April 1954. In hopes of a sighting, Carl Anderson, together with his family and some friends, set off for a camping trip near Desert Hot Springs. As the convoy of three cars neared a dirt road on their left, an "uncontrollable unseen force" started to turn Carl's driving wheel.

"I immediately thought that something had gone wrong with the steering mechanism," he reports. "And then a voice whispered in my ear:

'Turn here, drive three miles and stop.'" Had his wife Stella, sitting beside him, been responsible? She said not. "It seemed," he explained, "as if I had suddenly been bathed from head to foot in lukewarm water, and the voice had actually seemed to come from inside my head, neither in my right nor my left ear, but from somewhere inside my brain."

At the end of the three-mile drive, Carl and Stella set up a tent, which they shared with their daughter Betty-Ann and son Bobby. A stove was lit and a snack meal consumed. It was a beautiful starry night in the clear desert air. But alas, no flying saucers, so the group retired some time after midnight. Brothers-in-law Jim Stewart and Harold Spencer, and their respective wives Terry and Eleanor, bedded down in their cars.

"How long I slept I do not know," said Carl. "Suddenly I was wide awake and sitting upright. Stella and Betty-Ann were also sitting up, but Bobby was still sleeping. As the three of us sat there wondering what had awakened us, a miracle happened.

"The tent slowly began to disappear until it became absolutely invisible and, looking out across the desert, apparently hovering a few inches off the ground, was a large shining disc. The diameter of this craft was about sixty feet. . . . Five windows, or portholes, were visible from where we were. The unearthly vehicle glowed all over with a dull fluorescent light [and] a sort of halo seemed to surround the entire craft. I could not tell whether it had any landing gear. It appeared to hover about eighteen or twenty inches off the ground.

"I tried to move toward this object. I wanted to go over and touch it, but I found that I could not move an inch. I was completely paralyzed. Stella and Betty-Ann later said they had the very same experience. . . . I did however manage to roll my eyes enough to glance at my wrist watch. The luminous dial read three o'clock (A.M.). We did not know at the time just how long we remained in this paralyzed condition while we continued to watch and listen. We could now hear voices mumbling in a low tone, but could not tell, however, if the conversation was in English, as the sounds were very faint.

"After what seemed hours, we began to hear a slight humming sound like a generator running—a low droning, pulsating hum. The dim glow surrounding the saucer slowly took on an orange cast, then a bright red color. Then it started to rise straight up, very slowly at first, then faster and faster as it got higher and higher. The red light changed to a brilliant blueish white. Then slowly the tent began to reappear [and] we were free to move about.

"We sprang to our feet and looked out through the tent flap. The brilliant blue-white light was streaking across the sky and soon disappeared over the horizon near Mt. San Gorgonio. Betty-Ann's first words were, 'Daddy, where did the tent go? And why couldn't I move?' Harold and Eleanor had also been paralyzed and the car in which they were sleeping rendered invisible. But strangely enough Jim and Terry, being farther away in their car, had not even been awakened, and were dumbfounded when told of the saucer's visit.

"The next morning," said Carl, "the clock in my car, which had been at some distance from the saucer, was fifteen minutes faster than my wrist watch, indicating that it had stopped at three A.M. for a period of fifteen minutes. The paralyzing rays had evidently stopped it. Since my watch is self-winding, it must have started again when the craft took off."

In the late summer of 1955, while working at the U.S. Navy Yard near the No. 1 Dry Dock in Long Beach on an electrical installation, Carl suddenly felt suffused with a familiar warmth. A huge silvery disc appeared in the blue sky, observed also by his workmates. "It was of tremendous size and hovered perfectly motionless, [then] seemed to turn on its side and roll across the sky like a gigantic wheel. It stopped abruptly and shot straight out of sight [then reappeared], slowly circled, then started to descend [and] made several right-angle turns.

"As we watched, a jet fighter appeared, streaking swiftly toward this huge shining saucer, which was now hovering. On rushed the jet until it seemed it would crash into this monster from another world. Then quick as a flash the disc shot to one side and the jet missed it by a very wide margin. The speed of the jet took it way off over the city before its pilot could finally circle and start back. The first performance was repeated [and] the saucer avoided the plane. Making another side circle, the jet returned. This time its tactics were different. It went into a steep dive, then started to climb straight up [to] beneath the space visitor, and a third time it was a complete miss, as the saucer darted to one side then shot straight up and disappeared. . . . But as usual, not a word appeared in the press."

On October 2, 1955, eighteen months after the first encounter, Carl felt compelled to drive to the desert. Accompanied by his wife and Jim Stewart, they decided to spend a night under the stars in sleeping bags. They had planned to head for Desert Hot Springs but, again, the car seemed to have a mind of its own. "Upon rounding a sharp bend," said Carl, "we once more came upon what appeared to be a small dry lake-bed [and] we were surrounded by huge boulders. As I sat there wondering if this were my appointed destination, the motor stopped [and] I discovered to my amazement that the ignition key had been turned off. This we immediately took to be our answer—this was the spot where we would camp."

Shortly before midnight, a brilliant blueish-white light came streaking soundlessly toward the group and began circling overhead. Very slowly, it started to descend. "We were all now on our feet. The moon shone on this huge craft, and we could look up from beneath. It looked like a plate slowly falling. . . .

"The great craft was now scarcely two hundred feet overhead. We could now make out three round ball-like objects, equally spaced near the outer rim of the ship, from which the fluorescent glowing light appeared to emanate. The craft seemed to bounce up and down slightly, as if the Earth's gravity were gradually being canceled out. We could hear the pulsating hum. Each time the craft bounced, the hum would increase, then decrease. . . ."

Sketch by Frederic S. Aber

Suddenly panic-stricken, Stella ran toward the car. The craft immediately climbed rapidly but descended again when the others signaled to it with a flare. Jim burned his hand severely on the flare, whereupon the craft emitted a bright glow and disappeared. And then something miraculous occurred, as testified in his affidavit:

"This is to certify that I, James R. Stewart, did on or about the 2nd day of October in the year 1955 witness a huge object hovering above me on the California desert in a remote spot south of Victorville. I also had the uncanny experience of having a severe burn which I had suffered from a burning flare, miraculously healed, as this object changed color. . . ."[2]

The other witnesses also signed affidavits testifying to these extraordinary events, one of which—by Stella Anderson—is reproduced on p. 112.

CONTACT

Further encounters ensued, including a contact in February 1960. I have condensed the following report from a lecture given by Anderson in 1966:

"On the night—or I should say morning—of February 14, 1960, I was ushered personally aboard a 200-foot craft on the Mojave Desert, some ten to twenty miles north of the town of Yucca Valley. I remained on board this craft for two hours and twenty minutes, during which time I was given some very important information. And I was told that I was to take this information to some great scientists. And when I questioned this, the man who told me this informed me that the way would be made clear, that all expenses would be taken care of, and that I would go to Germany and talk with some noted scientists and physicists in that country.

"I asked why I had to go to another country [and] why I couldn't see physicists in my own country, because it so happens that in 1932 or 1933 I was employed by none other than Dr. Vannevar Bush [a pivotal pioneer of nuclear weapon technology]. At that time, he was with the Massachusetts Institute of Technology. I lived with him in his house in Belmont, Massachusetts, for two years. I was very well acquainted with him—he's one of our noted physicists and scientists. And I asked why I had to go to a foreign country to impart this knowledge [and] I was told that scientists here in my own country would turn a deaf ear to what I had to say, therefore I would have to go where people were capable of listening and understanding, and would accept the truth."[3]

Anderson flew to Germany on October 17, 1960, and participated in a UFO conference at Wiesbaden. Another participant was Dr. Hermann Oberth, one of the true pioneers of astronautics (whom I met in 1972 at his home in Germany). In 1955 Oberth had been invited by Dr. Wernher von Braun (his former assistant) to go the United States, where he worked on rockets at the Army Ballistic Missile Agency, and later with NASA at the George C. Marshall Space Flight Center in Huntsville, Alabama. Oberth returned to Germany in 1958.

PROPULSION TECHNOLOGY

The information imparted by Anderson at the 1966 Reno conference included much data relating to alien propulsion technology, based on the information imparted to him by his alien friends in February 1960:

"Most everything we read about the craft—the way they're propelled—we read it in terms of an electromagnetic field. This is not entirely true. There are two forces involved. There *is* an electromagnetic force field; however, there is also a very, very high-voltage static charge involved. . . . And it is this static charge that has caused the scorched bushes and the scorched grass, where these craft have landed and made contact. This is from the static charge, which contains billions [and] billions of volts. But as such, it is not actually a danger to human life because there is no amperage involved.

"Now many people wonder why these craft have been seen going through the sky at terrific rates of speed that have been clocked on radar and by other means, and being able to negotiate the seemingly impossible maneuvers and turns that they make—instantaneous stops and starts—traveling near the speed of light and making 90- and 45-degree turns. And they say these people cannot be human people inside these things, they must be machines, they must be robots, they could never stand the pressures that are being brought about during these quick turns and quick stops and starts. This [would be] very, very true, provided they use Earthmen's means and methods. But we know they are much more highly evolved—not only spiritually, morally, physically, but also mentally and electronically, and in every other thing that you can name they are much, much further advanced than we are.

"This is what they have done: they have made a vehicle and they have harnessed the forces of nature; they have copied a real planet. Now, the planet Earth that we know spins on its axis, which is nothing more in itself than a static generator—a huge static generator."[4]

During a Chamber of Commerce luncheon in Pueblo, Colorado, on July 22, 1952, Joe Rohrer of Pikes Peak Radio Co. recounted an interesting story relating to early knowledge of alien propulsion technology which endorses some of Anderson's claims: "A Californian air pilot told me that, in 1942, he had been right inside a giant saucer and seen giant flywheels sheathed in metal skins, and found that the motive force came from electrostatic turbines, whose flywheels create an electro-magnetic field of force, creating tremendous speeds. . . ."[5]

Anderson learned that part of the propulsion system of the spacecraft he went on involved a "wheel within a wheel," the principal process by which they derived their motive power. "This in essence is nothing more than a gigantic static generator," he explained. "One of these wheels turns in a counter-clockwise direction, the other in a clockwise direction. And when these two counter-rotating forces reach a speed equivalent with the [rotation] of the Earth or of the planet involved, and in direct relation to its mass, then a static charge is forthcoming to the extent that it is repelled away from the Earth.

"We know that the Earth has a magnetic field surrounding it. Now, when you are inside a magnetic field, you are in truth inside of a gravity field, because gravity, electricity, and magnetism are one and the same. . . . When you go into a gravity field, every atom, every molecule, every electron of your body is acted upon simultaneously with every atom and molecule of everything around it. And therefore, these people, being inside a gravity field, have no sense of motion, no knowledge whatsoever of quick turns, of stops and starts, because they in reality, from an atomic standpoint, are a part of the craft itself. . . .

"Now, another thing that our scientists do not understand is how these craft can travel with such fantastic speeds in our atmosphere without getting hot and disintegrating and burning up. Well, here again, it's because the forces of nature have been harnessed in this vehicle, and an ionization effect as such takes place with this static charge surrounding the craft—the skin of the craft—whereby you have several inches of complete insulation on the outside of the craft by means of a vacuum, in which your craft travels through a vacuum and carries its vacuum along with it all the time. It can never get hot, it can never get cold; it remains the same temperature always.

"So, you see, they have thought of everything. And they tell us that our science knows this, but it's being kept from us. . . . Now, when I took this information to Germany, I was received with open arms [by] various other physicists and scientists who were associated at that time, or who had previously been associated in one way or another—with the teaching staff or in an advisory capacity—with Heidelberg University, and who were in complete accord with what I had to tell them. And checking it out mathematically, Dr. Hermann Oberth said, 'My God, it will work! Why haven't we thought of this?'"[6]

Oberth was one of the few scientists to have the courage to speak out on the controversial UFO topic. In 1962, he wrote an illuminating article in which he refers to the Wiesbaden conference in general—and to Anderson in particular:

"As far as the so-called 'contact' persons are concerned (those persons who allege they have been passengers in UFOs or have spoken to space people)," he wrote, "I had expected to encounter swindlers, hysterics, or schizophrenics. But I must say that among these contact persons, Carl Anderson, particularly, made quite a congenial, reasonable, and clean-cut impression. Skeptics should understand that I studied medicine and began my professional career as a doctor in a military hospital for three years, where I also had the care of mentally ill persons [and] I would bet a hundred to one that some of the contact persons are normal and have seen and experienced *something*. . . ."[7]

Oberth was skeptical that aliens would look like us. But it is interesting to note that in the article his technical explanations for UFO propulsion parallel many of those revealed by Anderson in his 1960 presentation (which Oberth translated into German after the conference) and, more comprehensively, during private meetings with Oberth and other scientists.

"We cannot take the credit for our record advancement in certain scientific fields alone; we have been helped," conceded Oberth some years later. When asked by whom, he replied, "The people of other worlds."[8]

Regarding UFO sightings per se, Oberth calculated that 11% of reports resisted conventional explanations. "They cannot be hoaxes or lies because they involve responsible men such as senior air force officers, or radar readings, or photographs from responsible sources. . . . Furthermore, the reports check out against each other so well that a common origin is to be concluded from them. . . ." He then proceeds to describe the "state of the art"—at least, as it was in 1962:

"The discs always fly in an attitude as if the driving power were effective vertically with the plane of the disc; when they hover steadily over a certain area they are in a horizontal position; if they want to fly fast they tilt and fly with the broad side facing forward.

"In sunlight, which is stronger than the luminosity of the discs, they appear to have a metallic sheen. At night they appear dark orange or cherry red if their maneuvers are such that little driving power is required—such as hovering. Under such conditions they emit very little light. If more driving power is required, the luminosity increases and they appear yellow, then yellowish green, then green like a copper flame, and at the highest speeds or accelerations glaringly white. They also may suddenly light up brightly or darken, even disappear. . . .

"If we establish the working hypothesis that the UFOs are machines, we also have to assume the following:

". . . They are flying by means of artificial fields of gravity. This would explain the sudden changes of directions. If an apparatus built by humans were capable of changing its direction and speed as suddenly as do UFOs, the passengers would be pressed against the wall so violently they would be crushed to death. Artificial fields of gravity, however, would mean that the occupant would be rushing forward along with the vehicle and that between him and the vehicle no tractive force [the pulling force exerted by a vehicle, or machine or body] would even come into being. The hypothesis also would explain the piling up of the discs into a cylindrical or cigar-shaped mother ship upon leaving the earth because in this fashion only one field of gravity would be required for all discs.

"They produce high-tension electric charges in order to push the air out of their paths, so it does not start glowing, and strong magnetic fields to influence the ionized air at higher altitudes. First, this would explain their luminosity. Even the poles of our electric influence or induction machines glow in the dark. Secondly, it would explain the noiselessness of UFO flight. Our jet aircraft have a high noise level because they move through the calm air and create violent turbulences. The UFO, however, does not create turbulences near it because the air has the same speed it has, and the speed of the air decreases gradually with distance from the UFO. . . . Finally, this assumption also explains the strong electrical and magnetic effects sometimes, though not always, observed in the vicinity of UFOs. . . ."[9]

COLONIZATION

Anderson's particular alien contacts, who said they had come from Mars, explained that Earth had been colonized thousands of years ago by two extraterrestrial races which had amalgamated. These races supposedly had been responsible for the great pyramids. "Primarily, the pyramids were constructed for means of generating a huge amount of energy which was used to charge their crafts when they came here from outer space," he explained in his 1966 lecture. "The cosmic energy rays of the universe came down upon the pyramids [and] these rays, upon striking these sides of the pyramids—the sides being constructed at the perfect angle—were radiated off the apex and shot for many, many hundreds of miles out into space, just like a beam from a huge searchlight, only in this case being an invisible beam. And their craft would hover over this beam and re-charge their units.

"This was the reason why pyramids are built all around the earth—you can follow a circle around the earth. They're in China, they're in South America, they're in various places, [constructed] for the purpose of charging their units when they came here, and their energy was getting to such a low ebb that they needed charging [when they] had to go back again. Now, I was told that the 'wheel within the middle of a wheel' was, as I said before, an electrostatic generator. And this obviously has to have a means of turning it—a motive power. I was told that the central shaft, or column, of the craft, on which these two wheels were pivoted, was the true energy source. This was a type of battery with which we are not at this time familiar which would last for perhaps fifty or a hundred years, or more. But eventually they did have to be recharged.

"It's also been noted that many of these craft have been seen hovering over mountains—and the Rocky Mountains in particular—places where it is known that there are large deposits of quartz, or granite containing quartz crystals. And quartz crystals are a source of energy that never dissipates; it's like a battery that will never run out. And so when the energy source is harnessed from these millions of quartz crystals contained in a mountain, and especially a mountain whose peak is shaped more or less like a pyramid, so that this energy will radiate off the apex of the peak of the mountain, then they can do pretty much the same by charging a unit as they used to do from the great power-house of the pyramids."[10]

Another contactee from this era was George Van Tassel. Though I retain misgivings about some of his claims, his report of an encounter in August 1953 with a landed craft and its occupant—"Solgonda"—may be worth citing here.

Following the demonstration of a small device about two by two inches square and around a half-inch thick, with rounded corners, carried around the neck and alleged to make the aliens invisible when necessary, Solgonda demonstrated how the device was periodically charged:

"Suddenly he opened two opposite ends of it and pointed it at the granite rocks of the mountain. I saw a pencil lead-size stream of light between the object and the mountain. . . . Later he explained that he was charging the device. He said they charge various other pieces of their equipment over granite mountains. This is due to the piezoelectric effect set up by quartz in its granite matrix.

"When they discharge the 'crystal battery' by pressing on either side of it, it releases the charge into their electric body, or aura, and causes light to bend around them; therefore appearing to disappear to the limited physical vision of anyone who is watching them. . . ."[11]

Anderson said that the three aliens who befriended him—two men and a woman—looked identical to Earth people. "If you met them walking down the street or if you sat beside them in a restaurant, you wouldn't know any difference," he stated. Except for telepathy, that is. "They know all languages because they are the greatest telepaths. As you go to ask a question, before you can form the words on your lips, they have the answer."[12]

In *Alien Base*, I cited the fascinating case of Albert Coe, another of many claiming extensive contacts with aliens, in this case dating back as far as 1920 in Canada. Coe was informed by his alien friend (who claimed to live on both Mars and Venus) that Earth was colonized over fourteen thousand years ago by his race after their home planet—orbiting around the star Tau Ceti, some eleven light years from Earth—dehydrated. The only solution was mass migration to another solar system with a similar star—ours. Following a successful exploratory mission to Earth, during which contact was briefly established with Cro-Magnon humans, the expedition returned to their home planet. It was decided to colonize Earth. Tragically, only one of their huge spaceships survived the journey, the rest having been drawn into our sun, and were forced to settle on Mars. They overcame its harsh environment, then established bases on the high land of Venus, but mostly on Earth.[13]

Mars and Venus have frequently been cited by "contactees" as alien abodes or bases. Most astrophysicists, however, point out that the Martian atmosphere is too thin and cold, while Venus's atmospheric pressure is reported to be about ninety times that of Earth, with a temperature averaging around 464°C (867°F), a massive carbon-dioxide atmosphere (97 percent)—and no water. These findings are disputed by some, as we shall learn.

Probably the first person publicly to claim contact with aliens from Venus was Samuel E. Thompson, a retired railroad worker, who told a reporter that while driving to his home in Centralia, Washington, on the evening of March 28, 1950, he encountered a large flying saucer in a wooded area between Morton and Mineral. Two naked, deeply tanned children with dark blond hair which came to their waists were seen playing near the craft's entrance ramp. Thompson approached to within about fifty feet of the saucer, which emanated strong heat. Several naked male and female adults—humanoid, attractive, with refined features and also deeply tanned—then appeared at the craft's entrance. They beckoned Thompson to come closer.

Thompson claimed to have spent the next forty hours with the crew of twenty adults and twenty-five children. He found them "oddly ignorant, yet happy, cheerful, and gentle," as researcher Jerome Clark reports. They said their craft served as homes on Venus. They had stopped by on Earth, even though other Venusian saucers had been shot at by our military. Before leaving, Thompson explained that he wanted to go home to collect his camera. On his return, and prior to leaving, he tried to photograph the craft, but it was "just like trying to take a picture of the sun." The aliens themselves refused to be photographed. They told him he could contact them at any time, but that he had to keep certain information to himself. "If I'd tell everything I knew," he explained to Kenneth Arnold (the pilot who observed nine flying saucers over Mount Rainier, Washington, on June 24, 1947) and his wife Doris, "I never would get to see the ship again. I'd be watched every minute."[14]

Much of the additional information revealed in this case, unfortunately first published on April 1, 1950,[15] is seemingly absurd. But despite their understandable reluctance to accept a literal occurrence of the events described by Thompson, the Arnolds were impressed by his evident sincerity.[16] (Incidentally, Kenneth Arnold was a contractor at the time for Los Alamos National Laboratories, assigned to find out as much as possible about "flying discs," following the Maury Island incident of June 21, 1947, when several witnesses observed six craft circling above Puget Sound, Washington, spewing molten "slag"—much of which was collected—that occurred three days prior to Arnold's sighting.)

MARS

Fred Steckling, who had emigrated to the United States and worked with the U.S. Air Force in Germany, was a former chef and private pilot (with whom I flew on one occasion) and close associate of George Adamski, one of the first to claim regular contacts with aliens from Venus, Mars, and elsewhere in the solar system. Regarding the Martian climate, Fred pointed out to me a number of inconsistencies when we met in California a month after the Viking 1 lander had touched down on Mars in July 1976.

"On Mars," he began, "they've photographed sand dunes, and there's an area there that is the same size and same height as the sand dunes of

Colorado. The scientists are baffled by this, because with one-tenth of the atmosphere, which is supposed to exist on Mars, these sand dunes could never be there, because the winds wouldn't be strong enough to produce this kind of sand dune."

The winds vary from as low as 4 mph, gusting up to 50 mph, with occasional windstorms as high as 300 mph, apparently. Maybe, given the latter speed, sand dunes can be formed in such extremes? Fred made another point about the atmosphere, which seems harder to contest:

"In the Martian morning, they've photographed large patches of fog in the valleys. Now, in my standard pilot's book, it says that fog is a product of the temperature and humidity being nearly at the same point—called the dew point. So if the temperature is below freezing, there'll be no fog: it has to be above freezing to create fog, and the temperature has to be the same as humidity, so that if the temperature is, say, 40°—which is above freezing—and the humidity is 40%, you have fog. . . . If the temperature is below freezing, and the humidity is high, you still have no fog, because it will not be created. Consequently, if there are large patches of fog, there must be areas on Mars that warm up sufficiently to produce it. And from what they're telling us from the Viking Lander, so far, temperatures are too cold—it's always 20, 30, and 40 degrees below zero."[17]

A 2012 article on Mars in *Air & Space* gives the average temperature as −81°F (−63°C),[18] while the NASA Quest Mars current Web site states that temperatures may reach a high of about 70°F (20°C) at noon at the equator in summer, or a low of about −243°F (−153°C) at the poles. "In the mid-latitudes, the average temperature would be about −50° Celsius with a nighttime minimum of −60° Celsius and a summer midday maximum of about 0° Celsius."[19]

Contactee Apolinar (Paul) Villa, who took many fine color photographs of alien craft in New Mexico in the 1960s and had a series of encounters with their occupants, told me in 1976 that Mars was used as a base by his alien contacts. They said that the atmospheric pressure at ground level was equivalent to that at 12,000 feet on Earth. Life is sustainable there: cacti and other plants, for example, thrive.[20]

Dr. Lloyd V. Berkner had been executive secretary of the Joint Research and Development Board in 1946 (under Dr. Vannevar Bush) and, later, a member of the top-secret Majestic-12 group and an adviser to the government and other agencies on the space program—including the alien situation. Carol Honey, another close associate of Adamski, revealed to me that while working at Hughes Aircraft, he sneaked into a closed lecture by Berkner. The subject was Mars. "Berkner said that the atmosphere was a shirt-sleeve-type southern California environment. He very definitely believed that you could walk around on Mars and breathe. And this guy was Eisenhower's space adviser. . . ."[21]

VENUS

As for Venus, in 1921 Albert Coe's alien friend explained that although the planet was younger in evolutionary processes than Earth, "its higher regions are not too drastically different than the environment here." Only ten percent of the Venusian terrain is highland, and the highest point on the planet is the mountain known as Maxwell Montes, towering 35,400 feet above the planet's "sea level" and 27,000 feet above a huge highland region the size of Australia known as Ishtar Terra. In any event it seems likely that, with their highly advanced technology, aliens are capable of converting the hostile environment—which in any case may be less extreme in the highland regions than we have been led to believe.

Carl Sagan, a world authority on planetary sciences, postulated that "terraforming"—involving in this case the injection of appropriately grown algae into the Venusian atmosphere—"would in time convert the present extremely hostile environment of Venus into one much more pleasant for human beings."[22]

In his book *Why Are They Here?* Fred Steckling describes some of his meetings with aliens in downtown Washington, D.C., one of which took place on March 19, 1966. A main topic of conversation was the Russian *Venera* space probes, Venus 2 and 3, which had just reached the planet: an object about twice the size of a football had been ejected from the one-ton Venus 3 into the planet's atmosphere and achieved a soft landing by parachute system on March 1—man's first spacecraft to reach another planet. Reportedly, no transmissions were received. The alien explained, however, that the small device had been sending radio signals for some time, signals that had shaken up our scientists' previous beliefs about the planet (thus presumably had been censored). He went on to explain that a "magnetic shield" enveloping Venus served as protection from cosmic rays and "holds a very high temperature, as well as the natural electrical layers of the upper ionosphere. The protective magnetic shield is made artificially by the inhabitants of Venus." Fred's unspoken thought that this shield probably cut down radiation levels to a minimum was confirmed verbally by the alien. (Venusian gravity, incidentally, is 91% that of ours, thus hypothetical Venusians would weigh a little more on Earth.)

Shortly before this meeting, Fred had written letters to some newspapers, including *The Washington Post*, challenging several of the published findings regarding Venus. In late 1962, the U.S. space probe Mariner 2, during its fly-by of the planet, reported surface temperatures of 428°C (802.4°F)—above the melting point of lead. Following the later soft landing by the Soviet Venus 3 probe, the *Post* commented: "Our scientists were sharply critical of this landing, for they were not sure the craft was sterilized [and] feared the unsterilized spacecraft may have carried germs from Earth to Venus, which might have jeopardized the chances of finding life on the planet."

"I openly ask the scientists," Fred challenged, "What life do they expect to find with an 800° surface temperature? If the boiling point of water, for instance, stands at 212°F, why does the space craft, then, have to be sterilized, if at only 212° all germs are killed automatically?" The letter was not published.[23]

I should add here that Fred Steckling's son Glenn, currently a pilot with a major U.S. airline, also attests to a number of meetings with aliens living among us.

Another person claiming regular contact with Venusians during this époque was an American brigadier general. In a letter to Major Hans C. Peterson, Senior Air Traffic Control Officer in the Royal Danish Air Force (1949–1976)—Adamski's representative in Denmark—the general stated, in part:

"In regard to the space ships and their crews, so-called 'flying saucers,' what I am about to impart to you I am asking you as a fellow Veteran not to divulge the source. . . . Let me first state that through no effort or expectation on my part, I was contacted one night eleven years ago while working late in my shop to finish a printing job. They came to my shop door, insisted on my opening it, came in, looked around a bit, spoke no word, and motioned me to come outside. As I did so I became aware of a large object, a few feet overhead.

"I was taken aboard, and had my first experience of positive telepathy, a very informative few minutes. They left, saying they would return soon. They kept their word and they returned—I think I can honestly say a few hundred times since, in the past eleven years.

"They have requested that I act as their contact man with quite a number of our national and religious leaders, and my identity must remain a strict secret, except with their permission as in your case. You can understand that, if my identity and work were known, I would never have a single moment's rest, and would soon become worthless to both them and the problems I attempt to handle.

"Now to their ability to speak perfect English. If you, for instance, had been within close vicinity of Venus for 2,000 years, as the Venusians have the Earth, and had been able to hear any conversation in any language that was spoken on Venus, do you not think you would be able to speak their language quite fluently? Among their own people they use thought only, but we of Earth, because of our habit, they have learned our language so perfectly that if one of them was to step up and speak to you in your place of business or your home or on the street, you would not recognize him from one of your own people, and in appearance, probably the greatest difference would be his handsome features and perfect proportions physically. . . ."

It has been twenty-five years since the Russians and Americans—or any other nation, apparently—have sent a lander to Venus. In late 2009, however, NASA awarded the University of Colorado at Boulder (CU-Boulder) $3.3 million for a detailed, one-year concept study for a lander mission to Venus "to study the history of its surface, climate and atmosphere and to predict its ultimate fate in the solar system." The mission had been proposed by CU-Boulder Professor Larry Esposito, science team leader on the proposal. As part of CU-Boulder's Surface and Atmosphere Geochemical Explorer (SAGE) mission, the lander would descend onto the flank of an active volcano known as Mielikki Mons, which is about 200 miles across and

4,800 feet in altitude. Once the lander was in place, instruments would dig about four inches into the surface, then "zap the soils with two lasers and a vacuum tube shooting large pulses of neutrons, which would bounce back data to the lander with information on surface composition and texture," it was reported in 2011. The lander would be constructed to survive the harsh conditions on Venus for three hours or more. "Venus has gone terribly bad since it first formed," says Esposito. "The surface pressure is a hundred times that of Earth and its temperature is similar to that of a self-cleaning oven. . . ."[24]

According to Jet Propulsion Laboratory (JPL) planetary scientist Suzanne Smrekar, at eight miles above the surface of Venus, the carbon dioxide in its atmosphere becomes so dense that it turns "supercritical." "Supercritical carbon dioxide is a gas-liquid mix that can eat through metal, and SAGE is designed to keep this nasty stuff from entering the sealed vessel," explains Sam Kean. "For protection from the crushing atmospheric pressure—1,300 pounds per square inch—the lander will be roughly spherical. . . . The one redeeming quality of the heavy atmosphere is that it cushions the lander's descent. Terminal velocity on Venus is a leisurely 25 mph—so slow that the parachute is no longer needed after the spacecraft is 42 miles above the surface."

"Temperature is the thing that will kill you the quickest," claims Smrekar, who adds that to protect circuits and batteries, she and others have been testing advanced insulation materials such as lithium nitrate. But insulation, per se, would be insufficient, and planetary scientist Mark Bullock points out that such landers will require "active" cooling—that is, multi-stage refrigeration.[25]

Is Venus the veritable hellhole it's cracked up to be? Who are we to believe—the contactees, the "Venusians," or the down-to-Earth scientists? Could it be that official statements about Venus are deliberately distorted? In addition to Fred Steckling, others have come forward to dispute the official findings. John Lear, whom I first met in 1990, is a former pilot who has flown over 160 different types of aircraft in many different countries. The son of William P. Lear, designer of the Learjet, he is the only pilot ever to hold every airline certificate issued by the Federal Aviation Administration, and has also flown numerous missions for the CIA. He became interested in UFOs and the space program in the early 1980s. Behind the scenes, he has learned much about NASA and, in the following instance, about Venus in particular:

"In the late 1950s NASA was formed to compartmentalize, containerize, and sanitize information from all space platforms and vehicles," claimed Lear in an interview with Art Bell in 2003. "We sold NASA to the public, claiming that all information would belong to them, but they got very little, and even that was highly sanitized.

"Our first efforts were to keep the public from learning about Venus—a very similar planet to Earth, and its population very similar to ours, just [more] technologically advanced. . . . Starting with the Russian Venera 1 and U.S. Mariner 2, we made Venus look like a lead-melting, volcanic surface, spewing sulfuric acid into a pressurized atmosphere 90 times that of Earth. And as often is the case, we overdid it, and we wondered why nobody asked how a parachute survived a descent into 800-degree air."[26]

During my fourteen years with the London Symphony Orchestra, a fellow member learned from a scientist friend in the 1970s that the director of a top-secret U.S./German space research center in West Germany was of Venusian origin. This revelation, my colleague informed me, was restricted to a quorum of scientists at the center. The information supplied by the director proved invaluable in their research effort, which I assume was related to the liaison program. In the 1980s my friend had the opportunity of meeting the director over dinner in London, together with his scientist friend, and was satisfied as to the director's "credentials." Like some of the aliens in the Amicizia group (Chapter 13), the director enjoyed good food and wine. And why not?

EARLY INFILTRATION

In 1921, Albert Coe, then seventeen years old, was told by his 340-year-old (!) alien friend that, as early as 1904, the aliens replaced a hundred terrestrial babies and infiltrated their own. "In the base of each baby's brain was this little thing that recorded everything that that baby saw or did, from the time they put it there," Coe told Dr. Berthold Schwarz, a noted researcher and psychologist. "No one ever knew it was a switch." Subsequently, as adults, the aliens became active in every major nation on Earth.

Their main concern: that we were on the verge of discovering secrets of the atom, which could have disastrous consequences for our planet.

"You've just finished what you call a world war," the man explained, "and each of your wars gets a little more brutal and devastating than the preceding one. We're here to watch and see what you're going to do when you learn the secret of the atom. This is one reason we're here." Coe learned years later that in 1955 the aliens, alarmed about the escalation of nuclear-weapons tests, had set up a neutralizing screen, "in case one of these nuclear experiments of ours got out of hand—that it wouldn't start a chain reaction." One nuclear weapon, for example, had been exploded above the atmosphere in 1964, they said. Were it not for the neutralizing screen, the results could well have been catastrophic.[27]

PERSONAL ENCOUNTERS

Many years ago I co-authored a book, together with Lou Zinsstag, on George Adamski, examining the pros and cons of his claims.[28] Lou—a cousin of Carl G. Jung—had been Adamski's Swiss representative and, like most of the representatives, subsequently experienced encounters with aliens living among us. The first of Adamski's contacts occurred near Desert Center, California, on November 20, 1952, witnessed from a distance by six companions. The alien with whom Adamski communicated on that occasion—given the name "Orthon"—asserted that he came from Venus. The witnesses, two of whom (Alice Wells and Lucy McGinnis) I knew and found totally credible, subsequently signed an affidavit testifying to this significant event[29]—perhaps more significant than we realize, as I shall discuss later in this chapter.

Although described in *Alien Base* and in the book on Adamski I co-authored, since both are out of print I should mention here my two encounters with presumed aliens in the United States. The first occurred on November 13, 1963, while touring with the Royal Philharmonic Orchestra. During the five-hundred-mile or so journey from Tucson to Los Angeles in our convoy of three buses, we stopped at a restaurant near the Arizona/California border. Seated at a table with three colleagues, I happened to survey the customers waiting in line. My attention was drawn to an extraordinarily graceful, petite girl with blond bobbed hair and delicate pale features. The thought struck me that she might be one of those aliens living among us, so I telepathically transmitted the somewhat trite question: "Are you from another planet?"

There was no response. But as she left the line, she made a point of walking past our table, pausing to give me a lovely smile and gracious bow of acknowledgment before proceeding to another part of the restaurant, a "dead-pan" expression on her face. My colleagues shared my bemusement. Later, I was to be reminded of Adamski's description of one of the female crew members he encountered on board a large mothership in February 1953, with her "almost transparent skin."[30]

I do not know the precise location of the restaurant, but I do recall that as we departed in the buses, one of the highway signs nearby coincidentally indicated Desert Center. I had hoped to meet Adamski in Vista during our few days in Los Angeles, but unfortunately, owing to my schedule, it didn't work out.

In February 1967 I was playing with the London Symphony Orchestra in New York for a series of concerts at Carnegie Hall with Mstislav Rostropovich, the great Russian cellist. I had just returned from my first meeting with Madeleine Rodeffer, a close associate of Adamski, with whom (and others) she had observed the classic Adamski-type scout-craft at very close range in her front yard in Silver Spring, Maryland. On February 26, 1965, Adamski had taken 8-mm film of the craft as it described a series of maneuvers. Madeleine told me that she had had a number of encounters with aliens living in the Washington, D.C. area, and suggested that on my return to New York I should try to initiate a contact telepathically. So, on that late afternoon, between a rehearsal and concert, I sat down in the lobby of the Park-Sheraton Hotel at 56th Street on Seventh Avenue and transmitted a telepathic request: "If any of you people from elsewhere are in the New York vicinity, please come and sit down right next to me and prove it."

After about half an hour a man entered the lobby whose demeanor put me on the alert. Dressed in a charcoal-gray suit with a white shirt and dark tie, he could have passed for a businessman from Madison Avenue. He wore rimmed glasses and appeared to be about thirty-five years old and five feet ten inches in height, with slightly curly fair hair, a mild olive complexion, and perfectly proportioned features. He sat down beside me, took out a copy of *The New York Times* from his attaché case, and turned the pages over in a rather deliberate and superficial manner. After he had refolded the paper, I asked him telepathically if he really was from another planet, and if so, to please confirm this by placing his right index finger on the right side of his nose and—I vaguely recall—asking him to keep it there for a short while. No sooner had I transmitted the thought than he did precisely that.

I attempted more telepathy, but no further confirmation was forthcoming. Eventually he stood up, walked over to some display windows, and then gave me a direct and serious look before walking out of the hotel into Seventh Avenue. I never saw him again. I am often asked why I didn't try and engage him in a conversation, to which I can only respond that it seemed inappropriate. I assumed that, if conversation was to be on the agenda, he would be the one to initiate it.

"EARTH'S FUTURE IN SPACE"

Since that occasion, I have had two encounters reaffirming my conviction that aliens live among us, one of which occurred in Wrocław, Poland. I had been invited by the researcher Janusz Zagórski to give a presentation at the "X UFO Forum" ("X" meaning "10th" in this instance), which ran from May 6 to 7, 2006. I was also honored by an invitation to head a discussion on the UFO topic the evening before the conference, as guest speaker, at *Salonu Profesora Dudka*—Professor Dudek's Salon—organized by Józef Dudek, a Wrocław University professor well known as an outstanding mathematician and humanist. The aims of this prestigious Salon are to "integrate scientific, political, and cultural elites of Wrocław by means of organizing discussion meetings devoted to topics that are of vital interest to representatives of various disciplines and circles." The attendees, numbering about seventy (at a guess), included medical doctors, military personnel, politicians, psychologists, and scientists, some retired.

At 19:00, after being introduced to the assembled gathering by the chairman, I delivered my illustrated slide presentation, scheduled to last thirty-five minutes. An interval of forty-five minutes followed, allowing informal talks and refreshments.

From the beginning of the evening, I had been aware of an immaculately dressed, very composed man in the audience, sitting about ten feet from me. Slight of build, he was about five feet ten inches in height and wore a dark gray suit, waistcoat, white shirt, and dark tie. His complexion and hair were similar to the man in New York. I tried a bit of telepathy—to no apparent avail.

As the audience returned to their seats after the interval, I began taking a few photographs, hoping to capture an image of this man. I succeeded in taking a few shots of the audience seated to my right, but as I panned to the left—where the man was seated—a voice from the back of the room said, "The speaker is not allowed to take photographs." I apologized—to whomever.

What followed turned out to be a lively debate. I shall never forget the moment when a psychologist launched into a diatribe against the subject, his face purple with rage (and perhaps liquid refreshment), after which Major Jósef J. Makiela, a retired Polish air force pilot, countered vehemently by stressing how seriously the subject was taken by the military, and introduced a fellow pilot who had experienced a close encounter.

Participating contributors to the debate were encouraged not to exceed five to seven minutes. Both English and Polish were spoken. On my left-hand side sat a professional female simultaneous translator. Toward the end of the evening, the unusual man stood up and, as per protocol, announced his name (which I didn't catch) and gave his occupation—"doctor." He then proceeded to address the topic of "Earth's future in space." Obviously, I was all ears.

At the conclusion of the debate, I approached the man, proffering my right hand, which he held briefly and limply, with no handshake. "I think you have a great deal of knowledge," I said. He made no verbal response but continued looking at me very directly, his unblinking pale blue eyes betraying not a vestige of expression. I handed him my business card and he left the room.

After the debate and ensuing conversations with various guests, which finished after 23:00, I was taken back to my hotel in a suburb of Wrocław, part of the fabulous Wojnowice Castle, as guest of the proprietors, Iwona and Franciszek Oborski. On the twenty-five-kilometer journey, I vaguely recall struggling to recall what that unusual man had said.

Over drinks with a small group of attendees, we discussed the evening. I immediately alluded to the man in question. Franciszek commented that the man frequently attended the Dudek Salon, and invariably had something interesting to contribute. "Can any of you remember what he talked about?" I asked. It seemed that nobody—including myself—had a clue, other than that it had something to do with Earth's future in space. Bearing in mind that when I approached the man I had been extremely impressed by what he had communicated to us, I remain puzzled.

All subsequent efforts to obtain evidence were thwarted. I had asked a professional photographer who took a number of photos during the proceedings to send me some pictures. I never heard back from him. Janusz Zagórski sent copies of the photos he had taken, but unfortunately the unusual man does not appear in them. Furthermore, debates at Professor Dudek's Salon are usually recorded and speakers are entitled to a copy. I never received one, despite several requests. (It is possible that the event simply was not taped on this occasion.) Franciszek Oborski had offered to find out what she could about the man's background, but she was not in the best of health at the time and sadly died a few years later.

Whatever the background of this unusual man, it seems likely to me that he was one of a number of aliens who live and work among us. I nurture the impression that subliminally he had imparted some possibly important information regarding Earth's future, and then somehow "wiped" our memories thereof. For the time being, perhaps.

MOUNT PALOMAR

Many of George Adamski's associates and friends experienced encounters and sightings when visiting his home at Palomar Terraces, Valley Center, on the slopes of Mount Palomar, California. One such was Alan G. Tolman, who had served in the Korean War with the 3rd Battalion, 7th Marine Regiment, 1st Marine Division, when he had his first UFO sighting. Later he spent six years in aerospace research, including with the Douglas Aircraft Company in Segundo, California, where he worked in the Experimental Department as an electrician. In October 1955, assigned to attaching a special camera on the Douglas Skyrocket, he was approached while alone in the hangar by two intelligence personnel, one from the CIA

(Henry Harvey Hennes) and the other (unnamed) from the Office of Naval Intelligence. Somehow, the men were aware of Tolman's sightings.

"Both men encouraged me to speak up and tell more people of my sighting experiences," Tolman reports. "They told me that the CIA had three volumes of Intelligence Digests, which they said contained sightings and photos from all over the world [and] said that Earth was being looked over by people from other planetary systems." The existence of the Intelligence Digests was later confirmed (in a roundabout way) in a letter to Tolman from Vice Admiral C. S. Freeman, U.S. Navy (retired). I possess a copy of that letter.

Around the same period—1955–56—Tolman was visiting Adamski. "George had a fifteen-inch Newtonian reflector telescope in a dome, in a clearing just a short distance from his house. He also had a six-inch Newtonian telescope that he used with a German 3-inch by 4-inch plate-glass-type camera that he used to take flying saucer photos with in the early 1950s. One night, George let me use his six-inch telescope while he was in his house speaking with friends.

"While looking through his telescope, I saw a 'blueish' streak that filled the field of view, going from my right to my left and toward the clearing where George's fifteen-inch telescope dome was. I quickly looked up but saw nothing. Suddenly, I saw a blue-white flare, then a glow, near the fifteen-inch 'scope dome area. The blue-white glow was elliptical in shape. A grove of trees stood between me and the spacecraft, and the trees were sharply silhouetted by the ship's glow.

"I walked toward the craft, and as I got closer I could hear a soft, pleasing 'hum' sound. At about a hundred yards from the craft, I heard people that had just come out of a restaurant, down the hill from George's house, yelling loudly, 'There's a [flying saucer] on the ground!' From the restaurant parking area, the people had an unobstructed view of the craft.

"Suddenly, a man from the restaurant parking area came running toward me and almost knocked me down, saying 'There's a [saucer] out there.' He then disappeared. The craft increased in brightness, going from blue-white to an intense white that seemed to shimmer. The hum sound increased in frequency until I could not hear it anymore. The craft then shot straight up, making no noise, into the night stars, until it looked just like a star. It then shot off horizontally toward the horizon.

"I then went into George's house and told him what had just happened. He said he heard all the 'ruckus' outside, and then just looked at me and smiled. . . ."[31]

Adamski wasn't alone in photographing alien craft in this vicinity. According to Harold Wilkins, in December 1951 a U.S. Marine claimed to have overheard an interesting conversation at the Palomar Observatory, which then housed the world's largest telescope. The Marine stated as follows:

"I, and another Marine, were chatting to one of the Palomar professors when a friend of his arrived from Berkeley, California. He, too, is a professor. They began talking, and we listened in to what we were not supposed to hear. The Palomar man said that the U.S. Federal Bureau of Investigation had forbidden the publication of [certain] astrophysical photos taken at Palomar. 'Why?' asked the other. 'Well, they show things that the U.S. government thinks it wiser people should not know. They might cause panic. There are pictures of jet planes chasing flying saucers, and disintegrating in mid-air. There are [also] data about strange changes in the atmosphere, and the effect on other planets of radioactive emanations after the explosion of atomic bombs.'"

Wilkins also cites a tongue-in-cheek report by Walter Winchell, the well-known columnist: "June 30, 1952: Scientists at Palomar Observatory, Calif., are supposed to have seen a 'space ship' land in the Mojave Desert, in May last. Four persons stepped out, took one look, and went off again. The U.S. Army may officially announce it in the fall."[32] It didn't, of course.

COLLATERAL EVIDENCE

In *Flying Saucers Have Landed*, a best-selling book by Desmond Leslie and George Adamski, the latter's famous series of clear photographs of scout-ships and motherships, taken through his telescope, were first published. In the updated edition, Leslie reports that in 1955 his friend Patrick (later Sir Patrick) Moore, the iconic British astronomer who died in 2012, revealed that he too had been shown a set of photos of a "scout-ship," even better ones than those taken by Adamski and Stephen Darbishire:

"They were taken, I was told, by a world-famous American astronomer who desired to remain anonymous as he feared the ridicule of his colleagues. Patrick Moore has given a pledge of secrecy regarding this eminent man's identity [so] we compromised by referring to him as 'Dr. X.' At my request, Moore kindly wrote to Dr. X asking if I might be permitted a sight of his photos (while preserving his anonymity), but this, to my regret, was refused. However, I gathered that Dr. X had taken some of his series through a telescope, as had Adamski, and had once, when out for a walk, practically stumbled upon a UFO rising from the ground and had managed to photograph it close at hand."[33]

"THE NOBLE ONE"

In an unusual book on the early contactees, author Henry Dohan reveals that the aforementioned Orthon—the name given him by his terrestrial contacts, meaning "the noble one" in Greek—lived "on and off for about three years" in the Vista, California, area, spending much of his time with Adamski. Claiming to be around 360 years old in 1952, but apparently looking like a man in his twenties, Orthon was often pursued by both the FBI and CIA, according to Dohan.[34]

During a conversation with Adamski in 1959, Lou Zinsstag asked about the well-known painting of Orthon depicting him as appearing rather effeminate and undistinguished. "Orthon did not look like that at all," replied Adamski. "He had a very manly, highly intellectual face, but as his features were so distinct and characteristic, it would have been dangerous for him to have had them published." To Lou's surprise, Adamski then showed her a photo of Orthon's face in profile. Lou revealed to me that his most striking feature was a pronounced chin.[35]

"People may wonder what kind of person He [sic] was," writes Dohan. "I was never privileged to meet Him, but those who did say He is a most humble person with the most incredible powers." On one occasion while with Orthon, Adamski explained that he would need about four or five people to move a large solid oak table from a storage shed into the house. "Orthon told Adamski to go to the street and make sure that no cars were coming," Dohan continues. "Orthon put His hands on the top of the table and it began to float. He held His hand over the table all the way as He walked alongside it and it floated all the way from the storage shed into the house."

Yet Orthon was evidently very down to Earth. "On another occasion," writes Dohan, "Adamski had problems with the plumbing in the house near the foothills of Mount Palomar where he lived. Orthon volunteered to help since He [was smaller than Adamski] and He fixed the problem. I write this to illustrate the humility of such a great Man who was not too proud to go under a house to help somebody."

Dohan claims that Orthon left after three years and allowed people from Adamski's house to film the departure of his craft. "I saw this movie," he affirms. "The spacecraft rose in front of the camera to only a few feet above the ground, then it flew in a circle, returning again to the camera before it finally departed. In the beginning of that same movie was a short segment where [an object] the size of a fly kept jumping up and down in front of the windshield of the car in which Adamski was riding," Dohan continues. "Adamski asked the driver to stop the car [and] filmed the small saucer and followed it with the camera; and then, as you look into the sky, in the background of the tiny saucer was another one, an exact replica of the first one but many miles [sic] in size. The message they wanted to give us is that these [craft] can be built in all sizes."[36] In the Amicizia case (Chapter 13), very similar small "craft"—given the name "aniae"—were seen by various witnesses, two of whom I interviewed.

Born in Vienna, Henry Dohan was a textile and electrical engineer who achieved fame in 1961 for his invention of ladderless nylon stockings, based on research into "mass and macromolecular structures." After becoming an Australian citizen, he eventually moved to Southern California. He seems to have been respected, described for example in the Australian Parliament by Senator the Hon. G. Brown as "an inventive genius, with remarkable powers of concentration and unusual tenacity who finally triumphed over colossal difficulties. . . ."[37]

Dohan's use of the capital "H" in relation to Orthon seems to imply his belief that the latter had been Jesus in a previous life. An outrageous implication, to be sure. Yet I have often pondered on the possibility myself. In 1976 I asked Alice Wells, Adamski's closest associate for many years, if she thought this to be the case. She replied in the affirmative, without further comment. In Chapter 19, I cite various quotes from the Bible which tend to support the likelihood of Jesus's out-of-this-world provenance.

Fred Steckling relates that one of his alien contacts worked for several years on Earth, in many different environments, with both rich and poor people. "I have not hesitated to do any kind of job, regardless of what kind of work was involved, 'dirty' or 'clean,' as you may classify it," he told Fred. "The work has to be done, and without the dirty work, the clean could not exist."[38]

Which brings me back to Carl Anderson. He recounts how a trusted friend of his, a native American chief who lived in east Los Angeles, was camping one night in 1965 at Salton Sea (a National Wildlife lake recreation area where he owned quite a lot of land) when he and his wife witnessed at close proximity the landing of an alien vehicle. "The people came over and conversed with him in his own tongue—an Indian language. They told him they were coming here to study the ways of our people. They wanted him to find them a place to live, because they wanted to mingle among us and associate with the people of Earth, to try and find out what made us do the things we do; why we have wars, why we kill one another, and why we don't have any brotherly love. . . .

"So he got them a place to stay. But first of all he told them they had to put on different clothes. 'You're all dressed in white,' he said, 'and you'll be recognized right away as somebody different.' So they went to the store, after [my friend] had put them up in a motel for the night—a man, a woman, and three children. And their hair, it was so red![39] 'You're going to have to dye that hair a different color,' he told them, 'because it'll be obvious that you're not like people of Earth.'

"They're now living in a town in the east Los Angeles area. My son-in-law was driving a bakery cart, and he delivered bakery goods to them. The three children are going to a school in the Los Angeles County School System, and they got coached almost daily by their parents to make boo-boos—to actually make mistakes on purpose so that they won't be recognized as being out of the ordinary, because those children are such geniuses that they're almost incapable of making any mistakes. And as far as I know, they still live in the area. The man works putting vegetables on the counters of a large supermarket. . . ."[40]

Since the early days of the space program, we have received assistance from some alien groups—and hindrance from others. Citing the deflection from orbit of NASA's Juno 2 rocket in 1959, Wernher von Braun is reported to have stated: "We find ourselves faced by powers which are far stronger than we had hitherto assumed, and whose base is at present unknown to us. More I cannot say at present. We are now engaged in entering into closer contact with those powers. . . ."[41]

Date. *May 17 1956*

To whom it may concern;

This is to certify that I, Stella Dee Anderson, did on two separate and individual occasions, witness Spacecraft known as flying Saucers, in the Calif. desert. One near Desert Center, the other, south of Victorville Calif. on the dates of April 4, 1954 and on October 2, 1955 And that on one occasion, a beam or ray of some kind which I believe is unknown to earthly science, caused my husband, my daughter, and myself to be completely paralyzed until the Saucer left. During this period, about fifteen minutes, a tent in which we were, became invisible to the eye. And that on the other occasion, I witnessed the miraculous healing of a severe burn on the right thumb of my brother James E. Stewart, which had just been caused by a burning flare he was using to signal the Saucer with. This healing was accomplished, I believe, by the same ray or beam from this huge Saucer which was hovering above us. The statements herein contained, are true to the best of my knowledge and belief.

Stella D. Anderson

Signed this. 17th. . . day of. May. . 1956

Witness. *Herbert P. Smith*

HERBERT P. SMITH, Notary Public
In and for the County of Los Angeles, State of California
My Commission Expires July 27, 1958
9443 E. Flower, Bellflower, Calif.

One of five affidavits provided by witnesses to their observations of spacecraft in the California desert in 1954 and 1955.

George Adamski claimed that these strange symbols were inscribed for him by one of his alien contacts in the 1950s. Each symbol apparently represents a sentence. Note the array of planets in our solar system (top right, third line) depicting three alleged planets beyond the orbit of Pluto. Translations welcomed!

CHAPTER EIGHT
AIRBORNE ENCOUNTERS

Over a lengthy period, Britain's Ministry of Defence has released batches of its voluminous documents relating to unidentified flying objects, mostly comprising correspondence from members of the public and attendant inter-office memos. In August 2010, the sixth such batch (some five thousand pages) included an interesting if apocryphal story contained in a series of letters in 1999 from an astrophysicist in Leicester (name and address redacted).

The physicist's grandfather had served with the Royal Air Force (RAF) in World War II, and his duties sometimes involved being part of the personal bodyguard of Winston Churchill. On one occasion—according to his young daughter at the time—he was present when Churchill and General Eisenhower discussed an incident, alleged to have occurred during the latter part of the war, when an RAF photo-reconnaissance aircraft returning from a mission in either France or Germany was intercepted by an object of unknown origin, which "matched course and speed with the aircraft for a time and then underwent an extremely rapid acceleration away from the aircraft." The report continues:

"The encounter with the unknown object occurred close to or over the English coastline [and] was undetected until it was close to the aircraft. It was suddenly observed by the aircrew appearing at the side of the aircraft at a very high speed; then it very rapidly matched its speed with that of the aircraft [and] appeared to 'hover' noiselessly relative to the aircraft for a time. One of the airmen began to take photographs of it. It appeared metallic but its shape was not described. The object very rapidly disappeared, leaving no trace. . . .

"[My grandfather] was not present during the initial discussion when this event was communicated to the U.S., but he was present at the follow-up meeting when the response from the U.S. was received [and he] witnessed the discussion of the event by both Mr. Churchill and Mr. Eisenhower in the United States. . . . Mr. Churchill declared that the incident should be classified for at least 50 years and its status reviewed by a future Prime Minister. [He also] is reported to have made a declaration to the effect [that] it would create mass panic amongst the general public and destroy one's belief in the Church. . . ."

Said to have been "greatly affected by his experience," the bodyguard told few people about it.[1]

Another document reveals how some UFO reports from members of the public were taken seriously by the Ministry of Defence during the Cold War. Minutes from a meeting of the Joint Intelligence Committee in May 1959 state that Air Vice-Marshal William MacDonald discussed the matter at the highest level. He reported that UFOs had been observed by official and unofficial sources at a rate of one a week and disclosed that a sample of sixteen reports in early 1957 showed that ten had been identified—but six were not.

Also during the Cold War, and right up to 1991, RAF fighters were scrambled two hundred times a year to intercept unidentified targets penetrating U.K. airspace. Although some were anomalous, most turned out to be Soviet long-range reconnaissance or anti-submarine aircraft.[2]

AIR DISASTERS

In the late 1940s and 1950s, unexplained crashes of military and civilian aircraft proliferated dramatically. It needs to be stressed that hundreds of reports of UFOs from all over the world were coming in each *week* from trained observers—pilots in particular. In *Need to Know,* I cited numerous cases involving mysterious disasters worldwide, including many kindly supplied to me by Jon "Andy" Kissner, former Republican State Representative for Las Cruces, New Mexico,[3] and other cases reported by Harold T. Wilkins and Major Donald E. Keyhoe. The late American researcher Kenny Young also collated records of such cases, including the following sobering examples I have selected from the period June 3–8, 1951:

JUNE 3: A C-82 Packet cargo plane "fell apart in the sky" over New Boston, Texas, killing all aboard.

JUNE 4: A C-119 Flying Boxcar cargo plane exploded in mid-air and crashed, killing four crew. A crew member who parachuted successfully reported that the plane "just seemed to come apart around him and he found himself in mid-air."

JUNE 5: An F-51 Mustang, an F-86 Sabre, and an F-82 Twin Mustang were involved in a mid-air collision, killing two pilots.

JUNE 8: Eleven or more U.S. military planes crashed, some disintegrating in mid-air, including an AJ-1 Savage and an F-80 Shooting Star (the latter "falling apart"), and several F-84 Thunderjets, near Richmond, Indiana, killing three.[4]

Here follows another of Harold Wilkins's summaries, covering mainly the period between January and June 1954:

"RAF Meteor jet explodes and strews wreckage over Poulders Green, Kent. Pilot, gallantly remaining at the controls, is killed; Vampire jet cuts out at 15,800 feet and falls on ploughed field at Old Lackenby, Yorkshire. Pilot killed; Royal Danish Air Force grounds all its Thunderjets and Sabre jets after numerous disasters; British Undersecretary for Air says that 507 RAF jets crashed in 1952–1954 with great loss of life (112). Some crashes caused by engine-disintegration; Six-engined Stratojet, U.S. B-47, crashes at Townsend, Georgia, immediately after take-off. Four men lost; Skilled chief test pilot, Ed Griffiths, crashed in field and was killed at Rugby, England, only a few miles from his starting-point. He was testing a new Royal Navy propeller-jet, torpedo-carrying Wyvern, and had only time to radio his position before his sudden crash; Canberra jet bomber explodes in air over suburbs of Doncaster, Yorkshire. Crew of two killed. On the same day, a few miles away, at Six Mile Bottom, Newmarket, a second Canberra crashes, the crew of three missing; The bodies of two pilots were found in a Vampire jet wreckage at Lewes, Sussex."[5]

Obviously, not all these disasters should be attributed to alien hostility: many new types of aircraft were in service at this period, thus susceptible to accidents.[6] However, it is revealing to consider official U.S. Defense Department statistics for the period from 1952 to the end of October 1956, which I published in the second (and U.S.) edition of *Need to Know*. Out of 18,662 major accidents of U.S. Air Force and U.S. Navy military aircraft—mostly involving fast new jets (such as those scrambled in UFO interceptions)—1,773 were caused by "unknown factors."[7]

TEST PILOT ATTACKED

Lieutenant Colonel Roy Jack Edwards enlisted in the U.S. Marine Corps (USMC) in 1941 and served in World War II. A 1947 graduate and class-mate of President Jimmy Carter at the U.S. Naval Academy (a letter from Carter to Edwards is reproduced on p. 130), he also served in Korea and Vietnam.

In 1955, while stationed with the USMC at Edwards Air Force Base, California, test-flying the latest version (F-100C) of the Super Sabre jet, Edwards encountered a large UFO during a test flight in clear sky at about six thousand feet. On alerting ground control, the pilot was ordered to break away immediately and return to base, together with his "chase" plane monitoring the flight.

"His observation plane complied," reported his son Frank in 2008, when the story first came out. "However, my father told me that his raw intrepid instincts kicked in, thus he ignored ground control because he knew he probably wouldn't ever get another opportunity to confront a UFO—and pursued."

Edwards headed directly toward the stationary cigar-shaped and orange-glowing object, estimated to be about two football fields in length and slightly more than fifty yards in circumference, without any apparent source of propulsion on its surface area. "As he reached a range of about three or four miles from the UFO, it emitted a single burst of blue light, immediately rendering my father to instantly lose his ability to see and disabled his plane's communication equipment."

Although stripped of his vision and communications with ground control, Edwards managed to bank his jet slightly to starboard and to prevent his altitude from dropping. He considered bailing out but, knowing he had enough fuel, opted to "ride out some time," in the hope that the shock of whatever had happened to him and his plane would be temporary. Luckily, he regained full vision after about fifteen minutes and headed back to base—still minus communications.

During the debriefing by his commanding officer for disobeying orders, Edwards was admonished severely. He learned that the reason he had been ordered to return to base immediately was the fact that the same UFO had previously caused the deaths of three test pilots.

Edwards subsequently lost his status as a test pilot and was reassigned to a U.S. Naval Academy weapons department teaching position at Annapolis, Maryland. Furthermore, he was never again allowed to fly jet aircraft. After a few years at the Pentagon, however, he petitioned and was permitted to fly CH-46 Sea Knight helicopters with the U.S. Marine Corps.

Colonel Edwards did not discuss his experience until two years prior to his death in 2003. Interestingly, his military records list him as having been stationed with the USMC in Gifu, Japan during the period when he was actually at Edwards AFB.[8] Tactics such as these commonly apply to pilots who have close encounters with UFOs—as in the following case.

PILOT WITNESSES FLYING SAUCER CRASH

Before becoming a military pilot, Robert B. Willingham served with the U.S. Army during World War II and thereafter, until he was reassigned to Korea in 1950 as an F-51 Mustang pilot. Following a serious injury incurred during an attack on his ground position, he was flown back to the United States. In 1952, doctors having decided he was no longer fit to fly combat missions, he entered the Air Force Reserve, flying many types of aircraft, including F-51s, the F-47 Thunderbolt, the F-84 Thunderjet, and the F-86 Sabre.

In the early spring of 1955, stationed as an F-86 pilot at Carswell Air Force Base, Texas, one of Major (later Colonel) Willingham's missions involved an exercise escorting B-47 bombers as they flew into Texas from New York, heading for El Paso, from where they would then continue to Washington State, and then via the West Coast, Canada, and Alaska on a pre-designated flight path to the Soviet Union (in the event of a nuclear exchange). Each bomber was assigned four fighters.

The fighter escort squadron received an alert that the Distant Early Warning (DEW) radar system had tracked fast-moving unidentified traffic. Willingham then received a report from the radar operator aboard the B-47 he was escorting that the object appeared to be heading toward them from a northwesterly direction. "By his radar, he could tell it was coming our way," Willingham told Noe Torres and Ruben Uriarte, authors of an important book on the case. "I looked up and saw a big, bright object that looked like a star, but I knew it couldn't be a star." He estimated that it shot past at over two thousand miles per hour, within thirty-five or forty miles of their position.[9]

All four pilots escorting the bomber observed the UFO as it headed south toward the Texas/Mexico border. "At about that time," said Willingham, "it made a 90-degree turn to the right doing about two thousand miles an hour, and I knew it wasn't an airplane. We didn't have anything that could do that." The object then headed in the general direction of Del Rio, Texas. "There were a lot of sparks, and it tilted down by about a 45-degree angle." The object continued listing as it descended, and then no longer could be seen. Willingham learned that the radar controllers claimed it had crashed "somewhere off between Texas and the Mexico border."

During a debriefing later, two of Willingham's F-86 colleagues admitted to their base commander that they had observed the incident, though Willingham was the only one to speak up about it.[10]

CRASH/RETRIEVAL

Based also on the radio exchanges he was listening to, Willingham estimated that the object had crashed near Langtry, Texas. Knowing the area well, he requested permission from the flight commander to fly down to the crash site—about 150 miles away—and attempt to locate the object. Permission was granted. Approaching the crash site at about eight hundred feet, he could see the still-smoldering wreckage of a roughly disc-shaped object on the ground, just south of the Rio Grande river. He then returned to his mission.[11] He has implied that he used the excuse of being low on fuel to obtain permission to return to Carswell ahead of his colleagues, as he already had it in mind to procure a small plane and return to the crash site.

Determined to find out more, a few hours later Willingham asked Lieutenant Colonel James P. Morgan—who had flown with him on the mission—if the latter could fly him to Corsicana Air Field, some fifty miles away, where Willingham planned to pick up a light aircraft to survey the crash site. The two men flew out of Carswell Air Force Base in Morgan's Piper Cub. After arriving in Corsicana, Willingham ran into his friend Jack Perkins, an electrical engineer who had served in Willingham's Civil Air Patrol unit. After relaying the events of the day, Willingham asked if Perkins would accompany him to act as witness.

The two took off from Corsicana at around 14:00 in a very basic two-seat Aeronca Champion. "It was a nice little plane for landing and taking off in tight spaces," Willingham reflected. "You could land it in a hundred feet if you had to, but I had to make sure I had enough room for take-off, especially if you had a passenger." Two hours later, they arrived in the vicinity of the Langtry crash site. There they noted that a team of Mexican soldiers had cordoned off the area and were guarding the craft and wreckage. Based on Willingham's testimony, Torres and Uriarte describe the scene as follows:

"The UFO had impacted very close to the edge of a flat rocky ledge overlooking the Rio Grande river. [It seemed as though] it had first bounced and then skidded about three hundred yards generally toward the south, plowing up a mound of dirt ahead of it as it went along. The main object split into three large sections, and smaller debris was scattered all along the skid line. The top of the object, which was dome-shaped, broke off and landed about fifty feet beyond the main body of the UFO. The main section, which originally was a flattened disc between twenty-one and twenty-five feet in diameter, broke into two larger pieces and many smaller ones.

"The bottom part of the UFO, ripped into two large sections, was partially embedded against a sand mound, while the dome lay about fifty feet beyond it. Willingham and his partner noted a long plume of shiny metal debris that extended along the long furrow, where the object hit and skidded on the sandy desert soil prior to coming to rest. Judging from the length of the furrow, Willingham guessed the object was traveling 'pretty fast' before hitting the ground."

After landing, Willingham eased the Aeronca onto the rocky ledge between the crashed disc and the edge of a small cliff leading down to the Rio Grande.[12]

The Mexican military were "just looking at everything," Willingham recalled. "Of course, it was still red-hot, and they were staying back from it." At this time, a Langtry resident paddled across the shallow river to talk to Willingham and Perkins, relating his sighting of the flaming object, which had nearly clipped the top of his house. At first, the armed soldiers had assumed that Willingham and Perkins were part of an American recovery team they had been expecting. However, as the pilots followed the skid marks to the craft itself, they were ordered at gunpoint to leave the area, though they kept studying Willingham's Air Force uniform, as if still wondering if he was part of an official investigation.

Buying time, Willingham, who spoke Spanish, chatted with one of the officers, a Lieutenant Martínez of Mexico City, who offered to take Willingham closer to the main impact site. Perkins was not included in the invitation. As the pilot approached to within thirty-five or forty feet of the burning-hot object, two soldiers carrying rifles tipped with bayonets prevented him from getting any closer. Glancing in the direction of the separated dome section, he noted that it was more heavily guarded than the rest of the debris and was warned to keep away. Willingham also observed a number of Mexican government officials at the crash site.[13]

"It was at this point," Ruben and Noe told me, "that he [Willingham] saw the ET bodies, which is a fact he withheld from us during the writing of our book but later revealed on the Jeff Rense radio program on March

8, 2010. He disclosed for the first time his recollection of three strange, non-human entities that he saw inside the ruptured hull of the crashed UFO. Willingham said two of the bodies were badly mangled but one was fairly intact. The entities wore no clothing of any kind. He was fascinated by the arms of the creatures, which he described as being 'like broomsticks.'"[14]

As the light was fading, Willingham joined Perkins and headed toward their plane. Determined not to take off without having retrieved some evidence (he had not thought to bring a camera with him), he picked up one of the many fragments of shiny metal, still warm, wrapped it in his handkerchief, and put it in his pocket. They took off at about 16:30. After a refuelling stop near Waco, they headed back to Corsicana.

The following day, Willingham filed a detailed report at Carswell Air Force Base about the incident, which was forwarded to Colonel Miller, commander of the Air Force Reserve unit. At some point later, Miller summoned Willingham to his office. Also present were two of the other pilots he had been flying with during the initial sighting. After Willingham had related details of his experience in Langtry, there was little response. But he was later to receive several disturbing telephone calls from various personnel, including a general and a major in Air Force Intelligence, warning of "consequences" if he related to others what he had seen.[15]

THE METAL ARTIFACT

The curved metal artifact was about the size of a man's hand and half an inch thick, of a grayish-silver coloration and extremely light, with more than twenty precisely crafted holes in a honeycombed pattern on one side. (A sketch of the artifact made by Willingham in 1978 for a Japanese television program is reproduced in the Torres/Uriarte book.) Ridges on the other side or sides looked to Willingham "as if this piece had been broken off from a larger object. . . . The outside was kind of a dark gray and the inside of it was kind of orange-colored."

A keen metallurgist, Willingham ran a series of tests, including several with a cutting torch. At temperatures from 3,200 to 3,800 degrees Fahrenheit, the metal became hot but would not melt. "The cutting torch made the metal turn slightly blue for a while, but it did no lasting damage," he reported. "We tried grinders and everything else, but nothing would even touch it."

Most unfortunately—as it transpired—Willingham did not take any photographs of the metal. He flew the fragment from Texas to a Marine Corps metallurgy laboratory in Hagerstown, Maryland, where a major applied the same tests, with identical results. Further tests were needed, he said, after which he would get back to Willingham. The following day, the major phoned and apologized, explaining that he had to move out of the building. When Willingham called back later and asked to speak to him, he was informed that no such person worked there, and no records existed of either the metal or the tests carried out. A further visit to Hagerstown revealed only that it would not be in his best interests to pursue the matter.[16] Further warnings ensued. Two Air Force Intelligence personnel—a General White[17] and a Major Sealton—warned Willingham to tell no one, even if commanded to do so by a superior.

Within two weeks of the experience at Langtry, Willingham flew over the same area to see what had happened. Not a fragment of the device could be seen. As in other crash/retrieval cases, the entire site had been wiped clean by (I presume) a technical intelligence team,[18] also known as a "T-Force," usually assigned the responsibility of collecting flying discs at that time.[19]

In 1967, Colonel Willingham made the mistake of mentioning his experience to a reporter for a weekly newspaper in Pennsylvania. On retiring from the Air Force with many decorations in 1971/72, he was informed that he would not be receiving a pension. "Of course, they didn't tell me that it was because of what I said," he told Torres and Uriarte, "but I figured it out. Twenty-six years of service went down the drain. . . ."[20]

PROJECT BLUE BOOK

From about 1959 to 1963, Colonel Willingham was assigned to Project Blue Book, the third of the U.S. Air Force's official investigations into unidentified flying objects (1952–69). "Of the two thousand cases that my Blue Book team looked at, I would say that at least half of them were totally unexplained," he acknowledged—at variance, not surprisingly, with Blue

Book's official figures. The cases Willingham investigated were mostly on the East Coast, but occasionally he was ordered further afield, such as to Chile and Venezuela:

"We were contacted by people down in South America who had seen these objects flying around and were very scared. So I went down there in an F-100 [Super Sabre] and we flew surveillance, looking for the UFOs in the places where they had been seen. Some of these were night missions, flying up and down the coast, hoping to run into something. . . . If something was sighted at night, one of the planes would be sent out, and another would take off shortly afterward to provide cover for the first plane. We were armed, but we were instructed to fire only when we faced danger to our own plane. If they were doing something to screw up our airplane, we could fire."

He did not see any unidentified objects during these surveillance missions—officially logged as "test flights"—with the 192nd Interceptor Squadron.[21] Of incidental interest, a USAF cover reference for UFOs is/was "Unusual Helicopter Activity." Furthermore, I have learned that foreign cases were handled by Project Fang—not Blue Book.[22]

Willingham later learned about two other crashes of alien craft: one in North Texas, somewhere near Dallas, in the mid-1960s, when three alien bodies had been recovered. "They shut that one up really tight," he recalled. "It was hushed up very quickly." He was keen to visit the location, but access was denied. A second crash—also said to have involved the recovery of bodies—occurred in Colorado earlier in the 1960s. Yet again, the military clamped down on the incident.[23] He did not dismiss the possibility that the craft he saw might have been damaged by U.S. military intervention—a strong likelihood, in my view, given that since the 1940s quite a number of alien vehicles have been brought down to earth by the military.

Investigator Kevin D. Randle, who has served with the U.S. Air Force and the Army National Guard, involving numerous tours on active duty as an intelligence officer, believes the entire Willingham story to be a fabrication. He cites, for example, the lack of any military documents proving his service in the Air Force Reserve. All he could find in St. Louis, Missouri, where records of former military personnel are housed, was a record of

Willingham's service in the Army from December 1945 to January 1947. What few records Willingham has produced are dismissed as fabrications or irrelevant. One is a Reserve Order which, Randle reports, "seemed to indicate that Willingham had served twenty years of combined active duty and reserve time and would be eligible for a pension when he reached age sixty. That applies for those who have not done twenty years of active duty." And so on.[24]

Noe and Ruben sent me copies of several of the few documents pertaining to Willingham's service record which have been located. Though I am no expert, the Reserve Order does appear to have some questionable anomalies. But it has to be said that pilots and other military personnel who encounter UFOs frequently discover that many of their service records are either missing, or, as in the previous case of Colonel Roy J. Edwards, altered significantly.

Both Noe Torres and Ruben Uriarte find Colonel Willingham highly credible. So do I. "Originally," Noe explained to me, "we got started on the Robert Burton Willingham (RBW) case based on the recommendation of Dr. Bruce Maccabee [a retired U.S. Navy physicist], who had studied the case for years and considered RBW a credible witness with nothing to gain by lying. RBW showed us countless photographs and [pieces of] paperwork from his military days. . . . Randle contends that RBW never served in the U.S. Air Force or Air Force Reserve. When RBW has come forward with documents that show he served in these units, Randle has called them fraudulent.

"Ruben and I have cooperated one hundred percent with all Randle's many requests for information about the case over the past two years, but it became increasingly frustrating due to his unsupported dismissal of key documents and his closed-mindedness about the case. Someone specifically assigned the task of discrediting RBW could not possibly have done a better job of it. Randle has stated to us several times that RBW should be charged with violation of a U.S. law that prohibits persons from falsely claiming that they received certain military honors or medals. But Randle can no more prove that these claims are false than we can conclusively prove that they are true, since the military has conveniently lost most of RBW's service records.

"Willingham was ordered by military intelligence not to disclose, and he lives in fear about that to this very day. He has told us that 'they' have already tampered with his life, his military retirement benefits, etc. He admits to being deliberately vague and even misleading when Todd Zechel [ex-National Security Agency] and NICAP [National Investigations Committee on Aerial Phenomena] first contacted him in the late 1970s. If you read his 1978 affidavit, he does not give a date for the UFO crash. The 1948 date is something Randle injects to discredit RBW, but RBW never gave that date. . . . In his 1978 affidavit, he was being evasive in order to protect his own skin.

"We have spent hours face-to-face with RBW. He is a straight shooter, down-to-earth, matter-of-fact personality with an extremely conservative background. Like Randle, Ruben and I also wish we had more hard-core, indisputable documentary evidence regarding RBW's military service, but the fact is, we may never get it. . . ."[25]

LARGE CRAFT INTERCEPTED OVER THE U.K.

It was the height of the Cold War. On the night of May 20, 1957, Milton John Torres, a 25-year-old lieutenant serving as a U.S. Air Force fighter pilot with the 514th Fighter Interceptor Squadron in the 406th Fighter Expeditionary Wing, was on standby at the Royal Air Force base at Manston, Kent, when he received an urgent order to scramble and intercept an unknown object. He raced to one of the two F-86D Sabre jets on permanent five-minute alert at the end of the runway and took off.

"The initial briefing indicated that the ground [control] was observing for a considerable time a blip that was orbiting East Anglia," Torres later wrote in his unofficial report to the U.K. Ministry of Defence in 1988, released in a batch of documents in 2008:

"All the controlling agencies revealed that this was an unidentified flying object with very unusual flight patterns [and] motionless for long intervals. The instructions came to go 'gate' to expedite the intercept. Gate was the term used to use maximum power (in the case of the F-86D, that meant full afterburner) and to proceed to an Initial Point at about 32,000 feet. By this time my radar was on and I was looking prematurely for the bogey [unknown object]. The instructions came to report any visual observation, to which I replied, 'I'm in the soup and it is impossible to see anything!'

"The weather was probably high alto stratus, but between being over the North Sea and in the weather, no frame of reference was available—i.e., no stars, no lights, no silhouettes; in short, nothing. GCI [Ground-controlled Interception] continued the vectoring and the dialogue describing the strange antics of the UFO. The exact turns and maneuvers they gave me were all predicated to reach some theoretical point for a lead collision-course type rocket release. I can remember reaching the level-off and requesting to come out of afterburner only to be told to stay in afterburner. It wasn't much later that I noticed my indicated Mach number was about .92 . . . about as fast as the F-86D could go straight and level.

"Then the order came to fire a full salvo of rockets at the UFO. I was only a lieutenant and was very much aware of the gravity of the situation. To be quite candid, I almost s__t my pants! At any rate, I had my hands full trying to fly, search for bogeys, and now selecting a hot load on the switches. I asked for authentication of the order to fire, and I received it. . . .

"The authentication was valid, and I selected 24 [2.75-inch Mighty Mouse] rockets to salvo. I wasn't paying too much attention to [my wingman], but I clearly remember him giving a 'Roger' to all the transmissions . . . instructions were given to look 30 degrees to the port for my bogey. I did not have a hard time at all. There it was exactly where I was told it would be [on his radar]. The blip was burning a hole in the radar with its incredible intensity. . . .

"I had a lock-on that had the proportions of an aircraft carrier. By that, I mean the return on the radar was so strong that it could not be overlooked by the fire control system on the F-86D [and] it was the best target I could ever remember locking on to. I had locked on in just a few seconds, and I locked on exactly fifteen miles, which was the maximum range for lock-on. I called to the GCI 'Judy,' which signified that I would take all further steering information from my radar computer. . . .

"I had an overtake of 800 knots and my radar was stable," Torres's report continues. "The dot [on the screen] was centered and only the slightest corrections were necessary. This was a very fast intercept and the circle started to shrink. I called 'twenty seconds' and the GCI indicated he was standing by. The overtake was still indicating in the 7 or 8 o'clock position. At about ten seconds to go, I noticed that the overtake position was changing its position. It moved rapidly to the 6 o'clock, then 3 o'clock, then 12 o'clock, and finally rested about the 11 o'clock position. This indicated a negative overtake of 200 knots (the maximum negative overtake displayed). There was no way of knowing what the actual speed of the UFO was, as he could be traveling at very high Mach numbers and I would only see the 200-knot negative overtake.

"The circle, which was down to about an inch and a half in diameter, started to open up rapidly. Within seconds it was back to three inches in diameter, and the blip was visible in the blackened 'jizzle' band moving up the scope. This meant that it was going away from me. I reported this to the GCI site and they replied by asking 'Do you have a Tally Ho?' I replied that I was still in the soup and could see nothing. By this time the UFO had broken lock and I saw him leaving my thirty-mile range. Again I reported that he was gone, only to be told that he was off their scope as well. . . ."[26]

Torres had the impression the craft was moving at no less than Mach 10 (over 7,000 mph) when it disappeared. "It didn't follow classic Newtonian mechanics," he told reporter Billy Cox. "It made a right turn almost on a dime. The [RAF radar] scope had a range of 250 miles. And after two sweeps, which took two seconds, it was gone."[27] The pilots were then vectored back to Manston.

A CLOAK OF SECRECY

"Back in the alert tent, I talked to Met sector," the Torres report continues. "They advised me that the blip had gone off the scope in two sweeps at the GCI site and that they had instructions to tell me that the mission was considered classified. They also advised that I would be contacted by some investigator. It was the next day before anyone showed up.

"I had not the foggiest idea what had actually occurred, nor would anyone explain anything to me. In the squadron operations area, one of the sergeants came to me and brought me in to the hallway around the side of the pilots' briefing room. He approached a civilian, who appeared from nowhere. The civilian looked like a well-dressed IBM salesman, with a dark blue trenchcoat. (I cannot remember his facial features, only to say he was in his thirties or early forties.)"[28]

In an interview with *The Times* of London in 2008, the 77-year-old Torres—by then a retired professor of civil engineering—told defence editor Michael Evans that the man flashed a National Security Agency (NSA) identity card at him and warned that if he ever revealed what had happened, he would never fly again.[29] "He immediately jumped into asking me questions about the previous day's mission. I got the impression that he operated out of the States, but I don't know for sure. After my debriefing of the events, he advised me that this would be considered highly classified and that I could not discuss it with anybody, not even my commander [as in the case of Colonel Willingham]. . . . He threatened me with a national security breach if I breathed a word about it to anyone."[30] (In the *Air Force Times*, Dr. Torres elaborated that the agent had threatened to revoke his flying privileges and end his Air Force career if he talked about the mission.[31])

"He disappeared without so much as a good-bye, and that was that as far as I was concerned. I was significantly impressed by the action of the cloak-and-dagger people, and I have not spoken of this to anyone until recent years."[32]

Lieutenant Torres later became a range control officer at Cape Canaveral for the Gemini and Apollo space programs before flying 276 combat missions in the Vietnam War and earned thirteen air medals, including the Distinguished Flying Cross. He attained the rank of major prior to retiring from the military in 1971 and later became a professor of engineering at Florida International University, retiring in 2004.[33]

In other interviews, Dr. Torres expressed relief that he had not actually been ordered to fire upon the craft because he was certain he "would have been vaporized,"[34] and asserted his conviction that the craft was designed by an alien intelligence.[35] "My impression," he concludes in his report to the Ministry of Defence, "was that whatever the aircraft (or spacecraft) was, it must have been traveling in two-digit Mach numbers to have done what I witnessed.

"Perhaps the cloak of secrecy can be lifted in this day of enlightenment and all of us can have all the facts. . . ."[36]

JIMMY CARTER

August 18, 2000

To Lt. Col. Jack Edwards

It was great to talk to you earlier this month. I have your son, Frank, to thank for helping me get in touch with you after all these years.

You have my admiration and respect for your exemplary military career, and I feel personally honored to have been your classmate. Your outstanding accomplishments reflect well on the training we received at the Naval Academy.

Rosalynn joins me in sending you our warm regards and best wishes.

Sincerely,

Jimmy Carter

Lt. Col. Roy Edwards, USMC Ret.

████████████████████

Dallas, Texas 75231

A letter to Lt. Col. Roy Jack Edwards from former president Jimmy Carter. In 1955, while stationed at Edwards Air Force Base test-flying an F-100C Super Sabre, Edwards's jet was attacked by a large unknown craft, temporarily blinding him and disabling the aircraft's communications. The U.S. Air Force later falsified his whereabouts at the time of the incident.
(The Carter Center)

CHAPTER NINE
"A NEW WORLD–IF YOU CAN TAKE IT"

L ieutenant Colonel Philip J. Corso served on the staff of the National Security Council (NSC) and became an inter-agency coordinator for the NSC's Operations Coordinating Board—also known as the "Special Group," "54/12 Committee," or "5412 Group." As such, I learned, it was "the most clandestine, covert, and senior secret intelligence authorizing and controlling committee in the executive branch of the U.S. government during the Truman and Eisenhower administrations."

From 1961 to 1963, Corso acted as chief of the U.S. Army's Foreign Technology Division at the Pentagon. In 1997, his book—*The Day After Roswell*—caused a sensation with the revelation that he had been instructed by his boss, Lieutenant General Arthur Trudeau, chief of U.S. Army Research and Development, to steward alien artefacts from the Roswell incident in a reverse-engineering project that led to today's integrated circuit chips, fiber optics, lasers, and super-tenacity fibers.[1] Corso also briefed Robert F. Kennedy, during his term as U.S. Attorney General, regarding the Army's effort to seed extraterrestrial technologies into the private sector.[2]

Although Corso describes in detail his viewing of the recovered alien bodies at Fort Riley, Kansas, omitted from the book was his close observation of a grounded flying disc and, later, an encounter with an alien being, which occurred while he was in command of the Army's missile firing range at Red Canyon, White Sands, fifteen miles west of Carrizozo, New Mexico, in 1957. Corso's Record of Assignments (in my possession) shows that he served as Battalion Commander, based at Fort Bliss, Texas, from June 1957 through August 1958.

Described in a manuscript provided for me,[3] which Corso had intended for inclusion in his book, the separate events began with the intrusion and subsequent downing of an unknown craft.

"I took my small military plane with pilot and headed for the area where my radars had last located the object," he reports. "We flew over the site and I saw a bright, shiny saucer-shaped object on the ground." He assumed it was a missile booster.[4]

Later that day, Corso drove an Army car to the area where the unknown object had come down. "I asked Fort Bliss to send me an old World War II command car. It was built high off the ground, had large tires and four-wheel drive [which] was ideal for cross-country over the desert. So I set off for the area about ten to fifteen miles from the down-range launching sites and well within my area of jurisdiction. I decided to go alone. I took my belt with pistol and canteen, a map and a compass and a Geiger counter which we used to test stray voltage in the connection between the booster and missile. . . . When I arrived at the spot I had marked on my map, there was nothing there but desert. I sat in my command car and surveyed the area with binoculars. Finally, I saw something shimmering like a heat wave. . . . Suddenly it materialized.

"It looked like a metal object [shaped like] a saucer. . . . Seconds ticked away and abruptly it disappeared. I approached closer. I stopped and waited. Then again after about ten minutes it materialized in the same shimmering manner, then quickly it disappeared. I timed its appearance (forty-eight seconds). Again after about twelve minutes it appeared again. I picked up a desert rock and threw it at the solid metal-appearing object. The rock bounced off but made no sound. It disappeared again. I placed a large rock in the spot and some sagebrush. When it reappeared, it crushed both stone and sagebrush.

"By the time interval I figured, I had a total of about five minutes to observe the object in its solid state. On this appearance I gathered my nerve and went and placed my hand on it. In the hot desert sun it was cool; the surface was smooth, and felt like a highly varnished table top. It had no rough edges, no seams, and no rivets or screws.

"When it disappeared, I went back to my command car and sat to observe the see, no-see sequence. Each time it appeared to shake, but more like a shiver or tremble. Suddenly on the next appearance my Army compass started to spin and my Geiger counter began to fluctuate. I thought, discretion is the better part of valor. I started the engine, put the command car in reverse, and gunned it. After about three or four hundred yards, the engine stopped. The object slowly rose, turned on edge, and with a streak disappeared. . . . The bright-colored streak as it disappeared remained embedded in my memory. I started the engine and made four or five widening circles around the site. I stopped and got down, and thought I saw footsteps on the ground.

"They looked like they were made with a soft moccasin. I placed my foot alongside. I wear an 8C. They were half the size. I put the Geiger-counter leads on one. There was no reaction. I placed my compass. They were pointing east toward my missile firing sites, about ten miles away."[5]

Two days later, Corso was told to report to two range riders, who demanded to know what he had seen at the site. "A booster from one of my missiles," Corso responded. "There could be dire consequences for not telling us what you saw," threatened one of the men.

"I am the commander of this U.S. Army installation, and don't like threats in my command post," Corso fired back. "If I press this button, a dozen armed men will surround this office. Consider yourself in protective custody; you will leave when I say so. . . . Now, give me your identification and the name of your commanding officer." Over the phone, he explained to the officer that he had White House "Eyes Only" clearance and all other necessary clearances and therefore knew how to keep a secret.

Later, Corso flew over the area again to take another look at the object. But the area had been swept clean.[6]

GREEN TIME

"While I was in command of the U.S. Army's missile firing range at the Red Canyon range, I had one very annoying problem," relates Corso. "The range was part of the White Sands complex. I could not fire a missile unless they gave me what was called 'green' time. This coordination was necessary so there would be no radar interference. At times they held me up for hours, keeping hundreds of men on hold.

"One hot day, during one of these lulls, I was downrange in my command car, with two of my sergeants (my command post was a white shack on a high hill overlooking the range). . . ."

"First Sergeant Willis asked me if I wanted to visit the gold mine, only a few miles from the range area. . . . A mile or so from the 'D' Battery firing site, we turned off the dusty desert road into what seemed like a moon 'rille.' Dark rocks on both sides, then into a sloping area with a dark outcropping like a cliff. We stopped and walked about a hundred feet to a simmering pool of water. In the cliff area was an opening [where] we entered the mine shaft. . . . My men said antelopes, burros [small wild donkeys], coyotes, jackrabbits, birds, and even large rattlesnakes came here to partake of the cool water. It was like an oasis in the desert. . . .

"A week or so later, I was in my command shack during one of these White Sands-generated lulls. I decided to take a jeep and go visit the gold mine alone. When I arrived, some animals were around the pond. I drove up to the opening, went in, and sat down and cooled off in the natural air conditioning. The soft dripping water sound was almost hypnotic. I dozed off [but then] my instinct took over. My right hand slowly went to my holster. I drew my .45 and snapped off the safety. (Every other cartridge had a tip of pellets, like a shot-gun shell.)

"I drew the gun and rolled on my side. Suddenly, a word registered in my head—'Don't.' In mental telepathy I responded, 'Friend or Foe?' The reply came back—'Neither.' I was impressed. In the shimmering half light, bouncing off the moving water, I saw a figure that appeared transparent. It had on a helmet, silver in color, large slanted eyes. and a bright red spot on a band across the forehead [see sketch on the next page]. The message continued as our eyes met in the semi-light. 'Will you give me ten minutes, radar free, after green time?'

"I thought back. 'Ten minutes could be an eternity. What do you offer?'
"'A new world—if you can take it.'

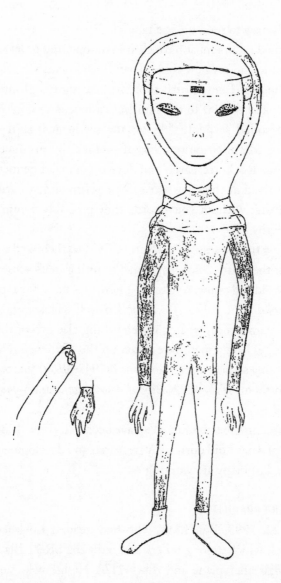

A sketch by Amy O'Brien based on Colonel Corso's description of the alien.

"I started the jeep, looked back, and saw a figure in the shimmering light of the mine opening. I saluted and took off.

"When I arrived at the range headquarters, Captain Williams reported, 'Sir, D Battery locked on, for sixty seconds, on an object fifty miles out, traveling three thousand mph.'

"'Tell D Battery to send me the tape.'

"The downed radars must have cleared an opening to let in a reported UFO. Did it pick up my new-found friend? Or enemy?"[7]

On the alien's helmet, Corso thought he caught a glimpse of something that looked similar to the familiar caduceus symbol—that of the tree and the coiled serpent.[8] "As for the (caduceus) sign of healing," he wrote, "we compiled quite a list of medical by-products and other advances of our R&D [research and development]. The mental conversation I dismissed at the time as figments of my imagination. In 1960 I discovered that without vocal cords they probably communicated by mental telepathy."

In pondering the request for "green time," Corso theorized that radar had caused loss of the craft's control systems, resulting in its subsequent crash.

"'A new world—if you can take it.' There was no other reply possible," reflected Corso. "The debris [from the Roswell wreckage], research and development, new concepts, etc., were nothing else except the beginning of the challenge. Many men have taken up the challenge. New developments are coming so fast, after a slow start (1947–1960) that we can hardly keep up with them. *If the alternative is destruction, we are progressing well toward 'taking it.'*

"Like Hermann Oberth said, 'We have been helped by those from outer space.' Most of what I did during my [research and development] tour were just concepts, but many are working out. . . ."[9]

INTERSTELLAR CAPABILITY

On March 23, 1993, Ben Rich, who had headed Lockheed Martin's Skunk Works, which among others had built the SR-71 Blackbird high-speed reconnaissance plane and the F-117A Nighthawk "stealth" attack bomber, gave a presentation to the Engineering Alumni Association at the University of California in Los Angeles (UCLA), of which Rich was an alumnus. Two researchers I know, Tom Keller and Jan Harzan, who also had graduated from UCLA, attended the illustrated lecture. Tom is an aerospace engineer who has worked, for example, as a computer systems analyst for NASA's Jet Propulsion Laboratory, and Jan is an engineer and senior project executive with IBM Global Services.

"We sat at the front of the audience, say about 150 to 200 folks," Tom's report begins. "I took a look around. The 200-or-so capacity auditorium was filled with what appeared to be aerospace-industry professionals, the press, members of academia, and a few military types in uniform sitting at the back—Air Force 'blue-suiters.' Knowing the history of Lockheed's activity in military intelligence, my guess was that there also were also a few 'spooks' there too."

"Please don't ask me any questions about the Aurora project," Rich announced in his introduction. (Aurora is reportedly the top-secret unmanned hypersonic reconnaissance craft that replaced the SR-71.) "I can't answer any and if I did, I'd be thrown in jail. There are some representatives of the CIA here who I recognize."

Rich continued for an hour reviewing the history of the Skunk Works, highlighted by numerous slides. "He described the U-2 reconnaissance plane and its successor, the TR-1 variants [and] the SR-71 Blackbird [and] the little-known D-21 supersonic spy drone that was carried atop an SR-71 mother ship," Tom continues. "The part of the lecture in which he truly beamed was the F-117 stealth attack plane (sometimes erroneously called a 'stealth fighter'). . . . All of these aircraft were *built* by the Skunk Works, not designed by them and then built by someone else."[10]

Clarence "Kelly" Johnson was the legendary designer of aircraft such as the above. Of related interest, the Lockheed A-12 reconnaissance aircraft (code-named Oxcart), of which thirteen were built at the Skunk Works for the CIA, preceded both the YF-12 interceptor and the SR-71 (ordered by the U.S. Air Force). Donald Phillips, who prior to joining the U.S. Air Force worked as a design engineer on the SR-71 project with Johnson, stated cautiously at a National Press Club conference in 2001 that he was aware of evidence that these aircraft had served in another capacity apart from their more routine missions. "Each pilot—and I knew a few of them—learned about the assignment immediately prior to takeoff, and there's strong evidence to suggest that there was a dual role in that they were monitoring some type of traffic to and from Earth. . . ."[11]

At one point in his memorable presentation, Ben Rich said, "If you can imagine it, Lockheed Skunk Works has done it," a phrase he later repeated on two occasions. And in his concluding comments, he added, "We already have the means to travel among the stars. But these technologies are locked up in black projects and it would take an Act of God to ever get them out to benefit humanity. Anything you can imagine, we already know how to do."

He then showed his last slide—an artist's conception of a flying disc zipping off into the unknown—and announced, "We now have the technology to take ET home." The reaction of the audience was nervous laughter, Tom recalls. "My interpretation was that this was Rich's way of saying, 'We can do it now.' A few others in the room, including my friend Jan, also took this statement very seriously. All you had to do was read between the lines.

"The talk concluded with some questions and answers and the formal part of the program was over. As soon as it ended, about thirty of us crowded around Rich like rock fans around the Beatles at their last concert. I was beginning to wonder if anyone else (except Jan, as he and I think alike) in the audience was having the same thoughts: Could Skunk Works be working on some otherworldly craft as we spoke?

"One man spoke up and said that he was a new manager at Northrop [which built the B-2A Spirit stealth bomber] and wanted Rich's advice. Rich pointed his finger at the man and said, 'Well, let me ask you a question: Is it possible to travel to the stars?' The man was taken aback a bit and then said, 'Oh, sure. It would just take a long time.' Rich replied, 'No, it won't take someone's lifetime to do it. There is an error in the equations and we know what it is, and we now have the capability to travel to the stars.'

"Rich went on to imply that various people at Skunk Works had been studying alternative propulsion technologies for interstellar travel [and] said they had, for example, determined that Einstein's equations dealing with relativity theory were incorrect. I asked him to clarify that. Did he mean that Skunk Works employed theoretical physicists, 'Einstein types,' to look for alternative means of space travel? Rich said 'Yes,' [then] went on to say that they had *proved* that Einstein was wrong. He made a mistake.

"I didn't know how that set with other people in the room, but to me that possibly meant that they had determined how it was possible to travel faster than the speed of light. It's important to keep in mind that Skunk Works is a fabrication outfit. They are not in business to be a theoretical think-tank. My take on this was that at Skunk Works they were looking for loopholes in Einstein's work that would give them a way of traveling at ultra-high, faster-than-light speeds, to the stars and back. I interpreted Rich's comments to mean that the scientists at Skunk Works had found such a loophole—and they were building or had built a craft to do it.

"One woman in the small crowd apparently had similar thoughts. She asked, 'Mr. Rich, when will the ETs go home?' Rich smiled, looked down at the floor, and said nothing. Some of us were left wondering what his response might have been had he been able to answer without fear of being sentenced to twenty years in Fort Leavenworth.

"As Rich was walking out of the door, Jan followed him and asked privately, 'Ben, what equations are you talking about?' He just looked at Jan, who then explained that he was interested in propulsion and wanted to know how UFO propulsion worked. Rich said, 'Let me ask you: How does ESP work?' Jan replied without thinking, 'All points in time and space are connected?' Rich shot back, '*That's* how it works!'

"Jan did not know if Rich was referring to his question or his answer. Rich then turned around and abruptly left the room. . . ."[12]

The great pioneer died of cancer in January 1995, aged sixty-nine.

CHAPTER TEN
GRAY LIAISON

The summer of 2009 brought me a promising letter. "I have a true story to tell [which] relates to my RAF Service, 1955–1957, and involves an alien situation at the camp where I was stationed," the writer began. "I need some advice and wonder if you have time for a chat? I would add that my involvement, with five of my RAF/Fleet Air Arm pals, fills the gap relating to Britain."[1]

My informant—"Thomas"—spoke guardedly about the gist of the "alien situation" when I first conversed with him on the phone, stressing that he was still bound by the Official Secrets Act. However, he wished to include the story in a book he was currently engaged in writing about his Royal Air Force career and requested my guidance on how to proceed. I agreed to visit him for a couple of days at his home in the West Country. Much of the information presented in this chapter is taken from Thomas's remarkable manuscript,[2] and from my regular communications with him.

Thomas began by giving me details of his National Service record. In March 1955, at the age of eighteen, he had been posted to RAF Cardington, Bedfordshire. He then was posted as Airman Second Class (AC2) to Padgate, Lancashire, for "square-bashing," consisting largely of .303 rifle/bayonet drill. Following that came trade training, in which Thomas and his colleagues were given a choice of five RAF trades. Thomas ticked off five "admin" jobs, and was assigned to the Equipment Provisioning and Accounting Section (EPAS) at RAF Creddon Hill in Hereford for five weeks' training. In due course, he was posted to RAF Weston Zoyland, Somerset, and nearby RAF Merryfield.

Located some four miles from Bridgwater, Weston Zoyland was originally a World War II airfield, opened in 1944 and used jointly by the Royal Air Force and United States Army Air Forces, primarily for transport aircraft. It was also used, I learned, as a secret base in that period by Britain's Special Operations Executive (SOE). After the end of war in the European theater, four fighter squadrons occupied the station briefly. The station was then used as a reserve RAF Fighter Command airfield, but little flying took place there until the summer of 1952, when Meteor and Vampire jets operated there in a training role. Canberra bomber/ photo reconnaissance and training aircraft were present during the mid-1950s. By 1958, no more aircraft used Weston Zoyland. During the relevant period, the commanding officer was Group Captain H. E. Hopkins. Today, several derelict buildings remain, excluding the hangars but including the control tower, which I explored in September 2010. Part of the airfield is used nowadays for microlights, and it is also a base for the Sky Watch Civil Air Patrol.

At the time of Thomas's posting there, Weston Zoyland had been taken over by the Fleet Air Arm (FAA). EPAS included a squadron leader in charge, plus a flight lieutenant, a couple of corporals, and the six airmen, including Thomas, who became firm friends with his colleagues.

One morning, the flight sergeant ("Flight") came over to the EPAS office and whispered to Thomas that he was to present himself in the squadron leader's office at 10:00, to say nothing to anyone, and to join his colleagues. The flight sergeant ordered the men to be on parade outside No. 1 hangar at 08:30 the following morning, dressed in their "best blues." At the appointed hour, the EPAS team assembled outside the hangar, followed by the squadron leader with three others, one in naval uniform. The team snapped to attention.

"Airmen," began the squadron leader, "you will all recall signing the Official Secrets Act. You will be here until the end of your service, by which time the matter you will be dealing with will have been resolved. Or should be. . . . Your duties will be extraordinary, to say the least."

No badges of any sort were to be worn. "To anyone in camp you will be rank-less and anonymous," continued the squadron leader. "On the left epaulette of both your new working blues you will find an orange band already in place. You will not remove them at any time.

"You will have no status whatsoever as far as any other personnel can see. Only yourselves and others involved on the project will know who you are, and from time to time that will include civilians as well as members of the armed forces.

"You will all receive a small pay increase and will deserve it. However, you will say nothing about it to anyone, even at home, if you go on leave. The increase will be on a scale higher than your actual rank. Simply follow orders quietly and responsibly and all will go well and smoothly. . . . You cannot go off camp in uniform, nor take your orange flashes off camp, nor will you say one single word about today for the remainder of your service, not even to your nearest and dearest. Is that perfectly understood?"

The team confirmed that it was. "Now, of course, you are all curious as to what the hell this all about. You will return to your billet, then change into your new shirt-sleeve order, with orange flashes worn as instructed. Be here at No. 1 hangar at 14:30 hours for a further briefing. Stay together and not a word to anyone, no matter who. . . ."

CODE ORANGE

Thoroughly bemused, Thomas and his colleagues—now effectively attached to the Fleet Air Arm—presented themselves outside hangar No. 1 at the appointed time. The squadron leader summoned the men into the hangar and ordered them to sit down on a row of six chairs—individually assigned with the mens' initials. Opposite stood a table with four chairs. A car drew up outside and the three men from earlier that day came and sat down, dressed this time in civilian suits. "One was tall and hawkish," Thomas reported, "and the other strongly built with a head of white hair. The naval officer sat away from them, allowing our squadron leader to sit beside him, but between him and the two civilians."

"You are now attired as you will be for the remainder of your service," began the squadron leader. "You each have certain things in common. For example, you passed your RAF entrance exams at the top of your classes, though of course you did not know that about each other. Equally, at your respective training camps you were recorded as best airmen in your Flight. . . . I shall not introduce you to the three gentlemen with me today. If any of you feel you know any or all of them by sight, forget it and say nothing.

"The task you are going to undertake may be quite easy, but it could become extremely difficult. We have known about it for some years and have made certain preparations at this airfield during the past six months. You may have observed activity at and near this hangar which appeared to be a building project. It is a secret project and all works have been carried out by military experts, some flown in from the United States and Canada. The men and women involved are no longer in camp."

The project henceforth was to be referred to as "Code Orange." "All personnel in camp have been told the airmen with orange flashes are on sensitive RAF work," continued the squadron leader, "and you are not to be interrupted, questioned as to your work or whatever. If you are questioned, then treat it as a breach of security, reporting the incident on the phone in your new quarters."

Thomas and another colleague, Alan, were assigned overall charge of Code Orange, within the camp perimeter. Next, one of the "suits"—the man with white hair—addressed the new team, after thanking the squadron leader for his briefing. "I work for the government as a scientist and feel satisfied that all has gone as it should here today," he began. "So, what is Code Orange about? It is about an incident that occurred in the American state of New Mexico during 1947, a most unfortunate incident that involved living beings from another world crashing to Earth, for reasons I will not go into here, and of deaths and casualties," claimed the man. "Code Orange is about ordinary country people on the spot at the time and of military personnel becoming involved under orders from their superiors within the military and within the government. Code Orange is about putting right, as best we can, a mess. . . .

"I am here to explain your part, and perhaps then we can learn more about how to take advantage of the alien technology as a priority over alien life. Whatever the outcome, Code Orange is about a strange craft and its occupants who did not complete their journey in New Mexico after all—well, two of them did not, and who knows if others got away? [There were] three craft on the 1947 situation, each with seating areas for three. Two dead bodies were recovered, two alive and still held by the military.

"Other craft have been sighted over many years and many have landed. They are not all from the same place, and are therefore of different races. The two aliens still held by the military are having, shall we say, an English holiday. It is too hot for them where they were and the wrong people are getting close.

"The aliens are vastly more intelligent than we are as a race. So despite considerable arguments, they themselves have forced a move, and months of talks and time-wasting have at last resulted in Code Orange. . . . The two aliens went silent, refusing to communicate unless they were moved. They do not speak and voice their words aloud as we do, but they converse with each other and us in silence. For want of a better expression, the term 'thought transference' will do, but they communicate mood too. . . . Your task is to look after them here—until they decide to communicate again, or not. You will be shown how."

"That was it, really," reflected Thomas. "The other two did not have anything to say to us. I remember sitting quietly, trying to take it all in. Then we were told to sort out our new billet at the side of No. 1 hangar and settle in immediately. . . ."

SUNRISE AND SUNSET

The office at Weston Zoyland was reached by the team directly from their billet, and another door led into the hangar. "A long desk with three chairs was along one wall, with two telephones, piles of notepads, pens, pencils, and a radio set and typewriter," Thomas reported. "Filing cabinets were ready for use and a screen 'looked into' the hangar, but was not 'on' at first. Fire buckets and extinguishers, tea and coffee facilities and water were laid on to a sink basin. A fairly ordinary situation then, but extraordinary was a metal cupboard with revolvers and ammunition and a set of white overalls for all of us."

Thomas's team had the use of other amenities nearby and were permitted access to the NAAFI (Navy, Army and Air Force Institutes) shop and the Mess at mealtimes, though only two at a time. The team received orders to man the office from 08:00 to 16:00 each day, until further notice. "At that time we organized two four-hour shifts, always with Alan or myself leading these in turn," Thomas explained. "We received phone calls on a regular basis to verify that all was well, from an anonymous female voice, the origin of which we were never told. We were given a password—'Sunrise'—and had to use it in reply to the woman's password—'Sunset'—which I will never forget."

SPECIAL DELIVERY

The team looked after the office and kept themselves fit by running or walking outside the hangar and in the large field adjoining it. Nothing relevant occurred until well into the second week, when a phone call came from a man advising Thomas that a Code Orange delivery was due on the Saturday of the following week. Early on the next Monday morning, the team was advised that their password would change to that of the project name. The usual female contact advised them that on Wednesday at 08:00 a special consignment would be arriving (at Merryfield).

Thomas told me that the special consignment, originating in the U.S., was delivered from somewhere in the U.K.—Scotland, he believes—by train, ending its rail journey at Ilton Halt, thence by a huge vehicle to Merryfield.

Like Weston Zoyland, Merryfield had been used in World War II by the USAAF and RAF, and then by the latter as an advanced pilot and training establishment with Meteor and Vampire jets until the end of 1954. During the following two years—which involved Code Orange—a detachment from an operational conversion unit, with Canberra jets, was often present. Then came the Royal Navy with Sea Venoms, until 1958. By 1961, it was abandoned until 1971 when, as Royal Naval Air Station Merryfield (HMS *Heron II*) it was used for assault helicopter training and exercises. Today, it remains an operational airfield and a restricted area, with security on the gate.[3]

About twenty feet high and eight to ten feet deep, the wooden crate was hauled on to the back of a large wide-load vehicle, secured with steel cable hawsers on its narrow end. "It didn't cause a lot of problems along those Somerset roads on its short journey to Merryfield, as one might imagine," Thomas explained to me. "However, some traffic problems delayed delivery."

"It was 11:00 when the two motorcycle MPs (Military Police) roared up to the doors of No. 1 hangar followed by the huge wide-load vehicle, all noise and flashing lights, then two more motorcycles with a staff car following," Thomas reports. "The hangar door slid smoothly shut on it." An hour or so later, the presence of a group captain in the hangar was announced to the team via phone. On being admitted to the office, he introduced himself, explaining first that a viewing screen in the office was now operational, enabling the men to see into the hangar. "The hangar had a pitch roof with rows of skylights and a pair of very large hangar sliding doors to the front," Thomas continues. "There were rows of strip lighting for night use. Our billet-cum-office was on one side abutting the west hall of the hangar with the one door between us. An orange six-inch-diameter circle was painted on it [and] the viewing screen had a small red light above it, no doubt showing it was 'on.' From within the hangar there was no way of knowing what was behind our door."

A large red-brick room had been built at the back of the hangar, within which was another room mainly made of glass or similar material. "Its rear wall, really a gigantic window, looked out across the Somerset countryside to a distant perimeter fence we were told was electrified," Thomas revealed. "We later learned that the electrified fence was only fixed about No. 1 hangar at Merryfield and that the fencing around the remainder of the camp remained normal. Just beyond this fence was another, some eight feet high but not electrified, and beyond it were fields and a river. Due to the slope from the rear of the hangar down to the river, the view was not despoiled by the fencing, nor could anyone else see in."

About fifty feet by forty, the glass room was divided in two by a dark glass partition. Normal daylight was adequate, but strip lighting was used at night. Other rooms in the hangar were color-coded differently, each with windows looking into the hangar. "Security was very tight. We could see two men on a high platform facing the hangar doors. . . . During a practice security drill, we had seen a row of vertical bars shoot up from the ground [and] at that instant two armoured vehicles appeared. . . ."

When the crate had been positioned in the hangar and the lid taken away, the day after its arrival, the team was allowed to inspect it. "Almost touching the sides was a gray, glistening metallic saucer of perfectly circular shape," Thomas describes. "It had what looked like a window all the way around but with no panes, just one strip of glass-like material, and we could see within to panels of instruments, screens, and three seats. At a nod from the group captain, four men in overalls ran across and within minutes the sides of the crate were on the floor."

It looked, said Thomas, like two saucers, one in the usual position with the other upside-down on top of it. "Strange though it may seem, I felt it was alive and thinking, silent but as if brooding. It was more 'alive' than any other inanimate object I had ever seen."

Three small seats with seemingly molded curved-topped backs—evidently not designed for adults of normal human stature—could be seen. No seat belts or any obvious "driving" apparatus were noted. As Thomas reveals:

"The panel of instruments facing the seats swept around the front half of the craft and was black or [very] dark gray. There were scores of 'keys' of the shape and size of our modern computers plus several screens of about one foot by six inches (30 × 15 cm), some vertical, some horizontal. Along the lower length of the panel was a 'desk' with more keys in neat rows and at each end a pale gray-colored list in some printed form of hieroglyphics . . . above the main panel was a larger screen, again dark, and of about three feet by two feet and fitted as a horizontal, like a modern TV screen."

The area behind the seats was relatively bare, with the exception of half a dozen circular "switches," almost flush to the wall.

Asked if the team could enter the craft, the group captain began by expounding on the actual event that had led to its recovery. The one in the hangar had followed two others down, one badly damaged with "bits strewn over the desert, the other badly damaged but intact," he explained. "This one came down of its own volition, that is, it was not shot at. . . . At that time it was on a set of tripod-type legs with a small disc at the end of each."

The group captain went on to explain that the craft had been opened by its occupants at the crash site in New Mexico. Two aliens were seen to emerge but a third remained inside—then simply stood up and "disappeared" and hadn't been seen since, despite the area having been searched for a week. The other two aliens were "seemingly unwell," said the group captain. They were easily apprehended and had no weapons. "If all three craft had three occupants, we have dead and alive evidence of six. It is known that one, apparently unhurt, left this craft and has since escaped detection somehow. The other two may have been thrown out from the two crashes and lost, or they also escaped. . . . On the third occupant's disappearance, the exit-cum-entrance facility was seen to close itself. It has not opened or been opened since. We just can't bloody well open the thing. The seal is absolute perfection. The metal and glass are absolutely unknown to us."

The other two damaged craft were kept in great secrecy at a certain U.S. base, the group captain revealed. "All I know," he said, "is that parts of its amazing system of navigation, and some sort of tiny technological 'brains,' which have to do with communication and pretty well everything else, are hastily being examined by various world scientists to see how we humans can benefit by them."

Later that day, the group captain explained to the team that visits to the craft at Merryfield were permitted, provided they were dressed in their "whites"—white overalls unique to the team—and that authorization had been obtained by their Code Orange contact. At Weston Zoyland—where the aliens were to be housed—the team agreed to eight-hour shifts with three men on and three off, with one of each three always by the phone. "So it was 0800 to 1600, 1600 to midnight, and midnight to 0800," explained Thomas. However, two officers and a scientist came on duty during the early shift's lunch break, allowing the team a two-hour respite.

NOT OF THIS EARTH

Some days later, an RAF "V" bomber—either a Valiant, Victor, or Vulcan, capable of delivering nuclear weapons but in this operation delivering two aliens—landed at Weston Zoyland with a two-fighter-jet escort. Thomas told me he was fairly certain that the bomber was a Vulcan. The team was told to remain in their office and await further orders. A few hours later, they were summoned, two by two, to meet the alleged aliens, now ensconced in a specially constructed glass container in the hangar at Weston Zoyland. Thomas and his colleague Alan were first. "Emotions welled up in me that I feel to this day," Thomas admitted.

"Two thin little people lay side by side. They were gray-colored and their heads seemed rather large for their bodies and were oval, or egg-shaped, with the large end at the top, a large cranium leading down to a small chin, and their eyes were large, limpid, and dark with no iris visible. Just dark, lustrous pools, wide open, rather like those of seals, I thought. There were nostril holes but no nose projecting from the face, and I could see a small mouth beneath. There were no visible projecting ears as we have.

"Sinewy arms stretched alongside their bodies and the legs looked skinny. They were very still. Unreal, I thought. . . . I looked at their hands. Four long fingers similar to us. But no thumbs. And four-toed feet.

"Just beneath the small chin of the body nearest to me a pulse was beating, and looking at the other being I could see the same. . . . I was actually looking at two people from somewhere else. Not of this Earth! I glanced across at the officer and met his eyes. He smiled and nodded, as if to say 'yes, this is real—they are alive.'"

Shaking, Thomas made for a chair and sat down, followed by Alan. They didn't feel it was appropriate to stare at the aliens too much. "They look so dignified," said Alan. One appeared slightly shorter than the other. They seemed frail, though Thomas sensed a latent strength about them.

Half an hour later, all of the team having seen the beings and returned to the office, the officer/instructor declared that he didn't know which sex the aliens were. He thought they wore a membranous covering, but added that the Americans hadn't been very forthcoming with their information. He suggested that the team gave names to the aliens if they wanted, but that officially they were referred to by their American captors as "G32" and "G33." Thomas speculates that the numbers might relate to the 32nd and 33rd aliens recovered by the U.S. military. The team elected to call them simply "G" and "L." (Much later, it was determined that G was male, L female.)

Thomas remains amazed at the aliens' ability to convey a sense of humor, or sadness, for example, without such feelings manifesting facially. As time went by, it became possible to "feel" their thoughts, and it was always clear what they meant. They did speak audibly on occasions—not that it helped. "The problem in our inability to converse by voice was that their language contained no vowels," he explained; "thus, if they spoke to us we would hear a series of unintelligible sounds not unlike the chattering of small animals." (However, the airmen later learned from their duty officer that although official communications from G and L did not involve actual spoken words, the Americans confirmed that they do have voices—presumably capable of communicating in English and other languages.)

Thomas and the others liked the aliens from the outset and grew to care for them deeply over the approximately twenty-month period involved.

One lovely summer's day, Thomas and Alan were sitting beside "the Grays" (as they apparently were referred to occasionally by the military, even at that time), surveying the countryside through the large window of their enclosure. "What is worrying you both?" "said" the aliens. "Is this not the kind of day when you should feel all is well?" The men were indeed worried—about the aliens. "Thanks to you airmen, we are doing well and recovering," the Grays responded. "You need not worry about us."

When communicating, G and L would put one hand on their chest, to convey who was "speaking." Then began a discourse, warning of Earth's future overpopulation, the poisoning of its environment, and so on. "We know your instructions are to inform your seniors of all we say. Do so. We will be telling them all we have told you when they pay their regular visits. . . ."

Like other alien groups, they confirmed Man's extraterrestrial genetic links.

"The majority of flora and fauna on this planet have evolved over millions of years. Humans were one of those that were genetically manipulated and thus you are related to another species as a planned experiment by beings from another world. Our presence here is of right, and we have visited before this time, many times. Our present role is to observe others who are here, to see that they are not destructive and to give you some of our technology in order that you will survive—if you have earned the right to survival as we judge it. That was the core of our message to Earth people and part of the reason for our arrival in your time of 1947, though we reneged upon that in that July month, and here two of us remain—at least for a little longer."

At this juncture, G reached out and clasped hands with L. "I felt there was significance in the comment 'at least for a little longer,' linked with the hand clasp," writes Thomas. "The two aliens had been held captive for at least eight years. Not much of an existence for people who know how to travel light years' distance, and had somehow done so to reach Earth."

The Code Orange team were never present when the aliens took their meals. Although some thin tubes were present in their glass enclosure, their purpose was indeterminable. Waste matter, perhaps? Eventually, G and L, having picked up the men's bewilderment, communicated some details. "You have been wondering if we feed, and how we do so. We know your seniors have not told you. Knowledge is important to all life. . . .

"We feed on blood, and water. Yes, I can feel your reaction, but our race does not digest solids. . . . Both liquids are available on this planet and we partake of small amounts of each in order to survive. We also breathe your air, though it is clearer in some regions of your planet than others. Your seniors obtain enough food for our needs and provide us with it in your absence."

Thomas told me he recalls that the blood—presumably from slaughtered animals—was obtained from a local farm. In an interesting letter to a magazine, written in 2001, he made some apposite references to the consumption of blood—without, of course, citing his own experience. "Over the years, certain peoples have been vilified by modern attitudes against the terrors of blood sacrifices," he wrote. "However, if genetically modified humans, ruled by their makers up to a time when they, our makers, leave the planet [and] have had at times to 'entertain' and consort with said makers, then they would have to provide the necessary correct food. . . .

"What if there was, or is, a race of beings which have evolved to feed on blood? As simple as that. It may appal some of us, even possibly most of us, yet we are talking alien creatures here. A race apart. Light years apart. Evolving on a planet or planets away from and not far from this Earth. . . . So along comes a race of beings which lives on blood from animals rather than the meat. And when they arrive as 'gods' or powerful beings, we in due deference feed them with what they require."[4]

In this context, G and L related how their people had influenced the Inca, Aztec, and Maya cultures.

For nutrition on their own planet, G and L indicated that they also consumed other liquids of varying thicknesses, from water through to heavy soups, plus a variety of what we would term "wines" made from fruits and vegetables growing on their own planet.

ESPIONAGE

When Thomas's leave period came up, he went to his home in Barnstaple, Devon. Waiting at Taunton station for the connecting train, he was approached by a well-dressed, well-spoken man who invited Thomas for a cup of tea. "I can always tell an airman," he said. Acknowledging the fact, Thomas explained that he was on 72-hour leave. Over tea, the man asked Thomas what he did in the RAF. He replied in vague generalities, mentioning Bomber Command and admin work. "Ah, so you are in the RAF but with the Fleet Air Arm crowd? Yes, I know all about that. An interesting posting, no doubt." Thomas gave nothing away.

As the steam train for Barnstaple drew in, the stranger invited Thomas to join him in a First Class compartment. Sitting opposite this man in an empty carriage, a strong feeling of unease crept over Thomas, particularly when the stranger placed a hand on his knee. "Don't worry. Here's my card. I am an MP [Member of Parliament]. My name is Tom Driberg."

The notorious homosexual MP for Barking, Driberg (later Lord Bradwell)—a member of the Communist Party of Great Britain and a close friend of the traitor Guy Burgess—had links with the Soviet KGB and its Czechoslovakian counterpart. Coincidentally, Driberg happened to be staying for the weekend at the Imperial Hotel in Barnstaple, and Thomas was invited for tea in his room at the hotel to show his paintings (which were never returned). Distinctly uncomfortable at the prospect, he nonetheless turned up and managed to resist Driberg's approaches, not least being his persistence in trying to gather information regarding the nature of Thomas's work.

Thomas was also invited, together with his girlfriend, to attend a play at the Queen's Hall Theatre. During the evening, a local couple who were friends of Driberg's introduced Thomas to Driberg's friend Lord Robens.

Alfred Robens (Baron Robens of Woldingham), a well-known industrialist, trade unionist, and Labour politician, was shadow foreign secretary at that time. After the show, a drinks party was held at the couple's home, during which Driberg made further "passes" at Thomas and offered to give him a camera to "record his activities at the camp." Thomas retorted that cameras were forbidden.

Back at Weston Zoyland, G and L expressed complete knowledge of, and disquiet at, the weekend's developments, though they were well aware that Thomas had betrayed nothing sensitive.

FURTHER EDUCATION

Sometimes days went by with nothing "said" by G and L. But over the months a great deal of fascinating information was imparted to the team, described by Thomas in great detail in his book. The aliens communicated that they had visited Earth over a long period. As a naturalist, the airman was delighted to learn a great deal about, for example, "mythical" sea creatures on Earth millennia ago. "The aliens, having visited Earth many times over many centuries, knew at firsthand about evolution and extinctions [and] spoke of other aliens who had visited Earth, carrying out their experiments. . . . It helped that G and L saw colors as we did and though their eyes were considerably larger they seemed to have eyesight and other senses akin to our own."

While careful not to reveal the location of their home planet (which had three moons and was in a solar system with five other planets of similar size), the aliens were forthcoming regarding a description of same, describing their planet in great detail, to which Thomas devotes considerable space in his book—describing numerous types of creatures, some very similar to our own.

The aliens reiterated that the overpopulation of Earth, combined with pollution, would lead to catastrophic consequences during the 21st century. Everything they had observed on this planet in previous millennia was recorded on crystals and retained on the "mother craft," which transported them and their smaller craft. "They could have shown us much on their screens in the craft still held in the camp," said Thomas, "but they did not completely trust our seniors, hence the craft remaining closed."

REASONS FOR ROSWELL

G and L discussed the so-called Roswell incident, which, as we learned earlier, was said to have involved three craft. "The remains of the damaged craft will continue to be examined, as will medical analysis of our people. Both have been examined so intensely since your year of 1947 that it is surely time our people were laid to rest and not be moved constantly from liquid solutions and frozen state to be further examined by your scientists and, we fear, at least one alien race your people consort with. . . ."

Following the ends of World Wars I and II, the aliens contacted our leaders—in 1919 and 1946 respectively—to openly offer their assistance, and to be seen to do so, but were rebuffed. So they informed the American and British military and governments of their intention to "offer scientific instruments to forward human progress rapidly and without cost. Thus did the Roswell event occur, with its subsequent spreading of falsehoods."

The Code Orange team were informed that the reason the aliens visited New Mexico owed largely to the siting of American military bases there, including one site that received and transmitted messages from beings other than themselves. They also said that New Mexico and a neighboring state had alien bases built into mountain sides beneath the ground (such as the Manzano Mountains, I learned from another source) and that a to-ing and fro-ing of American military and government personnel (the latter including numerous scientists, I have been told) had occurred up to the time G and L had been transported to Britain at their own insistence.

"Our own activities required monitoring by other than human beings," Thomas explained, "simply because Earth is a vital and necessary planet for others. We could not be permitted to despoil it, even though despoliation had begun and we were doubted as to our integrity and genuine concern for the planet and its myriad life forms. G said, much to our disappointment, that humans could be seen as a malign race, and we were partial aliens in any case."

CATTLE MUTILATIONS

G indicated that a number of beings of a certain race had been collecting samples of our animals and plants. This was mainly in the USA, the then-current project involving cattle, which they did not possess—but intended to. "They said the powers that be know about it," Thomas explains, "and compensation was paid to cattle owners who reported losses." It needs to be pointed out here that in this time period (1955–57) the cattle mutilation phenomenon was unknown to the general public. It was not until several decades later that researchers became aware of it. As Colonel Philip J. Corso reveals in his book *The Day After Roswell*:

"In 1997 this may sound like a nightmare out of a flying saucer horror movie, but in 1957 this was our thinking both in the White House [National Security Council Staff, of which Corso was a member] and in the military. We didn't know, but we had irrefutable evidence that EBEs [Extraterrestrial Biological Entities] were landing on farms, harvesting vital organs from livestock, and then just leaving the carcasses on the ground because they knew we couldn't do anything about it.

"The mutilations that interested the National Security personnel seemed to have the same kind of modus operandi. Whoever went after the animals seemed most interested in the mammary, digestive, and reproductive organs, especially the uteruses from cows. In many cases the eyes or throats were removed in a type of surgery in which the demarcation line was almost microscopically thin and the surrounding tissue showed that the incision had superheated and then blackened as it cooled. But the crime scene and forensic specialists noted that in any type of cut by a predatory animal or a human—even a skilled surgeon—one would find evidence of some trauma in the surrounding tissue [but] forensic examination showed no evidence of collateral trauma or even inflammation, [implying] the cuts to extract the tissue were made so quickly and wounds were sealed so fast that the surrounding tissue was never destroyed. . . ."[5]

"We asked would it not have been simpler to have had a farm on which all the necessary animals, and presumably plants too, could have been part of a humane project to avoid hurting cattle and such," Thomas writes. "We were told 'hurt' did not come into it. The aliens used what we now know as a form of laser [which] immediately kills the target. At least, they said, it was so in this instance, but the extremely intense beam was mainly used for surgical operations to heal. . . ."

Corso provides confirmation that what turned out to be a laser device was found by the Army "in the Roswell spacecraft and would later develop as a weapon in co-operation with Hughes Aircraft." As head of the Army's Foreign Technology Division, Corso himself assembled the information to support laser product development with military funds before the whole operation was turned over to one of the Research and Development specialists.[6]

THE PATH TO DOOM

Four hundred Earth years was the average life span for these aliens (as with certain other species).

G and L were adamant that all answers to our future and all the lessons of history had been written down for us to learn from and live by. "Each major culture and each primitive culture had its standards," explained Thomas, "but the move from a basic, primitive life to a life where selfish motives, however noble we tried to make them seem, prevailed, could and would lead to disaster and the final extinction of the human race." Our Christian Bible, supposedly, was the full account of ourselves, "the written path of homo sapiens."

There may well be many truths passed down in the Bible—as in many other religious documents—as I have remarked on later. But I find it puzzling that the aliens failed at least to acknowledge some of the inconsistencies in various translations of the Bible over the centuries. Exactly how much of it is factual? Thomas's team had no axe to grind in this regard. By their own admission, they were neither atheists nor "practicing Christians in the recognized manner," as Thomas puts it. However, G and L did indicate that we were a world of too many religions, and would suffer for being so. "They said the core of our numerous religions and creeds was a good and right way forward, but eventually humans would sacrifice their beliefs in a selfish manner, and our leaders would lazily accept this. . . .

"I remember how G placed his hand upon his chest and 'said' the incident at Roswell, New Mexico, and certain others, was a part of the 'Path to Doom' for the human race. He said items stolen from them at that time would show us how to live well and prosper greatly in a way that no human need ever go hungry or thirsty, and all human problems could be solved using their technology before the century we called the twentieth ended. But, he added, those in power will not wish it; rather would they have what they see as greater power."

The aliens acknowledged the existence of Jesus, furthermore indicating that the so-called "Second Coming" was already in force (as also implied by Henry Dohan in Chapter 7).

OFFICIALDOM FRUSTRATED

On several occasions, the duty officer complained to the team regarding official frustration at their inability to gain access to the inside of the craft. One of the team, Ian, said they'd done all they could—as would have been evident on the taped recordings of all their communications to, if not from, G and L. Several days later, the aliens responded, pointing out that the craft contained a self-destructive device which would operate if entry by any beings other than themselves was accomplished.

"They made it very clear," said Thomas, "that they could open the craft in a matter of seconds in human time, and seal it closed just as rapidly. Only massive power could open it falsely. They told us the problem at Roswell was that having come in peace to exchange thoughts and certain technology, the mechanism of self-destruction concealed behind the small panel, with what we called a pentacle on it, was switched off. It seems G and L and their missing friend switched theirs to 'on' again before the craft closed. . . . G and L told us they had no intention at this time to open the craft."

When I first met Thomas, he told me that this craft had come down of its own volition while the military combed the site where the other craft had crashed. He said that G and L were "upset about the cruelty and treachery of their American captors in betraying their word." Given their wide knowledge of human fallibility, one can only wonder at the apparent naïveté of G and L in this respect.

ANCIENT HISTORY

The aliens expounded on their presence here on Earth thousands of years ago. Like the species with whom Carl Anderson liaised (Chapter 7), G and L described how their own people had been present during the times of the many kings (named Pharoahs after 950 B.C.) who ruled Ancient Egypt, and how "the aliens were described as Gods, but of course they were not." Thomas's team was advised not to mock what is written in the

Bible, the Koran, the Talmud, or similar writings that foretell the future. "For example, the great flood did occur and destroyed cities and countries, but mountains were left dry and habitable.

"They told us that a simple, basic change in the Earth's axis angle had caused the vast flooding, and that included the destruction of the lost land of what we now call Atlantis, which lay close to what is the island of Cuba. They produced maps of those places and times showing Antarctica before it was ice-bound, and land bridges before the final dividing of the land masses which were one. They told us these maps exist today copied onto the skins of antelopes in our sixteenth century, but only one has been shown to present humans, yet thirty of them exist even now in the land known as Turkey.

"They explained how their presence in Central America at a place known as Aztlan was to obtain gold and to enrich cultures and races that preceded the Mayas, [and] the forefathers of Aztecs were the people of Aztlan and that the great floods drove them from their original, ancestral homeland."

The aliens needed gold—and later silver—exclusively as part of their craft's propulsion system.

THE MOTHERSHIP

At around 23:00 one pleasant warm night in 1957 at Weston Zoyland, Thomas became aware of a strange presentiment. "There was little sound to begin with," he wrote, "then a few shouts and the noise of vehicles, then the noise of a helicopter. But then our office phone rang. 'Code Orange! Code Orange! Have you any problems? I need an immediate appraisal of your situation.'

"Alan came rushing in, saying, 'Come outside quick! Lights, zooming about. Amazing!'" Thomas reported the matter, adding that he was going outside to see what was happening. "Watch the aliens," he was told. "Do not leave them alone."

"Our two friends were fine," noted Thomas, "seated up against their 'home' couches and staring ahead. I asked if they were all right and, receiving affirmation, went to look outside, leaving [colleagues] Keith and Cyril with them. 'Do not be concerned,' one said. 'We are passing messages to our people. You can so inform your seniors later.'"

The lights—a dozen or so glowing orange and green spheres a bit larger than a tennis ball, Thomas guessed—could be seen zooming and hovering in a controlled manner. Forces personnel rushed around, concentrating on the No. 1 hangar, its protective "portcullis" already up. One of the spheres came close enough to Thomas to touch. The only sound he detected was like that of a bumble-bee. They watched two of the green spheres bob and bounce along the top of the electrified inner perimeter fence; then they returned to the hangar and sat with the aliens, letting Keith and Cyril watch the display.

FAREWELL

"All is well," communicated G. "They will be away soon. Their purpose here has been fulfilled. We ourselves feel much stronger now. We are grateful to the six of you, and you will not be forgotten. Our messengers will return to their craft; there is much they have to do."

"Is there a craft visible then?" asked Thomas.

"There is. It is very high at present and therefore only visible above the rain clouds, but soon it will move lower, not of necessity but to show the humans watching that real power and science is ours, yet we remain peaceful. You should both be able to observe the craft in an hour from now, so you can remain at your post without missing the sighting. You may tell your seniors that the craft will be observable between the two settlements [Westonzoyland and Middlezoy] which lie each side of this military area."

An hour later, Thomas, Keith, and Alan went outside. "In front of us was an almost terrible shape, an intensely dark shape like a black thundercloud," Thomas recalls. "This was totally mind-chilling. . . .

"In front of us was a triangle. It was very, very big, dwarfing the V-bombers we [sometimes] had in camp. It was black, solid, and pulsing at about fifty feet from the ground, and it was creepily still, hovering and silent. No one spoke. . . . The lights appeared along it and what must have been windows lit up. The shape of the craft became more defined. . . .

"The lights, or windows, glowed yellow to orange, becoming richly colored but never reaching red. Eventually I felt there was a horizontal division and that I was seeing lights above windows. At first they played from right to left, 'disappearing' around corners of the triangle and back again; then, suddenly, all remained alight. There were no shapes of beings in any of the windows, we all agreed. . . . There was no sound, no engines or machinery sounds as with all of our own aircraft and vehicles. And our camp had gone silent. No [searchlights] were shone onto the craft and no aircraft took off, not even a helicopter. . . ."

As Thomas reports, this probably owed to the fact that most of the personnel in camp were asleep and, apart from those on duty, had simply not been told. "The huge craft then descended to almost ground level. . . . Then the lights began to flash again and the craft rose slowly. Violet lights showed beneath, emphasising the craft's triangular shape, and without any sound to suggest rapid acceleration it left Somerset at a speed I could not even have guessed at."

"That was frightening," said Keith. "I need a drink." So did the others.

The following day, the aliens at first seemed unresponsive. Eventually they responded that this would be their last day in camp, that they were now recovered and grateful for the care they had received. G put his hand on his chest and delivered a lengthy and interesting "speech" to Thomas and Alan, which included ominous warnings of dire things to come. "We, or those who work with us, will decide Earth's future, and all life upon it. . . ." Later, L communicated some concluding remarks:

"We owe the six of you so much. You will not be forgotten. We leave today, but be assured we will remain about and upon this planet. . . . Say nought about these days to others, even to denying our presence if asked—unless we bid it differently to one or another in the future—for at least a quarter of a century, even half a century. Remember what we have told you. . . . We cannot have all six of you here to say good-bye. Everything must appear as usual and as normal. So, tell the others and go about your lives."

Shortly afterwards, the duty officer and two "white coats" appeared. Alan and Thomas returned to their office. As they and his colleagues were finishing lunch, the fire drill bell rang twice. Together with the others they ran back to the office. "Gone!" shouted the duty officer. "Vanished! They damn well disappeared before our eyes! All three of us. Do you know anything about it? No, of course you don't. They were sitting there as usual. Saw them clasp hands—32 and 33. Then my head hurt and I saw the other two holding their heads as I was. Then 32 and 33 faded . . . and their couch was empty. Gone!"

And that was it.

———

There is much more to be learned about this truly extraordinary case in Thomas's book. Naturally, the questions arise: How much of the story is true? Although not a student of the subject, per se, he has read only a few related books. Apart from Roswell, for example, he was unaware of numerous other cases involving so-called "crash-retrievals" of alien craft and bodies.

Since his career in the RAF features in the book, it was incumbent upon Thomas to submit his proposal for review by the Royal Air Force Historical Branch. And having stated in his introduction that readers can take the story as either fact or fiction, the RAF understandably relegated its status to the latter. They could hardly have done otherwise.

Never will I forget the first time I heard the fundamental aspects of the story from Thomas in person. In spite of the many years that have gone by, he evidently retains a vivid memory of—and remains deeply moved by—these awesome events.

PART TWO

CHAPTER ELEVEN
THE OVERLORDS

M y study of the various types of alien encounters reported around the world includes a number of cases which initially I was tempted to reject on account of their absurdity. Yet subsequent reflection and comparison with other scarcely known cases reveal certain parallels that have caused me to change my mind. Sometimes, ludicrous, sinister, surreal—and even evil—elements feature in these cases. One such is that of Richard Höglund, a Swede whose encounters covered a lengthy period. First investigated by Ernst Linder, the case is barely known outside Sweden. What follows is taken largely from several reports provided for me by Håkan Blomqvist,[1,2] a leading researcher of contact cases, and from our many communications and discussions. He has written a book on the case in Swedish.[3]

Born in Stockholm in 1913, Höglund was a rock-blaster by profession. Though by all accounts a very down-to-earth man, he nonetheless had an uncanny ability to read people's minds—a talent that might have some bearing on his experiences. The story begins on the afternoon of December 9, 1965, the day before he was due to undergo surgery to remove a small kidney stone. He felt a sudden urge to take a long walk with his dog on a frozen lake, Grindhultsjön, just outside Uddevalla (near Gothenburg), where he lived with his wife, Gunvor.

As Höglund began walking on the lake, the dog began running in circles as though demented and had to be restrained with its leash. Suddenly, a whining sound came from above. Looking up, Höglund saw a saucer-shaped, translucent craft about five meters in diameter. "He could see figures moving inside," reports Håkan. "The object came closer to the ground in a spiraling movement. It stopped before touching the ice, and a dark tube was lowered from under the object. This tube was seemingly made of a soft material since it moved in the wind. He felt a breeze of hot air with a distinct smell of hyacinth. His first thought was that this must be a Russian machine. But he soon changed his mind.

"From the tube four entities floated down, as though they were in an invisible elevator, and walked up to him. They were three men and one woman. Other than for a translucent overall, they were naked. One of the men seemed old, while the others looked younger. They were of normal height, had very large, dark, somewhat slanted eyes and perfect teeth. Their skin had no blemishes and there was absolutely no hair on their bodies, not even genital hair.

"Richard was especially fascinated by their ears, which were large and pointed. The ear opening in the head was very large, as on a cat: he thought he could almost see into their heads. The men seemed very strong, like wrestler types, with bull necks. They had a slight Oriental look about them. The entities were covered by the clear plastic overalls which looked like they were held out from the body by air pressure."

Höglund became confused, though not afraid. Through sign language and drawings in the snow, the entities started to communicate with him. They seemed fascinated by his hair, and he had to remove his cap several times as they laughed and pointed at him. When he tried to touch their overalls, however, they quickly retreated, as if they did not want him to do so. Using a small black package, they sprayed something like a gas on everything, including the dog, before they touched it. The dog evidently objected, as the "gas" had a strong smell of hyacinth. Höglund himself smelled of hyacinth for several days afterwards, causing his wife to wonder if he had already bought flowers for the coming Christmas.

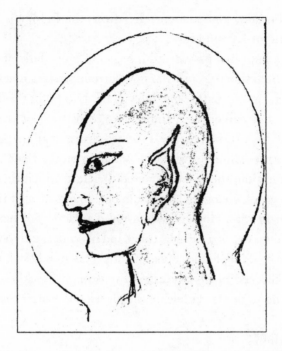

A sketch of one of the entities, as described by Richard Höglund. (Gösta Johansson)

Communications in sign language continued for a while as Höglund tried to explain a number of earthly pursuits, such as hunting and dancing. The woman meanwhile played with the dog, which was out of character since it normally became aggressive toward strangers. All this time, the strangers appeared to be walking on an unseen layer, as their feet did not touch the ground. When the woman patted the dog, she too leaned her knee against this unseen layer. On their left wrists the entities wore a broad, black bracelet with a yellow button, which when touched seemed to alter the effect of gravity on the beings.

The older man indicated that he knew about pygmies, by demonstrating how they hunted with bow and arrow. He also seemed to indicate that his people would come in "great armadas" in the future. After further communication, the older man returned to the craft and fetched an object the size of a cylinder or microphone, which he proceeded to run along Höglund's back. At this, he felt a sensation of warmth, vibration, and sudden relief from the kidney pain that had troubled him for fifteen years.

By now an hour had passed and it began to grow dark, at which point Höglund noticed that the craft was now surrounded by a blue phosphorescent light. The whole craft seemed to vibrate. Except for the dark cylinder underneath, it remained semi-transparent, consisting of two shells, the outer one rotating. Inside, the craft seemed Spartan: all that could be discerned were three shining "cylinders" standing on the floor. Terminating the communication, the entities entered the craft, which then took off at tremendous speed, changing color from blue to orange as it flew away.

The following day, Höglund was X-rayed at Uddevalla hospital. Much to the bewilderment of a Dr. Hartman and his colleagues, no trace of the kidney stone could be found. Subsequently, Håkan told me, all the X-ray plates were checked by Dr. Karl Erik Svensson in Stockholm, who confirmed that no stone was visible on the plates, taken after the encounter.

SECOND CONTACT

On August 24, 1966, Höglund felt a strong impulse to visit another lake outside Uddevalla. The urge was so powerful that it felt as if someone else was driving the car (a sensation recounted by Carl Anderson). Arriving at the lake, he saw the same kind of craft hovering above the water, beside which a man seemed to be suspended in the air. Spotting a small rowboat nearby, Höglund climbed in and headed toward the craft. He recognized the man as the same with whom he communicated during the first encounter. This time, he could hear the man speak (presumably in Swedish), though his speech did not synchronize with his lip movements and seemed to originate from the craft slightly delayed.

During this communication, Höglund learned that world peace was threatened because the USA and the USSR supposedly planned a war against China, and that he should go to the Bahamas to act as their contact man. He was given a metal plate with strange hieroglyphic-type symbols embossed thereon and instructed to wear it at all times. Höglund explained that such a mission was impossible; he was an uneducated man, did not speak English, and in any case had a wife at home. These objections were brushed aside, and Höglund felt obliged to comply with the order.

Following the encounter, however, he buried the plate in woods near the lake and then returned home.

Despite serious misgivings, Höglund and Gunvor went ahead with the plan. To finance their trip, they sold everything. On March 5, 1967, they flew via London to Nassau, thence to Little Exuma, a small island in the Bahamas where they had been told to go. Höglund did not bring the metal plate with him, however. During the flight, the couple noticed fourteen passengers dressed like priests, all similar in appearance, who supposedly disappeared in an unusual way on landing at Nassau. Apart from this incident, nothing unusual happened during the trip. The couple returned to Sweden. Ashamed to resettle in their home town, they bought a cheap house trailer south of Stockholm, where Höglund was able to find work once more as a rock-blaster.

SURREALISTIC DEVELOPMENTS

In ensuing months, Höglund became involved with *Ifologiska sallskapet*, a Stockholm-based UFO group which had become interested in his story. Among the members was a wealthy building contractor who offered to finance Höglund in the event he was ordered to the Bahamas again. He decided therefore to recover the metal plate. On the drive from Gothenburg, after picking up the plate, he stopped at a gas station, where an old man approached and asked him for a lift. Höglund consented, as he felt tired and thought it a good idea to have someone to talk with during the journey. The man was dressed in a black cape, boots, and a big slouch hat.

After a while, the man asked Höglund if he recognized him. He replied in the negative, but suddenly it dawned on him that the man was one of those dressed as priests on the outbound flight to the Bahamas. The man introduced himself as "Father Ra Paz" (later contracted to Rapas), and said he worked for "the Overlords," that is, the beings who had contacted Höglund on the two previous occasions. Rapas suggested a coffee break at a motel. He took off his hat but ordered nothing to drink. By now thoroughly confused, Höglund began to worry that the stranger might be an illusion, so when a boy passed their table, Höglund knocked the hat onto the floor. The boy, assuming himself responsible, picked up the hat and apologized. Father Rapas was no illusion.

Nothing had happened in the Bahamas, Rapas explained, because Höglund had not taken the metal plate with him. He was told that he must return to the Bahamas, this time not forgetting the plate. 7 × 4.5 centimeters in size and about one centimeter thick, with a coarse back, the plate appeared to be made of an aluminum-type material, engraved with three rows of cryptic symbols. At times, the plate became so hot that Höglund kept it in asbestos. He also said that it gave him rashes (caused by the asbestos, perhaps?).

After continuing the journey for a few more miles, Rapas suggested that he should take the wheel. Höglund pointed out that Rapas seemed rather elderly to drive—he guessed about seventy years old. "If you double that some ten times, you will be closer to the truth," came the riposte. Exchanging seats, Rapas proceeded to drive the old Volvo as if it were a racing car. Höglund protested, explaining that the police might have speed traps. "Don't worry," said Rapas, "I can sense where they are." Höglund fell asleep. When he awoke, the car was parked beside the road outside Sodertalje. There was no sign of Rapas, who had left a package of fruit on the seat.

AN ALIEN BASE?

The building contractor in the UFO group now agreed to finance Höglund's second trip to the Bahamas, the money to be mailed via a school teacher in Nyköping by the name of Tryggwe Glantz. Höglund and his wife returned to the Bahamas around the New Year period of 1967–68, staying initially in Nassau. When nothing happened during the first two days, Höglund lost his temper and threw the metal plate on the floor, shouting that he wanted nothing more to do with the whole business. That evening, he claimed to have been visited by three humanoid beings of rather oriental appearance but distinctly different from those encountered in Sweden. They delivered a sharp warning to Höglund not to act like that again.

On New Year's Eve, acting on instructions supplied to him by Rapas, Höglund went to the harbor in Little Exuma Island and contacted an old black man called Joe, who owned a boat. A girl called Li was also aboard. "Höglund was told to lie down in the boat, presumably so he could not see where they went," Håkan told me. "The boat was very fast." They arrived at a small island where, through an opening in elevated terrain, they entered a secret base. At some point, Li, presumably one of the "space people," demonstrated her ability to walk on the water outside the boat! Rapas, who had arrived before them, acted as a guide.

In the base, Höglund met twenty-three different supposed representatives from various planets. "Some were giants, some were dwarves, and others hermaphrodites," Håkan reports. "He was shown a three-dimensional 'film' of human history from the birth of Christ. During this experience he collapsed three times and had to be revived by Rapas. He was also shown a collection of weapons from all ages and given the mission of starting a peace movement in Sweden, though told that he himself should not appear in public to promote it."

"THE NEW GENERATION"

Back in Sweden, during a meeting of contactee-oriented enthusiasts in January 1968, a statement written by Father Rapas and dictated to Höglund (who did not attend) was read out. A new "international peace organization" should be started by the group, it began. With the approbation of the Overlords, the organization was to be named "The New Generation." The statement contained so much drivel that it is a wonder anyone took it seriously. Among Rapas's exhortations are the following:

"Your catchwords shall be: Freedom from violence, from hunger; we are all brothers and sisters. . . . You who have supported [Richard] shall not be forgotten, you shall reap a hundredfold, but if someone hurts him or his devoted wife, I say, they shall be revenged sevenfold." The group also received "Ra Paz's Rules"—sixty-five "philosophical points"—one of which is more than enough to suffice here: "If there should be interplanetary people among you, which I believe is rather rare, don't let them go to heaven but bring them down to Earth again and demand more work of them."

Most members of the group felt uneasy about Rapas, his threats, and the "New Generation" and their platitudes. The building contractor, for instance, had been asked to pay thousands of kronor without knowing what he was really supporting. And Höglund, thoroughly disillusioned, became reclusive. As a result, the group split up, though Tryggwe Glantz continued to act as spokesman. Interviewed by a Swedish newspaper in mid-1968,

Glantz was quoted as saying that the now 600-member organization had been created by "the West Indian peacemaker Ra Paz" as "a worldwide peace movement in the spirit of Martin Luther King." The article went on to mention the organization's plans for a large meeting in the fall that year, to be attended by the singer Harry Belafonte; Ralph Abernathy, a leader of the American civil rights movement and assistant of Martin Luther King Jr.; and King's wife Coretta. The meeting never happened. In the article, Rapas is referred to as a wealthy industrialist who, during his travels around the world, had seen so much misery that he decided to devote his wealth to charitable causes.[4]

BACK IN THE BAHAMAS

The aliens encountered by Richard Höglund in the Bahamas were of human appearance, with "thin, pointed features, deeply tanned, with a somewhat Oriental look, long tapering fingers and dark eyes," Håkan learned. "They all seemed perfect—not a blemish on their skin. He never saw the beings from the initial contacts in Sweden again. . . ."

During the New Year period of 1968–69, Höglund and his wife returned to the Bahamas. One night, he told Gunvor that she could meet one of his contacts at a discotheque in Nassau. Gunvor protested at visiting such a venue, but her husband insisted. They found a table on the second floor and Höglund began looking around for the man. He left the table and returned with a man dressed in an ill-fitting brown costume, Håkan learned from Gunvor:

"The man just nodded his head in a short greeting to Gunvor. He was rather short, his skin had a peculiar suntan, and he had a slight Mediterranean or oriental look. The clothes were too large for his rather thin body. The man returned to his table. Richard explained that the man was one of 'them.' When Höglund and Gunvor started dancing, the man came up and watched them very closely. He looked straight into Gunvor's eyes. There was a sort of hypnotic power in his eyes. 'I will never forget those eyes,' she said."

The man showed Höglund a photograph of his family and house, supposedly on another planet in our solar system, which Gunvor recalled her husband referring to as either Venus or Saturn—she couldn't be sure which.

During this and another trip to the Bahamas (there were three in all), Höglund met others like himself who acted as couriers for the "space people." One was a Russian, another an African-American named Loftin Anderson, with whom he became good friends. Anderson, it transpired, was an agent for the Central Intelligence Agency. During 1968, Little Exuma was swarming with CIA agents, Håkan reveals. "Anderson had informed the CIA about the [alien] base. Later he was found dead with a bullet hole in his head. He had been killed for 'treason.'"

Several photographs were taken of Höglund in the Bahamas. The entities themselves, however, could not be photographed. "Instead, there was an illuminated square on the photo where one of them had been," Håkan explains. "Höglund remembers one episode when he sat on a bench, talking to one of them. Suddenly a stranger walked by and Höglund felt very embarrassed as it appeared as though he was talking to himself. These people had the ability to disappear into thin air."

Another peculiar feature of the aliens was that they never seemed to sleep or eat, though they did drink—and even smoke. Also, Höglund never met any women among them.

A coincidental element in this saga is the Mafia. "Lou Chesler was the front man in the Bahamas for the big Mafia boss Meyer Lansky," Håkan told me. "Richard and his wife found an ad in a Swedish newspaper in the autumn of 1968 about work in the Bahamas. They applied, and as they had been there before they got the work through a Swedish man. Richard was to be butler and his wife housekeeper at the Chesler residence in Nassau. They worked there for a couple of weeks before being forced to leave because of new laws by the government. During those weeks Richard met the visitors several times."[5]

Höglund was allowed the use of their cars and drove an unused but old model of a black Cadillac (like those reported in other cases involving the proverbial "men in black"). "The strange thing was that it couldn't be crashed," said Håkan. "It had a sort of magical 'eye' that steered it. When you learned the trick it was very easy, he claimed."

In a letter sent from the Bahamas in early 1969 to a friend in Sweden, Höglund wrote: "I cannot and am not allowed to disclose what we are doing here, but I can tell you this much: we are in a school here, and as you can understand, the teachers are interplanetary."[6]

DISTURBING DEVELOPMENTS

The building contractor having withdrawn his financial support, Höglund had to rely on his alien contacts for funding. "Obviously," Håkan commented, "this group had unlimited economic resources.

"One day a man from a car firm visited Höglund and gave him a new car. He said it was paid for and was to be delivered to him. Before the third trip to the Bahamas, Höglund contacted a friend who was to take care of his apartment, pay the rent, and care for the indoor plants. The payment for this service would be sent from the Bahamas, to a special bank account. Höglund paid just five kronor into the account before he and his wife left. On the very day that they went to the Bahamas, someone paid 1,000 kronor into this account. Every week it increased by a few hundred kronor, but the receipts never stated who had put the money there. No money ever arrived from the Bahamas.

"When Höglund and his wife returned, they were very anxious as they thought they must owe their friend [who had looked after the apartment] a lot of money. When the friend explained that there was always money in the account, they first thought he had given it himself, but later they realized that some of their ['space'] contacts must have made the payments."

Following the leak of information about the Bahamas base to the CIA, the aliens moved their base to an area outside Mexico City. Henceforth, Höglund's foreign trips were to Mexico. He was often away from home for a month at a time. After the third and final trip to the Bahamas, Gunvor no longer accompanied her husband. In October 1968, during the Olympic Games in Mexico City, Höglund claimed to have been taken to the new base. He became very upset as he was not allowed to attend the Games!

"I had the feeling he was afraid," Höglund's friend Dr. Karl Svensson revealed to Håkan. "He told me in general terms that he had been in Central America. I don't think he really knew where he was. . . ."

Further contacts also took place in Sweden. Höglund's wife always knew when a visit was forthcoming because her husband became restless and got up early. He claimed to have been taken on board spaceships during this period, but information on these contacts is scanty. "He took his car to a secret location south of Stockholm, where he was picked up by a craft," Håkan told me, referring to the first trip. "He was blindfolded and had to lie down on the floor. The craft was very small—he couldn't stand up." After that first trip, he became nauseated, but later adjusted to these experiences.

In the early 1970s, Höglund said that he had been operated on by his contacts, as Gunvor related to Håkan:

"He had a lot of headaches before, and took pills. One day, when I was going to work, he said that someone is coming and something is going to happen. He didn't always tell me when they were coming, but this time he told me not to come home too early from work. After that day he never had any headache. They did something to him and he said he would not have survived otherwise. It was some form of tumor, which was removed. I looked at his head but there was only a slight blemish. He was a bit pale and tired afterwards, and was told to rest a few days."[7]

Höglund's contacts reportedly continued until his death, from a heart attack, on October 23, 1977. He was sixty-four.

ALTERNATIVE SCENARIOS

There is the possibility, of course, that Richard Höglund might simply have been insane, or been suffering from delusions engendered perhaps by the tumor that had been "operated" on. This might explain at least some of his claims, but not according to those closest to him, including his wife. Nonetheless, there are a number of alternative explanations for his seemingly fantastic and farcical assertions. First is a hypothesis that he might have been spying for a foreign power such as the USSR, using the "alien" element as a cover.

Höglund was a Communist, Håkan told me. There was much Soviet infiltration of Sweden at that time, he notes, and Höglund had a friend who worked at the Swedish Navy base in Musko. He also had Soviet contacts. "Was he just a member of the Communist party, or an agent?" asks Håkan. After all, he had been asked by his "alien" contacts to obtain a map from that base. It is not known if he succeeded. But in any event, such a request, combined with his "translating" or decrypting some form of codes, raises suspicions, as does his trip to Mexico City in 1968 during the Olympic Games, when Soviet penetration and subversion were at a peak.

"Höglund acted as a courier for his contacts," Håkan emphasized. "He translated coded messages in the form of numbers. The codes disappeared in a few days (invisible ink?). He went to different places, like airports, to deliver envelopes with information for his contacts. Many of his activities sound like ordinary espionage. I believe the UFO story was a cover for probably Soviet espionage. His order to start a peace movement also indicates this."

What of the car given to Höglund in Sweden? In checking Soviet activity at the time of his contacts, I noted that the KGB (the national security agency of the USSR from 1954 to 1991) had an auto dealership in Sweden—the Materco Bil Ab—with offices in four cities, used as a cover for espionage activities. In 1971, the Swedish newspaper *Dagens Nyheter* reported that police frequently followed Soviet "car salesmen" to "mobilization centers, radio stations, and other sensitive defense installations." Pilots complained that radio transmissions emanating from the auto company, beamed to Soviet warships in the Baltic, disrupted their communications.[8]

Prior to the contacts, Höglund and his wife had seen an advertisement for land in the Bahamas, and he wanted to build a hotel there. Håkan wondered if the order to go to the Bahamas might have been a cover to persuade his wife to accompany him. The fact that one of Höglund's financiers was a building contractor also raises suspicions in this connection, though that financier had withdrawn his support after the first Bahamas trip.

There is also the question of Höglund's psychic abilities. By all accounts, he was a gifted telepath, and in my opinion this might have been a reason for the contacts—whatever the nature of those contacts. Moreover, he had other paranormal abilities. "I thought, before, that there was no psychic component prior to the contacts," Håkan said to me, "but his wife told me that he sometimes went off and talked in a strange tongue. Also, he wrote a strange story about nuns and monks in the Middle Ages during one of his previous incarnations. So, he was, after all, a mystic. That changes the whole picture. . . ." Also, Höglund excelled at telling stories (not lies), according to some.

Although Håkan believes the espionage hypothesis to be a possibility, he concedes nonetheless that there are aspects of Höglund's story which are difficult if not impossible to explain exclusively in terms of Soviet espionage, a vested interest in the Bahamas, his psychic abilities, or his talent for telling stories. In June 1984 he interviewed Gunvor, then in her fifties. "Like her husband, she is very down-to-earth and practical," he explains. "She confirmed almost all the details of the contacts."

When Gunvor first heard about her husband's experience in 1965, she was stunned. "I believed him, though," she told Håkan, "because Richard never lied to me. He was almost cynical, and believed neither in God nor the devil."

"If several of the people involved in the affair hadn't been very close friends of mine, whom I have no reason to doubt, I guess I would never have started an investigation in the first place," Håkan declared in 1984. "But there are just too many witnesses involved to dismiss the case." Gunvor herself not only encountered one of the extraordinary beings in the Bahamas—which left her in a state of shock—but also with Richard at their apartment near Stockholm. She described these men as "beautiful, and tanned," though, unlike the man in the Bahamas, "extremely well dressed."

NO WAY OUT

Most of those who knew Höglund—including his wife—were reluctant initially to go on the record under their own names, out of what seems a genuine fear of his sinister contacts. Höglund himself was both afraid and mistrustful of them. "I'm not allowed to say anything," he admitted to Håkan, during their one and only communication, by phone, in 1973. "People would be shocked if they knew of these things. I've already said too much." Fourteen months before he died, he reiterated these concerns in a phone conversation with a friend of Håkan's. "What I have gotten into is negative," he lamented. "You become very isolated. I warn you against going deeper into this."

Asked why he did not simply stop working with the beings, Höglund explained that he "would go the same way as Loftin Anderson. There is a way in but no way out." During the first few years of his contacts, he felt that he owed them some help in return for healing his kidney. Later, things got worse. "You don't know what kind of a hell I'm into," he remarked. In the event he could take it no longer at some point, he carried a suicide pill around with him.

Höglund obtained very little information from his contacts. If he asked something, he said, they would return the next day after consulting with the Overlords. Nonetheless, the Russian friend of Höglund's (mentioned earlier), who claimed contact with the same beings, said that Höglund seemed to know more about them than he did, after working for them for twenty years.

"They are totally without feelings and can witness the most brutal torture," Höglund once revealed to a friend. "It means nothing to them." He felt like an animal in their company. In some ways, he said, they seemed stupid, and not even telepathic. They claimed to come from another planet and were here to prevent a third world war. But Höglund speculated that their real objective was to take us over from the inside—by infiltration.

A DIFFERENT EVOLUTION

Rather than emissaries from another planet or planets, is it perhaps more likely that the group involved with Höglund following his initial encounters in Sweden was of terrestrial, rather than extraterrestrial, origin? Also, there are parallels with reports of the notorious "men in black"—MIBs. In his initial appraisal of the case, Håkan cites John Keel, the well-known author and leading investigator of the MIB phenomenon. "On a number of occasions," wrote Keel, "I actually saw the phantom Cadillacs as advertised, complete with sinister-looking Oriental-like passengers in black suits. On Long Island, following the directions given me in an anonymous phone call, I pursued one of these cars down a dead-end road where it seemingly vanished into thin air. . . ."[9] The black Cadillacs are not necessarily phantom, anyway, since Höglund had been lent one to drive in Nassau.

Howard Menger, an American who claimed to have acted as a liaison for the "space people" in the 1950s, and who is the subject of a chapter in my book *Alien Base*, was informed by his contacts:

"My friend, this Earth is the battlefield of Armageddon, and the battle is for men's minds and souls. . . . There is a very powerful group on this planet, which possesses tremendous knowledge of technology, psychology, and, most unfortunate of all, advanced brain therapy. They use people not only from this planet [but also] other people of your own planet, who live unobserved and undiscovered as yet, to dupe your peoples into a distorted concept of a truth which enveloped your planet thousands of years ago [in order] to attain their own ends."[10]

It is difficult to know how much credence can be placed in all this, but it certainly resonates with Höglund's experiences, and indeed those of others, such as the Amicizia group (Chapter 13). I spent a lot of time with Howard Menger, and though I am certain that some of his later claims were fantasized, I do believe he had genuine contacts with beings who, whatever their origin, were highly advanced, mentally and technologically—and capable of space travel. He told me that he grew skeptical of their professed "Venusian" or "Martian" origin, speculating that they may have been from Earth, the remnants of a highly advanced civilization, such as the mythical Atlantis, said to have existed thousands of years ago.

"Most of this is myth, but suppose Atlantis was real?" Howard suggested. "The people might have gone under the ocean and have cities there. It's very possible. UFOs have been seen going into the ocean, and coming out. It's possible they don't want us to know that they live here on this planet, that they would throw us off the track by telling us [they come from] Venus or Mars." He thought it likely, however, that they had bases on those planets.[11]

Höglund claimed that Little Exuma Island in the Bahamas was "swarming" with CIA agents when the location of the alien base was leaked to the agency. Again, Menger has some pertinent points in this regard, relating to the MIB. "Around this great country of ours is a jungle, whether you know it or not," he declared in 1967, "and there are specialized men who know how to deal on the same level with these people on the outside trying to get in and conquer us. That's the only way we will ever survive, so don't knock the CIA please."[12]

The Overlords—the four beings encountered by Höglund during his initial encounters in Sweden—seem a quite different, possibly truly alien, species, with their large slanted eyes, large pointed ears, and lack of hair. It is impossible to reconcile this description with the KGB hypothesis. Furthermore, there are a number of similarities in Höglund's account that match some little-known reports by others; for example, Håkan reminded me that in the case of José Higgins, who encountered two strange, tall humanoids in Brazil in July 1947, the beings were covered in a kind of inflated, transparent suit, which enveloped them from head to foot.[13] Höglund's humanoids, likewise, were covered by transparent coveralls which looked like they were held out from the body by air pressure.

Regarding the beings who liaised with Höglund and others, I feel that Håkan Blomqvist's original hypothesis remains valid. "My personal speculation," he wrote in 1984, "is that these entities somehow belong to this Earth but are of a different evolution. In Theosophical literature there are frequent mentions of two other physical evolutions sharing this planet with us. They are possibly neither good nor evil but can be 'used' by those who know. . . ."[14]

CHAPTER TWELVE
RELUCTANT GUINEA PIGS

I t was the summer of 1968 in London's West End. Leonard Mantle, a gardener for the City of Westminster, was busy spraying the roses in Soho Square when a stranger bade him "good morning." In a busy public square, especially in summer, it was not unusual for tourists to stop by for a brief chat.

"I looked up and saw a man there, very immaculate, with a dark gray suit and an about-town shirt," Leonard told me, in one of two interviews at his home in 1978. "I thought I'd better just carry on. The next thing he says is, 'Obviously you're enjoying your work?' To which I replied, 'Well, yes, of course.' And when you're seeing people rushing to work, you just carry on doing what you're doing."

"You're not aware of time," the stranger commented. "You seem to be more acutely aware of that than most people."

"Well, time is important," replied Leonard, somewhat bemused.

"That's a very true statement," replied the man. "But people's concept of time is entirely different."

The stranger introduced himself as Iso Khan. Leonard inquired if he was on holiday. "Oh, no," came the reply. "I'm just on a visit—sort of." Asked if he traveled a great deal, Khan confirmed that indeed he did, adding that he had met people from all walks of life.

"It would appear there hadn't been any part of the world he hadn't been to," said Leonard. "At this point I excused myself, as it was my tea break, but suggested that he come back after I'd had my break. So I had my tea and came out of the hut, which is in a picturesque place in the middle of Soho Square.

"And, naturally, I never thought he would be there. I'd watered the rose beds, so I thought I'd get the mower out and start mowing the grass. I went up and down a few times, then got back to the seat. And there he was, sitting on the same seat. 'They're quite nice straight lines you've made with that cutter,' he said. I replied that I liked to see them straight as it makes the grass look good."

At one point in the conversation, Khan implied that he came from another world.

"His knowledge of things was so overwhelming," Leonard emphasized. "It seemed as though he knew *everything* pertaining to our world: its formation, the psychology, the arts, literature, culture—not only our cultures but cultures I'd never heard of. He seemed to be familiar with every aspect of our world. 'How could you possibly know what happened a hundred years ago unless you were there?' I asked him."

"Well, it is a question of time," he responded. "Your whole concept of time is a man-made thing. Time, according to you, is being born, living, and dying; getting up, working, and going to bed. That is your concept of time."

Leonard pointed out that, from his personal experience, he however had always been aware that there is "another time—a time where you sort of step out of yourself."

"Yes, then you are going into time," came Khan's cryptic response, alluding briefly to a "sixth dimension," which meant nothing to Leonard at the time.

Another meeting took place the following day in Park Lane. "I had to go onto the central reservation, watering all the way down and picking up the Coca-Cola cans and various things that visitors had thrown all around Marble Arch by the fountains," Leonard explained. Khan seemed determined to accompany him. Leonard's superintendent, who was checking progress at the time, just glanced at Khan, assuming him to be a member of the public. "So, it wasn't as though it was a hallucination and that he was invisible to anyone but myself," Leonard impressed upon me.

Khan alluded to our exponential developments in technology. "The tragedy of things here is that your technology has advanced too fast," he pointed out. "You will not be able to contain it."

"Well, I know we've got the atom bomb and the hydrogen bomb," responded Leonard.

"It's not only that," said Khan. "Your world is being destroyed without those things. You don't need to have a worldwide war between two major powers to eliminate this world. That is entirely unnecessary. . . . The men who count *know*—they know they cannot contain what they have made," adding that, at any given time, "a chain reaction could take place."

"He never alluded to pollution of rivers or seas, or oil or anything like that," Leonard explained, "just that the rate of pollution in the environment was now so rapid that it was highly improbable we would last for more than five hundred years—even without any wars."

PSYCHOLOGICAL PROBLEMS

Leonard became so concerned by these encounters that he decided to inform Scotland Yard, headquarters of the Metropolitan Police, responsible for law enforcement within Greater London (excluding the City district).

"I was fed up with the whole thing," he told me. "So one evening I went on my bicycle to Scotland Yard, and there was a sergeant sitting there. 'Look, Sergeant,' I said, 'do me a favor, could you possibly let me see someone high-up I could talk to?' So he just looked at me and said, 'Do *yourself* a favor—just go home.' 'All right,' I said, 'I'm going.' So I walked toward my bike, and I thought, no—so I went back. 'Piss off!' he said.

"I must be sincerely honest about this. Iso Khan, wherever he comes from, whoever he may be, certainly hasn't done me any favors—because I went to Epsom." (The name of this town in the county of Surrey was often used as a euphemism at that time, owing to the notorious prevalence of its psychiatric hospitals.) Leonard's general practioner, Dr. Rydall, had recommended psychiatric evaluation.

"I was there three days and they said I could go home for the weekend. They said I was emotionally upset and just needed rest." He spent a total of six weeks in Epsom, returning home each weekend. "They didn't keep me there, fortunately, but once you get that label stuck on you. . . . So what have I got to thank him for? I'm quite philosophical by nature and of a logical mind, but there are times when I thought, My God, this fellow has done me irreparable harm, in a way. I thought maybe it's this obsession of mine about the time thing, or that it could all be illusory—hallucinations."

Len related to me one of several instances when he claims to have experienced a "time shift."

"A neighbor from my block of flats in Clapham was just coming out of Hannell's grocery store, and I was standing outside. As he was walking, and before he got to the door, I was suddenly there and opening the door for him! And he started scratching his head, looked at me again and again. The same thing happened again in the afternoon when he was coming down in the lift. And he looked at me again in disbelief. If you're behind someone and all of a sudden you're in front of them, how can you explain it?"

FURTHER MEETINGS

The first of several further encounters with Iso Khan took place in the summer of the following year (1969), in Marble Arch, London. As usual, Khan was immaculately dressed, with what Leonard thought looked like a suit tailor-made in Savile Row, and handmade shoes.

"You're a fine one, you are," began Leonard. "I had a breakdown last year. Will you tell me something: Why, of all people, did you pick on me?"

"Oh, no," replied Khan, smiling. "I haven't only picked on you. There are three other people." The other three apparently had been selected from another country or countries.

"But why in this country then am I the only person? I'm cutting the grass, watering the roses, digging the flowerbeds—you know full well no one is going to believe me."

Kahn laughed. "It's the obvious thing you do: pick the lowest common denominator. The lower down you are, the lower intellectually people *think* you are, and the less likely they are to believe you."

"That's not very complimentary to me."

"It's logical to follow. Who's going to believe you? The only important point is that *you* are aware of time. And we know this."

"Come off it. How could you possibly know?"

"We have an inbuilt register. If we walk near people, we can calculate the intelligence level of that person. You're very intelligent, and you have six senses. We have nine. . . ."

"But why pick on me? Look what I'm doing—old trousers, great big boots, and messing around with mud—of all people, why me?"

Kahn replied that he'd talked to other people and had met with a negative response.

At one point during the several days of meetings that year, Leonard invited Khan to his home in Dolman Street, Clapham North, southwest London. "He was reluctant at first. And I said 'Why don't you? There's nothing to stop you.' And so he agreed."

Khan declined Mantle's offer of food and drink. He behaved impeccably, and liked his host's three cats, which he petted. But his telepathic ability was disturbing. "He knew what you were going to say before you opened your mouth," Leonard explained to me. "It's like being dissected brain-wise."

One of the many topics discussed was our space program. "A very primitive way of getting off the ground," commented Khan. "There are far better ways of getting around."

"Give me an instance."

"Well, our spacecraft are relatively simple. Our technology is completely different from yours. We work with an electro-magnetic field. The craft can either be [disc-shaped] or cylindrical. The principle, in effect, is that you have two magnets: one on the bottom and one on the top. Do you understand magnetism?"

Len replied that he knew very little.

"Well, if you have two magnets and you push them together, they repel each other," Khan explained.

"I know that well," rejoined Len, "for the simple reason that I had a Black & White whiskey promotion toy involving two small magnetized dogs which pushed one from the other."

"Well, the principle is the same. There's a magnet on the bottom and one on the top. And we have a cylindrical column which is a mercury barometer. A long thing comes down like that, and up, and it's used when we enter barometric pressure." (I presume on entering a planetary atmosphere.) Khan added that a "dimensional field" was also involved.

In our last interview, Leonard expanded a little on the propulsion aspect, struggling to comprehend what he had been told. He referred to a "hydro-electric magnetic field," and thought that "the top half of the cylinder-type central column was identical to the bottom half." Takeoff was at a "terrific rate," which occurred "when the top half hit the bottom half."

It should be borne in mind that Leonard had no scientific education and thus conceded that, although blessed with a good memory, he might easily have been mistaken regarding some of these explanations. It is equally worth pointing out that he was not a "ufologist," thus unfamiliar with any of the numerous books on the subject: he hadn't even bothered to see *Close Encounters of the Third Kind*, he assured me.

Queried about his extraterrestrial origin, Khan said he came from a world very much like own, though lacking in pollution. His race was about 5,000 years ahead of ours. He claimed to be around 150 years old.

"You know," he added, "your people are under an illusion. You seem to think that people from other worlds have got all sorts of funny faces."

I asked Leonard for a detailed description of Khan.

"He was debonair, slim, and about five feet eight. He had straight brown hair, immaculately well cut, and a sort of pointed, aquiline nose, high cheekbones, and a very determined chin. His eyes were greenish: it wasn't so much the color but their expression. They never darted about and were static—very calm. He didn't seem to blink. His teeth were absolutely perfect—nothing irregular at all. If you saw him, you'd say: there's a very smart, well-groomed business man—you wouldn't say handsome. He had the look of a man who knows where he's going."

Khan invited Len to examine one of his hands. "The pigmentation—it's the same," Len declared.

"Not quite. Our pores are a little bit larger."

Khan was conversant with many of our languages. "In the acquisition of a language, it doesn't matter whether it's Chinese, Russian, or any other," he explained: "to us, any forms of language or speech are relatively simple."

He spoke English "in an educated way," said Leonard. "Only once did he ever make a mistake. Instead of saying 'I don't understand you,' he said 'I have not the meaning of your words.' That was the only time *ever* that he said something that was not compatible with the ordinary way of speaking English.

"He had a very reassuring type of smile—and a sense of humor. He also seemed compassionate about us, almost as if he felt sorry for us in a way.

"Since he had been responsible for my breakdown, I told him that the least he could do was to prove to me that he was who he said he was.

"I had a Dynatron record player," Leonard continued. "I've always been passionately fond of music. I had an album of Nat King Cole numbers, and 'Let There Be Love' was playing."

"That's quite nice," Khan commented. "I'd like to hear that again."

"Yes, well, hang on. . . ."

"There's no need for that," rejoined Khan, making a slight gesture with his hand.

"The pick-up arm lifted itself up and it moved back, which is impossible because the record should have finished first—it had one more track to go. So I said, 'Well, do it again!' Sure enough, it came back and started again. So then I took off all the other records, left this one on, and told him that he could stop any track he didn't like. And sure enough he did—and he never touched the thing. And what's more, it happened for several days after he'd left, witnessed by my wife.

"It was absolutely incredible—you just don't know what to think; you're so nonplussed that you begin to doubt your senses. 'There are probably people in a laboratory who would have the answer to this,' I told him, 'who could probably do it with an electronic beam. But if you say you really are from somewhere else, just do something that nobody on this Earth can do; say, fly up to the top of the house.'

"'Well, how about this?' he responded.

"And without making any effort, he just sort of rose up to about two feet off the floor."

"'How about that?' said Khan.

"Then he went right around my octagonal table at the same height!"

Khan explained that his people had discovered inadvertently that they were able to do this about fifteen hundred years ago. While walking in a group, they suddenly noticed that they were taking more prolonged strides, followed by levitation just above the ground. (Advanced yogis are also reported to have achieved this ability.)

Ironically, the demonstrations—convincing though they were—did nothing for Leonard's equilibrium, resulting once again in his return to the psychiatric hospital for two weeks, unable as he was, yet again, to convince anyone of the reality of his experiences.

Was Mantle mental? I do not believe so. Having spent quite a lot of time with him and his wife, I remain impressed by his total sincerity, by his erudition, and—incidentally—by his talent as a jazz pianist.

— —

The night of November 22, 1977, was very clear, with an almost full moon. Barbara Beavers was relaxing in her bedroom with yoga exercises in her Yucca Valley, California, apartment. Suddenly, through her westward-facing window, she noticed an erratically moving light describing various maneuvers. It then approached and appeared to hover over the apartment building, forcing Barbara to stoop at her window to continue observing it.

The bedroom had become suffused with a blueish light, and even when she closed her eyes it felt as though a spotlight was shining on her face. The light in the sky then moved northward, so Barbara went to her living room window, which also faced west.

"At this point," writes Shawn Atlanti, the investigator who in 2002 kindly sent me this unpublished report, "she glanced at the clock on the north wall of the living room and noted that it read 11:45. She then 'heard' a voice which said: 'Barbara, come to Desert Christ Park.'"

Desert Christ Park, overlooking the high desert town of Yucca Valley, is dedicated to "Peace on Earth and the Brotherhood of Man," featuring over forty statues and images portraying scenes of Christ's life and teachings. The walk from Barbara's apartment was slightly uphill, and it took her fifteen or twenty minutes over the mostly unpaved, sandy roads. "Reaching the parking area, she heard a sound like rushing wind, looked at the mesa to the north, and saw a glow which resolved itself into an almost transparent half-dome with translucent panes, four in number on the side that could be seen.

"The upper portion of the vessel appeared to rotate clockwise, in the direction opposite to that of a disc on the underside. When the craft came to rest, hovering a few yards off the ground, the rotation ceased. The light from the upper portion was a soft electric blue-white: the underside had the same hue but was darker than the upper surface, from which it was separated by a rim-like projection that glowed like white heat.

"The craft hovered about twenty feet over the witness, and an aqua blue beam was directed from the lower disc to the ground. Barbara was illuminated by a blinding light and the same voice that she had heard in her apartment spoke in an English accent: 'Are you prepared for this visitation?' Accompanied by a rosy flickering of the surface, a ramp then came down from the upper portion of the vehicle. A voice, sounding like an intercom, warned her not to stand under the ship or to touch its exterior. Ascending the ramp, she walked through an automatically opening door into an inner room."

Barbara was instructed to remove her clothes, place them in a "sanitizer" compartment (in common with the Dworshak brothers and others), and then to stand before a six-foot-high black screen. "She was told to put her hands at shoulder height and her forehead against the screen. The voice said, 'Keep your eyes shut, and press the activator button.' She had the sensation of being illuminated, until a tone stopped. This process was repeated in the reverse position, with hands on hips.

"On instruction, she removed a suit from a locker. The material felt soft—like a liquid. She donned the suit, zipping it from wrist to elbow, ankle to knee, and from waist to shoulder. The suit had a wide belt, with metal bars, about three inches long, around the entire waist. Carrying a helmet, she walked into 'central control,' where she was met by four humanoids.

"Two of these beings, a man and a woman, were quite human-looking and appeared to be identical. They both had light brown-blond hair, with flecks of gold throughout, in a 'geometric' cut. Their eyes were the color of topaz and their pupils had serrated edges. They had honey-color complexions. Both wore the same type of garment with some type of insignia (whose appearance Barbara could not recall).

"The two other beings contrasted sharply—both with each other and the first pair. One was about four to four and a half feet tall, with well-defined pupils in slanting eyes. His head was disproportionately large for his body, his frame thin and gangling with long arms. His complexion was pale—almost translucent. He wore a white suit.

"The fourth creature was quite tall, with ebony skin, full mouth, blue, slanted eyes, larger than those of the first two, and a Roman profile. His suit was black."

Their ages were indeterminate. Portraits of them, as shown in slides to the Yucca Valley UFO Club, depicted the "human" pair as well-endowed physically.

"Since they spoke in a language unknown to Barbara," Shawn's report continues, "the woman came forward to serve as a translator. At this point, Barbara was moved to tears, but after recovering her composure was given information about the ship and its occupants. She was also given an arrowhead-shaped device out of which the language of the occupants came out as English, having been translated by the main computer and relayed to the object held by Barbara.

"Like everything in the ship, the 'translator' had a crystalline appearance and was said to be 'photochromic glass.' By means of this device, Barbara was told that the ship had an outer and inner shell, with seven 'pressure' panels on the outside. These panels were plated with gold 1.25 hundredths of an inch thick. Between two gold layers was a layer of silicon. It was possible to see out clearly, but not in [as reported by the Dworshak boys]. The computer was made of pure rock quartz, 47% silica and 53% oxygen.

"The ship had a central cylinder containing an all-crystal interior cylinder. Graphite fibers provided reinforcement at stress points. The fuel was carried in a lower portion in a sort of 'cloud chamber' and consisted of plasma and electromagnetism. The temperature of the central portion was 0.01° greater than absolute zero. The computer stated that plasma was the first state of matter in the universe. The vehicles produced their own external clouds. Their communications were by neutrinos that traveled faster than light. When the speed of the neutrino decreased to that of the speed of light, it 'died' and remained in a cloud until reactivated.

"In their charts, communications, and central section, glass fibers were used to bend light, and with lasers to make holographic images, so that the crew could see outside the entire ship.

"A disc about the size of a silver dollar, called a hologram disc, was put in a small panel with a viewer. This disc contained the contactee's 'life readout' and voice-print. The voice-print was displayed on the oscilloscope screen on the small panel. On a large circular screen was displayed her form, with its 'Kirlian' aura.[2] She was told to look closely, and could observe the 'chakras' associated with various glands. 'Certain humans emit low-frequency radiation,' she was told, and was informed that when the vibrations and the mind were in exact accord, the individual's psychic abilities were heightened."

Barbara was asked if she would agree to be a "coordinator, transmitter, and receiver." Her mind, said the aliens, would be taught to receive signals in codes, color, pictures, emotions, music, and symbols. She replied that she could not and—like Leonard Mantle—asked why they did not make contact with someone more educated. They replied that it was "difficult to make contact because such people did not have time to meditate and attain the serenity to elevate their minds." An undisclosed geographical factor was also said to be involved.

"She was told that they were more or less innovators and hoped to make communications possible between our world and worlds older than ours which were more advanced, as well as with younger worlds. Some of the older worlds were becoming so mechanized technically that they desired interchange to gather as much as they could of nature." A corollary here can be inferred in the case of Julio Fernández and his dog, who were abducted by tall humanoids in the province of Soria in Spain, in February 1978. They explained to Julio that they were seeking the "warm human qualities" which had atrophied in their race. "They didn't have a Beethoven" was how Julio put it.[3]

Barbara was also informed by the aliens that they wanted a mixture of our people, such as astrophysicists and doctors, to visit their world. "She was then given 'perception tests' to determine her response to novel sights. One scene, in space, appeared as if the observer was moving through the stars. The stars forward were blue and green and formed oval bands of color. The stars to the side were yellow and went by like elongated streaks to disappear in back with a reddish color. She was then asked to count flashes of dots on a screen and to give the apparent degrees of the dots shown (in positions like the numerals of a clock). Other tests involved describing shapes.

"Additional technological information revealed that the photo-chromic glass and films were five times lighter, but seven times stronger, than steel. Under pressure, the outer hull of the ship would weld back together if scratched. The hull acted as a heat conductor so that they could enter the clouds of Jupiter and Venus."

"You will be led," Barbara was told. "You will know those to talk to and those not to. You will not find this a pleasant thing. Your mind can be trained, and will be." Barbara replied that she would not do it. "We think you'll change your mind," came the reply.

"The boarding procedure was then repeated in reverse," Shawn relates. "The ramp let Barbara down and then retracted. The craft began to spin and took off slowly. She found that her watch had stopped and recalled that she had been warned to take all metal from her body. She then retraced her steps back home, where she asked the lady in the adjacent apartment, Evelyn Whitfield, what time it was, and was told 2:30 A.M.

"Barbara reported that after the experience her teeth became sensitive, she needed new glasses, and that various electrical devices in her apartment appeared to have been affected. Her TV set needed degaussing; certain tapes no longer played properly—nothing would play soon after—and the refrigerator freezer stopped working. . . ."[34]

CHAPTER THIRTEEN
AMICIZIA

S panning at least forty years, this is the saga comprising a large group of people in countries such as Argentina, Austria, Chile, France, Germany, Italy, Siberia, and Switzerland who were involved in an extensive alien liaison program. In Italy, those most deeply involved named the group *Amicizia* (pronounced ami-cheet-siya)—"friendship." In Germany, France, and the former Soviet Union, it was known respectively as "Freundschaft," "Amitié," and "Дружба." The most extraordinary case I have ever investigated, it is at times outrageous, farcical, and ludicrous—though always compelling. I would not be including it here were I not convinced of its relevance to our assessment of aliens and their motives regarding Earth.

Preliminary contacts seem to have been initiated in Italy in April 1956. One of those first contacted was the late Professor Bruno Sammaciccia, a Catholic scholar who authored 160 books on religious matters. Holding degrees in psychology and psychiatry as well as many academic and theological awards, he also contributed extensively to a history of Amicizia, compiled by Professor Stefano Breccia and another major participant, Hans (surname withheld), though sadly both Bruno and Hans passed away prior to publication.

Stefano, who died prematurely in March 2012, was also deeply involved with the group, from 1962/3 to 1997, and many of his experiences were shared with colleagues and friends—in particular Giancarlo De Carlo, an accountant. One of the most remarkable men I have met, Stefano generously allowed me to quote from his book *Mass Contacts*, from my numerous interviews with him at his home in Italy, and from our regular communications. As he wrote in a foreword:

"All of us were moved by the deep morality and sincere humanity on the part of the aliens. These were people who simply could not imagine doing any evil to anyone, people who liked eating well, drinking, even smoking, who enjoyed playing the violin [in one case] and tennis, and driving luxurious cars and executive airplanes (in the 1970s, when very few people in Italy could own a personal plane). . . . They lived most of the time in their huge underground bases, but some of them lived among us, inside our society, playing every kind of role in it. One was a university researcher, another one the manager of a rather important textile company in the center of Italy, a third one was a senior manager in one of the largest German telecommunications (TLC) companies, and so on. . . .

"It was an explicit decision by the Amicizia people to keep everything concealed under the strictest secrecy, and there were very good reasons for that. Actually, once in a while something would emerge publicly, but always in a vague and uncertain way. Many European scholars were aware that something was happening . . . but nobody, outside our group, has ever had even the slightest idea of how big and how important it all was.[1]

"We had direct, face-to-face meetings with the Friends (also called W56), who are extraterrestrials coming both from planets in our own galaxy [and] from other galaxies," a participant who prefers to remain anonymous told researcher Nikola Duper in 2008. "Here on Earth they reached the maximum number of two hundred, living inside underground and undersea bases, some of them along the Adriatic coast, at a depth of about twelve miles. The first, 'historical' base was located under the area of Ascoli Piceno, a small town in central Italy [in the mountainous Marche region].

"'Friendship' gathers together various extraterrestrial populations that are different from each other, both as regards physical characteristics [and] provenance (there are Friends from other universes and dimensions).

However, all share a fundamental choice toward 'Good.' . . . The population whom we personally interacted with is composed of individuals (men and women, like us) who are physically very beautiful, some about three meters [9.84 feet] tall, while others are tiny. . . . What is important is what they represent, beyond the various typologies and endless 'folkloristic' singularities. . . . The Friends are not the only extraterrestrials who have come to the Earth. Individuals from various other populations are among us, because the Earth is a very particular planet inside the economy of this part of the Universe."[2]

There is, reportedly, an ongoing conflict between these species regarding the future of our planet.

The humans involved—hand-picked by the aliens—were not cranks. Professor Breccia, for example, was a retired expert in artificial intelligence and computer sciences, and has given lectures on didactical methodologies at the British Telecom training center, and on fractal analysis at the University of Novosibirsk and the Soviet Academy of Sciences. He was also a qualified pilot. Amicizia, he confirmed, included a psychiatrist, two cardiologists, the respected aerospace journalist Bruno Ghibaudi, the distinguished diplomat Alberto Perego (who authored several pioneering books on UFOs), an archaeologist, some twenty engineers, several accountants, an expert in military logistics, bank employees, two members of the United Nations Food & Agriculture Organization, five university professors, a Court of Assizes judge, the executive vice-president of one of the largest multi-national companies in the world, two future Nobel laureates, four generals, and a few politicians.[3]

Others included Gaspare De Lama, a well-known Italian painter, and Professor Paolo Di Girolamo, a distinguished cartoonist I had the pleasure of meeting in Rome, who gave me a copy of his book in which his experiences are recounted.[4]

THE EARLY ITALIAN SCENE

According to Bruno Sammaciccia and his friends Giulio, an engineer, and Giancarlo, an accountant, a series of poltergeist-type phenomena, including "automatic writing" of elaborate instructions, preceded initial in-person meetings with the aliens, which happened in April 1956. The group had been directed via a map to the Rocca Pia castle (*Fortezza Pia*) overlooking Ascoli Piceno. Nothing happened on this occasion, although the group felt suffused with "euphoric sensations of well-being and health." The following day, they drove to the top of the road leading to the castle. "All of a sudden we saw some spots of light moving in the [evening] air," Bruno reports. "We heard a voice, coming from nowhere, a very calm and strong one: 'Now, my friends, stay calm, because I am going to have one of us appear. Are you ready?'"

Giulio expressed concern that strangers might observe what was going on. "Be sure that while our friends are with you, nobody else will be allowed to intrude," the voice explained. "If they do, we will divert them." A man then emerged from behind the castle wall, followed by another. One of the men was very tall, the other very short. "We were just in front of the main entrance, and they came toward us, speaking our language perfectly," reports Bruno. "As they approached, we saw that one of them was more than 2.5 meters [8.2 feet] tall, and the other about one meter [3.3 feet] tall. The latter had a high-pitched voice, as dwarfs often do, but his body was perfect and his voice that of a man of authority."

With very few exceptions, the aliens did not use names. For reference purposes, Bruno and his friends ascribed names to these and others. The tall one in this case became "Sinas," the short one "Sajù."

"They both shook hands with us, very gently, [perhaps because] they were very strong. We felt at that moment a strong sense of love. . . ."

The men remained seated, talking with the aliens on nearby steps—the tall one some steps down, the smaller one a few steps above—for over an hour and a half. "How many things they told us! That theirs was an important mission, that they had been here for many years, that he [Sinas] had been here three times, and that three or four centuries ago he had been in Central America, because in that area were bases operated by other aliens [perhaps the group featured in the previous chapter, who said they lived for up to four hundred years?], that there was a war, unknown to us. He said they usually keep to desolate areas where nobody could see them, so that they would not bother anybody, and at the same time they would not be bothered by anyone. . . . They were perfectly aware of our history, our religions, and our philosophies."

"This Earth was made for the good, but the men who inhabit it are transforming everything into bad," asserted Sinas.

"We are not here to conquer, we have nothing to conquer: our interests arise from the fact that your Earth lies within our stars, and so we are concerned with it. I do not live on a planet, but everywhere I happen to travel.

"This is a critical point in your history, a turning point in your technologies, but because of your childish enthusiasms you are forgetting your moral values . . . everything arises from morality, and everything is done because of it. For this reason, we had, and we are still having, many problems with your people in the Middle East, and you too are going to be in trouble with them in the near future."

The meeting ended at 03:00. Two days later, another meeting took place on Colle Orlando, a small hill to the south of Pescara. The men had taken a transistor radio with them, via which the aliens were able to communicate by superimposing their voices over whatever was being broadcast. They also had the ability to make use of various gadgets with phenomenal qualities. One of these entered the ground in front of the men and disappeared. "That particular place had been transformed into a kind of facility for us," explained Bruno. A subterranean base was built there so that when the men came to within thirty kilometers of it, they would be able to communicate with the aliens by telepathy. Other means to do the same—such as small rectangular metallic plates (similar in function to the one given to Richard Högland, described in Chapter 11) and other devices—were also provided. Months of further communications and meetings ensued.[5]

One night at the Ascoli Piceno castle site, Bruno and his friends, forewarned via the communication implements of an imminent contact—to include three of the craft and some alien newcomers—suddenly noticed that the sky seemed to change. In the distance, three tiny pinpricks of light approached. "The ground under our feet started to tremble, so strongly that Giancarlo was thrown off balance and fell down," Bruno reports. "It lasted some fifteen minutes, during which Giulio took shelter inside the car and Giancarlo sat on the ground. . . . They were almost hysterical.

"All of a sudden, two of the lights grew larger and disappeared. We realized that they were the spaceships we had been waiting for, and that two of them had already entered the underground base." The third spot of light just switched itself off. A few moments later, "Gallarate," Sinas, and another alien appeared, together with an extremely tall one, calling himself "Dimpietro," who they had also met before. The latter was over nine feet tall. (Stefano Breccia told me he once encountered him negotiating a corridor in Bruno's house in Montesilvano—bent double!) Some others were even taller.

"We were happy being with them," continued Bruno, "but at the same time felt a bit uneasy, because one could never tell what was going to happen when Dimpietro—a notorious practical joker—was around. . . . All six of us sat on the ground. Dimpietro took a big cigar out of a box. He threw the empty box away, admonishing us to pick it up before leaving. Then he broke the cigar into four parts, keeping one for himself and giving us the other pieces. Then he lit the cigar with a flame coming out of his forefinger, laughing at us!"

In the meantime, some other aliens walked past and disappeared behind the castle wall. Curious, Bruno began to follow them, but was stopped by Dimpietro. "Where do you suppose they are going?" he said. "They are entering our base."

"But I can't see them going in."

"Well, we like to be a bit spectacular at times."

"Does the door close after each one of them?"

"No, it doesn't."

"Then may I go and have a look?"

"You're welcome to."

At this point Dimpietro picked up Bruno with one arm and Giancarlo with the other! "When we got to the entrance, I saw an opening in the ground, like a vertical tunnel heading downward. I thought that the tunnel might have weakened the castle foundations, and, as if reading my thoughts, Dimpietro said: 'Do you believe that we are such fools? We have taken care to strengthen the structures, so there is no risk.'"

Dimpietro entered the base and bade Bruno and his friends farewell, bending down in order to embrace them. "Please, let the world know that we have come here with a great love toward you. You speak about love, but you do not know what love is. It is the very basis of life itself."[6]

INSIDE THE BASES

In due course, Bruno and his friends were allowed to visit the base. Bruno and Giancarlo met at the appointed time in front of the castle and were told to wait. Giulio did not show up, having mistaken the date. They were told to go to the right side of the castle and to stop at a certain point in the pathway. "I started feeling the ground under my feet trembling," Bruno reported. "I feared that maybe there was an empty room under us, and that the ground was going to collapse into it, because of our weight." To the contrary, the ground itself opened, and another alien—"Meredir"—came out and told the group to proceed toward an empty area in the center of the hole through which they were about to descend. They were told to place their feet in certain areas where nothing was visible. "I did so," said Bruno, "and felt as if some invisible step was preventing me from falling into the pit. Then this invisible floor started lowering into the vertical corridor. . . ."

Their descent came to a stop inside a huge subway with crystal-like walls, filled with a soft light. No lights as such could be seen, and they learned that none of any kind was used. "This place is filled with a peculiar radiation that interacts with the energy of the photons," explained their guide. The light was of a beautiful pale blue and the air very clear and scented. No shadows could be seen anywhere.[7] However, Stefano—who has been inside a base on many occasions—disagrees. "First, the shadows were colored—not dark," he told me. "And they were in different respective positions from the shadows cast by our sources of light. We have a main shadow, but their light comes from everywhere, so the shadows are distributed."[8]

The group was met by Sinas and another man. "It was a pleasant feeling, walking with these three friends of ours, inside that huge structure," Bruno writes. "I was feeling calm with a sense of well-being as I was breathing [their] air. They explained that the air was different from that available in our towns; it was full of negative ions, which were the cause of that sensation." He was told to touch his hair, and found that it was stiff and brittle, as though frozen, a result, he was told, of his being "detoxicated."

Via a viewing screen, the group was shown a room in which young boys appeared to be studying. Their height apparently varied from two to two and a half meters. "For us, they are boys," said the guide. "One is fifteen, some are thirty, and another one is ninety-five years old [!]. Biological growth is slower than yours, but achievements are quicker."

Many of the "boys" had short hair. "They showed a benevolent countenance," Bruno continues. "Some had brown eyes, others very light-colored green/blue eyes. They were of different races, and I was told that there are actually many different people, but that in most cases only their [physical appearances] are different—not their biological functioning."

The group was offered a pleasant drink, made from a mixture of fruits, which apparently had a detoxicating effect. After learning and observing many fascinating things, Bruno and his group left the base at three o'clock in the morning.[9]

No women were seen, though Bruno encountered them on other occasions. "I've seen at least six women inside their bases," he wrote. "They were really beautiful, and you could feel a strong sense of femininity emanating from them. Giancarlo once fell in love with one of them. . . ." Neither women nor men had a problem with nudity among themselves, though never among terrestrial guests.[10]

Stefano related to me how, during the early 1970s, the W56—"W" from two VVs for "double victory" and "56" for the year it started—informed him that they had built a base about 975 to 1300 feet in depth, directly beneath the ground-floor apartment he rented at that time in Bologna! "When they wanted me to come down," he said, "they made a circle of light appear in the floor and the ground then opened up somehow and I was taken down as though in an elevator, with no visible means of support. Over a period of three to four months, I spent a lot of time at the base—at times sleeping there—having many discussions. In this particular base there were no women, though I think that was just coincidental."[11]

Such is their technology that they are able to fabricate bases in a short space of time. "Our friends were able to generate what they called a 'magnetic tress,' i.e. a structure where the lines of force were strictly twisted around each other," Stefano explains:

"Such a thing had the property of 'opening' matter, compressing it sideways, squashing it in on itself. Translucent, almost crystal, walls were the result, with [enormous] density, a Young's modulus [a measure of the stiffness of material] equally high, and of unbelievable strength. In this way they were able to open the cavities that would become their bases, evidently without damaging the surrounding tectonic structures—on the contrary, probably strengthening them.

"Such a structure remained stable while the fields that had generated it were active: it was sufficient to switch off these fields, a finger over a switch, to revert at once to the *status quo ante*. In a similar way, they opened passages to access their bases when needed, closing them immediately when no longer in use. Only very rarely (very small bases just under the ground) were stable corridors used. . . ."[12]

Stefano informed me that the major W56 base beneath Italy exceeded 186 miles in length and 62 miles in width, with a 980-foot-high ceiling. This huge base, he says, was not for living quarters but for the machinery essential for their operations.[13]

In April 1972, Bruno, Giancarlo, and two other friends, Assad and Gustav, were re-invited to a base under the beautiful mountain chain of the Monti Sibillini National Park in Umbria. On emerging, the men found that several days had passed, whereas they were certain not more than a day had elapsed. "Our friends then told me," he explained, "that inside their base, gravity was twenty percent less than usual; therefore, one could move more easily [and] the heart beats with less strain."[14]

TELEPATHIC INDUCTION

"To what extent were the aliens you encountered telepathic?" I asked Stefano.

"I know of up to 150 individuals claiming to be with Amicizia. I don't *think* they were telepathic. They said that, to produce telepathy, they had to use specific devices that were able to induce telepathic capabilities in human brains using a kind of implant. I have seen one of these implants—known as an 'ania'—and it is jet black, of a polyhedron shape. It looks like it's 'eating' light. It generates a huge quantity of reflective light—much more than incidental light. In the case of the W56, this object was inserted under the skin immediately behind the ear, and yet it dissolves into thousands of very small biological robots that disperse in the body. So you couldn't find anything if you looked with X-rays.

"Bruno had been implanted in this way—they asked for his permission before doing it—so he could receive telepathic messages. Once when we had invited him and his wife for lunch, and I had gone to pick them up at their home in a nearby village, during the trip back to my house Bruno said, 'I see that your wife is preparing something with mushrooms. Please tell her that my wife can't eat them.'"[15]

FINANCIAL PROBLEMS

On several occasions, the aliens asked Bruno to obtain literally tons of fruit and vegetables, and sometimes fish, for delivery to one of their bases. Bruno and his colleagues were told to hire trucks and drivers, ensuring that the drivers were never present when it came to collection time. The food was then "collected" by means of "tele-transportation" and beamed to their bases! The drivers, having been persuaded to join Bruno and his friends at nearby cafés, could never understand how such a huge amount of food could have been collected so quickly.

Payment to Bruno and others was sometimes by precious stones or—in one case—platinum ingots. On the latter occasion, at Bruno's villa in Montesilvano, the ingots reportedly just fell from the open sky into the garden, which when collected filled ten boxes weighing about 150 kilograms. Luckily, Bruno was able to sell them to a wholesaler who didn't inquire as to their origin.[16]

Bruno was asked by the aliens to build a large villa for them—under their guidance—on top of a high hill to the west of Montesilvano, beneath which they had a base. With three floors, it had many meeting rooms, large convention rooms, cubicles for individual study, and even a small observatory on the roof. They needed the property, they said, as a center of operations, to introduce new people to Amicizia and to develop some technical projects, and as a business enterprise.[17]

When the W56 saga ended, Bruno suffered great financial loss as a result. "I had to sell everything," he explained, "two buildings belonging to my wife, a couple of agricultural sites, and above all, I had to sell the large villa I had built, and in so doing I made no more than a tenth of its value, because I had to sell everything in a hurry."[18]

"W56 *sometimes* supplied Bruno with platinum and gold," Stefano told me, "and—aware that the operation was costing us a lot of money—they once gave Giancarlo a device made by them which was capable of generating diamonds. But there were two problems. First, the device was absorbing a huge quantity of electricity from the cables surrounding the area—without any direct connection—so that people living in the area started receiving huge bills from the electricity company! The second problem was that, although the device *was* actually generating diamonds, they were in the shape of an ellipsoid 20 centimeters long and 10 centimeters wide! So nobody would believe they were real diamonds and they couldn't be sold: it would be too dangerous to try, because of criminals and so on. So one night, Giancarlo and I took a boat, went out a couple of kilometers from the coast, and threw them into the sea! It was an example of the aliens' inability to comprehend our situation."[19]

What these aliens did provide, however—and in abundance—was a phenomenal amount of knowledge, inspiration, and, in many respects, protection for those involved with the Amicizia group. And it needs to be pointed out here that, on at least two occasions since 1956, they had prevented a nuclear war on Earth. "They did so by transmuting the fission-able metals inside the warheads into lighter substances, so that no nuclear reaction could take place," Bruno was told.[20]

W56 CRAFT

The technology of the W56s was almost indistinguishable from magic. "Very seldom did they explain something," writes Stefano in a more recent treatise—"Their Technology"—to be included in a second book on the Amicizia case.[21] "Most of the time they made use of Maieutics [the Socratic mode of inquiry, serving to bring a person's latent ideas into clear consciousness], where a concept is not blatantly exposed to pupils, but [discovered] by themselves."

Stefano learned that W56 and other groups use many types of craft, from small "scouts" to huge motherships. The scouts are not transportation devices per se, but mainly mobile laboratories, and even weapons systems. Surprisingly, they are made mostly of pure iron, though certain parts are manufactured from various alloys. "There is a peculiar 'field' that connects all the pieces together," Stefano maintains. "When this field is switched off, the pieces fall apart." And the scouts are not stored in hangars. "Thanks to their technology, the W56s ask their machines and robots to build a new scout when one is needed." Each time it is designed in accordance with its specific mission. "When the mission is over, the scout is simply dismantled. That's why we see so many different types of craft: each one of them has been built having in mind the peculiar activity it had been designed for.

"Scouts are not even always meant to be manned devices: many are totally automatic in their operations. And scouts are not always flying saucers: they may vary from 'aniae' [see earlier], less than a millimeter long, to craft several kilometers long." Some scouts are not material craft, per se, but "physical properties forced into a small amount of space"!

Stefano has ascertained that the propulsion systems vary "from pure aerodynamics to magneto-hydrodynamics to electrostatic or electrodynamic effects, to electromagnetic effects or to extremely complex sets of fields generating relativistic effects. These are what we call flying saucers or flying cigars. I do not know much about the latter. . . . Of course, there are also differently shaped objects, such as triangles, squares, cubes, spheres, and the like. . . .

"Usually the power source is an internal one. In flying saucers it consists of three or more objects, similar to cigarettes in shape and dimensions, but much heavier. They are called mother cells and produce a high-frequency current through their extremities . . . it seems that the intensity of electrical current flowing through the poles is astonishing [and] one wonders how such a huge amount of current can flow through such small surfaces. What I do know is that it is always necessary to have something that absorbs the energy they generate, otherwise they could explode.

"A scout is never switched off, even in the rare cases when it is on standby. Thanks to their superior technology, no maintenance is required even in the long-lasting interstellar or even intergalactic craft that they use for their major 'displacements.' Re the latter, their propulsion system relies on greatly distorting the space-time geometry, requiring awesome amounts of energy that, in a kind of perpetual-motion machine, the W56s are able to extract from the distortion process itself . . . there is no practical limit to speed [except] the rapidity with which the internal computers are able to interact with the surrounding environment. That is the only practical limit, because operations depend heavily on it."

"SCOUTS"

Of mostly circular (sometimes elliptical) planform, flying saucers have diameters ranging from about three to five hundred or more meters. "The ratio between the diameters of the outer rim and of the inner cabin depends on several factors, and may range from, say, 1.2 to 10 or even more," explains Stefano in his treatise. "Also, the ratio between the outer diameter and height depends on several factors, and may range from, say, 0.05 to 3. So, we may have extremely 'flat' discs, or objects that we would not call 'discs' because their height is much more than their diameter. In some cases there is no central cabin . . . mostly [when no one] is inside."

No fixed portholes or doors exist. When one is needed, it is simply "created," Stefano asserts. The iron can be rendered transparent, thus it is possible to create a "porthole" at will. "It must be said that, most of the time, it makes no sense to look outside, because the outer disc prevents one from looking down. It can be rendered partially transparent, but that would interfere with the propulsion. A major problem, when flying low over ground, is that a scout encounters serious problems in acquiring information about its immediate environment; therefore, in such circumstances small devices are usually ejected that monitor the local situation and transmit the data back to a central computer. . . .

"The control panel of a small scout is a rectangular area [which] is very small—about 50 centimeters wide and 35 centimeters high. It is a touch panel, and it only ever shows the information that is required and the commands available in that situation. That means that its contents are continually changing, both owing to a decision by the central computer or upon a request by the pilot. Commands are activated by pressing the touch panel.

"It is theoretically possible to drive 'by thought,' but rather cumbersome and therefore seldom applied. It is also possible to drive without the help of the central computer, but it is extremely difficult and occurs only when a new pilot is trained. Typical commands a pilot may want to enter are: climbing to a certain altitude, then deciding where he wants to go, either selecting from a list or entering the name of a place; or entering the name of an 'anchor,' then selecting the time required to reach the selected spot and eventually adding some details about how the flight should be effected. . . .

"'Anchors' are to a certain extent similar to our 'VORs' [very high frequency omnidirectional radio range][22] used in general aviation, a kind of radio-homing device, although working on totally different principles. It is possible to create an anchor on a certain point, at a certain height, give it a name, and from that moment on it will be available to all scouts, because the local computer will transmit this information to a central computer that will make it available to other scouts, if required. . . .

"There are some minor operational details which I have not included here, including allowing oneself to be recognized by the computer (not everyone is entitled to pilot a scout), managing environmental conditions, and the like. But, again, each operation consists of selecting an option from a list. For instance, for most scouts it is better not to land, but to hover about half a meter above the target, in order to avoid heavy exchanges of power. An actual landing is rather complicated, and is usually assigned to the computer."

The craft are not pressurized like ours. "Because of its propulsion criteria," Stefano explains, "a scout, even in space, is always surrounded by an envelope of atmosphere; therefore, if opening a 'door' while in space, the internal atmosphere would leak out at such a slow speed that it would take weeks to empty. If necessary, of course, it can be emptied within seconds.

"Just like inside the bases, the air itself is luminous: there is no concentrated light source. This generates peculiar effects on shadows that I have not quite understood. . . .

"Light appears to be generated from nowhere," as Stefano told me. And the flooring of a craft with which Stefano was familiar "appeared to be metallic, but was rather soft and looked like plastic."[23]

Most amazingly, certain scouts of about nine meters in diameter can be compressed in some way to a diameter of some forty centimeters, with a corresponding reduction in their mass and inertia. Nicknamed "pocket scouts," when reduced they can be kept and transported in a square rigid bag about sixty centimeters wide. "Having got to a rather wide clearing," writes Stefano in *Mass Contacts*, "the small scout was taken out from its bag and put down with care. Then one had to get at least twenty meters away, if possible concealing oneself behind a tree or a wall.

"Acting on a switch inside the bag, the scout would at once get back to its original dimensions (with an obviously violent blast, pebbles shooting [around] like bullets followed by an inverse air displacement, a loud sound, and leaves flying around). Shortly, this quietened down and the scout was ready to be flown. When [the mission] was over, the inverse operation typically generated lower gradients of pressure, therefore was not so violent as the first one. In both instances, noticeable variations in the air temperature were felt.

"I have never understood the use of such devices: it would have been much easier to have a scout, on auto-pilot, following its owner at a great height, then have it land when necessary. . . . Probably there was a reason behind such complicated devices, but no satisfactory explanation was given."[24]

"BELLS"

According to Stefano, this was the common name—*campane* in Italian—given to flying-saucer scout craft. Much of what he has learned attests to the validity of a number of George Adamski's disputed claims and provides valuable new scientific and technical data. "Although usually no two scouts are identical to each other," Stefano reports in his treatise, "some general outlines may be described. The first is that Adamski's bells look squatter than those of the W56s." [See below.]

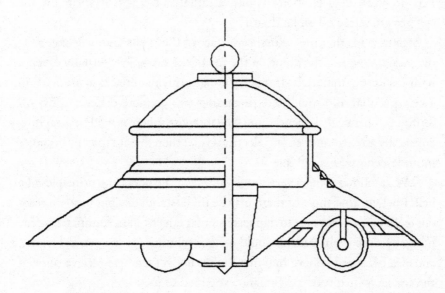

"The height-to-diameter ratio is around 0.6. This second image (below) refers to a typical W56 bell":

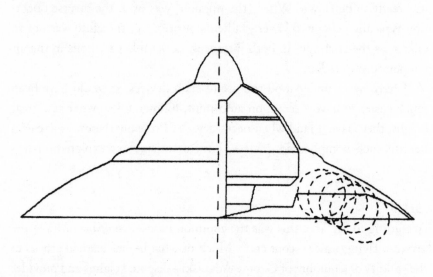

"It may be seen that the proportions are slightly different: the height-to-diameter ratio is around 0.4; moreover, usually the mechanism to extend/retract the three spheres under the disc behaves in a different way: in the Adamski bell, the spheres go up and down vertically, parallel to the scout axis; in W56 devices, there is also a radial movement. [Normally, the spheres are retracted on landing.]"

Stefano adds that the main disc surface of the "bells" is made of cobalt/magnesium, while "the dome on the top of the tower is externally covered with insulating material: strangely enough, this material is again iron, in a very peculiar allotropic state [including two or more different physical forms of a chemical element]," and "the topmost sphere is made of graphite, crossed by an extremely strong electrical flux; therefore it typically becomes incandescent, with a red hue.

"What follows is but a very rough outline of the operating principles of a bell. I believe that most of them may be understandable, but in some cases our technology is not able to duplicate similar effects. I am summarizing my notes, because their content would be too technical for the general reader, and also because I believe that mankind is not yet ready to receive some of the concepts involved." As Stefano explained to me:

"The three spheres under the main disc are hollow and filled with nitrogen at a very high pressure [via an internal radial magnetic field that forces nitrogen into a 'doughy' state, in order to increase its density]. This gas is taken out and pumped along the three rings at the base of the cabin. It circulates in the same direction on the first and third rings and in the opposite direction in the second ring. It is pushed by ultrasonic pumps and contributes to the maintenance of the electrostatic field around the craft.

"The rings on top of the cupola are made, alternately, of metal discs and isolating discs, perpendicular to the 'torus' structure, and it rotates in the same direction as the second ring. Then, under the disc itself, there are two more rings, one over the other—the highest one a bit smaller than the lower one—and the lower one rotates in the same direction as the second ring, and they are made of isolation materials. Then there is a central column. The main idea of the operation is that the topmost ring generates the 'suspending' operation, while the other rings generate electrostatic fields. . . .

"The spheres must be polarized differently from one another: this may reflect on the direction of flight. In an actual landing, spheres are usually retracted: if this is not possible, their polarizations are equated to that of the outer disc. If this precaution is not taken, a really hard landing would take place, with no damage to the craft but probable injuries to its occupants.

"When taking off, some time must elapse before the craft's gravity escapes the local one, because the change of polarization requires a big exchange of electrical charges. During this time, the craft floats almost at random, owing to the interaction between its polarization and the local electrical field. That is why Adamski reported that, after takeoff, he felt a push and acceleration. And the reason he got an electric shock [when he first approached a landed craft near Desert Center, California, on November 20, 1952] is that, with the rotating electronic field and the one electrostatically generated by the lower rings, the outer rim is 'charged,' owing to currents running around it. If the current is not steady, the magnetic field itself is not steady, and it generates a secondary field on the outer ring that becomes charged electrostatically. . . . *We* are not able to store such a large amount of electricity—but that was back in that period."[25]

Ian Taylor, a well-informed student of the subject, related to me how in around 1976 he was shown two approximately ten- by eight-inch glossy black-and-white prints of "what at first looked like an illuminated lamp-shade that was out of focus. Both prints seemed the same but there were minor differences as I recall," he said. "I asked [the source] what it was he was showing me, after which he turned over the prints to reveal what I gathered was an official USAF seal, in a blue ink, slightly faded but clearly legible. I have seen official military seals before and this looked pretty authentic. He asked me to examine the shots more closely. . . .

"It soon began to dawn on me that I was actually looking at what appeared to be night-time shots of a shape that was almost identical to Adamski's classic Scout, albeit seemingly slightly more compressed, but that could have been down to the printing processes in the darkroom or for whatever other reason. What I was looking at was the shape of the craft in its familiar outline as a white illumination made up of parallel, horizontally opposed bars of light of an almost neon-like intensity. It soon became apparent that what I was looking at was the magnetic energy field of excitation circumnavigating the underlying form, or something to that effect.

"I asked where he had gotten these images and he said they had been smuggled out of the USA a few years back by a colleague who had known people in the U.S. Air Force who had had access to certain classified material, and that he had been given the prints as something to own, but never to make public. . . . I have to admit that I was completely taken aback by the sheer clarity and definition contained in the shots. As I was well into photographic techniques and special effects in my work in the creative business, I had a suspicion these would have been copies taken from the original negatives rather than original prints, but it was difficult to say."[26] (See photo section.)

"OVERALLS"

For me, the most astonishing mode of alleged W56 transportation was a one-piece apparel, referred to as "overalls." "Typically, the W56s used these overalls—not scouts—to move from one place to another," Stefano told me. "The suit was a biological entity/device for supporting its occupant, from any point of view: nutrition, elimination of waste, and so on. Under the ten-centimeter-thick soles were two propulsive devices. From my point of view, they were rather elementary, as the propulsive system wasn't so difficult to use. It generated two identical 'pushes' from your feet toward your head, or vice-versa."[27] In *Mass Contacts*, Stefano expounds:

"The overalls were biological entities, strictly personal, which acted as [both] defensive and transportation systems. They were to be worn over the naked body, protecting the occupant against practically any external danger.

"There was a whimsical system for managing inertia: the overall was able [incrementally] to adjust its inertia up to unbelievable levels. . . . The propulsion system was really rudimentary, based on two 'pushes' applied perpendicularly to the soles, and the only control system was a button on the belt which was able to modulate the intensity of the two pushes (identical to each other). Pushes could be both positive (upward) and negative (downward). The pilot's skill lay in graduating the strength of pushes and in carefully orientating his feet. . . .

"Needless to say, more than once, funny episodes took place; for instance, one morning in Munich, Germany, passers-by were astonished by the sight of a distinguished elderly gentleman who, upside down, was flying randomly at a height of a few meters, from time to time bumping into buildings in his path!

"The overall would tune itself to its owner's identity, which it was able to recognize, not through DNA but thanks to a biological principle still unknown to our scientists. A different occupant would have been considered a potential enemy. . . ."[28]

It is worth noting that, though relatively rare, sightings of "flying humanoids" have been reported in other countries. In an article published in 2007, researchers Ruben Uriarte and Steven Reichmuth describe a series of sightings in Mexico of what they categorize as "unidentified flying humanoids" (UFH). "A number of UFH sightings have been reported over the skies of Mexico since the year 2000," they report:

"Mexican citizens equipped with home video cameras have recorded flying silent humanoids, often wearing an apparatus on their backs or around their waists. Sometimes they appear to be in a sitting or reclining position. They hover or move silently, regardless of wind direction, displaying definite flight control characteristics. They have been reported predominantly around Mexico City, notably over Cuernavaca, just southeast of the capital city. Sometimes they are reported to accelerate to 100 mph or more, but more often they are filmed hovering. . . ."

Uriarte and Reichmuth checked the possibility that such sightings were related to people flying with the aid of "rocket belts" propelled by hydrogen peroxide. They consulted Juan Mañuel Lozano, CEO of Tecnologia Aeroespacial Mexicana (TAM), which manufactures such belts. Lozano denied that TAM was responsible and said he was unaware of any other company in Mexico that made such rocket belts. On viewing video footage of some of the Mexican incidents supplied by Uriarte, Lozano—himself a pilot and parachutist—declared his bafflement:

"I don't have an explanation for the 'thing' that is seen in the video. It is clear that it is some kind of human form, but this is not a parachutist, this is not a rocket belt or jet pack, and this is not a craft that is known around here . . . my rocket belt only flies for thirty seconds. No other rocket belt in the world can fly for more than thirty seconds."

As Uriarte and Reichmuth confirm, the UFH objects were recorded on video flying for much longer than any human-designed rocket belt. "UFHs have been observed and videotaped flying effortlessly at well over 300 feet high [and] flew totally silently, as opposed to the 150 decibels produced by rocket belts," they point out. "If alien in origin, are these some sort of flexible kinds of individual transport? What could these objects do that good old-fashioned flying discs cannot do as well?"[29] How prescient. To the best of my knowledge, neither Uriarte nor Reichmuth were aware of the Amicizia saga. *Mass Contacts* was not published (in English, at least) until 2007. And they were certainly unaware of the following, which is published here for the first time.

Stefano claims that "overalls" are capable even of transporting an occupant to another planet—at least in our solar system—and related to me how one of his friends had once visited Mars, allegedly discovering that the temperature was less cold than, and the percentage of oxygen well above, that which is officially stated.

"GIANTS ON THE EARTH"

To return to the W56 aliens, the gigantic Dimpietro had rented a small house owned by an elderly woman in the country near Forlimpopoli, at that time a small village some thirty kilometers north of Rimini. He liked to cook his own meals and, by way of relaxation at night, sometimes played his violin (which he had made himself) in the grounds surrounding the house! "Think how small the violin would be for a 3.5 meter-tall man!" remarked Bruno Sammaciccia.[30] Indeed. As a violinist myself, I surmise that, given his proportionately larger hands, the instrument he made must have been larger than our full-size instruments—possibly the size of a viola. Dimpietro refused to be disturbed during such periods.

Bruno had been asked by Dimpietro to rent a large car for him and remove the front seat so he could sit directly on the floor. On one amusing occasion in 1957, Bruno invited Dimpietro to his flat in Milan. Before being introduced to Bruno's wife, Dimpietro tactfully sat on the floor to avoid alarming her. "When this happened," explained Bruno, "my wife had just come home after her shopping, found this incredible being seated on the floor of our kitchen, got frightened and ran into the bedroom, locking the door behind her. I had told her about our friends, but she had never met any of them. At the time, I was walking in the neighbourhood with my dog Dik, and deciding to return home, I looked for the caretaker to let me into the building, but he was nowhere to be seen. So I rang the bell at the intercom, and my wife Alessandra opened the door.

"As I entered my flat, Alessandra told me that there was 'somebody' in the kitchen; Dik had already gone there himself. When I entered the kitchen, I found Dimpietro seated on the floor and Dik sitting beside him. My wife, still terrified, [returned] to the bedroom. Dimpietro remained seated, without uttering a word. Then he got up, his head just touching the ceiling. 'How will we talk to each other?' I asked him, 'with a megaphone?' 'That's why I sat on the floor,' he replied. 'So sit down again,' I said, which he did. 'Your wife is terrified of me, but do I look as though I would terrify anyone?' 'It's not that. . . . She knows you're a man from another world, and she's very upset.'"

Dimpietro asked for a cigarette. Bruno offered him one, but it was declined. "These are for children," he complained. "Downstairs, you'll find a car parked just in front of your building; here are the keys. Do not get upset when you see that there's no driver's seat, because I need to sit directly on the floor of the car. You'll find some cigars inside the glove compartment." Bruno found four cigar boxes, and returned with one of them.

"Call your wife in," said Dimpietro. "We have to calm her down and convince her that I'm not aggressive." Alessandra returned to the kitchen, still nervous. Hands shaking, she made some *napoletana* coffee, with Dimpietro ensuring she knew how to prepare it properly and to serve him without sugar in a larger cup than the others. Next he made himself a *frittata* (a kind of Italian omelette). "We offered him some bread," said Bruno, "but he refused, because he said he wasn't yet accustomed to our bread. Instead, he asked for some wine. In my kitchen was some white wine, and I knew that he drank only red, so I phoned a nearby grocer and in a few minutes we had a bottle of Corvo di Salaparuta [a fine Sicilian wine]."

"Would you allow me to drink directly from the bottle?" asked Dimpietro. "I'm used to doing it this way. If you like, I'll pour some wine into a couple of glasses for you, and then I'll drink from the bottle." He drank the rest of the wine in three mouthfuls. Bruno asked if this could be harmful. "No," came the reply, "you must understand that it is not the quantity that hurts, but the quality."

After another smoke, it was time for Dimpietro to leave. "He knelt on the floor," said Bruno, "embraced my wife with great delicacy (she was still a bit upset because of that unusual dinner), and told her: 'Remember, I do not eat women, I only eat peppers, pasta, and some sweets at times. . . .' He kissed her on the forehead. It was a strange vision, I can assure you, looking at this extremely tall man, kneeling on the floor and trying to calm down my poor wife.

"It was three o'clock in the morning, and he had to drive the car, parked in the street. Luckily it was night, and nobody was around: of course, he couldn't use the elevators, so Dimpietro, Dik and I went downstairs, with great care. He opened the car door, and as there was no driver's seat he entered just as if going to bed, sat on the floor and finally forced his legs on both sides of the steering wheel. 'Do you have any problem with the pedals?' I asked him. 'Not at all; if necessary, I can use my hands to operate them.'

"He started the engine and began to move. I asked him, 'Do you know the way?' 'I know every street, even the alleys,' he answered, and sped away."[31]

What if Dimpietro had been stopped by the police? And surely individuals as tall as Dimpietro, "Mr. Kenio" (see photo section), and other colleagues would stick out in a crowd? Apparently not. Stefano related to me several instances where some of his friends had been shocked to see these particular aliens mingling in crowds—yet no one else even noticed them.

Regarding the height of Mr. Kenio, according to a study by Teresa Barbatelli of the photograph—based on estimated measurements of the nearby pine needles at the time and some railings in the background and other factors—he was about 3.07 meters (10 feet) tall.[32] The original photo, taken circa 1976 by Bruno Sammaciccia at the large villa in Montesilvano built under instruction from the W56s, Stefano told me, belongs to a Swiss person who keeps it in a bank security vault.

Our attitude toward aliens is determined by preconceptions in assessing their appearance, origins, and motives. We balk at the idea of aliens as tall as three meters or more. But there have even been very tall Earthmen, the current tallest being Xi Shun of Inner Mongolia, at 2.36 meters (7 feet, 8.95 inches) in 2005.[33] And if the Book of Genesis is to be believed, "There were giants on the earth in those days, and also afterward, when the sons of God came in to the daughters of men and they bore children to them. . . ."[34] Is it possible that the giants were the same species as the W56s?

In 1959, Leon B. Visse, an expert on histones—proteins connected with cellular genetic material—was invited to a compound (almost certainly the Aerospace Medical Research Laboratory) at Wright-Patterson Air Force Base, Dayton, Ohio. Here he was asked to perform an experiment on the histonic weight of some particular cells. An astonishingly low weight—far lower than human cells—was found. Visse then was escorted into a room where the corpses of two seven-foot-plus humanoids lay, evidently having been killed in an accident. They had high and broad foreheads and very long blond hair, Jean-Charles Fumoux relates. The eyes slanted upward, giving them an Asiatic look. The nose and mouth were small, the lips thin and perfectly delineated. "Despite slight differences in their facial appearances, the two humanoids looked like twins."

The bodies had been preserved in formalin but remained perfectly white, apparently lacking the (melanin) granules which cause normal human beings to tan in strong sunlight. Their very light blue eyes looked no different from normal, reported Visse. The hands were human-like if slender, while their feet were absolutely flat, with small toes.[35]

Los Alamos National Laboratory (LANL), New Mexico, which specializes in High Science, has a visiting scholar program, especially in fields such as physics and the theoretical sciences. I have learned that in the 1960s, a visiting scholar attended meetings seemingly wearing nothing more than a white lab coat. He was nine feet tall, with very blond hair and blue eyes, and seemed very secretive. (The lab coat apparently wasn't sufficient to cover his private parts!) While visiting, he lived at LANL under considerable security. "Everyone was told he was a Russian physicist and that explained his peculiarity and the security," I learned, "but those few lab scientists that met him whispered between themselves that he was not even human. . . . One day the visiting scholar was simply gone." And in 1988–89, what were described as "a bunch of Russians"—about nine feet tall with blond hair—had moved into a forty-unit apartment complex at the LANL. Whoever these guys were, it's unlikely they originated from Russia.

In the autumn of 1999, a man and his wife hiking in New Mexico's Santa Fe National Forest encountered a nine-foot-tall, extremely blond-haired man walking toward them—stark naked. "He seemed to float over the ground as he strode along and walked right past them, within a foot or so, with his head down, not saying a word. They turned in amazement, and after twenty or thirty feet he stopped and turned around to look at them. They took off up the trail, not looking back again."[36] In both these instances, the apparent lack of embarrassment at appearing either near- or stark-naked appears to be shared by the W56 aliens.

A Dayton, Ohio-based reporter related to me an intriguing case revealed to him by an officer serving at Wright-Patterson Air Force Base who admitted that while working at the Medical Center as a radiologist, evaluating X-ray scans of patients as part of his job, he came across some extraordinary abnormalities displayed in one particular scan of a patient's spine. The officer was struck by its symmetry and flawlessness. "I mean that normal spines have all sorts of flaws, nodules, bends, and twists," he explained. "This spine was absolutely perfect." The officer tracked down its owner and learned that he held the rank of major, was over six feet tall, blond-haired, blue-eyed, with perfect proportions, a ramrod-straight posture, and he "looked to be taken from a page about the Aryan master race."[37] The reporter contacted me because he thought there might be a connection with the reference in my previous book to the U.S. Air Force Space Command list of "Non-Terrestrial Officers," discovered by the well-known hacker Gary McKinnon.[38]

A CHILEAN COMPONENT

In 1999–2000, Chilean National TV produced two one-hour segments on the Amicizia case. Antonio Huneeus, Chile's leading civilian UFO researcher (now living in America), has enlightened me regarding an Amicizia group of aliens who are said to have established a base on Friendship Island, off the country's south coast. "I worked on that series as the journalistic producer for all their American segments, although I was not involved in the Chilean cases," Antonio pointed out. "It was a very high quality and serious production. I do believe there was something to the case. . . .

"The main witness who claims there was an alien base on the Friendship island was a well-known radio broadcaster (Oscar de la Fuente, I believe) who was terminally ill and claims he was miraculously healed in the base. He told his story in detail in the TV program.

"The producers of the show got the support of the Chilean Navy and searched for the island. They eventually located what they believed to be the island but didn't find any traces of an alien base. There was also the allegation of a mysterious ship called *Mytilus*, which would transport people to the island and was not registered with the Navy as required by Chilean law. That part of southern Chile with literally hundreds of small islands would provide a perfect site for an alien base since it's so remote."[39]

ENTER THE CTRs—AND UTIs

One of the many problems associated with—and to their credit acknowledged by—those involved with the W56 group is the alleged conflict between the W56s and a large group of aliens aiming to dominate Earth—the so-called "CTRs," named after the Italian word *contrari* ("enemies"). In conversation with one of the W56s at the Zanarini coffeehouse in Bologna in 1967, Stefano was informed as follows:

"The CTRs are the result of an experiment [by W56] that has run out of control. They are robots, in the full meaning of this word, even if centuries ago they [began] biological reproduction. To you, at this point, it's no longer possible to discriminate between a natural being and a biological robot . . . you would agree that a synthesized human body, with a conscience and a will imposed from outside upon a pre-existing amorphous structure, might be called a robot."

The man went on to explain that he and his colleagues, however, were able to determine such a distinction. "We do not consider this situation as a war, because no war can exist between natural [and artificial] beings."[40] "The reason the CTRs are here," Stefano told me, "is to study us because they understand that there is a difference between them and us. They were created—I don't know where—and distributed in the universe. They want to understand how to cover the gap between themselves and us. . . ."[41]

The CTRs—encountered by Stefano and his colleagues on a number of occasions—created divisions within Amicizia. On several occasions, for example, *doppelgänger* of some of the participants supposedly were "produced" to sow confusion and dissension among the group. Some—including Bruno Ghibaudi—even left the group, no longer able to cope with the situation. "Our colleagues were not able to adhere to the teachings of our friends, and our group started to disintegrate," explained Bruno Sammaciccia. "The CTRs, little by little, were seizing the opportunity, altering documents, changing memories, even wiping out somebody's memories . . . as easily as if they were showing a movie."[42]

Discrediting of participants—supposedly initiated by the CTRs—was rife. Owing to his wealth, apparently, Bruno Sammaciccia was once falsely accused of having swindled an elderly couple of money. The case came to court and Bruno was convicted. He appealed the sentence, however, and in December 2000 was proclaimed totally innocent of all charges.[43]

In November 1978, the whole central part of the Adriatic Sea erupted, as confirmed in numerous contemporary news reports (some of which are reproduced in the book). "It lasted a full couple of months," Stefano reported. "Huge columns of water tens of meters high suddenly arose; unprecedented waves and strange lights were seen at night, and both civilian and military radars got unexplained echoes." One fishing boat sank inexplicably, with the loss of two fishermen, though they had not died from drowning. "The results of the autopsies conducted on their bodies were never released, and fishing activity stopped almost completely. In the meantime, over land and sea, hundreds of UFOs and their occupants were seen by all kinds of people, from policemen to farmers."[44] What on earth was happening?

Far beneath the seabed along this stretch of the Adriatic lay one of the W56's larger bases, at a depth of about twelve miles from the surface. Paolo Di Girolamo writes as follows: "The CTRs were able to enter and destroy most of the W56's bases [with casualties on both sides], including the largest one, which stretched from Ortona to Rimini, and from the center of the Adriatic to the center of Italy . . . the W56s themselves had forecast: 'You'll see waters rising [and] boiling over the place where we have built our big base.'"[45]

Stefano was skeptical about the reasons for this scenario. "Officially, there had been a terrible battle between the CTRs and the W56s," he told me. "The latter said they had been defeated and went away, promising that they would return at the beginning of the new century. That's the official version. My opinion is that, on the contrary, it was false information in order to justify their interruption of the contact with Bruno and his group. Because, actually, they never went away. . . ."[46]

Stefano related to me two experiences he had while flying in aircraft, the first of which occurred near L'Aquila on May 17, 1981 (entered in his pilot's logbook, which I examined). "I was piloting a C-Falke-70 powered glider, registration I-IMAD, at an altitude of about a thousand meters above the ground, when a fast-flying disc, stone-colored, flew below my starboard wing, generating a great deal of turbulence. My starboard wing went up, the nose went up—and I was in an incipient spin. Probably for structural reasons, that aircraft could not do a spin. So I applied full power, full right rudder, pushed the stick forward, and the aircraft got back to normal. But all the way back to L'Aquila I continued to be in strong turbulence."

Usually, UFOs do not affect the atmosphere in this way, therefore Stefano believes the craft was based on aerodynamic principles. However, there have been occasions when severe turbulence and other disturbing effects have been encountered by planes confronted with craft of non-aerodynamic shape, such as those reported in Ireland in 2004.[47]

Stefano's other experience occurred in 1997—as a passenger. "At that time," he told me, "I was working in Córdoba, Argentina, so typically was flying from Rome to Madrid, then Madrid to Buenos Aires, and from there to Córdoba. On that occasion in 1997, I was flying in a Boeing 747, which I knew to be an old plane. As managing director of my company, I was flying First Class. We were probably in the mid-Atlantic, when all of a sudden there was a sudden movement of the aircraft—not turbulence—as though something was wrong. At the time, I was listening to some classical music. Then 'Sigis'—one of the aliens I had known—announced via the headphones, 'Don't worry. We have the situation under control.'

"When we landed at Buenos Aires the next morning, as we disembarked from the plane I noticed on the port wing that a panel—about 3 × 3 feet— was missing on the upper side. I guessed it was metal fatigue, but normally, had that been the case, all the other panels would have gone too—the corrupted airflow should have taken away the other panels, depriving the wing of lift. But it was just that one. That means they were looking after me. So, you see, they never went away. . . ."[48]

To further confuse the issue, according to Bruno Sammaciccia there was yet another group of ETs operating during this period, which he called the "UTI." "I don't know what he meant with those initials," Stefano writes in his treatise, "but UTI was a group in a way on a higher level than the W56s and CTRs, whose activities they were supervising, taking action when they believed that one of the two groups was going beyond certain limits. Once, the UTIs reproached the W56s for something they'd done, and Bruno was seen weeping because he couldn't accept that his friends had been reprimanded." According to Stefano, an Austrian general he knew was among those in regular contact with the UTIs.[49]

PHYSIOGNOMY, CLOTHING, AND CUSTOMS

"From a physiological point of view, the [W56s] are roughly identical to us," Bruno learned:

"They breathe oxygen, though they need a slightly higher percentage than we do. Most of the oxides in our atmosphere are poisonous to them, [so] they take some substances that enable them to safely metabolize those oxides. Their blood is identical to ours, has the same color, only there are many more proteins. . . . The main difference consists in their liver, which changes its dimensions and functions according to the environment. Acting like a sponge, when its services are not required it atrophies to the size of a fist. When they live here on Earth, their liver is very active and works as a filter for the toxins they receive in our environment. Their legs and arms are very strong [and] their brain is somewhat larger than ours, but they maintain that this doesn't necessarily imply that they are more intelligent than us."

Most of the aliens with whom Bruno liaised had blond hair, and a few, black with a blueish tinge. Hair and eyelashes were thicker than ours, and some of the men sported stiff beards. "Their eyes are gray, blue, and some black with a blueish hue. . . . Their hands are slim, just like their bodies, with long fingers ending in nails that are some four or five millimeters longer than ours."[50]

The W56 aliens do not use water to clean themselves. According to Bruno, they enter a kind of unit in which they are engulfed in "vibrations," resulting in foam that exudes from their body, rendering them totally clean. "Their suits are living entities that adapt themselves to the body they cover." "This is a strictly personal process," Stefano points out; "one cannot wear the clothes of someone else." Once a month, the suits are "purified" within a peculiar machine for a few minutes.[51] Defecation apparently occurs only once a week.

They slept only two or three hours a night. Dimpietro—and probably others like him who claimed to have spent several centuries on Earth— slept for longer.[52]

Mating is the same as on Earth, though apparently they often use a form of artificial insemination and the child is born in a special device.[53] (According to Stefano and others, they are totally compatible in this respect: some have even interbred with Earth humans.) Directly over their skin, a very tight overall was worn, a "second skin" intended to protect their body against adverse temperatures, while also eliminating bodily impurities and preventing toxins from reaching their skin, Bruno learned. Over this "skin" they wore a one-piece suit, tight at the neck, wrists, and ankles, ending with shoes that formed part of the suit, and soles some five centimeters thick. These suits were colored, usually in every hue of gray, green, red, and blue, sometimes white, with a rigid collar often bordered with pale orange on the neck. They seemed to attach importance to the color of their clothes: when making important decisions, for example, they would wear translucent, almost pearl-colored suits with "moving" colors (perhaps similar to "shot" silk?).[54]

No government, as such, exists. Neither do the W56s possess a formal civil code; as a highly developed people, they know instinctively how to behave. "Our formalities are unknown to them. They do not have lawyers, courts, or the like," Bruno explains. "To them, doing evil is plain absurd: they cannot lie; they cannot hurt anybody, nor anything."[55] According to Stefano, however, in some circumstances killing can be justified. "One of the W56s once told me that it is not fundamentally evil to kill a man (within certain contexts)," he says.[56]

As for their religious attitudes, Bruno (the Catholic scholar) reports that they see "God" in everything, from the smallest insect to the cosmos. "Their religion is not as full of rituals as are ours: to them, it is just a deep feeling," he writes.[57] Stefano believes their creed is similar to that of classical yoga philosophy. I concur. Having read numerous books on these matters since my student days, I have always been particularly drawn to this philosophy.[58] "Although respecting whatever creed of our planet," wrote Stefano, "the W56s maintained that there is no need for rituals, worship, or asking for grace. God is within us. . . ."[59]

The W56s speak a wide variety of our languages and are adept in numerous dialects. The man interviewed on tape by Stefano in Bologna, for example, was fluent in Chinese, English, German, Hindi, Italian, Latin, Russian, and Sanskrit.[60]

Regarding Sanskrit, Stefano gave me some splendid examples of references to "cosmic vehicles" and "space ships" in the *gveda Samhit*, including the following:

"O twin-leaders, your objective is clear; you have thrown open the routes of space. The pilots of your space ship have harnessed engines for your onward journey, the engines that take you safely . . . without accidents. Both of you have been conveniently seated in your richly decorated three-shafted craft, going along a direct path through space."[61]

———

Many of Stefano's experiences and projects were shared with his friend Giancarlo, the accountant mentioned earlier. But the lengthy contacts took their toll. Eventually Stefano terminated his participation with the W56s, as it began to impact on his professional career. "You cannot live a quiet life when you are regularly meeting aliens!" he explained to me. "And after forty years I decided to quit."[62]

In edition to the material cited in this summary, *Mass Contacts* features an interesting foreword by Roberto Pinotti, one of Europe's leading investigators. Though not directly involved with the W56s, he became aware that something exotic was going on in 1969, while studying political science at the University of Florence. At the time he was also general secretary of Centro Ufologico Nazionale, a leading Italian group. He learned from his professor that an underground alien base existed near Pescara, information acquired from important and well-connected sources.[63]

In *Mass Contacts*, Stefano Breccia also includes a very interesting background history relating to various extraordinary individuals, including George Washington, who over the centuries seem to have been inspired by advanced beings from elsewhere. He also writes about some of the post-World War II contactees, such as George Adamski, Truman Bethurum, Dan Fry, and George Hunt Williamson, and devotes about ninety pages to the so-called "Ummo" affair. The latter is a complex and sometimes seemingly ridiculous saga beginning in 1965, when hundreds of physicists, engineers, biologists, astronomers, and selected people all over the world interested in the subject (including Stefano) began receiving strange letters from these people, individually typed, in many different languages, though primarily in Spanish. The information and diagrams covered mostly scientific and technical aspects of their craft, plus aspects of their culture and language—and much else besides.

Like a number of other researchers, I remain skeptical about the "Ummites," though I retain an open mind. Stefano shares my skepticism about many aspects. However, he describes personal experiences in *Mass Contacts* that tend to suggest that—like the W56s—something quite extraordinary was going on, which simply can't be a hoax (by Earth humans, at least).

With regard to the Amicizia saga, Stefano wisely cautions us not to take everything at face value. He was concerned, for example, when the W56s requested some of their contacts (including himself) to bring them certain potentially harmful substances related to their technology. As Hans explains:

"They use a lot of mercury in most of their applications, so that Earthlings trying to [duplicate] their technology had to cope with this metal: *horresco referens*, a device based on a nitrogen plasma generator, with mercury pipes, that became solid thanks to a liquid air envelope . . . mercury is an expensive substance, not readily found in great quantities, moreover a toxic substance. We have also been working with asbestos and radioactive compounds such as radium, barium-strontium niobate and with hyper-voltage generators (beyond one mega-volt), so we were used to being careful."[64]

"Who knows if there is anyone who actually [understands] the knowledge of what Amicizia has meant, *in toto*?" asks Stefano. "Who knows how many persons, all over Central Europe, are acquainted with it? . . . Too many have died during this period, even those foreign to it; too many people went mad, and too many have ruined their lives."[65]

Recently, in delving through one of my files containing correspondence between George Adamski and his Swiss representative Louise "Lou" Zinsstag, by happenstance I chanced on an Amicizia connection. "I want you to know what a singular experience I had during a short visit to Italy," Lou wrote to Adamski in July 1962. "A very good journalist named Bruno Ghibaudi wrote a whole series of articles in one paper, publishing all kinds of intriguing contact stories and also photos from other people. Among them were those of a young artist, Gaspare De Lama, from Milano, which were so interesting that I wrote to him. My Italian being rather poor, I asked a friend of mine, Curt Zäch, to accompany me to De Lama. We met him, his wife, and his mother. They are very sincere and trustworthy people; poor but of good breeding, well educated and hospitable. . . . De Lama tells an amazing story. He forbade me to write to anybody about it except you.

"His first question was regarding your pamphlet on the spaceships being useful in case of cosmic wars. He had heard this from Alberto Perego through a friend, but was not sure. When I confirmed it and said that [Adamski] took this seriously, he murmured: 'I knew that Adamski is no fool. . . .'

"He then proceeded to show us his photos. This man has been able to photograph saucers since February 1962, in seven series, one of them in color: 'A friend of mine pilots them and sometimes lets me know when they're coming and where I can take pictures. He is an Italian like me, called Franco. He works with people from another galaxy. These people have subterranean bases here on Earth. . . .'

"I asked him why his space friends were here and why they hid under the Earth. 'In the first place, they explained that they are kind of like military people and would have to hide everywhere. They are not here to make war on us, they came to fight—not with weapons—a bad race who came to this planet some time ago in order to force us to make war with each other. . . .'

"He himself has not yet had any contact. But Franco gave him some letters written by space people. They look most intriguing [though] did not much resemble the 'letter' from Venus which you showed me here in Basle [see p. 113]. I was all the more astonished when De Lama added (almost with your own words): 'You see, those signs are whole sentences. Such a letter may contain the contents of a whole book. . . .'"

In *Alien Base*, I alluded to the testimony of Ghibaudi, citing a series of photographs he had taken of alien craft on the shores of the Adriatic coast in Pescara in April 1961, one of which shows a bizarre-looking craft with what appear to be "wings" and "fins" set at a non-aerodynamically high dihedral angle (see photo section). A respected science journalist, Ghibaudi was a familiar figure on Italian television and radio at the time, specializing mostly in aerospace matters. Later that year, he was introduced to several of the W56 aliens, with witnesses present. They explained that although nuclear weapons remained one of the principal reasons for their increased presence, there were other reasons he was forbidden from disclosing (the alleged conflict with the CTRs undoubtedly being one, I would assume).

Ghibaudi learned that the aliens' reluctance to reveal themselves more openly was based not only on the danger that would ensue from public panic, but that their open appearance among Earth people would inevitably lead to negative comparisons.

"Do not let us forget," he pointed out, "that between their science and ours there is a gap of thousands of years, and for this reason an 'official' mass descent of space beings from other planets would inevitably bring about comparisons between their worlds and ours [and] there are cosmic laws which prevent the more evolved races from interfering, beyond certain limits, in the evolution and development of the more backward races. . . ."[66]

CHAPTER FOURTEEN
ALTERNATIVE SPACECRAFT

E arly one evening in November 1950, eighteen-year-old William "Blackie" Raulerson and his schoolmate Tommy Brown were hunting on north Merritt Island, west of Cape Canaveral, Florida. Suddenly, they heard a "noise winding up like a turbine" emanating from the southeast. Raulerson told *Florida Today* reporter Billy Cox that a "radial wing" aircraft approached slowly from about two miles away until it was directly overhead, some sixty feet off the ground. He estimated that it was about ninety to a hundred feet in diameter.

Behind the aircraft's twelve- to fourteen-foot-high windows of blueish tinted glass could be seen "about a twenty-eight-foot-long console cabinet with instrumentation," Raulerson recalled, as well as six human-appearing crew members, wearing "light blue-looking flight suits with square, black collars, about six inches [high]." The crewman he saw most clearly had "reddish blond hair—it looked like a crew-cut," he told Cox. The vehicle "glowed" from the inside, but had no running lights: the only exterior light was "a fourteen-inch diameter hole on the bottom that was this solid, flaming red. But there was no exhaust coming from it."

The encounter lasted about four minutes. "Then it took off real fast, to the northeast," said Raulerson. "There's not a day goes by that I don't think about what I saw." Sixty-five years old when he gave this interview in 1997, he was then the owner of two light aircraft and had been a pilot for forty years.

"What makes Raulerson's tale a bit different from the rest," Billy Cox points out, "is its location—north Merritt Island, just west of modern-day Kennedy Space Center, roughly four months after the United States entered the rocket era with ignition of the Bumper sequence from the Cape."[1] That was in July 1950. Although Launch Pads 1 to 4 were then barely under construction at Cape Canaveral, the Army scheduled launches of two modified German V-2 Bumper rockets as first stage and a "Without Any Control" (WAC)-Corporal rocket as second stage.[2] The space program was under way. And it was constantly monitored by beings from elsewhere.

Raulerson's early description of a red-haired alien is supported by the testimony of others, such as the Native American friend of Carl Anderson (Chapter 7) and by Apolinar (Paul) Villa (also Chapter 7), who had encounters with aliens in the 1950s and 1960s. In June 1963, for example, he witnessed the landing of a large disc in New Mexico from which emerged four men and five women, ranging in height from seven to nine feet. Some had red hair.[3]

In December 1959, Omar Bowley, of Cocoa, worked as a blockhouse and pad inspector for Northrop, mainly during the Snark rocket tests. "Off duty, having pulled over in his car to watch a late-night launch not far from pads 3 and 4," reports Billy Cox, "Bowley watched as three glowing objects—'with edges slanted like pie plates and if you turned one upside down on top of the other'—descended upon the launch area from the north." As Bowley reports:

"They were in a triangle formation, one in the lead, two in back. They were off-white in color, I guess, and absolutely noiseless. It was astounding. When the rocket launched, the first one turned over on its side in a vertical position and followed it, then the second vehicle followed, then the third, in single file. One was near the front, another was near the middle, and the other was near the back end. They all went out of sight together.

"There was one other fella pulled over at the time. He was in a Jeep, sort of a mustard color. I remember he looked at me and said, 'You didn't see anything at all, nothing occurred here. If you say anything, you'll be in deep trouble.' So I didn't say anything. But I never forgot it. . . ."[4]

CLANDESTINE RENDEZVOUS?

In June 1967, NASA's John F. Kennedy Space Center issued an ambiguously worded management instruction from Director Kurt H. Debus—applicable to all organizational elements—to "establish procedures for handling reports of sightings of objects such as fragments or component parts of space vehicles known or alleged by an observer to have impacted the earth's surface. . . . Included are reports of sightings of objects not related to space vehicles." Under Definitions (a) and (b), the latter specifies "Unidentified Flying Objects." Procedures for handling reports included the instruction: "Under no circumstances will the origin of the object be discussed with the observer. . . ." UFO reports per se were to be reported to Patrick Air Force Base (Florida) Command Post.[5]

In late December 1967, Jim Oglesby lived in Orlando, Florida, working as a clerk in the machine shop at the Bendix Corporation Launch Support and Logistics Office Modules at the Kennedy Space Center. His brother-in-law, Jon Baker, had invited him to join his family for New Year's Eve weekend celebrations at their mobile home in Bithlo, eighteen miles east of Orlando. On the early evening of December 30, Jon and Jim were chatting in the kitchen while the family watched a classic Christmas movie in the living room. "Suddenly, a flash of amber light reflected through the kitchen window that faced east," Jim reports in his book. "I reached around and flung wide the front door, my heart pounding, as I expected to see a meteor hit the ground.

"Instead, my attention was drawn to an amber basketball-sized swirling mass, suspended in midair less than a hundred feet above and east of the mobile home. At first glance, I thought [it] might have been the phenomenon [known] as ball-lightning. . . . The mysterious anomaly maintained the estimated hundred-feet distance; however, just before it vanished, its amber color illuminated the upper round structure, the underside, and the lower outer rim of a pewter metallic craft that measured perhaps forty-five to fifty feet in diameter. The unknown craft glided soundlessly as it banked and headed due east, and vanished." Both Jon and Jim's sister also witnessed this event.

At one point, a beam of deep-red cone-shaped light emanated from beneath the craft, tracing the ground as it continued eastward. "The red beam winked out, then on, then off again," Jim continues. "I concluded that whether remote-controlled or piloted by an occupant, the craft was under intelligent control and beyond our technology. Then a pattern of flashing red lights appeared where the red beam had just winked out, just above the shadowy tree line that lined up within the two poles that flanked the driveway.

"I stood in amazement as I watched the configuration of flashing red lights rotate in a 6-5-4-3-2-1, 1-2-3-4-5-6 pattern around the outer perimeter of a solid structure. Moments later, a second craft with an identical band of flashing red lights that flashed to and fro around the craft's middle, floated in from the left and glided alongside its companion. Now, the flashing red lights that rotated back and forth around the middle of each unidentified craft did not conform to any terrestrial navigational protocol that I had ever observed on aircraft before.

"Both craft hung there in the air just above the tree line; then the craft on the left rose and, on cue, the second one descended. Then the twosome reversed the process and, in one harmonious rhythmic motion, both craft floated and swayed back and forth (like leaves caught on the wind), as they dropped below the dark topography.

"As both ships descended, the frequency of the red lights increased back and forth in a horizontal pattern around the middle of each, and as the twosome dropped out of sight there was a moment of awe as I stared out there where something most extraordinary had just happened.

"I was not close enough to see the saucers touch the ground, but I watched the flashing red lights through the open space between the stand of trees in the distance, until the flashing red lights dropped out of sight. At that point, it was speculation if the two unknowns had touched down. . . ."

A short while after, six helicopters (believed to have been AH-1G Huey Cobra's) "fanned out in an ever-widening circle, their bright beams [directed] on the dark terrain below as they moved back and forth above the general area for three or four minutes, while two F-106A Delta Dart jets [also] flew low over the UFO targets' area. . . . After a brief scan of the area, the choppers resumed single-file formation and headed back in the east-south-east direction of their original approach. The jets banked, came back for another pass before heading back in the same direction as the choppers. . . .

"Two ships from parts unknown had apparently landed on the ground and possibly were still there! Why call off jets and choppers right in the middle of their special task-force operation? The answer would become clearer, but for the time being common-sense stated that either they found nothing upon arriving at the 'hotspot' and called back to base, or the pilots were ordered back to base whether they located and/or identified the craft(s) or not. . . . At my urgent request, Jon and I hopped into his pickup and took to the back roads and the general area where the incredible incident had just happened. Although this was Jon's neighborhood, driving blindly through unfamiliar territories turned out to be a futile effort." The two were forced to give up the search and head back for home.[6]

Back at the mobile home, Jim remained on the porch from where the observations had been made, anxiously awaiting any further developments. "From 7:10 to 7:20 P.M., Saturday evening December 30 until 1:50 A.M., New Year's Eve," he reports, "I stood in one spot, my attention riveted out there, waiting.

"At 1:50 A.M. one of the craft began rising from the area that had harbored it for the best part of six hours [*sic*] . . . the flashing red lights that circled the lone ship's outer perimeter moved faster and faster in the 6-5-4-3-2-1, 1-2-3-4-5-6 sequence as it climbed steadily above the dark terrain below. Then the ship shot straight up, paused, accelerated to a greater height until [its] outer structure transformed into a glowing white magnificent craft [which] shot straight up again, paused, then accelerated in one final ascending burst of speed, covering a vast distance. . . ."

At this moment, a fiery object could be seen rising from the ground above the Atlantic Ocean: coincidentally, a Minuteman II missile had just been launched from its underground silo at Cape Canaveral Air Force Station. As if in response, the strange craft "zipped to the right, [then] to the left, performed a vertical Z-pattern all in one continuous flowing streak of light, [then] drew near the cone section of the fast-rising missile, [then] streaked off to the south and vanished."[7]

TOP: Leo Dworshak (left) and his younger brother Mike, whose contacts with an extra-terrestrial group, beginning in 1932 near their family farm in Killdeer, North Dakota, spanned many years. The men are shown here in their Navy and Army uniforms at the outbreak of World War II. BOTTOM: Pierre Monnet, who encountered four alien human beings and their craft near Orange, France, in July 1951, and was arguably the first witness to claim what later became known as "missing time." He is shown here at his home in Sorgues, near Orange, during an interview with the author in July 1978. *(Timothy Good)*

OPPOSITE AND THIS PAGE: Examples from a series of seven photographs taken by Italian engineer Giampiero Monguzzi, in the presence of his wife, during a climbing trip on the Cherchen glacier, to the south of St. Moritz, on July 31, 1952. The couple were partially paralyzed during the encounter, but Monguzzi managed to take some clear pictures as they lay close to the ground. The two photos opposite (enlarged by the author) depict the astronaut walking around the craft, as if inspecting it. The final photo above is one of two photos showing the craft taking off. *(Giampiero Monguzzi)*

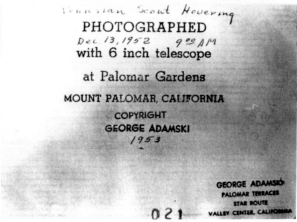

TOP: One of George Adamski's iconic photographs of alien craft. Taken through his 6-inch telescope on December 13, 1952, at Palomar Gardens, California, the craft is an estimated 27–30 feet in diameter. Adamski ensured that all his photographs were copyrighted on the back, as may be seen in the example (BOTTOM). Professor Stefano Breccia provided the author with much information pertaining to the construction and propulsion of these and other similar craft. *(George Adamski Foundation)*

TOP: President Eisenhower at the press conference in Washington, D.C. on February 9, 1955, announcing his trip the next day to Georgia for a few days' "quail hunting." On February 11, it was reported that the president had come down with a cold. He was not seen again for 36 hours, having secretly been flown in Air Force One to Holloman Air Force Base, New Mexico. *(The Dwight D. Eisenhower Presidential Library and Museum)* BOTTOM: An artist's conception of Air Force One and the disc which landed at Holloman Air Force Base prior to Eisenhower's arranged meeting with aliens. *(Leonard Griffie)*

TOP: Eisenhower's Air Force One, *Columbine III*, a Lockheed VC-121E Super Constellation, used in the flights to and from Holloman Air Force Base. *(U.S. Air Force)* BOTTOM: MSgt. Leo Borega, who served as a guard to three presidents, confirmed that Eisenhower flew in *Columbine III* to Holloman AFB. *(U.S. Air Force)*

TOP: A reconstruction showing the second of two discs that landed in Bexleyheath—a suburb of London—in July 1955. This craft was witnessed on July 17 by Margaret Fry, her doctor, one of her sons, and many others. *(Timothy White)* BOTTOM LEFT: Margaret Fry, at home in Bexleyheath many years after the incident. *(Timothy Good)* BOTTOM RIGHT: George Adamski, one of the first to claim regular contact with aliens. He liaised with high-ranking officials in this connection, possessing a passport bearing special privileges and a U.S. Government Ordnance Card which gave him access to numerous military bases.

TOP: Josef Wanderka, a former member of an anti-fascist sabotage group, who in 1955 claimed to have driven his motorcycle up a ramp into a flying saucer in the Vienna Woods! This photo was taken in 1954/5. BOTTOM: A sketch by Wanderka depicting his daring entry into the craft.

TOP: A photograph taken at the Ristorante La Cisterna, Rome, on June 14, 1959. From left to right: Dr. Alberto Perego, a distinguished diplomat who wrote the first books in Italy on the alien subject and became an early affiliate of the Amicizia/W56 group; the Mayor of Florence; Louise Zinsstag; and George Adamski, who had his first meeting with Pope John XXIII during this period. BOTTOM LEFT AND RIGHT: The gold medallion given by the ailing Pope John XXIII to Adamski, during his second private meeting at the Vatican, on May 31, 1963. The coin bore that date, and was not available officially until two weeks later.

TOP: One of a number of photographs taken by Gaspare De Lama, a well-known Italian artist, associated with the Amicizia group from 1960 to 1965. This photo was taken in Milan. *(Gaspare De Lama)* BOTTOM: Paolo Di Girolamo, the well-known Italian cartoonist, who was also involved in the Amicizia saga. He is shown here in his studio in Rome in 2010. *(Timothy Good)*

TOP: Professor Stefano Breccia (1945–2012), an expert in artificial intelligence and computer sciences who lectured at the Soviet Academy of Sciences and a number of universities. One of the many hand-picked people involved for decades with the Amicizia enterprise, he regularly liaised with aliens who had infiltrated Earth. He is shown here at his home in Chieti, Italy, during one of the author's visits in 2010. *(Anne Martin)* BOTTOM: Stefano Breccia, at the time of his early meetings with aliens in the Pescara area of Italy.

BOTH IMAGES: Two of a series of 20 photographs taken in the late 1960s by Stefano Breccia of low-flying craft, near Montesilvano, north of Pescara. The craft shown nearest to the ground was approximately 12 feet in diameter. The other photo is interesting for its emanation of light (plasma?) surrounding the left side. Two other craft seem to appear in the distance. *(Stefano Breccia)*

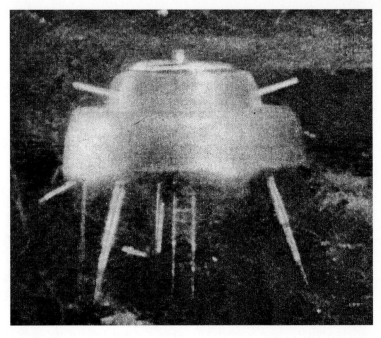

TOP: A bizarre flying craft photographed by science journalist Bruno Ghibaudi on the shores of the Adriatic coast at Pescara, on April 27, 1961. A few months later, Ghibaudi began a lengthy series of meetings with several aliens from the Amicizia group. *(Bruno Ghibaudi)* BOTTOM: A photograph submitted anonymously to the Italian magazine *Domenica del Corriere* on June 23, 1963. The craft allegedly landed in woodland on a hill in Genoa. "I saw it together with a garage worker not many days ago," claimed the photographer. "For personal security reasons I cannot give my name." The craft is similar to the one encountered by Antônio Villas Boas in Brazil in 1957. *(Domenica del Corriere)*

"Mr. Kenio," one of several giant aliens associated with the Amicizia group. According to a study by Teresa Barbatelli, this man was 10 feet (3.07 meters) in height. The photograph was taken circa 1976 in Montesilvano, Italy, by Professor Bruno Sammaciccia, a Catholic scholar who authored 160 books on religious matters and held degrees in psychology and psychiatry. The original photo/negative is held in a Swiss bank security vault. *(Bruno Sammaciccia)*

TOP: A bizarre "twin scout" craft, used by the Amicizia/W56 group and seen on many occasions in Italy's Abruzzi region. This sketch is based on a sighting near Aveyron, France, on February 11, 1967.
BOTTOM: Professor Hermann Oberth, the great pioneer of space travel, who was given information on alien spacecraft propulsion, thanks initially to Carl Anderson, whose contacts asked him to pass the information in person to Oberth, Dr. Wernher von Braun, and other scientists. This photo was taken at Oberth's home in Germany in 1974. *(Timothy Good)*

A photograph sent to Canadian aviation authority Robert Bracken by a Royal Canadian Air Force officer. The experimental flying disc—which betrays no sign of a conventional powerplant—was a real aircraft developed and test-flown by De Havilland (Canada). Bracken was not given the name of the man beside the craft. *(Courtesy of Robert Bracken)*

TOP: On the night of May 20, 1957, Lt. Milton J. Torres, then serving as a U.S. Air Force fighter pilot at Royal Air Force Manston, Kent, was scrambled in an F-86D Sabre jet (not the aircraft shown here) to intercept an unknown craft orbiting East Anglia. On establishing visual contact, he was ordered to prepare to fire a salvo of rockets at the gigantic UFO, which then disappeared at phenomenal speed. On landing, Torres was warned by a National Security Agency agent never to discuss the event with anyone—even his commander. RIGHT: Fred Steckling, who began flying airplanes at the age of sixteen. He later migrated to the United States and became one of George Adamski's principal associates, claiming a number of encounters with aliens in Washington, D.C. and elsewhere.

TOP: Leonard Mantle, the gardener who claimed several meetings with an extraterrestrial human being in London in 1968/69. *(Timothy Good)* BOTTOM: Pamela Handford, formerly with Britain's Secret Intelligence Service (MI6), who participated in a NASA conference at Anacapri, Italy, in June 1984, during which she learned in person from Neil Armstrong that when he and Buzz Aldrin landed on the Moon in July 1969 they encountered large alien spacecraft, which they found "menacing." *(Timothy Good)*

TOP: Richard Höglund, a rock-blaster by profession, whose sinister encounters with aliens in Sweden and other countries—including the Bahamas—began in December 1965. BOTTOM: Capt. Joseph W. Kittinger, Jr. (right), renowned for his record-breaking free-fall jump from a Project Excelsior balloon at 102,800 feet in 1960. Formerly attached to Holloman Air Force Base Missile Development Center in 1954–58 (during the period of Eisenhower's classified visit), he also became associated with Dr. J. Allen Hynek (left), a consultant on UFOs to the U.S. Air Force and CIA, with whom he discussed the subject at length. *(U.S. Air Force)*

A sketch based on descriptions by numerous witnesses in central England who on Decem___ __9, 1987, observed two very large objects "20 or 30 times the size of a normal aircraft" displaying six ___ ___hts at the front, two red at the back, with a large bright white light at the side, emitting a const___ hum and flying very slowly and low from Newark, over Nottingham to the Derbyshire border, then ___ck east over the south of Nottingham. *(Tony Rose/Nottingham Evening Post)*

"We already have the means to travel among the stars. But these technologies are locked up in black projects and it would take an Act of God to ever get them out to benefit humanity. Anything you can imagine, we already know how to do. . . ." Ben R. Rich, who headed Lockheed Martin's Skunk Works which developed stealth aircraft, during a presentation to the Engineering Alumni Association at the University of California in Los Angeles, of which Rich was an alumnus, on March 23, 1993. *(Denny Lombard)*

A sketch by Jean Gabriel Greslé, a former French air force, U.S. Air Force, and Air France pilot, who together with six witnesses observed this enormous structured craft in Gretz-Armainvilliers, near Paris, on the evening of November 5, 1990. "It must have been at least a kilometer in length, and had triangular substructures," he told the author. *(Jean Gabriel Greslé)*

An enlarged and light-enhanced Polaroid photograph taken on January 12, 1988, one of a remarkable series taken by Ed Walters and witnessed by others over a considerable period at Gulf Breeze, Florida. The craft appeared to be about 15 feet in diameter. Light emission underneath is possibly plasma-related. *(Ed Walters)*

An artist's impression, based on descriptions by 22 witnesses, of a gigantic craft which was observed in three main areas along the 134-mile stretch of the Klondike Highway in Canada's Yukon Territory on the evening of December 11, 1996. Estimates of the craft's actual size—determined by triangulation—ranged from 0.55 miles to 1.3 miles in width. *(MUFON UFO Journal)*

Laurance S. Rockefeller (1910–2004), who sponsored a briefing document, *Unidentified Flying Objects: The Best Available Evidence*, with contributions from leading researchers. "The public interest in UFOs and extraterrestrial intelligence obviously remains high as evidenced by the recent cover story in *Time* magazine," wrote Rockefeller in February 1996 to President Clinton's Assistant for Science and Technology. "I do believe that the evidence presented indicates that this subject merits serious scientific study."

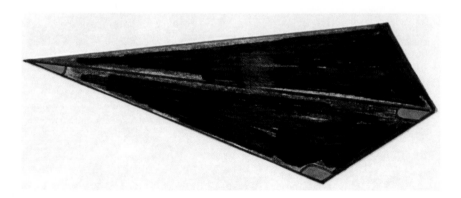

A sketch by Edward Bradley of the craft that passed over a suburb of Birmingham, U.K., at 20:30 on March 28, 2002. "It was a huge craft and very, very low indeed," he told the author. "Lengthwise I would have to say it would have fit comfortably into a reasonably-sized football ground. It was very close to the tops of the houses in the street. . . . There wasn't a soul about in the street at all, and no one to speak to or say, 'Did you see that?'" *(Edward Bradley)*

Kirsan Ilyumzhinov, former president of the southwestern Russian region of Kalmykia and current president of the World Chess Federation (as of April 2013), who claims to have been taken on board an alien spacecraft during a business trip to Moscow in September 1997. "They are people like us," he told a journalist. "I talked with them. I understood that we are not alone—we are not unique."

This painting depicts a huge craft—estimated at some 300 feet in length and width—encountered by a musician in the small hours of October 2, 2004, driving on a rural road in Bristol, Tennessee. As the object passed over him at about 100 feet, his skin burned and tingled. "He also noted that the sound seemed to [permeate] throughout his body," said MUFON Tennessee state section director Kim Shaffer. The witness awoke the next day suffering from serious medical symptoms. *(James Neff)*

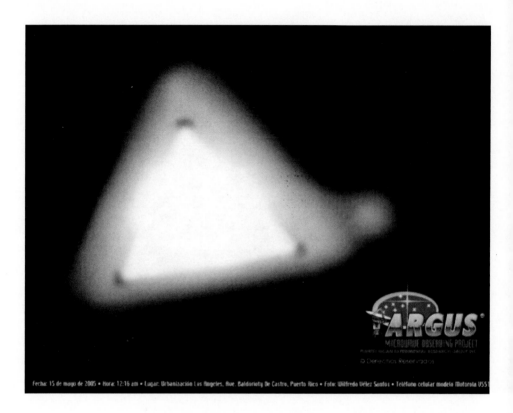

Fecha: 15 de mayo de 2005 • Hora: 12:16 am • Lugar: Urbanización Los Ángeles, Ave. Baldorioty De Castro, Puerto Rico • Foto: Wilfredo Vélez Santos • Teléfono celular modelo Motorola V551

A large triangular craft photographed by one of the witnesses near Luis Muñoz Marín International Airport, San Juan, Puerto Rico, on the night of May 15, 2005. The witness later experienced adverse physical symptoms, though he recovered. Two years later he and other witnesses encountered the same or similar craft on several occasions, twice during flights in American Eagle airliners. *(© Argus)*

A sketch by Finian Handley of the black triangular craft he and a passenger in his taxi observed while driving through Whitchurch, a few miles from Monmouth, Wales, on the night of September 26, 2008. The triangles were only a meter or two apart. Later that night, now alone in his cab, he saw two "orbs" hovering just above the trees in Chippenham Park, Monmouth, which "transformed" into triangles. *(Finian Handley)*

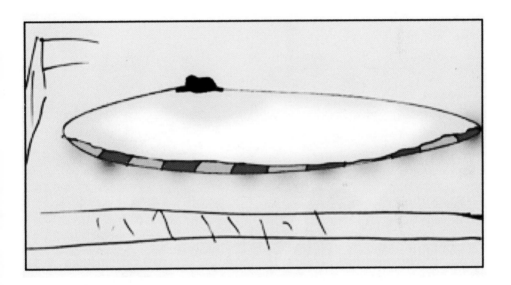

OPPOSITE AND THIS PAGE: Roy Shaw and his border collie dog, who were terrified by a 100-foot-long craft with flashing red and blue lights around the edge which landed in Phear Park, Exmouth, Devon, on the night of February 6, 2010. When a "white shape" came toward them, they bolted for home. Another man walking his dog also saw the object. *(Simon Horn/Exmouth Journal)*

Russian Prime Minister Dmitry Medvedev (left) with President Vladimir Putin. Following a television interview on December 7, 2012, a journalist interviewed Medvedev, supposedly off the air. At one point the prime minister was asked if the president had been handed secret files on aliens when receiving the briefcase needed to activate Russia's nuclear arsenal. "Along with the briefcase with nuclear codes," responded Medvedev—apparently seriously—"the president is given a special top-secret folder [which] in its entirety contains information about aliens who [have] visited our planet [and] a report of the absolutely secret special service that exercises control over aliens on the territory of our country. . . . I will not tell you how many of them are among us because it may cause panic."

During Easter 1968, Jim read an article in a special edition section of the *Orlando Sentinel* entitled "UFO tracks Minuteman Missile over Cape Canaveral," written by Dick Young. Unfortunately he lost track of the newspaper. Several years later he researched microfilm at both the *Sentinel* and Orlando Public Libraries' system main branch. The newspaper was intact, with the exception of the special edition—of course.[8]

In 1968, further sightings occurred in the same general vicinity. On February 17, Jim approached an intense flashing blue light which appeared to be reflecting off the metallic surface of a disc, as well as "patches of a deep glowing red." He then perceived "an aerodynamic structured craft perhaps fifty to sixty feet end to end, with each end tapered down and expanded to fifteen to twenty feet in height at its center.

"It had not occurred to me at the time that the glowing red that encircled the strange-looking sleek object might have been a 'force-field.' As I stood there just staring at the glowing aura, the hair on the back of my head literally stood on end. While the adrenaline soared through my body, I pivoted my body around and tried to walk away from the remote probe and the unknown ship, but I could not bring myself to take another step, [though shortly] I managed to force one foot in front of the other and made my way back to the car with considerable effort."

It was now a little over half an hour since Jim first observed the craft. On his way home along State Road 420, he caught sight of a glowing red cigar-shaped object as it floated up from a field and glided alongside the car, paused, tilted upward, then vanished into the sky.[9]

At sundown the following day, Jim's brother Gary showed up at the former's residence in Orlando, and the two drove off in Jim's car to the corner of State Road 420 and Fort Christmas Road, in search of more strange craft. "We stood there for several minutes, and the FBL appeared in the same location as it had done the previous night—the flashing light reflected off the dark metallic surface," Jim reported. "I pointed it out to my brother—no response. He just stood there staring at the blue light as it dropped silently below the dark tree line deep into the field and west of our location.

"I approached the fence, as I had the previous night, and climbed over, my brother close behind me. I began walking in the direction where the 'small wonder disc' had just disappeared below the dark topography. Moreover, like the previous night, while relentless howling winds whipped across the field and rattled the clusters of saw palmettos, I ventured a short distance and paused, [with] the same feeling I had the previous night. . . . We were being watched. My brother must have sensed something too, because he seemed ready to bolt." The men returned to the car and headed for home.[10]

At around 19:35 the next day, Jim returned to the same observation post. As he passed by Lake Louise and rounded a curve, the same, or similar, flashing blue light hovered about two hundred feet ahead, then paced the car along Fort Christmas Road for a mile or so. Just over a week later, as he arrived at the same observation point and at the same time as previously, fifteen to twenty cattle were bellowing and running around, terrified, as a blue pulsing light hovered above. The light vanished, and moments later a jet flew fast and low over the area, then made another pass before heading away.[11]

On March 4, 1968, about two hundred yards southeast of the previous area, a B-52 bomber appeared above the tree line. As it headed west, a brilliant flash of light emitted from its underside, illuminating the terrain below. "The bright cone-shaped lights flashed twelve times in three-sequence increments," Jim believes. Presumably, photographs were being taken.

The following night, at the same location, a car driven by a man with a woman beside him pulled up alongside Jim. The man asked Jim what he was doing out there. "Do you believe in flying saucers?" retorted Jim. The woman snickered, but the man sat there silently. "I pointed in the general area where I had watched a B-52 rise above the tree line over there [pointing], and I thought the crew had taken pictures of something on the ground. . . ."

"The area you're talking about is the Canada Ranch, where I live," the man volunteered. "I'm Ben Canada." And at that moment, the Air Force B-52 appeared again above the tree line. Again, brilliant flashes of light illuminated the ground in the same sequence.

Jim asked Canada if he'd been missing any cattle recently. "Come to think of it," he responded, "last week I found a young heifer, a healthy animal, standing out in the middle of the pasture. How she managed to get out of the high, well-built pen that I had her in that night was beyond my comprehension." He added that large numbers of animals had recently been unaccounted for, and that many farmers and ranchers from the area and the St. Cloud area had had meetings with the Cattlemen's Association to try and solve the problem, without success.[12]

On the evening of March 20, 1968, Jim felt compelled to go outside— "drawn" to the front of his mobile home. A disc, roughly two feet in diameter, was hovering outside the living room windows.

"A flashing blue light emitted from a thin rod atop the disc, perhaps an eighth of an inch in circumference, two or three inches long, and positioned near the outer edge of the probe. The blue light pulsed at a slow steady rhythmic rate, and the flashing rate reflected off the disc's dull burnished metallic surface. . . . Suddenly, the disc shot away and out of sight [and then] reappeared to the right of the cypress trees behind the trailer and headed in a northeast direction until I lost sight of it."[13]

Six days later, while visiting his parents in Orlando, Jim was struck suddenly with a bad headache and a simultaneous compulsion to leave the house. He got in his car, heading for a 7-Eleven store to get some pain-killers. On returning to the car, he heard his full name called out, loud and clear—in similar vein to the communications reported by Carl Anderson (Chapter 7).

"A case could be made that I was 'hearing voices,' the skeptic might say," Jim acknowledges, "but I know the difference between hearing voices in my head and having my name come through in a clear audible tone. . . . I headed east on Virginia Avenue, all the while wondering what was going on, [then] realized the headache had stopped. Moments later, I rolled to a stop at the Bumby Avenue and East Colonial Drive intersection [and] felt compelled to look out the window and up. The remote disc hovered above the traffic signal, its signature blue light flashing with a steady rhythm. I turned right and twenty minutes later turned left onto State Road 419 [and] spotted the disc as it glided along above the field [and] began moving slowly until it disappeared into the stand of trees that it had vanished into on March 18."[14]

One of the most interesting events occurred during the night of September 15 that year. Jim, together with his mother Naomi, niece Michelle, and Bendix electrician Larry Kelly and a friend, were standing by the big metal gate at the usual observation post when an amber cone-shaped beam of light appeared a hundred feet above the orange grove. "I proceeded to run as fast as I could through the sandy open lane that extended north through the middle of the grove," said Jim. "Moments later, Larry and his friend had caught up with me. I took off, running west over the white sandy trail. . . . Suddenly, I stumbled headlong into a pile of cast-off tree debris, [followed by] Larry and his friend."

By now, Jim's eyes had adjusted to the darkness. Fifteen yards away could be seen the faint outline of a cigar-shaped craft which "blended almost seamlessly into the dark terrain. Faint phosphor-green patches of light flickered and danced around the ship's midsection." An eerie stillness permeated the immediate surroundings and a "strange energy" seemed to emanate from the hovering craft. "I was ready to bolt—then vehicle headlights unexpectedly illuminated the darkness." The dark blue or black vehicle headed toward the craft.

"I turned and ran as fast as I could toward the big gate. I could hear Larry and his friend right behind me running as fast as they could to keep up with me and put as much distance behind them and what they too had observed. . . . My mom and niece obviously sensed that something was not right and both headed for their car."

Jim speculates that the dark sedan driver was most likely a government, military, or NASA official sent to rendezvous with the spacecraft in "a sparsely populated nondescript dot on the map named Bithlo. . . . During the Apollo program, the ETI [extra-terrestrial intelligence] took full advantage of the perfect meeting place, situated between the back end of fenced-in orange groves, with 'No Trespassing' signs and near the shoreline of a pristine kidney-shaped body of water named Lake Pickett. . . . After each meeting, the human officials and ET emissary/emissaries had exited the open wire gate west of the main gate, turned right, driven several miles, intersected with Highway 50, another left turn, and from there proceeded to their destination—the Cape and/or Kennedy Space Center. . . .

"Whatever 'agreements' have been made between the extraterrestrial intelligence and United States Government and NASA officials, we may never know. The fact that 'agreements' did take place is known, and surely the extraterrestrials waited and watched from a distance as the historic lunar event unfolded on July 20, 1969, as Neil Alden Armstrong and Edwin Eugene Aldrin, Jr. became the first humans to land on the Moon. . . ."[15]

APOLLO 11

In *Apollo 11: The Untold Story*, a British documentary first shown in July 2006, "Buzz" Aldrin revealed that their spacecraft had encountered a UFO during its flight to the Moon. "There was something out there that was close enough to be observed, and what could it be?" he began. "Mike [Collins] decided he thought he could see it in the telescope [and] when you made it real sharp it was sort of bell-shaped. . . .

"Obviously the three of us were not going to blurt out, 'Hey, Houston, we've got something moving alongside of us. . . . Can you tell us what it is?' We weren't about to do that, because we knew that those transmissions would be heard by all sorts of people and, who knows, somebody would have demanded we turn back because of aliens, or whatever the reason. . . ." The event remains unexplained, as confirmed by Dr. David Baker, Apollo 11 Senior Scientist.[16]

I happened to be touring the USA with the London Symphony Orchestra at the time and, together with my colleagues, sat spellbound as we watched the live transmission in Chicago. I recall hearing one of the astronauts refer at some point to a "light" in or near a crater during the transmission. According to an Associated Press report, the astronauts sighted strange lights inside a crater near the point where their lunar lander was due to touch down the next day. On their first orbit around the Moon, Armstrong described a mysterious bright light on the inner wall of the crater Aristarchus, located north of their flight path. "It seems to have a slight amount of fluorescence to it. The area in the crater is quite bright," he reported to Houston. "That area is definitely brighter than anything else I can see," confirmed Aldrin. "There doesn't appear to be any color involved in it. It looks like an eerie sight [site?]."[17]

Two former NASA employees, Otto Binder and Maurice Chatelain (the latter a former chief of NASA communication systems), confirmed that Apollo 11 encountered "other" landed spacecraft on the Moon.

"These babies are huge, sir . . . enormous," Mission Control was informed by the astronauts, according to Binder's sources. "Oh, God, you wouldn't believe it! I'm telling you there are other spacecraft out there . . . lined up on the far side of the crater edge."[18]

The Soviets were the first to publicly confirm the incident. Physicist Dr. Vladimir Azhazha, a professor of mathematics at Moscow University, stated that Neil Armstrong relayed a message to Mission Control that "two large, mysterious objects were watching them after having landed near the lunar module." This and related messages were censored by NASA. Another Soviet scientist, Dr. Aleksandr Kazentsev, claimed that Buzz Aldrin had taken color movie film of the spacecraft from inside the module, and continued filming them after he and Armstrong went outside. The alien craft departed shortly thereafter.[19]

All the original Apollo film material is located in NASA's Film Archive (Building 8), located in the Johnson Space Center (JSC), Houston. In 1970–71, Donna Hare worked for Philco-Ford, a NASA contractor, in the photo lab at Building 8 and in different areas of the company, both on- and off-site. On one occasion, she told Steven Greer's Disclosure Project, she entered a restricted area of the lab (she held a Secret clearance) unrelated to her work with Philco-Ford. A friend there directed her attention to a mosaic of photographs taken from a high altitude—possibly via satellite.

"In one of the photo panels I saw a round white dot," she related. "And I said to him, 'What is that—a dot on the emulsion?' And then he's grinning and says that dots on the emulsion don't leave shadows on the ground. And there was a round shadow at the correct angle with the sun shining on the trees. . . . I was pretty startled because I had worked out there several years and had never seen anything like this. And I said, 'Is this a UFO?' And he's smiling at me and says, 'I can't tell you that.'"

The man told her that photos of such objects were always airbrushed out prior to being distributed publicly.

From another employee at JSC, Donna Hare learned that some of the astronauts who wanted to talk about their experiences with UFOs had been threatened and coerced into signing statements agreeing not to do so, on penalty of losing their retirement pay. "One gentleman that I knew very well was in quarantine with the [Apollo] astronauts [following their return from the Moon]. He said that just about every one of them had seen things when they went to the Moon. In fact, one said that craft were on the Moon at the time of the landing [Apollo 11?]."

Hare also met a security guard who claimed that one day some soldiers in fatigues had ordered him to "burn a lot of UFO pictures." Although forced not to look at them, he was tempted to glance at one, showing a UFO on the ground. "Shortly thereafter," Hare reports, "he was hit on the head with a gun butt, and he still had the scar on his forehead."[20]

In *Inside the Space Ships*, George Adamski describes his second flight in a spaceship in 1953, during which he was shown parts of the Moon. "In some of these places, there was still a very small growth of vegetation perceptible," he commented. "Part of the surface looked fine and powdery. . . ." [21] Which is precisely how Neil Armstrong described it during his first steps on the Moon in July 1969: "The surface is fine and powdery."

During another flight to the Moon, in August 1954, Adamski was shown (through a viewing screen) parts of the other side, featuring a temperate section which included a number of thickly timbered mountains, as well as lakes, rivers, vegetation, and even a city.[22] Though these claims were ridiculed at the time, photographs of the other side taken by Apollo 8 and 10, for example, clearly show what looks like moss, or vegetation of some sort. I purchased a large print from Hasselblad of the Schmidt crater (taken from Apollo 10) which displays a pronounced dark green surrounding the crater—itself a mixture of white, fawn, and pink colored areas.

In *Above Top Secret*, I cited the testimony of a friend of mine who had participated in a NASA conference in Italy in June 1984, during which she learned from Neil Armstrong that "other" spacecraft were on the Moon when they landed. At the time, I was not permitted to include either the name of my source nor many other details. However, since she passed away a number of years ago, I am now able to do so.

My source was Pamela Handford, who had served with Britain's Secret Intelligence Service (MI6). I once asked about her background in the clandestine organization. "Bearing in mind that I am still firmly bound by the Official Secrets Act," she explained, "all I can tell you is that I trained with the School of Military Intelligence, in those days at Maresfield Park, and did my parachute training with the London 21st. I was trained for the

Russian front, learned Russian, and came under MI6's umbrella. Because of the sensitivity of the field work, I can tell you nothing more. . . ."[23]

The NASA conference was held at several venues, including the old castle Maschio Angioino in Naples and the Europa Palace Hotel in Anacapri. Some astronauts attending were staying at the Vittoria Excelsior Hotel in Sorrento, Pamela said. Her impromptu presentation was entitled "Man: An Extraterrestrial Experiment."

"It was only a very short stop-gap, and I probably scribbled the gist of it on a piece of hotel writing-paper," she explained. It so happened that Pamela's suite (Room 131) adjoined that of Neil Armstrong (Room 132). At one point during the conference, Pamela overheard a conversation in the next room between Armstrong and a Professor Herbert Schwartz, the gist of which went as follows:

SCHWARTZ: What really happened out there with Apollo 11?

ARMSTRONG: It was incredible—of course we had always known there was a possibility—the fact is, Herb, we were warned off. There was never any question of our building a space station or a Moon city.

SCHWARTZ: How do you mean, "warned off"?

ARMSTRONG: I can't go into details, except to say that their ships were far superior to ours, both in size and technology. Boy, were they big—and menacing. No, there is no question of a space station.

SCHWARTZ: But NASA had other missions after Apollo 11.

ARMSTRONG: Naturally, NASA was committed at that time and couldn't risk a panic on Earth. But it really was a quick trip and back again. . . .

At a cocktail party later that day, Pamela confronted Armstrong. He confirmed that the story was true but refused to go into further detail, beyond admitting that the Central Intelligence Agency was behind the cover-up. Officially, however, he denies the incident. "There were no objects reported, found, or seen on Apollo 11 or any other Apollo flight other than of natural origin," he told me.[24]

In 1995, I asked Pamela if she still stood by her claim. "Yes, Tim," she replied, "I still stand by the Armstrong report. Like Martin Luther, 'I can do no other,' perfectly placed as I was in the next suite—and in the light of the cover-up the United States still has in place, it surprises me not that Neil Armstrong denies it."

Pamela added that, according to her information, since the early 1960s "the States has had contact with a superior extra-terrestrial planet."[25]

I made four requests to NASA for details of this conference. The first person with whom I communicated politely explained that she had been unsuccessful in accessing any information. No replies were forthcoming from my additional three requests (via a different NASA inquiries Web site). However, my girlfriend tracked down online the proof that a conference had taken place. The Journal of Space Law for the relevant period reviews the "International Symposium on Space Lab held in Naples and Capri from 11–16 June 1984," noting that "The Second Forum was held in the Europe Palace Hotel in beautiful Anacapri and dealt with the utilization and the legal/economic aspects of space systems." Unfortunately, other than mentioning the participation of the European Space Agency (ESA) and NASA, none of the contributors is listed.[26]

Thus forearmed, I sent a Freedom of Information Act request asking NASA for details of the speakers. They eventually responded by citing several library sources, one being the Canada Institute for Scientific & Technical Information, from which I purchased a copy of "Earth-oriented Applications of Space Technology," listing many of the attendees at the Second Forum only.[27] No mention is made of Buzz Aldrin, Neil Armstrong, Professor Herbert Schwartz, or Pamela Handford.

SPACE DEFENSE

According to Lieutenant Colonel Philip J. Corso, the intelligence officer who headed the U.S. Army's Foreign Technology Division at the Pentagon, in 1961 NASA "agreed to cooperate with military planners to work a 'second-tier' space program [which was] covered up by the civilian scientific missions. They agreed to open up a confidential 'back-channel' communications link to military intelligence regarding any hostile activities conducted by the [aliens] against our spacecraft. . . .

"What NASA didn't tell military intelligence, of course, was that they already had an even more classified back channel to [former CIA director] Hillenkoetter's working group and were keeping them updated on every single alien spacecraft appearance the astronauts reported, especially during the early series of Apollo flights when the [alien] craft began buzzing the lunar modules on successive missions after they thrusted out of earth orbit. Even though military intelligence was kept out of the operational loop between NASA and the working group, I and a few others still had contacts in the civilian intelligence community that kept us informed. And the Army and Air Force managed to find at least 122 photos taken by astronauts on the moon that showed some evidence of an alien presence. It was a startling find and was one of many reasons that the Reagan administration pushed so hard for the Space Defense Initiative in 1981."[28]

The Hon. Paul Hellyer, former Canadian Minister of Defence under Prime Minister Lester Pearson and Deputy Prime Minister under Pierre Trudeau, found Corso's book so compelling that he decided to check its credibility with a retired American general. "Every word of it is true, and more," responded the general. "We then spent twenty minutes discussing the 'and more,' to the extent that he could without revealing classified material," Hellyer confirms in his latest book. "He told me that there had been, in fact, face-to-face discussions between the visitors and U.S. officials. . . ."[29]

In 2004, President George W. Bush announced his "Vision for Space Exploration," calling for humans to return to the Moon by the end of the next decade.[30] The plan was canceled in 2010 by President Barack Obama, citing cost and danger.[31]

In 2006, the Bush administration stated its intention to dominate space, rejecting any new treaties that would limit the United States' extraterrestrial activities, warning that it would oppose any nations that tried to get in its way. A policy statement signed by Bush asserted that, in its own national interests, the U.S. had the right to conduct whatever research, development, and "other activities" in space were deemed necessary. As journalist Andrew

Buncombe commented, "When proposals to ban the weaponization of space have been put forward at the [United Nations], the United States has routinely abstained. But last October [2005], the U.S. voted against a U.N. resolution calling for the banning of weapons in space."[32]

GORDON COOPER

In early 1978, NASA issued an information sheet by way of response to inquiries directed to the White House as well as NASA on UFOs. "NASA is the focal point for answering public inquiries to the White House," it begins. "NASA is not engaged in a research program involving these phenomena, nor is any other government agency. Reports of unidentified objects entering United States air space are of interest to the military as a regular part of defense surveillance. Beyond that, the U.S. Air Force no longer investigates reports of UFO sightings."[33]

In his autobiography *Leap of Faith*, astronaut Gordon Cooper describes the landing of a flying disc at Edwards Air Force Base on May 3, 1957. At the time, Cooper was assigned as test pilot and manager, with top-secret clearance, to the Fighter Section, Experimental Flight Test Engineering Division, and he recounts that his camera crew came running in to tell him what had just occurred:

"They told me they had just finished their work when the saucer flew over them, hovered over the ground, extended three landing gears, then set down about fifty yards away. They described the saucer as metallic silver in color and shaped somewhat like an inverted plate. . . . They said they had shot images with 35-mm and 4-by-5 still cameras, as well as motion picture film. When they had tried to approach the saucer to get a closer shot, they said it lifted up, retracted its gear, and climbed straight out of sight at a rapid rate of speed—again with no sound. They estimated the craft to be about thirty feet across. . . ."[34]

On July 14, 1978, Cooper attended a meeting of the Special Political Committee, United Nations General Assembly, in Miami, chaired by Secretary-General Kurt Waldheim, specifically to discuss the UFO question, following repeated requests by Sir Eric Gairy, Prime Minister of Grenada, for a full debate. Later that year, Cooper wrote a letter to Ambassador Griffith, Mission of Grenada to the U.N., setting out his position, prior to the debate, which was held in the General Assembly on November 27 that year:

"I believe that these extra-terrestrial vehicles and their crews are visiting this planet from other planets, which obviously are a little more technically advanced than we are here on earth. I feel that we need to have a top-level, coordinated program to scientifically collect and analyze data from all over the earth [and] to determine how best to interface with these visitors in a friendly fashion. . . . I have not yet had the privilege of flying a UFO, nor of meeting the crew of one."

He went on to add that, while serving with the Air Force in Germany in 1951, he had "two days of observations of many flights of them, of different sizes, flying in fighter formation . . . over Europe. They were at a higher altitude than we could reach with our jet fighters of that time." In referring to astronauts, Cooper revealed that "There are several of us who do believe in UFOs and who have had occasion to see a UFO on the ground, or from an airplane. There was only one occasion from space which may have been a UFO."[35]

Gordon Cooper was more forthcoming in a recorded interview in New York five years earlier. "I myself have encountered some of their craft while flying in space," he told a reporter. "NASA knows this and the American government knows it too. Yet they continue to keep their silence, probably in order to avoid confusing the public." He went on:

"For many years I have lived with a secret, in a secrecy imposed on all specialists in astronautics. I can now reveal that every day, in the USA, our radars capture objects of a form and composition unknown to us. . . . I was furthermore a witness to an extraordinary phenomenon [that] happened a few months ago in Florida. I saw with my own eyes a defined area of ground being consumed by fire with four indentations left by a [craft] which had descended in the middle of a field. Beings had left the craft—there were other traces to prove this. They seemed to have studied the topography; they had collected soil fragments and eventually returned to wherever they had come from, disappearing with enormous speed. I happen to know that the authorities did just about everything to keep this incident from the press and TV. . . .

"Flying saucers are a reality—I won't stop repeating this," Cooper concluded. "The public must be prepared to make contact with people who, sooner or later, will be compelled to interfere. The salvation of us all depends on it."[36] During my correspondence with Cooper, he neither confirmed nor denied the statements contained in this interview.

I am intrigued by Cooper's remark in his letter to Ambassador Griffith: "I have not yet had the privilege of flying a UFO." A few years ago, a respected colleague informed me that, following the U.N. meetings, Cooper had vented his frustration at the seemingly invincible task of convincing U.N. delegates of alien reality. What would it take, he said to the researcher—a landed flying saucer? He went on to claim that he had been in a position to actually pilot a flying disc and land it himself. An outrageous claim to be sure. Yet from a few other reliable sources I have learned that a number of astronauts and pilots—not exclusively in the United States—have flown alien and/or replicated alien vehicles, as we shall learn later.

COSMIC JOURNEY

In *Alien Contact*, I discussed at length the official plan by the U.S. government, NASA, Rockwell International, and other organizations for a space-related traveling exhibition, to include five to six thousand square feet of UFO-related materials. A synopsis is warranted here.

In 1989 I had been approached by Robert Kirchgessner, director of a special group associated with Ringling Brothers and Barnum and Bailey International, who had invited me to become the "Official Consultant on UFO Research" to the Special Development Group. A personal meeting in Orlando, Florida, was a prerequisite. We agreed on a date—October 12. However, although I was on a research trip in Gulf Breeze, Florida, at the time, difficulties with airline schedules arose and to my everlasting regret—as it transpired—I was obliged to cancel the appointment.

On my return to the U.K., Kirchgessner explained that the project had reached a critical stage. Could I recommend someone else? I didn't hesitate to name my friend Bob Oechsler (pronounced "X-ler"), a former NASA engineer who had worked on the Space Shuttle arm at the Goddard Space Flight Center in Greenbelt, Maryland. As it transpired, the Cosmic Journey exhibition was to include a mock-up of the shuttle. Perhaps also owing to his background in the Air Force, Bob turned out to be the right man for the job: he had joined in 1968, serving mostly with the American Forces

Radio and Television Service in the continental United States. During the Vietnam War he served in Cambodia, Laos, and Thailand, during which period some of his work required top-secret clearance, when each month he was flown by helicopter into the demilitarized zone (DMZ) to film classified prototype weapons systems. On returning to the U.S., he spent a year and a half at Wright-Patterson AFB.

Bob's meetings with the Special Development Group took place in Orlando on November 1 and 2, 1989. After signing a non-disclosure agreement, he was briefed on the project. "Cosmic Journey," as it was called, would be a review of, and a future look at, the space programs of the United States and the Soviet Union. The board of advisers included former astronauts Alan Bean, Eugene Cernan, Charles Conrad, Alexei Leonov, and Thomas Stafford. The project had the approval of President George Bush, Vice President Dan Quayle, and the National Space Council. The latter was chaired by the vice president and included the Director of Central Intelligence, the Secretary of State, and the Secretary of Defense.

With the co-operation of NASA and Rockwell International, the exhibition was to include a full-scale mock-up of the Shuttle, a 15,000-square-foot "space camp," representations of alien life-forms, and, I was told, a "post-show exhibit of five or six thousand square feet on UFOs." Additionally, the program was to involve a tri-level educational curriculum for twenty-five thousand schools in the United States, due to commence on New Year's Day 1990.[37]

On November 13, 1989, Bob reported to the Pentagon for a meeting with Thomas P. Stafford, Lieutenant General, USAF (Ret.). A former fighter pilot (who flew F-86D Sabre jets among others), he later became an astronaut, piloting Gemini VI for the first rendezvous in space and commanding Gemini IX. He was also the commander of Apollo 10 in May 1969, the first flight of the lunar module, performing the first rendezvous around the Moon and the entire lunar landing mission, apart from the actual landing itself. He logged his fourth space flight as Apollo commander of the Apollo-Soyuz Test Project mission, July 15–24, 1975, a joint space flight culminating in the historic first meeting in space between American astronauts and Soviet cosmonauts.[38]

Stafford turned out to be the intelligence community contact for Cosmic Journey. Following some bizarre sensations generated by an unusual type of detector at the security check, Bob proceeded to the general's office, accompanied by a guard. Stafford discussed exhibits for the project, asking Bob where he planned to obtain material for the kiosks to show UFO case histories and photographs. Stafford indicated that NASA and the CIA's National Photographic Interpretation Center (NPIC) would be good places to start.

"One of the more intriguing elements of the discussion," Bob told me, "involved an exhibit showing an alien/ET corpse.

"As a reference, the general showed me an eight-by-ten-inch color photo of what appeared to be an alien in a cryogenic tank; a space-age-looking coffin with blue tube lighting inside the clear lexan cover. . . . It was difficult to see too much in the way of detail, so it's virtually impossible to know if this was real, and the general didn't enlighten me. . . . It looked like one of the so-called 'gray' types, but the chin was much more sharply pointed than is usually described. I could see evidence of the 'bug' eyes, but there was a sort of covering over them. . . ."

The general seemed to be concerned about using the real thing versus a mock-up, querying Bob about his thoughts on public perception. Bob suggested that displaying a companion autopsy report with color photographs might lend credibility. The possible exhibition of an actual alien corpse was proposed quite seriously. "As a matter of fact," Bob added, "I got the impression they had a lot of bodies to choose from! The general also had the same concerns about showing a real, versus a mock-up, craft, [and] I suggested that the real thing would be preferable if on-board access for the public could be achieved.

"The other primary areas of discussion involved my robotics experience and the minor role that I had played in the development of the space shuttle arm, which was initially designed to provide life support to astronauts and a diagnostic instrument for repairing satellites in orbit."[39]

Bob had expected further contact with General Stafford, but none was forthcoming, probably related to the fact that funds for the project apparently stalled. In late 1996, I invited Stafford and his wife Linda to drinks and dinner at his hotel in London. It was a great privilege listening to this modest pioneer as he answered my questions about the flight to the Moon in Apollo 10 in May 1969. Naturally, at one point during the meal, I asked about Bob Oechsler's claim to have met him in the Pentagon back in 1991. "Bob *who*?" he expostulated. He denied having met him or even having had an office in the Pentagon at that time.[40]

For a while, I believed Stafford. However, a combination of several circumstances, including Bob's unwavering insistence that he had indeed been invited for a meeting with Stafford in the Pentagon, caused me to change my mind.

During the second week of January 1990, Bob was billeted at NASA Ellington Field (also known as Ellington Air Force Base), near the Johnson Space Center in Houston, where he was asked to assist in reconfiguring the movements of the shuttle arm from a zero-gravity environment to that of ordinary gravity, according to the project's requirements. But first, he told me, he was required to become accustomed to how it worked in "microgravity." Together with some astronauts and engineers, he was flown by helicopter to a NASA facility about twenty miles southwest of Ellington, where he changed into special clothing in preparation for entry into another room. He stepped through a hatch into this other room—and became airborne!

"It was weird, because it's like the loss of equilibrium and everything," he explained. "Obviously the astronauts had done a lot of training; they were so accustomed to it, and they were laughing at me. . . . You learn to skip around [and] it takes about fifteen minutes to become accustomed to the biomechanics [and] feels almost similar to getting into a pool of water—the arms tend to swing out."

No more than about eight astronauts or engineers worked on a variety of projects in the chamber at any one time, Bob told me. The chamber measured about thirty feet long, twenty feet wide, and nine feet high. Recessed in the ceiling was a strange, plasma-like light, which Bob felt was responsible for generating microgravity. Everyone was wearing the same clothing. "Several of the others I knew, but they really wouldn't let us talk among ourselves. It was pretty much forbidden to talk about anything that had to do with what we were doing."

In January 1990, Bob was invited to visit a North American Aerospace Defense Command (NORAD) installation in the Gulf of Mexico. He traveled in one of three sleek, black NORAD helicopters. "You couldn't see where the door was until it popped open," he said. The helicopter was relatively quiet, sounding "more like a humming noise." Bob believes that a highly advanced type of propulsion was being utilized, possibly deriving from alien technology. In any event, the over-500-mile flight lasted amazingly no more than forty-five minutes, a speed well in excess of that of the world's officially fastest helicopter, the Sikorsky X2, which in 2010 reached the unofficial speed record of 288 miles per hour in level flight. The X2 is known as a "compound" helicopter: in addition to two four-blade main rotors set one above the other, it also features a "propulsor"—a six-blade propeller that produces forward thrust.[41]

Of related interest, in a 2002/2003 Discovery Wings Channel program on the future development of the U.S. Army's Boeing/Sikorsky RAH-66 Comanche helicopter, former Director of Army Acquisition Bud Foster revealed: "I think Comanche will be flying in 2050. In my opinion it is the last pure helicopter the Army will ever develop. We may be into antigravity machines after Comanche."

The black helicopter landed on what looked like an oil-rig platform, possibly twenty miles south of Pensacola, Florida. It turned out to be a NORAD facility. Bob was taken to a control room with consoles and a huge screen, the latter seemingly with a three-dimensional quality and displaying about a third or fourth of the southeast quadrant of the United States. "It had altitude to it as well, and the entire area was covered with a grid that was moving," added Bob. At one point, a series of "blips" moved across the top part of the screen:

"There were five, as I recall [and] they were labeled, like a typical radar screen where blips usually designate aircraft . . . these particular ones that were up top were all labeled ASC. They didn't have any specific numbers—just ASC. I overheard someone say, 'Alternative Space Craft.' And they came down and spread out—all five of them. Two immediately went off the screen to the northwest and one came around the Gulf 'horn' . . . almost as if they were following the shoreline. There was one—possibly two, I forget—that stopped what looked like just across the border of Florida into Georgia [and] as soon as it stopped, it glowed; there was like a red glow that came off of it. I don't know what that meant. . . ."

After about 45 minutes at the NORAD facility, Bob and the others were flown back to Ellington.[42]

Plans for the Cosmic Journey exhibition were temporarily shelved in early 1990, ostensibly for budgetary reasons. And the project directors denied that they ever had any plans to exhibit anything other than mock-ups of aliens or flying saucers. They also denied that Bob Oechsler was ever employed as a consultant. NASA, too, denied that Bob had visited the places he said he went to.

On June 5, 1991, I had a brief meeting with astrophysicist Colonel (later Brigadier General) Simon "Pete" Worden, at that time Director, Advanced Concepts, Science and Technology, National Space Council (NSC), Executive Office of the President. The meeting took place in the NSC offices at the Old Executive Office Building (now the Eisenhower Executive Office Building) adjoining the White House. I asked Worden if he knew anything about the fate of the Cosmic Journey project, and if he was aware of any plans to include "extraterrestrial hardware" in the exhibition. He replied that he knew of no such plans, and that the exhibition had been canceled owing to the Spanish government's withdrawal of its financial support. He promised to keep me informed if he learned anything more. I did not hear from him again.

In February 1992, I wrote to Vice President Dan Quayle (Chairman of the NSC), seeking information on the status of the project, alluding to the alleged plans to feature an extraterrestrial body and/or craft. I received a reply from Jack Schmidt, NASA Exhibits Coordinator. "There were plans to have the exhibition at Expo '92," he wrote, "but negotiations between Feld Productions, Inc. and a group of Spanish investors were not successful. At that point further development of the exhibition was terminated. . . ."[43]

A CLANDESTINE SPACE PROGRAM

In October 2010, Simon Worden—as Director, NASA Ames—revealed a joint project with DARPA (Defense Advanced Research Projects Agency) called the Hundred Year Starship. "The human space program is now really aimed at settling other worlds," he explained. "Twenty years ago you had to whisper that in dark bars and get fired." He went on to mention some nearer-term projects that NASA is exploring, not necessarily related to the Starship program, one of which was "electric propulsion."

"Anybody that watches the Star Trek Enterprise, you know you don't see huge plumes of fire," Worden added. "Within a few years we will see the first true prototype of a spaceship that will take us between worlds. . . ."[44] But as Lockheed Skunk Works genius Ben Rich had declared, during a lecture at the UCLA School of Engineering as far back as 1993: "We already have the means to travel among the stars."[45]

In the late 1980s, the Electric Propulsion Study was conducted by Science Applications International Corporation (SAIC), a leading U.S. civil and military R&D company, for the Astronautics Laboratory (later part of the Phillips Laboratory, currently merged into the Air Force Research Laboratory's Space Vehicles Directorate). The study's primary objective was to "outline physical methods to test theories of inductive coupling between electromagnetic and gravitational forces to determine the feasibility of such methods as they apply to space propulsion." In simplified terms—an antigravity propulsion system.[46]

In his ground-breaking book *Secrets of Antigravity Propulsion*, physicist Paul LaViolette recounts much information acquired from sources knowledgeable about Project Skyvault, a highly classified program set up in the early 1950s to develop exotic propulsion technology. One of these sources—"Tom"—stated that NASA is "essentially a public relations organization or a front that obscures U. S. Marine Corps space research." Tom had served with the Civil Air Patrol (CAP) and had been the recipient of the prestigious Michelson Award, as a result of which he was selected in 1963 to represent Idaho, together with CAP representatives from all the other states, to visit Chanute Air Force Base, Rantoul, Illinois. One day, about eight generals appeared onstage in an auditorium for a "no holds barred" question-and-answer session. A representative asked about U.S. Marine Corps Major Donald E. Keyhoe, who had been censored for his pioneering books on UFOs and outspoken comments in the media.

"One of the generals responded that they had a way of taking care of people who gave out a little too much information," LaViolette relates. "He said they would use physical injury or whatever was necessary to make them shut up, indicating they would kill a person ('extreme prejudice,' if you will). Someone else started to ask more about UFOs. . . .

"One of the generals said the United States had a defense system in place at the time that consisted of a number of satellites, in orbit not only around Earth, but also around Mercury, Venus, Mars, and a few other, more distant planets they couldn't talk about. He said the satellites together functioned as an early warning system, that they were afraid of the 'people out there' because they didn't know very much about them. This satellite system was built to observe three possible sources: missiles that might come from the Soviet Union, missiles that might come from China, and intrusions of aliens coming in toward Earth.

"Someone asked why the generals were being so candid. According to Tom, one responded by saying, 'If you want, you can go ahead and tell people what we've told you, but they're not going to believe you. Besides, if you did get anyone to believe you and they came back to ask us, we would just deny it. So we have nothing to lose by telling you this.'[47]

"In the late 1950s NASA was formed to compartmentalize, containerize, and sanitize information from all space platforms and vehicles," claimed John Lear to Art Bell in 2003. "We sold NASA to the public, claiming that all information would belong to them, but they got very little, and even that was highly sanitized." He added:

"We set up operations in Pine Gap, Australia, to preclude any prying eyes figuring out what we were up to. We regularly 'eliminated with extreme prejudice' anybody who was part of the operation and made the least little tiny threat about disclosure or dissatisfaction with the operation. Any space mission that included Mercury, Gemini, Apollo, Mariner, Voyager, Clementine, and all the rest, all the data initially came transmitted to Pine Gap, then it was relayed to JPL or wherever, after sanitizing. We had a little trouble with amateur radio operators, but we figured out how they [were able] to intercept these signals [and] managed to deal with that."[48]

Paul LaViolette also learned from Tom about rumors indicating that the world's first satellite was launched, not by the Soviet Union in 1957, but by the United States in 1948, using a modified V-2 rocket. He also indicated that, independent of NASA, the U.S. Air Force has its own shuttle fleet, allegedly launched from Johnston Island AFB in the Pacific Ocean (717 nautical miles, or 823 statute miles, west-southwest of Honolulu). From 1976 to 1978, while working for the Air Force, Tom learned from a captain who had just returned from the island that the United States already had a base on the Moon. "The captain said that from looking at the cargo manifest for one of these shuttle launchings, one could conclude that provisions were routinely being shipped out," reports LaViolette. "This was several years after the Apollo program had been terminated, the last Apollo mission having been completed in December 1972."[49]

In this connection, President Ronald Reagan makes an intriguing observation in his diary entry for June 11, 1985: ". . . Lunch was with five top space scientists. It was fascinating. Space truly is the last frontier and some of the developments there in astronomy etc. are like science fiction except they are real. I learned that our shuttle capacity is such that we could orbit 300 people."[50]

The last space shuttle flight took place in July 2011. Meanwhile, according to an officially approved leak in November 2011, China intends to launch up to twenty spacecraft in the next ten years, at a cost of about $50 billion. Furthermore, it plans to build orbiting laboratory modules and a manned space station. "While the Chinese media and leaders speak with one voice about China's 'peaceful development in space,' the U.S. is not so sure," reports British journalist Michael Sheridan, adding that America "has no plans for manned space missions following the last space-shuttle flight."[51] Which is far from the truth.

In May 2012, the second demonstration mission for NASA's Commercial Orbital Transportation Services (COTS) program took place when Space Exploration Technologies (SpaceX) Falcon 9 rocket and Dragon spacecraft lifted off from Cape Canaveral Air Force Station. "Today marks the beginning of a new era in exploration," declared NASA Administrator Charles Bolden. "A private company has launched a spacecraft to the International Space Station [ISS] that will attempt to dock there for the first time. . . . Under President Obama's leadership, the nation is embarking upon an ambitious exploration program that will take us farther into space than we have ever traveled before."[52] Dragon successfully completed key on-orbit tests—including docking with the ISS. SpaceX aims to begin sending astronauts to the space station by 2015. In the meantime, the world's astronauts will rely on Russia's Soyuz for ISS transport (at a cost of $63 million per seat).[53]

It is my belief that U.S. Air Force Space Command (AFSPC) is in charge of a clandestine space program. I also remain convinced by the claims of Gary McKinnon, arrested in 2002 for having hacked with relative ease into numerous classified U.S. military networks—including that of AFSPC—searching for information relating to UFOs, for which he long faced extradition to the United States (vetoed in 2012 by Britain's home secretary). While studying AFSPC data, Gary uncovered a list of officers' names under the heading "Non-Terrestrial Officers."

"What I think it means is, not Earth-based," he explained. "I found a list of 'fleet-to-fleet transfers' and a list of ship names. I looked them up. They weren't U.S. Navy ships. . . ."[54]

"On finding the first image on my PC," Gary told me in 2006, "the Earth—or at least a blue and white planet with no continents visible—filled two thirds of the screen. Midway between the 'camera' and the planet hung a cigar-shaped object with geodesic domes above, below, and to the left and right. I didn't see any rivets, seams, or telemetry antennae. . . ."

CHAPTER FIFTEEN
TECHNOLOGY TRANSFER

On returning from the United States to his native Germany in 1959, following three years of studying information on alien spacecraft supplied by his own and other governments, the outspoken pioneer Professor Hermann Oberth revealed to newsmen waiting for him at the Frankfurt airport that there was a "world-wide effort to learn how anti-gravity could be put to use as a form of energy," adding that he expected "men would be traveling to the Moon in electrically driven devices within five to ten years."[1]

Captain Bill Uhouse served ten years as a fighter pilot in the U.S. Marine Corps, then four years with the U.S. Air Force as a civilian at Wright-Patterson AFB, flight-testing exotic aircraft, including—he claims—flying discs. "While I was at Wright-Patterson," he told Steven Greer's Disclosure Project in 2000, "they had selected several of us, and they reassigned me to A-Link Aviation, which was a simulator manufacturer. At that time they were building what they called the [Link] C-11B [jet flight trainer] and F-102 simulator, B-47 simulator, and so forth. They wanted us to get experienced before we actually started work on the flying disc simulator, which I spent thirty-some years working on. I don't think any flying disc simulators went into operation until the early 1960s—around 1962 or 1963. . . .

"The simulator that they used was for the extraterrestrial craft they had, which is a thirty-meter one that crashed in Kingman, Arizona, back in 1953.[2] That's the first one that they took out to the test flight. This ET craft was a controlled craft that the aliens wanted to present to our government. It landed about fifteen miles from what used to be an Army airbase. But that particular craft, there were some problems with—getting it on the flatbed to take it up to Area 51, which was just being constructed at the time. They couldn't get it across the dam because of the road. It had to be barged across the Colorado River, then taken up Route 93 out to Area 51.

"There were four aliens aboard that thing, and [they] went to Los Alamos for testing. They set up Los Alamos with a particular area for those guys, and they put certain people in there with them—astrophysicists and general scientists—to ask them questions . . . there was only one alien that would talk to any of these scientists [and] the rest wouldn't talk to anybody . . . first they thought it was all ESP or telepathy [but] they actually speak—maybe not like we do—but they speak and converse. But there was only one who would.

"The difference between this disc, and other discs that they had looked at, was that this one was a much simpler design. The disc simulator didn't have a reactor [but] we had a space in it that looked like the reactor that wasn't the device we operated the simulator with. We operated it with six large capacitors that were charged with a million volts each . . . the largest capacitors ever built [and] they'd last for thirty minutes, so you could get in there and actually work the controls and do what you had to do. . . .

"In the simulator there are no seat belts . . . the same thing with the actual craft [because] when you fly one of those things upside down, you just don't feel it [because] you have your own gravitational field right inside the craft. . . . There weren't any windows. The only way we had any visibility at all was done with cameras or video-type devices. . . .

"I'm sure our crews have taken these craft out into space [and] it probably took a while to train enough of the people, over a sufficient time period. . . . The design is so exacting that you can't add anything—it's got to be just right, [for example] where the center of the craft is, [such as] the fact that we raised it three feet so the taller guys could get in. . . .

"I ended up in a meeting with an alien [named] J-Rod—that's what they called him. I don't know if that was his real name. . . . The alien used to come in with [Dr. Edward] Teller and some of the other guys, occasionally, to handle questions that maybe we'd have. [But] if it wasn't specific for the group, you couldn't talk about it. It was on a need-to-know basis. And [the alien] would talk, but he'd sound just like as if you spoke—he'd sound like you. . . . His skin was pinkish, but a little bit rough. . . .

"Over the last forty years or so, not counting the simulators—I'm talking about actual craft—there are probably two or three dozen, and various sizes that we built. I don't know much about the [ET] ones that they brought here [except] for that one out of Kingman. . . ."[3]

In Chapter 4, I alluded to President Eisenhower's several meetings with aliens in the 1950s. One of these, in April 1954, had been witnessed by a number of people from various walks of life, including Gerald Light of Borderland Sciences Research Associates. Riley Hansard Crabb subsequently became director of that organization, which he renamed Borderland Sciences Research Foundation. In the early 1960s, Crabb and his wife were visiting a fellow researcher in California, with a background in space sciences, who showed them a letter offering him an unusual job with an engineering firm in the Denver area.

"The date of the letter was August 1961," Crabb reported, "and it outlined a proposal to set up an antigravity research project aimed at building flyable hardware using the radical new source of propulsion. This group of physicists and engineers were confident they had some sound theory, derived in part, as I recall, from the researches of Wilbert B. Smith, the late Canadian [government] flying saucer expert; and they also had plenty of research money, freed by Congress after President Jack Kennedy's message to that body in May 1961. Our UFO researcher friend declined the job offer. I don't believe he even bothered to reply.

"He was reminded of it four years later, when he attended the Flying Saucer convention in Reno, Nevada. While there, he was approached by a distraught woman, well dressed and in her mid-fifties, who insisted on talking to him in private. It turned out that she was the widow of one of the leading engineers in the antigravity project. The group had achieved one hundred percent of their objective.

"Theory was carried through research and development to where a two-placer was designed, built, disassembled, hauled secretly to a deserted spot in the New Orleans area, reassembled, and successfully flown to a pre-determined landing site in Florida.

"The widow then told our friend that within two days of the successful test flight of the man-carrying Flying Saucer, all of the leaders of the group had died violent deaths. Subsequently, several of their widows had died under unusual or mysterious circumstances, and she was constantly on the move, in fear for her life. In fact, she said, she had been warned by a friendly and inebriated government agent—or at least by one who identified himself as such—to forget her married name and the fact that such a man as her husband had ever existed."[4]

An unlikely tale? Perhaps not. I have previously cited a number of observations reported by qualified personnel of disc-shaped craft being test-flown as far back as the 1950s, and also alluded (in Chapter 4) to a transfer of alien technology during the Eisenhower administration.

In *Secrets of Antigravity Propulsion*, Paul LaViolette traces the history of research into "antigravity," focusing for example on ground-breaking experiments into "electrogravitics" by the physicist Thomas Townsend ("Towny") Brown, who in 1928 patented his invention of a "gravitator" motor. Later, Brown developed further projects, and there is evidence that he was involved with other top scientists in the highly classified so-called "Philadelphia Experiment" in 1943.[5]

"In an effort to secure government funding," LaViolette reports, "Brown wrote a proposal in 1952 urging the Navy to initiate a highly secret project to develop a manned flying saucer as the basis of an interceptor with Mach 3 capability and proposed that this might follow along the same lines as the Manhattan [Engineering] District Project, which developed the atomic bomb. . . . This confidential January 1953 submittal was code-named Project Winterhaven." And in 1960 he produced a report titled "Electrohydrodynamics," proposing a vertical takeoff aero-marine vehicle powered by a high-voltage "flame-jet generator."[6] The design is remarkably similar to that of George Adamski's iconic "scoutcraft." Interestingly, Adamski himself was averse to the expression "antigravity." In his final book, published in 1961, he wrote that "many writers have referred to 'antigravity' devices, and in our scientific researches the idea has been introduced that gravity can be wrestled to a standstill. This is not an efficient approach.[8]

"Space ships that today are visiting our world from other planets operate on a 'pro-gravitic' principle, *using* the natural forces instead of attempting to fight them. Since these ships operate on electrostatic power, it would be useless for them to fight the geomagnetic forces, since Earth's geomagnetic field alone has an electrical potential of billions of volts. . . .

"A flying saucer, or 'pro-gravitic' craft, operates by generating its own gravitational field, which surrounds it in a generally spherical pattern. This field is adjusted to resonate, or blend in harmony with the planet's geomagnetic field. The resonating gravitational field causes the ship to be weightless. In this weightless or balanced condition, the ship, wherever it may be, can be moved by a relatively slight thrust. . . . Within its self-generated pro-gravitic field, the saucer can travel at a rate exceeding the speed of light!"[7]

A privately owned London-based aviation intelligence firm, Aviation Studies (International), evidently took Brown's efforts seriously. And in an edition of their *Aviation Report* in October 1954, the company, citing Brown's Winterhaven project proposal, indicated that the Pentagon was on the verge of funding the development of electrogravitic aircraft.[8] LaViolette adduces numerous other examples proving that such craft were literally taking shape. In another *Aviation Report* (December 9, 1955), it was stated that companies studying the implications of gravitics included Glenn Martin, Convair, Sperry-Rand, Sikorsky, Bell, Lear Inc., and Clarke Electronics. And in an article two months later, *Aviation Report* quotes Glenn Martin as alleging that "gravity control could be achieved in six years," but that it would necessitate a type of highly classified effort along the lines of the Manhattan Engineering District Project. The report also confirmed that research was also being conducted in Britain, Canada, France, Germany, and Sweden. One year later, Aviation Studies confirmed that "Electrostatic discs can provide lift without speed . . . and a program in hand may now ensure that development of large-sized discs will be continued."[9]

"In secret studies and laboratories of the mighty of this world," reported Adamski to his co-workers, following his return from a world tour in

1959, "it is already quite well known how to make use of certain sources of free energy; for instance, canceling gravity, devices for creating electro-static magnetism, etc. They already have models for antigravity cars and antigravity-propelled objects in disc form. But none of these methods for application of a kind of free energy must be revealed to the public, because such a society in possession of these advanced methods would soon escape from economic control."

Coincidently, LaViolette points out that, around 1959, openness about gravity technology programs decreased substantially.[10] Since that period, it has remained among the most highly classified, so-called "deep black" Special Access Programs (SAPs). Periodically, however, witnesses come forward who have observed test flights of highly advanced craft.

A CANADIAN DISC

Also in 1959, the Avro VZ-9AV Avrocar, a disc-shaped, jet-propelled vehicle designed by John Frost and built by A. V. Roe Ltd. of Canada, was first "flown." It was powered by three Continental J69 engines driving a central fan which provided "a peripheral air curtain and ground cushion for vertical take-off and landing (VTOL) operation."[11] Following unsuc-cessful trial hovering flights, the program was canceled a few years later, despite extravagant claims made for its performance. A 1955 CIA memo-randum notes, interestingly, that "Mr. Frost is reported to have obtained his original idea for the flying machine from a group of Germans just after World War II. . . ."[12]

In the opinion of several experts, the VZ-9 was a smoke screen. Lieu-tenant Colonel George Edwards (USAF, retired), for example, is said to have revealed that he and others involved in the project were aware from the outset that it would never be successful. "Although we weren't cut in on it," he stated, "we knew that the Air Force was secretly test-flying a real alien spacecraft. The VZ-9 was to be a cover, so the Pentagon would have an explanation whenever people reported seeing a saucer."[13]

Robert Bracken, a Canadian aviation authority, sent me a photograph of an actual flying disc (reproduced in the photo section), the negative of which had been loaned to him in 1995 by a Royal Canadian Air Force officer who had served in the 1970s. "It is not the Avrocar, but it is a real 'aircraft,'" Bracken explained, "with a round 'fuselage,' twin triangular fins with racing stripes, and what looks like a converted F-86 or CF-100 canopy on top. I asked him all about this 'aircraft': he would not say much, but suggested [the photo] was taken at De Havilland."[14]

In conversation with a uniformed officer at the Fort Eustis Museum, Virginia, where one of the Avrocars is displayed, researcher George Myers was informed that the VZ-9 was the initial step to a successful program in which a disc-shaped aircraft flew to twenty thousand feet. It is quite likely that this is the craft depicted in the photograph, which evidently betrays no signs of a conventional powerplant.

AREA 51

In the early 1960s, Mike Hunt, who held a "Q" clearance from the Atomic Energy Commission and an inter-agency top-secret clearance, observed one such craft, at Groom Dry Lake in Area 51, which he guessed was twenty or thirty feet in diameter. He also claimed to have been present on several occasions when the "flying saucer" was taking off or landing, although he was never allowed actually to observe it. Hunt believed that a highly secret program known as "Project Red Light" or "Redlight"—connected to the discs—was in operation at Area 51 at that time.[15]

"We talked about Area 51 years ago, and at that time I only knew it as a place where we tested our most advanced aircraft," a friend informed me. "In fact, right up to my retirement two years ago, that was what I knew. At the end of my career, there was a program I was on that required a new development at Area 51. *Aviation Week* reported the existence of this building and the UFO enthusiasts who spied on Groom Lake caught sight of [it], and others wondered what it might be. In fact, it was business as usual with ground support for flight tests.

"Just yesterday I spoke again with a retired Lockheed mechanic [who] told me that he had worked with half a dozen other men at Area 51 in the nineties. Within five working years of working on that project, six of his buddies had died of cancer. He, however, did not have that problem because he said that he had only worked there about two months, whereas they stayed for two years. . . . Apparently his diabetes has affected one of his legs, which now needs to be amputated. So with a bleak and possibly short future to look forward to, he told me that the reason he left after two months was because the project scared him. The government had disassembled a flying disc and was building tooling to reassemble the thing. It was very large and had more height than the typically depicted flying saucer. He said that it was definitely not from here. He left the program as soon as he could. . . ."

FURTHER DEVELOPMENTS

In a publication of Borderland Sciences Research Foundation in 1967, an article on the infiltration of the U.S. government by aliens, based on a lecture by one Gordon Shandley, created a stir. "Those familiar with this field took Mr. Shandley's entertaining revelations in their stride," explained the writer, "but the 'newcomers' received the shock of their lives as they listened to this Army Air Corps pilot (1941 clearance Top Secret) expound matter-of-factly on the various types of UFOs as casually as though he were discussing the latest models put out by General Motors.

"Most of Mr. Shandley's research in this field stresses the scientific and technical side; but his association with George Adamski, prior to the latter's death some time ago, acquainted him with the philosophical and religious framework of space. . . .

"Mr. Shandley's elaboration upon the nature of the spaceships revealed that the large mother ships rarely come into the Earth's atmosphere. The saucers are contact discs operated by remote control from the main ship. . . . An ionization force is placed around the ship to protect it. A magnetic screen will plow a path ahead of the ship in its course through space. . . . Apparently the space people have gained comprehension of an unbelievably complex array of one-inch-thick invisible lines of force, none of which touch one another. If these lines do cross, a death ray is produced inimical to anything in its path.

"Although Earth has been visited by beings from other planets since the time higher forms of life developed here, their most recent attention has been sparked by our atomic explosions and the radar we bounced off the Moon. . . .

"It seems that our government is as infiltrated by spacemen as it is supposed to be by Communists—only with better intentions. Their purpose is to aid us spiritually and technically. Mr. Shandley spoke of having consulted personally with at least six individuals from other planets who in an unobtrusive way volunteered information aiding him in his research. Scientific laboratories have also received the benefit of extraterrestrial knowledge. Mr. 'Man-from-Venus' will pose as a second or third laboratory assistant. Then, when his suggestions have been adopted, he will quietly melt away and move on to some other spot. . . .

"John Q. Public, though conceding God's place in heaven, was nevertheless jolted on learning that said heaven was more thickly populated than was formerly suspected . . . several brisk questions were directed to Mr. Shandley regarding the credentials of these interplanetary visitors. . . . Mr. Shandley calmly replied that their identity was confirmed by Government top brass, and more than this he could not part with as things were coming dangerously near to trespassing on Top Secret territory. The U.S. government, while completely cognizant of interplanetary beings, has formulated a twenty-year education program for the public. . . . The idea is to break everybody in gradually, by emphasis on outer space exploration, rockets, etc., through news and TV media, which will in time lead to an admission of the true nature of these strange objects. . . . Until this period of time is up, the Air Force officially will continue to manifest a state of amnesia on UFO reports."[16]

WHITE SANDS

One of my sources served with the U.S. Army from 1969 to 1972. "In my initial six months of service," he reported to me, "I was assigned to the Pentagon in a position that was reasonably uninteresting. During that time, living in and around Washington, D.C., I met with a gentleman who was working the electrical side of hot-rodding VW Beetles. Mine was one of his projects. . . .

"One evening, over a couple of beers, he showed me photos of a 'hot-rod' version of a flying saucer he took at White Sands Missile Range. He had been employed by a contractor involved in a construction project there in the late 1960s, and the photos I was shown were less than three years old. The photos depicted the saucer-shaped craft maneuvering at about two thousand feet, then flying and hovering at fifty to a hundred feet, and landing. The closest shot was taken from about thirty feet away, when the hatch opened.

"There were no images of the personnel piloting the saucer, but he made it clear to me that these vehicles were ours, or at least under U.S. military control. The craft parked gave one the impression that the disc was about eighteen feet in diameter. My presumption here is based on my calculation from a three-foot-wide hatchway. It was a medium silver/gray color. The surface skin had a texture—not a rough profile texture, but a smooth and sort of porous-looking texture. To me, it looked like a sheet of aluminum or titanium that had been overheated, then cooled slowly rather than quenched. I recall that the sunlight reflected oddly on the craft, [giving] a pale orange-ish/silver-ish appearance. I drew my rendition in PowerPoint [see below], which has limited tools."[17]

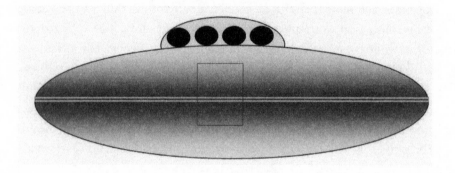

"Could you help me to distinguish between the types of craft that are constructed here, 'under license' as it were, and the 'real McCoy'?" I asked Fred Steckling in 1976.

"Well, as far as I have found out from my sources," he replied, "the Air Force has managed to build several types of these scout ships, and they are not quite as sophisticated as the ones that they have on other planets. They look the same, and they do move around in our atmosphere, but they are not quite as capable of going twenty thousand miles per hour in our atmosphere, because the knowledge that we have so far is to extend force-fields around this vehicle to protect it from any friction, and blend it. Actually, when the spacemen move with this spacecraft, it blends with our atmosphere; it does not force itself into the air, like a jet does, and we do not quite have this knowledge.

"I only know that what we have at the moment is a craft that uses mirror systems . . . we have a craft that looks like a doughnut: it has a hole in the center and it has a different arrangement of mirrors built in, so that when the craft is up about two, three hundred feet, hovering, they can, by reflecting the light around it, camouflage it with the background well enough so that if you really didn't know, you wouldn't see it. . . .

"George Adamski said to me, before he passed on [in 1965], that 'the Boys' [as he called his alien friends] had just returned from Russia and they told him that the Russians had developed a scout ship that looked like the one from Venus. It could move around in our atmosphere quite well, and they were going to work on a modification which would take approximately nine months and then they could go to the Moon with it. By 1966, the ship should have been ready to go to—we had not yet landed an astronaut there so, technically speaking, the Russians were capable of visiting the Moon long before we had our astronauts up there. . . .

"I know that nations work closer together than we think. This atmosphere of 'communism' as the enemy, the escalation of war material, and so on, are a clever set-up to keep our industries from going bankrupt. In other words, 'no breakage, no makeage.' So you know they're working together. . . ."[18]

LOCKHEED SKUNK WORKS

Brad Sorensen, an aviation designer who works mostly for aerospace companies, reported to aviation illustrator Mark McCandlish that during an air show at Norton Air Force Base, California, on November 12, 1988, he was invited by a wealthy former secretary or undersecretary of defense to visit a huge hangar at the base, surrounded by a cordon of military police armed with M-16s. Sorenson's companion asked one of the guards to fetch an acquaintance of his, the man in charge of the show. When he appeared, it was clear that the two men recognized each other. Queried about Sorensen's presence, the retired Defense source said Sorensen was his "aide." Reportedly, the men were then escorted into "the Big Hangar" (as it was called) and shown some highly classified exotic aircraft, including three fully functioning flying saucers.

"At this point, the story becomes somewhat confusing," explains Richard Dolan, the distinguished historian and researcher. "Sorensen originally told

McCandlish and others that the exhibit of exotic craft took place within the Big Hangar. In later tellings, he added a twist: that in fact the demonstration did not occur at Norton. Rather, the group was escorted aboard an Air Force passenger jet and flown fifty miles northwest to Palmdale. They arrived at the Lockheed Skunkworks facility at the west end of the complex, and it was here that the entire exhibit was held. It appears Sorensen was originally trying to withhold certain pieces of the story.

"They entered the Lockheed hangar, and it was obvious that the exhibit was for politicians and military officials who were cleared for high-security information. As McCandlish and aviation researcher Michael Schratt later put it, 'the express purpose of the exhibit was to garner additional support for classified "black," or SAR "special access required" programs.'"

As soon as they walked in the huge hangar, Sorensen received a warning from the former Defense official. "There are a lot of things in here that I didn't expect they were going to have on display—stuff you probably shouldn't be seeing," he advised. "So, don't talk to anybody, don't ask any questions, just keep your mouth shut, smile and nod, but don't say anything—just enjoy the show."

Among the first craft they were shown was a flattened football, diamond-shaped craft, known as the Pulser or "Flaming Pumpkinseed," an unmanned vehicle supposedly capable of launching nuclear warheads within less than a tenth of a second (an absurdly short time). According to Schratt, eighteen of these vehicles were built during the Reagan administration.[19] Sorensen told McCandlish that after he had been shown this and other craft, he noted a large black curtain dividing the hangar into two different areas. "Behind these curtains was another big area, and inside this area they had all the lights turned off.

"So, they go in and they turn the lights on, and here are three flying saucers floating off the floor—no cables suspended from the ceiling holding them up, no landing gear underneath—just floating, hovering above the floor. They had little exhibits with a videotape running, showing the smallest of the three vehicles sitting out in the desert, presumably over a dry lakebed—some place like Area 51. It showed this vehicle making three little quick, hopping motions; then [it] accelerated straight up and out of sight, completely disappearing from view in just a couple of seconds. . . .

"They had a cutaway illustration [showing] what the internal components of this vehicle [referred to as 'the Alien Reproduction Vehicle' (ARV) or 'Flux Liner'] were, and they had some panels taken off so you could actually look in and see oxygen tanks and a little robotic arm that could extend out from the side of the vehicle for collecting samples and things."[20]

The three craft were of different sizes—24, 60, and 130 feet in diameter. Nearby, a general was addressing a group of people, referring to the craft and citing various attributes, including an extravagant claim that they could perform at "light speed or better," Dolan learned from McCandlish. "It had extraordinary acceleration and maneuverability, able to move from a ground-level hovering position to 80,000 feet within 2.5 seconds." (A pre-posterously precise time.) "Sorensen noted that the [ARV] looked 'ancient' and as though it had been used extensively. . . . In 1992, McCandlish met a man named Kent Sellen who had been a crew chief at Edwards AFB years before," Dolan learned. "In 1973, Sellen unintentionally went into an area where he saw a craft exactly matching the description of Sorensen's [small] ARV. At that point, he was thrown to the ground at gunpoint, blindfolded, taken into custody, and interrogated about his presence there and what he thought he had seen. Sellen even provided McCandlish with details and data about the object that had been unknown to Sorensen."[21]

McCandlish learned some pertinent information from Sorensen relating to aspects of the ARV's propulsion. Inside the craft was a central column, for example, containing a type of vacuum chamber:

"Brad maintained that inside this big vacuum chamber that's inside everything else—inside the flywheel, inside the secondary coils of the Tesla coil, inside the crew compartment—there is mercury vapor. Mercury vapor will conduct electricity, but it produces all kinds of ionic effects. These little molecules of mercury become charged in unusual ways, and if you fire a tremendous amount of electricity through mercury vapor that's in a partial vacuum, there is something special, something unusual [that] happens in that process."[22]

It is pertinent to point out here that, in conversation with the gardener Leonard Mantle in 1969, some of the technological information imparted by "Iso Khan" chimes with Sorensen's description. For instance, Mantle learned that the propulsion system of the craft used by Khan's race included a cylindrical column that contained mercury (Chapter 12). And in Chapter 13 we learned that the "W56" aliens required mercury for many of their applications, including craft, the propulsion of which they revealed to several of their contacts as part of a technology transfer.

George Adamski was the first to publish details of a central column inside smaller spacecraft, describing how "a pillar about two feet thick extended downward from the very top of the dome to the center of the floor. Later I was told that this was the magnetic pole of the ship, by means of which they drew on Nature's forces for propulsion purposes, but they did not explain how this was done." He did learn, however, that the top of the pole was positive while the bottom was negative. "But, when necessary," his host explained, "these poles can be reversed," and added that the central pillar served a double purpose, "as a powerful telescope, with one end pointing up through the dome to view the sky, and the other pointing down through the floor to inspect the land below. . . ."[23]

VANDENBERG AND EDWARDS AIR FORCE BASES

In 1986, Peter Biagio Tresca, an aerospace engineer, was joint director of Lawrence Engineering and Supply Inc., based in Burbank. Tresca's daughter Teresa, who worked for her father at the time, recalls seeing blueprints on her father's desk that depicted what looked like a type of flying saucer. "Apparently the government had made them," she told me. "I wanted to take the blueprints and show them to my teacher at college, but they weren't allowed out of the office.

"My father used to take me to air shows, and in August or September 1988 he took me to a restricted show at Vandenberg. And I saw the demonstration of a flying saucer—like the one on the blueprints. I was busy watching a display of jets when it suddenly came in from the left, came in front of us, and then took off again. I didn't hear it approaching."[24] Her husband, British UFO researcher Philip Waterhouse, fills in further details:

"She said the craft approached from near some hangars and hovered silently at about ten feet, apart from a relatively high-pitched humming noise. Then after about five minutes the craft pitched up and shot off into the sky to the right of where they were standing. There were only about twenty people, including her father and herself, who were witness to this event.

"She said the craft was about twenty or twenty-five feet wide and about ten feet high. What is interesting about her description is the fact that the bottom was bowed upwards, which is fairly uncommon. And the craft appeared all in one piece, though it seemed to be sectioned in a circular way, with a dome on top. It was silver-colored all over, apart from the [indented] parts, which could have been shadows."

Teresa's sketches of the side, top, and bottom of the craft appear below:

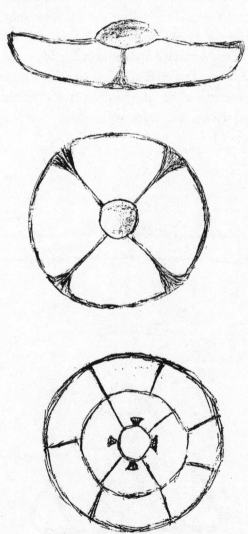

"What is also interesting to me and what originally caught my attention when she described her visit there," Philip continued, "was the fact that before the flying saucer was viewed, she and her father and others were witness to other stealth aircraft—and one triangular craft.

"She said the triangular craft was completely silent without any discernable humming—only the [displaced] air traveling around it. The craft hovered at about nine feet, tipped forward and backward and turned around its axis, rose another ten feet at least, and then took off silently at great speed.

"She described the craft as being a dull black (not shiny) with a pitch-black smoky non-see-through dome on top. She also saw what she described as discernable undercarriage arms underneath, which were of a darker-colored black. The craft also had what appeared to be 'lights' at each triangular corner—although she didn't see any light as such. They were of the same smoky dull appearance as the domed canopy on top."[25] [See sketches below.]

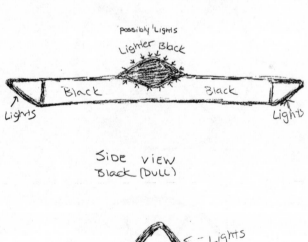

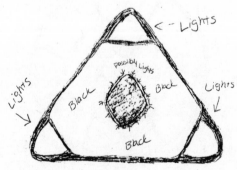

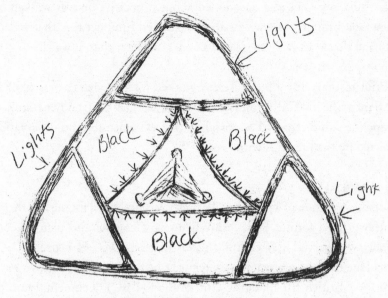

UNDERNEATH SIDE.
→ INDICATES Lights possibly

Toward the end of the following summer (1989), Teresa accompanied her father to Edwards Air Force Base to attend another restricted air show. The same number of people was present. She saw more of the conventional stealth-type aircraft, and what appeared to be the same black triangle. The saucer-shaped craft did not make an appearance.

"What was the level of security?" I pressed her. "Did you need any special access?"

"My dad did," she replied. "I would ask him questions, but he never really told me anything—he was really 'hush-hush' about it all."

"And it was just a relatively small number of people at these two air shows?"

"Yes. I would say about fifteen or so—mostly men. Apart from my father, there were other 'big-wigs' from Lawrence Engineering, such as Fletcher Seymour, Ray Barker, Ray and Mary Smith. . . . Of course, there was also a lot of military there."

"But weren't they concerned?" I asked, incredulously. "You were just with your father, and you were let in on it, so to speak?"

"I think my Dad was questioned about it because he was walked off. They took him off somewhere and questioned him, because that was the last time that I was able to go to a show. And after that, it was like everything was hush-hush."[26]

Prior to marrying Philip, Teresa worked for five years as a sheriff for the Santa Clarita (California) Sheriff's Department. I find her testimony compelling, and it provides corroborative evidence for the observations reported by the previous witnesses.

LOS ALAMOS

The demonstration of a much smaller craft was described for me by Gregory Molesworth, a former U.S. Army lieutenant colonel and platoon commander who served in Vietnam. In Washington, D.C., in February 1994, he told me that eighteen months previously, he had been working as a sound man for a British Broadcasting Corporation (BBC) documentary on the Strategic Defense Initiative (SDI). While filming at Los Alamos National Laboratory, he witnessed the demonstration of a four-foot-diameter disc, radio-controlled via a joystick in a metal-lined laboratory. As "foreign nationals," British participants were not allowed in—and Molesworth himself was threatened if he tried to film anything.

CALIFORNIA BASES

"I have been reading recently about all the alleged underground alien labs and facilities and took particular interest in a rumor purporting an underground base of this kind to be located in the Lancaster/Palmdale area near the Tehachapi Mountains," begins a narrative from "Alex R.," a woman who together with her friend Annemarie had a somewhat disturbing experience in the early 1980s.

Annemarie had purchased some undeveloped land in that area. She herself, however, had not yet seen it: her husband Ken had bought the property and confirmed that it was in an ideal location, then deeded it over to her after they divorced, giving her a rough map with some landmarks to assist her in locating it.

"We drove the nearly two hours to Lancaster/Palmdale and began our search. The map was not much help, however, because it had been made when the area was still undeveloped. And most of the natural landmarks were gone—removed to make room for houses. Every time we found what looked like a road which would take us somewhere, it turned into a dead-end. The area we were in was now full of cul-de-sacs for the housing development that would soon be built on it. After about two and a half hours of driving, we stopped for a cool drink.

"We got back on the main highway and decided to look for dirt roads in the hope that the land was still undeveloped and that we had missed it. . . . At last, a broad, well-kept dirt road appeared. At first we thought it might be the entrance to someone's farm or ranch but, since there wasn't a mailbox, we decided to proceed. After about half a mile, something odd happened: the dirt road became a wide, beautifully paved asphalt road, with a single white dividing line. We were astounded at this but were glad, as the dirt road was taking its toll on Annemarie's car.

"We had driven about two miles when, up ahead, we saw what looked like a dust storm coming out of the mountains. Annemarie slowed down, and we watched. It was not a storm but a vehicle, a car, coming toward us at full speed. 'Let's get out of here!' I said. 'I don't think that would be a good idea,' said Annemarie. She came to a complete stop, right in the middle of the road. 'Are you crazy?' I said. 'Stay calm and let me do the talking,' she said.

"The car, a drab olive green late-model sedan, was, by now, up on the road, still driving full speed. They were heading directly for us. I was afraid that they would not stop in time and would hit us. The car stopped, brakes screeching, within inches of us, and two men got out. A third man remained in the car. They were young men, in their mid-thirties, dressed in pale blue coveralls (no name plates or insignias) and baseball caps. One had sandy-colored hair, the other was white-blond. The third man was in the front seat of the car, talking on the radio-microphone. All wore wrap-around sunglasses. Somehow, I knew that we might be in terrible trouble and that we were somewhere we didn't belong.

"The sandy-haired man came up to the driver's side of the car; the blond one was on my side, the passenger side. He kept his right hand in his pocket at all times. I wondered if he was carrying a gun. 'Good afternoon, ladies!' said sandy-hair. 'Where are you going?' Annemarie showed him the map. 'We're trying to find my property,' she said. 'Can you help us?'

"He studied the map. 'You haven't been here for a while, have you?' he said. 'All of these places on the map have been removed or destroyed.' He looked at the map again. 'This place looks like it might be on the other side of town. Why don't you look there?' He was extremely polite, smiling all the while he spoke, yet he terrified me and Annemarie. The blond man never spoke, nor did he smile or look at me. The third man remained on the radio. 'We'll be happy to escort you ladies back to the main road.'

"Though it sounded like a polite suggestion, it was actually an order to leave now. Annemarie said nothing, merely backed up slowly and drove back, still slowly, to our place of entrance into this 'forbidden' area. The men and their car stayed close behind us and followed us for several miles. Annemarie and I did not speak during this time. I think we were too scared. Then, instead of going back to the main part of the city, she took the next freeway on-ramp and headed back home. I noticed that she kept looking in her rear-view mirror. 'Someone is following us,' she said.

"I was too frightened to turn around, so I lowered my sun visor and looked in the vanity mirror. There, a few car lengths behind us, was another late-model sedan, medium blue in color, being driven by a man in a green coverall, wearing a cap and wrap-around sunglasses. His two companions were dressed the same way. 'They probably want to make sure that we go back home and don't try to come back,' said Annemarie. 'Ken told me that he had heard about the government using parts of that area for secret experiments,' she said."

The car followed the ladies until they were halfway home, then began to back off and eventually disappeared. On arriving home, Annemarie dropped Alex off. They agreed to meet later for dinner at a local restaurant.

"We were now curious about what had happened and wondered if we should go back or if we would be able to find the road again. We lived in the San Fernando Valley and were not at all familiar with the Antelope Valley area. We then got further into our mutual interest in UFOs [and] jokingly considered the possibility that the 'men' we had seen were really aliens.

"We left the restaurant at about 10:30. The restaurant is situated in a very busy traffic area and is also near a freeway and a very well-known and very busy motor hotel. There is constant noise and traffic at all hours. It is *never* quiet there. However, this night, things were to be different.

When we came out of the restaurant, the street was deserted. This was on a Saturday night, one of the busiest nights of the week for this restaurant. There were no cars going by, no people, no sounds of traffic. In fact, there was no sound of any kind.[27] When Annemarie and I spoke to each other, our voices sounded hollow, far away." Neither of the ladies had ever seen it so quiet.

"Then, as if on command," Alex reported, "we both looked up. There, at a level just over our heads, across the street, was a spacecraft.

"We could not see the craft itself very clearly, but it was outlined by white lights that ran all around it. It was the shape of an elongated triangle. It remained in its position for what seemed a few minutes. Then it moved away. Suddenly, as if someone had turned up the volume on a TV set, all the normal sounds returned.

"We walked to our cars and Annemarie checked her watch. 'Oh, my God!' she said. 'What time do you have?' I looked at my watch and was stunned. It was 12:35 A.M. We had been looking at the spacecraft for two hours and five minutes!

"That was the final straw and all the fright we wanted to have for one day. We agreed never to go out to look for that 'forbidden' area, and Annemarie sold her property soon after this incident. There may be more than just rumors about what is going on in the Tehachapi Mountains. . . ."[28]

Tom Keller (who features in Chapter 9) has worked for British Aerospace, Douglas Aircraft, and NASA's Jet Propulsion Laboratory. In *The Total Novice's Guide to UFOs*, he writes extensively about Antelope Valley, described as "a hotbed for the aerospace industry."

"When I lived there," he reports, "Lockheed Martin, Boeing, McDonnell Douglas, and Northrop Grumman all had multiple facilities there." He mentions a base at the northwest end of the Antelope Valley in the foothills of the Tehachapi Mountains, known as "The Anthill," and another area known as the Tejon RCS [radar cross-section] Facility. Both are owned by Northrop Grumman. Another site is the Helendale Avionics Facility, owned by Lockheed Martin Skunk Works. Observations of flying discs and other unusual craft have been observed periodically over the years.[29]

Researcher Bill Hamilton reports the observation, in the Antelope Valley in October 1988 by two witnesses known to him, of a large boomerang-shaped craft, estimated to be over six hundred feet in span, traveling very slowly. "A second and identical large object joined behind the first one," he reports in his book, *Cosmic Top Secret*. "The trailing boomerang was followed by approximately fifteen to twenty disc-shaped objects in formation. . . . Two additional witnesses saw the boomerangs pass over the valley from a side view to the east, [and these] were also sighted in Fresno later that same evening. The objects rose in altitude to clear the Tehachapi Mountains to the north, flying directly over the secret Northrop 'Anthill' facility. . . ."[30]

In 1988, Hamilton learned from a Northrop source that "during the early era," a disc obtained from aliens via an exchange program had been sequestered underground at Edwards AFB. He also learned from several other sources that construction of underground facilities at the base began in the 1950s, and that a disc or discs had been stored in a hangar at the North base or underground.[31]

PROJECT AQUARIUS

William J. Pawelec, a former U.S. Air Force computer operations and programming specialist with numerous credentials in security technologies and access control systems, who died in May 2007, also confirmed the alien technology transfer. "I would say this is international in scope," he told Steven Greer of the Disclosure Project, during an interview that Pawelec had specified not be released until December 2010. "If you look at what layers of influence we have here, either at government or corporate level, I would say that at the corporate level we have to look primarily first.

"If you're talking about new propulsion technologies, we would first only look to the aerospace industry. I've had deep discussions with some people over a long period of time who—either they or their fathers—had worked for various aerospace companies and had been directly involved with the research as far back as the early 1950s on into the 1960s. And then by the 1970s they felt they had overcome most of the problems in reverse-engineering technologies from what, interestingly enough, they never call them UFOs; they call them AVCs—Alien Visitation Craft."[32]

A trusted source of mine—the same aerospace journalist who supplied me with a great deal of information on these matters for inclusion in *Unearthly Disclosure*—has hinted that in the 1980s a few aerospace companies, principally Lockheed and Northrop, had established underground plants inside the Tehachapi Mountains which produced top-secret, high-tech flying machines, allegedly produced by the Air Force's "Project Aquarius" in conjunction with aerospace and electronics companies. The huge amounts of money involved were distributed and sequestered in the black budget.

This exchange program purportedly involved a species of the so-called "grays"—aliens who claimed to have first come to Earth just after World War II and began establishing many underground and undersea bases around the world. These were located in areas such as Alaska, Australia, the Caribbean Sea (south of the Florida Keys), the Manzano Mountains near the nuclear weapons storage area at Kirtland Air Force Base, New Mexico, and the Monongahela National Forest in West Virginia. Several other bases were located around the world, mainly in Asia. From the information made available to me, I have deduced that the largest undersea base was probably located in the Milwaukee Seamounts, 32°46′ latitude, 171°91′ longitude, in the Pacific Ocean some 1,700 miles west-northwest of Honolulu.[33] By 1973, they had come to stay.

Highly telepathic, the beings were about four and a half feet tall, featuring large heads; large almond-shaped black eyes; vestigial mouths, noses, and ears; and very thin hands with no thumbs.

The alien crafts' propulsion systems "interacted with the magnetic fields existing throughout space and around celestial bodies," they claimed. Enormously powerful electrical charges were generated in tube-like toruses ranging around the insides of the hulls. The toruses were superconductors, made of materials not found on Earth. They were non-resistant to electric current, allowing the current to run free, and forever. Magnets inside the tubes converted the current into plasma jets. Each ship had several such systems to provide energy for different purposes. The build-up of magnetic fields around the ships, when their propulsion systems powered up, sometimes made them glow.

Air Force development of its own flying discs owed to their having studied recovered alien craft, a number of which had been brought down by the military. Although it was ascertained that a plasma field surrounding the craft shielded it from guided missiles, oddly enough bullets, shells, and cannon fire could cause severe damage and/or bring down such a craft (as another source confirmed for me), at least in the early days. As Colonel Philip J. Corso states, in later years hostile alien craft could be brought down by advanced particle-beam weapons, such as those fired from Blue Gemini satellites, as part of the Strategic Defense Initiative (SDI).[34]

The discs reverse-engineered by the USAF were technologically inferior to those of the extraterrestrials, I learned. Nonetheless, the aliens acknowledged that they had underestimated us in this regard and were said to have been impressed. Design and production were said to be almost totally automated. One craft, apparently a two-seater, was described as appearing like two soup-bowls fastened together rim to rim, seamless, with no sign of windows and three slender landing legs which retracted into slots. Entrance was via a hatch under the hull.

Propulsion was also said to involve plasma: indeed, it has been described as a "plasma-propelled magneto-hydrodynamic vehicle," and in water a "magnetohydrodynamic vehicle."[35] A vertical tube, some three feet in diameter, extended from the top of the cabin down through the floor. A superconductor torus of hot plasma circled the horizontal rim of the inner and outer hulls, generating a powerful propulsion field that interacted with Earth's ambient magnetic field, propelling the craft. Another hot-plasma superconductor torus circled the craft vertically. The craft's CPU (central processing unit) was alleged to make billions of calculations per second, manipulating the plasma flow to counter G-forces.

The American pilots wore special helmets that afforded "enhanced reality" for use in the plasma environment. Each helmet is unique to the pilot who wears it, reading his brain's "electromagnetic signature." The craft also utilized biocomputers. Viewing ports in the hull appeared only when required. Weaponry consisted of a very powerful beam that focused a mixture of photons and free electrons onto the target.

I do not know how much of this information is factual. But based on my acquaintance with the source for many years, I feel that, even allowing for disinformation, it is substantially true.

ITALIAN LIAISON

In Chapter 13, I detailed some of the wealth of information provided for me by Professor Stefano Breccia regarding the propulsion systems of the Amicizia (W56) craft. On one occasion, he was given the opportunity of a flight in a craft, together with his German engineer friend Hans. No aliens were on board, but both the craft and its occupants were monitored at all times. Stefano told me that a safety precaution involved jumping on board with both feet—presumably to avoid an electric shock (as explained in Chapter 13). Hans took the controls, while Stefano (a licensed pilot of conventional aircraft) was content to make calculations relating to co-ordinates, etc., on his calculator. "I did not want to pilot the craft," he told me frankly, "but I asked the W56s to show me the co-ordinates.

"The control unit, on a ledge inside the flange, was most interesting, partly owing to its small size—about that of a PC keyboard. It had virtual images, like modern mobiles, but no keypads. (Today's mobile phones would not work in a craft, incidentally.) I used my Olivetti 22 typewriter to make notes.

"The floor was of metal but rather soft and looked like plastic. Light appeared to be generated from nowhere—it's the air that's 'lit.' Shadows go in the opposite direction from what you would suppose. There were no portholes, but the metal of the craft could be made transparent, enabling one to see either outside or inside. The seats weren't very comfortable, owing to a triangular-shaped back. And there was a strange instrument that gave off different colors to different portions of air inside the cabin: it's used for giving an idea of electrical, magnetic and gravitational fields inside—a global measure so you can decide which color should be attributed to a particular thing. . . .

"The trip was from Pescara to Moscow, Cairo, then back to Pescara, and the computer showed geographic co-ordinates. We found out that the craft did not travel in a straight line to its destination, but in a curve, which we thought strange. We flew at a very high altitude and at a speed of six to seven thousand kilometers per hour. There was no sensation of movement. Actually, it wasn't so interesting—I find it more exciting in ordinary planes!"[36] This may seem somewhat blasé, but less so if we take into consideration the many years Stefano spent in close proximity to both the aliens and their craft.

Stefano gave me additional details pertaining to the piloting of their craft, which bears comparison with data provided by the previous source:

"One could just touch certain lighted areas (which today we would call diodes) on a panel in front of the seat which at all times presented one with the only available option in that specific situation. Then it would change—depending. You could choose four different possibilities for going from one place to another: (1) Limiting the amount of energy dissipated; (2) When emphasis is on the duration of travel; (3) When the pilot decides what to do at each moment—or 'manual override'; (4) Totally remote control, e.g. if the craft comes up against an obstacle, such as a mountain, say, the obstacle (or part thereof) is destroyed. When the computer is involved, it ensures that such obstacles are avoided.

"For example, when some Italian military pilots were being trained by the W56 to pilot their scoutcraft, at a certain point south of Calabria they detected a ship which they weren't sure of, sixteen kilometers away at a bearing of 234°. The pilots decided to try to land on the ship, piloting normally without the computer. In doing so, they realized it was a naval ship of undetermined nationality. As they descended, the pilot encountered difficulties so decided to engage the computer, which made the craft land on the ship.

"Of course, people on the ship, seeing this craft, reacted. And as they were military, they started firing at the craft. The pilots panicked so, via remote control, the W56 remedied the situation, pressing the 'fly away' option, in which the computer has control. So, when taking off from the ship, the craft destroyed part of the gun that was firing at them. Of course, the W56s—overviewing the situation—reprimanded the pilots, as they had not been in any danger at all."

The reason given by the Amicizia for the transfer of their technology, Stefano revealed to me, was to have humans performing as well as they did, for example with regard to the "CTR"—the *contrari*—and other groups who opposed them. Furthermore, the W56 group fully expected our pilots to defend themselves against the CTRs. "*These* types of craft," Stefano emphasized, "could not be captured or damaged by our weapons."

"How many of your country's pilots have flown these craft?" I inquired. "My guess," he responded, "is that, among the Amicizia group, ten to fifteen Italian pilots have been trained to fly them."[37]

———

How many other countries have acquired alien technology? I do not know. But Paul LaViolette confirms that Canada and a number of European countries have been involved in top-secret research programs since the 1950s, and Fred Steckling cited American–Soviet collaboration. Germany, I assume, would be high on the list, based on Hermann Oberth's testimony and that of others. There is also hearsay evidence, cited later, that the United States has shared much information with the United Kingdom.

In any event, as time passes, it will become increasingly difficult to differentiate between "theirs and ours" and—perhaps more pertinently—between "friend or foe". . . .

CHAPTER SIXTEEN
LEVIATHANS OF THE SKIES

It was the late spring or early summer of 1956—probably May—when a huge disc-like object was seen by thousands off the northeast coast of Aberdeen, Scotland. One witness is my friend Ian Taylor, who gave me an extremely detailed account of this remarkable, yet now little-known, event.

At around 08:30 Ian was on his way to catch the bus to school, not that far from Aberdeen Airport. A keen plane spotter, as he scanned the mostly clear skies for contrails he noticed what first appeared to be a balloon hovering in the direction of the city. "The object seemed to be stationary, around the one o'clock position to the vertical, but I remember being aware of some gentle sideways movement coupled with similar vertical transitions too," he told me. By 10:30, at which point Ian was enjoying a break in the playground, the object still remained in the sky, causing him to wonder why, if it was a balloon, it hadn't drifted. It was still there at lunchtime.

"I noted it maintained a different elevation, and immediately became aware of two sets of contrails in the sky, heading up from the south in a northerly direction, toward the city. I noted they had a twin exhaust exit, and that immediately suggested Meteor jets. I knew this type of aircraft had an operational ceiling of around 42,000 feet and that they would probably have come from RAF Leuchars in Fife, near St. Andrew's. It soon became obvious they were heading toward this object's position.

"Both aircraft then began to separate from their close formation to form a huge circle in the sky, which on reflection I would have estimated to be in the order of two miles in diameter. Both aircraft performed this maneuver for about two to three minutes at least, leaving this incredible graphic imprint in the sky which would have attracted considerable attention for miles around. The aircraft eventually broke away and headed south.

"Sitting at the core of the contrail pattern was this object, and I immediately began to suspect something wasn't quite what it appeared to be. Firstly, the object looked considerably smaller than before. Then, within a short space of time, it seemed to increase in size to return to what was first observed, but perhaps not quite as large. As the contrails began to spread out as they tend to do with upper windshear effects, I noted a barely perceptible drift westward of the contrail ring. As the contrail ring began to drift further westward, this object still maintained its position. I still observed this unusual, slow bobbing and oscillating motion associated with it. And then, when the ring continued moving in a westerly direction it began to obliterate this object and within a few minutes the object was lost to sight, soon to re-emerge as the contrail disc continued moving with the upper air stream.

"I instinctively knew this object was much higher than the contrails by quite a considerable margin and therefore much, much larger than originally considered and it began to become clear that the circling jets were well below this object and that it had in fact ascended to what might be regarded as a safe altitude above the jets. It must have seen them coming."

On returning to his school, Ian noted that the mystery object remained in the sky, maintaining its position and altitude. By around 14:30 it had disappeared. According to the front-page story in the *Aberdeen Evening Express* (date not known), thousands of people had witnessed the object. Furthermore, its first sighting had been reported north of the city at about 07:00. Photographers from the *Express* had attempted to capture the object with their large plate cameras fitted with standard wide-angle lenses, Ian reports, but "failed to get any image worthy of publication."

Two years later, Ian befriended James Stewart (long since deceased), a research scientist with the MacCaulay Soil Research Institute in Aberdeen, who also had observed the strange craft. He had driven home from the Institute to fetch his theodolite (a surveying instrument for measuring horizontal and vertical angles with a rotating telescope). "What he told me was fascinating," said Ian:

"He drew what he had observed through the device, describing the object as being rounded underneath, and the top—at least what could be seen relative to the observable angle from terra firma—came to a rounded point from what appeared to be a gentle upward sweeping transition from the outer rim. He went on to say it had a beautiful golden metallic luster with high reflectivity values and totally absent of appendages, graphic markings, or symbols. Like me, he was quick to detect its motion characteristics describing, as I had observed, this swaying motion coupled with a slow and gentle vertical bob.

"What he then went on to say threw me completely. He had calculated its overall diameter as being in the order of anywhere between 780 and 800 feet. And like myself, James was convinced enough to reach the conclusion that the arrival of the jets was no mean coincidence; and, as we both recognized the aircraft type, he was quick to assume they would have been taking footage with their nose-mounted gun-cameras, whose field of capture was a five-position lens system, as I recall from *Jane's All the World's Aircraft*, each lens position allowing a level of overlap to create a near panoramic template."

Years later, Ian joined the Royal Air Force for a period of three years, specialising in air defence work. After training at Compton Bassett in Wiltshire, he was posted to RAF Buchan radar installation, some thirty miles north of Aberdeen. "A few weeks after I settled in my new role," he recounted, "all the new conscripts were dispatched to RAF Leuchars in Fife. It was on that visit I took the opportunity to step out of the crowd and discuss with one of the host Hunter jet pilots the 1956 sighting, even though I knew he would not have been there at the time. I remember vividly his expression of bewilderment at my question, clearly struggling to offer a response in a manner appropriate to the occasion, especially so from a lowly SAC [Senior Aircraftman] radar operator.

"He eventually responded by saying he knew nothing about such an incident, smiled slightly, and then moved away to attend to the rest of the party. Naturally I didn't pursue the matter, as it was clear he intended the conversation to end there. Two days following the trip to Leuchars, during what I recall was a day watch for the crew I was attached to, the NCO [Non-commissioned Officer] of the watch came up to me when I was on the radarscope to say I had to report to the Squadron Leader of the watch once my break time came along. Somewhat mystified, no reason having been given, I went to his office as requested. As it happened, this officer was ex-aircrew and a fellow Scot, very well liked among the ranks as well as by lesser mortals like myself. I knocked and entered, stood to attention and all of that and then awaited his address.

"What happened next completely floored me, and it was clear I was in some sort of trouble. Obviously, the officer I had addressed at Leuchars had reported to the base commander about my questioning over the 1956 UFO incident in relation to Leuchars. That inquiry quickly got back to Buchan, probably long before we left Leuchars to return to Buchan, and most likely reached the ears of a senior controller, which then had been passed down the chain of command to this officer. As the officer at Leuchars had access to all the names of the team visiting that day, my name came out of the hat as being the defaulter. The following is more or less what was said to me and, I might add, in no uncertain terms . . .

"'It has been brought to my attention that you have been asking questions during your recent visit to Leuchars in regard to UFOs, in particular an incident that took place in the past that you claim had involved the Royal Air Force. As a member of the Royal Air Force, and subject to your position at this base as a radar observer, bearing in mind you have signed the Official Secrets Act to which you must adhere under all circumstances, you must never at any time, on or off the base, discuss the topic of UFOs. This is a subject of the highest sensitivity and you have no authority to discuss any issue relating to it whilst in this service.

"'If you at any time see fit to pursue the matter, make no mistake you will face a charge of the highest magnitude. The business of UFOs may be of casual interest to you, but whatever you see, hear, or learn of the subject during your time at this base is never to be discussed with other air force personnel, and certainly not with any civilian agencies beyond the perimeters of this establishment.

"'It is my understanding that you are a competent, extremely pleasant and reliable individual with an interest in music,' conceded the squadron leader. 'Don't let that standing be compromised by neglect of duty and of the things you may learn in your role in the air defence system.'

"It was a serious 'hands-off' call, and it left me somewhat shaken but not entirely stirred," Ian reflected. "I had no option whatsoever other than to comply with what was in effect an official order. That they reacted in the manner they did sent clear messages that the military did indeed take the UFO status quo very seriously. . . . It has long been my belief that this particular sighting represents what I would consider the most significant daytime happening to have taken place in U.K. airspace following the end of WWII, in terms of the actual size and shape of the aeroform, the sheer duration of the event, and how it behaved during the timeframe, its altitude and, more importantly, the intervention of the military, who of course denied any involvement whatsoever. . . ."

MOTHER SHIPS

With regard to the enormity of alien craft, in 1963, during a private meeting in London, which included two high-ranking British officials (Chapter 19), George Adamski described the "mother ships" in considerable detail, which he said served all the needs of space travelers for long journeys through space. "These gargantuan vessels varied in size," reported my friend Emily Crewe, who was present at the meeting, "but none ever landed on terrestrial ground. They were approximately one to three thousand feet long and hundreds of feet in width. They had many decks, and vast spaces to section off the life support systems, for the growing of foods and the freeze-storage of these supplies. They contained water purified in tanks so big, large sea creatures could swim in them, but this water was fresh and taken from terrestrial waterways such as ours here on Earth." The water could also be recycled; for example, in our skies.[1]

In 1965, not long before he died, Adamski revealed additional details to Fred Steckling, some at variance with what he had stated two years earlier. A main base for these giant craft on Earth, he claimed, was alleged to be in a deep ravine some two hundred kilometers west of Mexico City, in very rugged terrain virtually inaccessible except by helicopter. Some of the craft were claimed to be several miles in length and "stacked side by side with their noses pointing to the ground, not actually touching the ground but about three feet above the ground, pointing downward, while the rest of the craft pointed at a slight angle straight up into the air, as if held by some magnetic beam," Henry Dohan reports. "Near each nose was a hatch and steps of a sort for descending out of the cigar-shaped craft." Top-level meetings with several of the world's leaders were said to have been held in this remote location.[2]

POLICE PATROL

In the small hours of one night in the early 1980s, two Metropolitan Police officers were on patrol in Middlesex, Greater London. "I was a young Police Officer on night duty in a marked vehicle," Robin Perry wrote to me. "It was the Area Car—an old SD1 Rover—and I was the R/T [radio-telephone] operator, being driven by my colleague. We were traveling very slowly at about 3 A.M. from the White Hart roundabout along the Ruislip Road, Northolt, toward Greenford. Someone had been setting fire to parked cars at this location in recent days, so we were skulking along the road keeping a watch for any dodgy-looking characters. I have to point out that, back then, the road and pedestrian traffic at this time of the morning was almost non-existent—not as it is today.

"As we were driving along I noticed a large orange light in the sky over to our left—toward RAF Northolt[3]—and brought it to my driver's attention. The strange thing is that when we started to talk about it, the object flew directly toward us. As it did so, it flew over a large open park area which was on our left side, leading directly onto the Ruislip Road (Rectory Park).

"As it got closer, I could see that it was a huge black triangle with a light on each point and an orange ball on the middle underside. It was very large, and I estimated it to be at least the size of two football pitches (there were a number of pitches that it flew over toward us). It was very low and made absolutely no noise. It was so low, I couldn't see any of the sky around it.

"The object flew alongside our vehicle on the near side, matching our speed. I was leaning out of the car window and waving at it. We carried along the Ruislip Road for about three quarters of a mile with this thing still flying alongside and matching our speed, which was still slow. It was barely skimming the rooftops of the houses as it did so. My driver then stopped the car in the middle of the road opposite Greenford [Assembly] Hall and we both got out. The triangle then hovered directly over us at no more than thirty feet, or the height of the Hall to our left. It was huge, dead still, and silent. The driver even turned off the car engine, and we could still hear nothing.

"I then turned on the blue light on the roof and was waving up at the craft, but got no response. After a few minutes (yes, minutes), it turned around and then slowly glided away back along the Ruislip Road. After a couple of hundred yards, it suddenly shot up into the sky at an unbelievable speed and disappeared from view. We sort of 'came to our senses' and jumped into the car and drove around the corner to Greenford Police Station. We told the Station Officer—an old 'sweat'—who advised us to keep quiet, otherwise face ridicule from our colleagues. However, I called RAF Northolt straight away and had an interesting conversation with someone who claimed to be in their flight [control] tower. He basically stated that they too had seen it, had no idea what it was, and it was not worth filing an official report. So I never did.

"I know it sounds far-fetched, and I can't explain why neither of us tried to radio for other units to join us. We also passed neither other cars nor pedestrians throughout the whole incident. Just as a footnote, about a week or so later a very distressed driver burst into Greenford Police Station in the early hours of one morning claiming that his vehicle had been buzzed by a bright orange light as he drove along the Ruislip Road. This time, the Station Officer did report it, and that incident made the front page of our local newspaper. . . ."[4]

FURTHER EVENTS IN THE U.K.

An enormous craft, described as "looking like a flying fairground," was reported high in the sky over Exmouth, Devon, on the night of August 4, 1987. Gordon Baker viewed the craft from his garden, and was joined by his wife Gloria and a neighbor, Heather Palmer, as they took turns at viewing the craft through binoculars. The object looked like two cross-shaped objects joined together (see sketch on the next page).

'FLYING FAIRGROUND' IS SEEN OVER TOWN

From the Exmouth Herald, *August 7, 1987*

"It was definitely not an aircraft," insisted Mr. Baker. "There was no sound whatsoever. I believe the object was traveling at about thirty-five thousand feet. Then I heard the noise of a jet aircraft. I saw it pass under the lit objects, and I even checked with Exeter Airport to see if the pilot had reported seeing it. They said they had not received any reports. However, a man in air traffic control said he had a couple of objects on his radar, but did not know what they were. We watched it for about fifteen minutes until it disappeared on the horizon. I don't know what it was, but it certainly had hundreds of lights on it."[5]

Further witnesses came forward following publication of the report in a local paper, including former RAF technician Tony Millington and his wife Claire. "It certainly wasn't an aircraft," he said. "It is very difficult to say how high they were, but there was no noise at all. That is what seemed so odd to me. As we watched, the two objects seemed to get close together. . . . We watched [them] for about fifteen minutes before they disappeared over the horizon toward Haldon Hill. The lights were uniform in brilliance."

A Ministry of Defence spokesman evinced little interest when contacted.[6]

Of the hundreds of British reports of large craft sighted that year, one of the most interesting came to me from Barbara Forrest, of Brierley Hill, West Midlands. At around 19:00–19:15 on November 19, 1987, Barbara's 27-year-old son Brett spotted two very bright lights in the sky, one small and one large, close together, from outside the three-story block of flats where she resided in Moor Street. "My son said that they seemed to join together, and then it took on the shape of a diamond and became brilliant," she wrote to journalist Peter Rhodes of the *Wolverhampton Express & Star* two days later, asking to be put in touch with me.

Brett and Barbara sent me colored sketches, depicting how the craft appeared in three stages, finally coalescing into a huge elongated triangle with a series of grooves underneath, colored black, silver, and bronze. As Barbara recounted for me:

"The craft came over the street light where he had been watching it for quite some time. Brett thought he had to tell someone or he would never be believed, so he ran down the grass embankment to my living room window, knocked very hard, and as I opened it he said, 'Mom, look up!' And there it was, massive, wonderful—and frightening! Here was something that in the first instance had been two very bright lights, very still in the night sky, then the whole thing lights up in the shape of a diamond. Then it starts to move, and as it came nearer and lower it dimmed its lights. It passed right over the block of flats where I live.

"I was amazed at what I saw—a great floating airship all lit up underneath with many, many white lights. There was no noise. It was massive. That thing was so low, it was unbelievable. I watched it go right out of sight as it went in the direction of the High Street. There were two aircraft in the vicinity at the time, with their normal red and green lights."

Her first sketch depicts what she saw as the craft was directly above her, with black serrated edges "which when a little distance away looked as though they were kind of grills. The inner part of the craft was a gray or silvery color. There were strips underneath. The lights were fluorescent, very white and bright." The second sketch—varying from her son's depiction—shows the object "seen floating silently away. One could no longer see the individual lights or the shape of the craft. . . .

"This thing must have wanted to be seen, otherwise it would just have zoomed away. It seemed to follow my son. I have never seen anything like it in all my fifty-seven years. In actual fact, this is starting to worry me now . . . perhaps whoever was in that floating city may not like us very much."[7]

Brett's sketches of the craft appear on the next page:

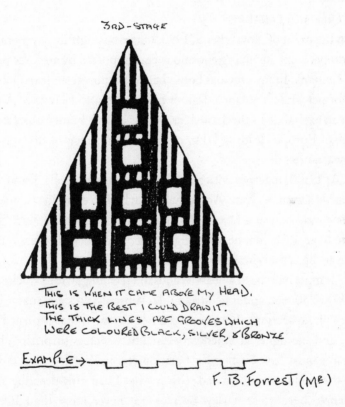

1ST - STAGE

THIS IS HOW I FIRST SAW THEM.
UP IN THE SKY

2ND - STAGE

THESE OTHER LIGHTS
LIT UP AROUND THE
ORIGINAL TWO

3RD - STAGE

THIS IS WHEN IT CAME ABOVE MY HEAD.
THIS IS THE BEST I COULD DRAW IT.
THE THICK LINES ARE GROOVES WHICH
WERE COLOURED BLACK, SILVER, & BRONZE

EXAMPLE →

F. B. Forrest (ME)

I had a lengthy correspondence with Barbara, but it was years before we finally met, together with her son, at a conference in Stourbridge organized by UFO Research Midlands in July 2005. My conviction in their sincerity was reinforced.

Three weeks following the Brierley Hill sighting, another event occurred, one of numerous reports from Nottinghamshire at that time.

"It was obvious to all the witnesses that it was not a normal aircraft and it immediately drew their attention," reported a journalist. "Most reports say there was a deep humming noise, faint but distinct. All agree that the object was huge [and] most say that a jet aircraft was seen shortly after the UFO."

"I knew it was huge, twenty or thirty times the size of a normal aircraft, and it made a distinctive deep throbbing noise," said Edward Fell, of Long Eaton.[8] (See photo section.)

FRANCE AND CANADA

On the night of November 5, 1990, numerous sightings were reported over Europe, some involving enormous craft reported by air force pilots as well as civilians. In my previous book, I cited a report from Jean Gabriel Greslé, a former French air force fighter pilot (who also flew U.S. Air Force jets on an exchange in the 1950s), as well as an Air France captain. He is now one of Europe's leading UFO researchers. A précis of this important case is warranted here.

At 19:00, together with six of his martial-arts pupils, Jean was standing outside a gym in Gretz-Armainvilliers when an enormous crane-like object came into view at a height of around three hundred meters. "It projected two huge, divergent beams of light, not quite touching the ground," he told me at the actual site in November 2004.

"It must have been at least a thousand feet long, with a thickness of about 200 or 250 feet, and it had triangular substructures and many, many lights [see photo section]. I ran around a tree to watch it as it turned its back on us, and the lights dimmed very quickly, which is surprising, because the beams must have been at least a kilometer in length—then it disappeared in the clouds. . . . It carried with it what I can only describe as a 'zone of silence,' because as it flew over us—at never more than 100 mph—we suddenly didn't hear the nearby traffic. And I had the impression that my mind was blanked out. . . . It was absolutely incredible—like a city floating through the clouds!"[9]

The following report was sent to me by Dr. Richard Haines, the well-known researcher, whose past employment includes posts with the National Research Council, Boeing Airplane Co., and at NASA's Ames Research Center, where he served as Chief of the Space Human

Factors Office and in other research positions. Co-author of the report was Bernard Guénette, a professional computer graphics expert—and a witness to the event.

On November 7, 1990, between forty and seventy-five people, including Royal Canadian Mounted Police (RCMP) and Montreal Urban Community Police (MUCP), witnessed a huge aerial object, beaming shafts of light, which hovered at around six thousand feet above downtown Montreal between about 19:30 and 22:00 EST. Many of the witnesses were located on the 17th floor of the International Hilton Bonaventure Hotel. Three journalists from *La Presse* arrived at the scene. One, Marcel Laroche, took two photos of the craft, but owing to cloudy conditions only the light beams could be seen. One of these photos was published in *La Presse* the following day. "The lighted object had six lights on the perimeter of a large circle with a ray of light emitting from each one," stated the paper. "Most witnesses described the rays as white, while some also claimed they saw blue, yellow, and red lights."

An Air Canada pilot who witnessed the event from the rooftop of the Hilton Hotel estimated the altitude of the object at between eight and ten thousand feet. While driving home from work between 22:30 and 23:00, a M. Pierre Caumartin saw "very big and strong lights" in a boomerang shape low in the sky. On arriving at his home, not far from the Longue-Pointe military base [CFB Longue-Pointe], he watched the object hover near the Hydro-Quebec Longue-Pointe power station. When he got out of his car, he heard a "purring" sound and thought the object was a dirigible, with only its gondola visible below the cloud base.

As Dr. Haines points out, CFB Longue-Pointe contains "forty-eight regular forces, detachments and units, of about 1,900 persons, twenty-five reserve units, and ninety-seven cadet corps with 7,500 persons. It also supports three military schools. No one at the base could be found who saw the aerial object on November 7. A power failure (*hors tension*) was experienced between 23:08 and 23:50 at the Longue-Pointe military base. The base is fed by a 12,000-volt lead from the Hydro-Quebec-Longue-Pointe power station. It is the only one which broke down on November 7 [and] a check of the operating records of telecommunications networks [etc.] did not uncover any unusual malfunctions. . . .

"Perhaps of equal importance with the overall scope of the aerial phenomenon was the almost total lack of official response to it. No action of any kind was taken by personnel of the St. Hubert military base after they were notified of the aerial object hovering above the center of the city. As far as is known, they did not even report it to the North American Aerospace Defense Command (NORAD) coordination center."[10]

THE WILLIAMSPORT WAVE

On February 6, 1992, the Pennsylvania Association for the Study of the Unexplained (PASU), headed by Stan Gordon, began to receive numerous reports of a series of low-level sightings in the vicinity of Williamsport, Pennsylvania, which had occurred the previous day. To assist in his investigations, Gordon sought the collaboration of Dr. Samuel D. Greco, a retired Air Force major and aerospace engineer who served as the Pennsylvania state section director for the Mutual UFO Network (MUFON), which liaised closely with PASU.

The wave of sightings on February 5 occurred from about 18:00 to 19:00. "Two different kinds of object, boomerang- and triangular-shaped, had been seen in the evening sky, and there had been numerous persons who had witnessed the sightings," Dr. Greco reported. "All the sightings followed a similar pattern. Apart from one, all originated in the houses of the witnesses." Typical descriptions follow:

- A loud or heavy rumbling noise above the house which shook or vibrated the building and rattled its windows
- Witnesses would then leave the house, see the object, and alert others
- Object usually boomerang-shaped. One witness, who stood directly underneath, described it as triangular-shaped. A few other shapes were reported (see sketches). Lights or portholes on the craft could be seen
- The span of the boomerang-shaped object was variously estimated at 100 to 600 feet
- The object moved very slowly, at low altitude, often surrounded by moving red and green lights

- Animals displayed irrational behavior
- Object disappeared suddenly

"There were no aircraft in the sighting area reported either by commercial air sources, the Federal Aviation Administration, or the USAF," concluded Dr. Greco. "The witnesses were ordinary people going about their daily lives [who] were considered reliable, honest, and sincere [and] did not want their names released to the public."[11]

Dr. Greco's diagrams of the various shapes of craft—seen in one day alone—appear below:

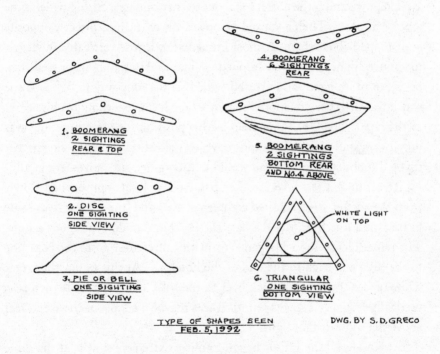

4. BOOMERANG
6 SIGHTINGS
REAR

1. BOOMERANG
2 SIGHTINGS
REAR & TOP

5. BOOMERANG
2 SIGHTINGS
BOTTOM REAR
AND NO.4 ABOVE

2. DISC
ONE SIGHTING
SIDE VIEW

3. PIE OR BELL
ONE SIGHTING
SIDE VIEW

WHITE LIGHT
ON TOP

6. TRIANGULAR
ONE SIGHTING
BOTTOM VIEW

TYPE OF SHAPES SEEN
FEB. 5, 1992

DWG. BY S.D.GRECO

CYPRUS

During the night of 11/12 September 1992, according to a witness who contacted me the following month, aerial objects, including an enormous structured craft, appeared above Le Meridien Hotel, located some fifteen kilometers east of Limassol, southern Cyprus. I shall refer to the witness (an accountant) as "Andy," as he insisted on anonymity.

"At approximately 10:50 P.M.," he reported, "I went out on the balcony of my room to listen to the music being played by a hotel group on the ground floor. From the balcony there is a panoramic view of the hills to the north—about three miles away—but the sea is obscured by the east wing of the hotel. It was a completely clear night with an almost full moon. As I sat at the table facing north, I saw a white light approaching from the northwest. I assumed it was an aircraft heading for Larnaca, but it suddenly stopped. I then thought it must be a helicopter, because it rose vertically and stopped again. I then realized that there was no sound coming from the 'craft' and also that there were no lights. . . .

"I kept watching the object for about twenty minutes, during which time it was stationary. Then it started to move away to the hills directly opposite and stopped above them. Almost immediately it rose vertically, in stages, to a much higher point and stopped again. . . . After an hour or so it then began to move again and cruised (which is the only way to describe the way it traveled) back to approximately where it started, though a bit nearer to the hotel. The UFO remained in this position for some time, but was not always stationary—it would move *very* slowly at times, so slowly that if you did not concentrate you would hardly notice any movement at all.

"At about 2 A.M., several other pale yellow lights approached slowly from the northeast—I counted eighteen in all—and [the nearest five] came to halt on a line from the sea past the hotel and inland for about a mile. The remainder were in a [square] formation stretching from the coastline to the hills and back to the end of the hotel. . . . At this point, the larger white object then moved back over to the hills and stopped. It then rose vertically—again in stages—until it was maybe a couple of thousand feet above the most distant light. . . .

"At 4 A.M., all the UFOs began to move extremely slowly, at the same speed, toward the sea [and] as I glanced over the top of the hotel, a huge object appeared out and over the sea, climbing very slowly. It is difficult to describe the shape of this object because of the light, but the moonlight illuminated the right-hand side and part of the side facing me. Also, there was a narrow band of light across the middle of the object, and as it got higher two other bands of light appeared to be switched on above and below the first one.

"I must emphasise that the speed at which this thing was moving was very slow, as though it was in trouble or very heavy. It appeared to be wider at the base [see witness sketch below]. I would say it was much bigger than the hotel. Meanwhile, all the other UFOs were patiently following at some distance. . . . It climbed really slowly and was upright, travelling vertically but at an angle above the sea."

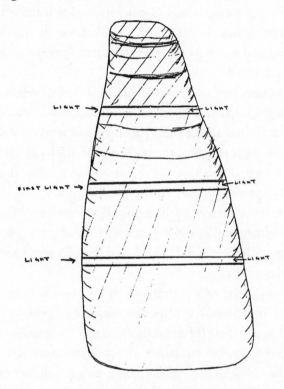

"There was no noise. Then the most extraordinary thing happened. . . .

"When the huge object was just gaining height, a missile appeared to be fired at one of the yellow UFOs which were still over the hills opposite me. It came from behind one of the hills and went sharply up, trailing a yellow flame. As it approached the UFO I prepared for an explosion, but the yellow light of the UFO went out for a split second, there was a white spark, and the missile seemed to be deflected toward the hotel, to the left of where I was standing on the balcony. I watched the missile, which was glowing or burning red, go past and just over the hotel, heading out to sea. It was about the length and half the height of a single-decker bus, and horizontal in flight.

"When the missile was fired, all the UFOs, including the massive one, stopped moving for fifteen minutes. The latter just remained suspended in the sky. Then they all began moving again, upwards and outwards over the sea, still at the same slow pace. This went on until 4:40 A.M., when a vivid green and blue semi-circular object appeared over the sea above the wing of the hotel, below the huge UFO and between it and the hotel. It was much lower and was flashing blue and green intermittently; at times the colors intermingled . . .

"At 4:45 A.M. another missile was launched at the last yellow UFO (the nearest one to the hills) and the same thing happened as before, except that when the deflected missile came past the hotel, it was not glowing red like the first one, only yellow at the rear end. At 4:50 A.M. all the UFOs were getting higher in the sky, but it was noticeable that the huge one was *not* getting appreciably smaller the higher it got.

"[The huge object] seemed to me to look like some kind of transporter, because of its lighting, color, and shape: it was dull and workmanlike with only three strips of light—at least that I could see. By about 5:00 A.M. the UFOs had almost gone.

"It is only conjecture on my part," Andy concluded, "but I think the huge UFO had landed by the Limassol power station just along the coast or beyond it, and stayed there for about three hours. The smaller yellow ones were a protective force, and the larger white ones were the reconnaissance craft. What the object of the exercise was is purely a matter for speculation, but maybe the power station had something to do with it. . . . The only other thing I can think of is that the huge object was perhaps being repaired, because the difficulty it seemed to have climbing could suggest some sort of malfunction."[12]

My first line of inquiry was Headquarters, British Forces Cyprus at the Akrotiri Sovereign Base Area, which occupies a large area mostly contained on a peninsula some 25 kilometers to the south and west of Le Meridien Hotel. "I can assure you that the sitings [*sic*] were not as a result of any British Forces Cyprus exercise," stated Squadron Leader J. A. Bartram RAF, Office of the Commander. "It would appear that other people did sight unusual aerial phenomena on the night in question [and] this was reported in the Cypriot papers. . . ."[13]

In late November/early December 1992, I spent a week in Cyprus and interviewed people in the area, including an assistant manager at Le Meridien. A local researcher had not heard anything about the event, and my appeals for witnesses—on CyBC radio and television and in *The Cyprus Weekly*—drew a blank. I was unable to get an appointment at the Limassol power station, but the following year my friend Graham Sheppard, a former British Airways senior captain, visited the station and was told that nothing unusual had been reported on the night in question. Although there were reports of UFOs around that time, neither of us could find anyone who could corroborate the main event. One possible explanation may owe to the closely knit Greek-Cypriot community who, I gathered, are "quite sensitive about things of this nature."

I should mention that earlier in the year, on the night of January 24/25, 1992, many residents of Larnaca, Limassol, and Palechori observed a brightly lit craft, estimated at about fifty meters in length. Some said it was soundless, while others thought they detected a low hum. Beginning at 23:00, the sightings lasted for two and a half hours.[14]

I met Andy in my apartment in December 1992. He appeared nervous. As he had explained earlier: "I am very concerned about the consequences arising from publication, particularly the security implications, not only for me, but also for Cyprus . . . especially as missiles are involved."[15]

I wrote again to British Forces Cyprus in 2003, asking if any further information had come to light, querying the possibility that the event might have been related to an air-defense exercise. "Your request has been exhaustively investigated by RAF Akrotiri," came the reply, "but, regrettably, unit records are unable to throw any further light on the events [and] hold no information on live weapon training for the night in question."[16]

If a hoax, one would have to question the motive. A desire for money and notoriety, at least, can be ruled out. Having met the witness and corresponded with him over a period of time, I retain the impression that he was describing a real event, one that—as in so many other cases—left him profoundly disturbed. Furthermore, reports of this type of craft were very rare in 1992. But as we shall see, sightings of similar types increased in ensuing years.

SHROPSHIRE, U.K.

In *Need to Know*, I cite the penetration in the small hours of March 31, 1993, of two Royal Air Force bases—Cosford and Shawbury—by a large triangular craft, and (in the second edition of that book) reproduced a minute from the Ministry of Defence's [MoD] Head of Secretariat (Air Staff) to the Assistant Chief of the Air Staff (ACAS). "Some of the reports state that the object was moving at a very high speed, while some say that it was hovering or moving very slowly," the minute concludes.

"Many of the reports refer to the object being very large, flying low, and making a low humming sound. My staff have spoken to a number of the military and police witnesses, many of whom commented that the object was unlike anything they had ever seen before; a Met Officer at RAF Shawbury reported seeing the object projecting a narrow beam of light at the ground at a height of four to five hundred feet and estimated its size at somewhere between a C130 [Hercules] and B747 [jumbo]. . . . If there has been some activity of U.S. origins which is known to a limited circle in MoD [Ministry of Defence] and is not being acknowledged, it is difficult to investigate further. . . ."[17]

On the night of March 30, sixteen-year-old Darren Perks had an encounter with what was either the same or a similar craft. "At the time of the incident," he told me in 2005, "I was preparing to enter the Army Air Corps. Since the age of twelve I had been a member of the Royal Air Force's Combined Cadet Force (CCF), in which I had already made the rank of flight sergeant. Being in the CCF, I had flying experience and extensive knowledge of all military aircraft of the current time and post cold-war era. I also had good knowledge of civilian and/or non-fixed-wing aircraft [and] I was a frequent visitor to RAF Shawbury airbase. . . .

"At approximately 11:00 P.M., I was walking home from my part-time job at the Shrewsbury Superbowl, in the northern outskirts of Shrewsbury. At the time, my parents owned a local pub called the Harry Hotspur, and it was only six hundred meters from my work along Harlescott Lane. As I got to within a hundred meters of my home, my eyes caught a slow-moving structured object, about three hundred feet up, moving from left to right—south to north. At the time, the weather was clear and there was no wind and also no traffic passing me on the road, so my surroundings were very quiet.

"It was a black triangle shape, approximately 200 feet in length and 150 to 200 feet in diameter. It was [clearly] defined, and [it] blocked out the stars. As I continued to watch this strange craft, a brilliant white beam of light appeared from it and started to sweep the ground from left to right as if it were looking for something in the fields. On the two rear points of the triangle, I noticed a faint red or orange-colored glow. At one point, the craft stopped moving and just hung in the sky, still not making any sound at all.

"The triangle was moving very slowly—I would say about walking speed—and I could hear nothing but a very low humming sound that was irritating to hear. I also felt warm, and the sense of being watched, or at least that whoever or whatever was controlling the triangle knew I was watching it.

"Opposite my house at the time was rough ground and fields, and the triangle continued to move north over them with the white light flicking back and forth randomly. At this point, I estimated that I had been watching this craft for about two minutes when all of a sudden it shot off to the north at incredible speed, making no sound at all.

"I knew that this was not a military or civilian aircraft, and I rushed into my house and woke up my parents to tell them what I had just witnessed. All of us then went outside to see if we could see the craft, but there was nothing.

"I never told the authorities because I didn't know what to do, and during my time in the military I never spoke of the incident as I didn't want to be ridiculed. However, it's only been in the last two years that I found out about the RAF Cosford [Staffordshire] and Shawbury [Shropshire] incidents, and that what I saw was linked to [other] sightings over the U.K. that night.

"Ever since the incident, I have had a feeling of knowing that the craft will come back. It makes me feel uneasy, but at the same time I want to know where it was from and why it was here. I can't explain it, but I have it in my head that in 2012 something is going to happen and that it's linked to what I witnessed. It's a feeling that never goes away, and when I go back to the spot where I witnessed the incident I get an overwhelming sense of uneasiness to this day. I think the military in the U.K. and the United States know of these craft but are keeping it under wraps away from the public so as not to alarm people. . . ."[18]

Roger Wise and his partner were traveling along the Telford Road, Bridgnorth, on September 16, 1996, at about 23:00, when an extraordinary craft, similar in some respects to the one in Cyprus, appeared. "The object was an incredible size, flying slowly from the east," Roger recounted for me. "It was low in the sky, rectangular in shape, rather like a skateboard moving sideways, with window lights/portholes all around it, with more than one tier. This, with several levels and the size, looked like the equivalent of a battleship.

"It then appeared to slow and from the mid-front released a fully lit spinning circle which spun off at top speed—like a flying saucer—toward the west and Clee Hill in a matter of seconds. The main UFO then turned around and went off back toward the east."[19]

YUKON TERRITORY

In some previous books I have referenced the encounter with three UFOs reported by the crew of a Japan Airlines Boeing 747 cargo flight over Alaska, en route to Anchorage, on November 17, 1986. During the encounter—which was tracked on radar—Captain Kenju Terauchi caught a brief glimpse of the main object's walnut-shaped silhouette, judging it to be twice the size of an aircraft carrier.

On the evening of December 11, 1996, a huge craft, estimated by witnesses at the time to be "larger than a football stadium" (see photo section), was seen in three main areas along the 134-mile stretch of the Klondike Highway in Canada's Yukon Territory. The majority of the twenty-two witnesses elected to remain anonymous.

"There was no sound at all coming from the object," reported the principal investigator, Martin Jasek of UFO*BC, and the craft had a "huge, and long, row of lights around it. When a witness happened to point his flashlight at the craft, it started speeding toward him.

"A beam of light emanating from the bottom of the UFO swept the ground once directly underneath the object. Was it a search beam? Looking for him? The UFO then drifted slowly to the right. There were other beams emanating from the craft as well: a greenish phosphorescent color beam shone horizontally out the front (right); two beams at the back (left) rotated slowly to a horizontal position. All the beams could be seen clearly, as there were ice crystals in the air."

The only witness to give his name was Don Trudeau, a trapper, who had a very close encounter with the craft near the village of Pelly Crossing. In company with many other witnesses, he was unable to determine its precise configuration, but based on the width of the rows of lights, he came up with a length of three quarters of a mile. Estimates of the craft's actual size were determined by triangulation. "This method was employed six times to obtain six estimates for the size of the UFO," explained Martin. "All revealed staggering results: the UFO ranged anywhere from 0.55 miles to 1.3 miles in length!"[20]

ARIZONA AIR DISPLAY

One of the most widely observed incidents relating to enormous craft, of varying shapes, occurred on the evening of March 13, 1997, when thousands of eyewitnesses across Arizona—mostly in the Phoenix area—reported having seen a mile-long, V-shaped formation of lights, seemingly connected and flying relatively close to the ground. In addition to members of the public, witnesses included F-16 pilots from Luke Air Force Base and a retired pilot in Scottsdale who held ratings in Boeing 747 and DC-10 airliners. Together with others, the former airline pilot observed a huge formation of orange lights, attached to what looked like a structured object "at least a mile in area."

A chevron-shaped craft, like "a carpenter's square set at 60 degrees" and estimated to be at least two city blocks in length, was observed by Tim Ley who, together with members of his family, watched as it passed over their home. As it did so, the family felt a sensation "almost like stage fright."[21]

Ten years later, Fife Symington III, former governor of Arizona, admitted to having seen an enormous triangular craft during the extraordinary air display that night. A cousin of the late Senator Stuart Symington, former Secretary of the Air Force, the governor had hitherto publicly ridiculed the incident at a press conference. "Unless the Defense Department proves us otherwise," he stated during a CNN interview, "it was probably some form of alien spacecraft."[22] This is how he described what he saw to journalist Leslie Kean, author of a *New York Times* bestseller on UFOs:

"Between 8:00 and 8:30 on the evening of March 13, 1997, during my second term as governor of Arizona, I witnessed something that defied logic and challenged my reality: a massive, delta-shaped craft silently navigating over the Squaw Peak in the Phoenix Mountain preserve. A solid structure rather than an apparition, it was dramatically large, with a distinctive leading edge embedded with lights as it traveled the Arizona skies. I still don't know what it was. As a pilot and a former Air Force officer, I can say with certainty that this craft did not resemble any man-made object I had ever seen."[23]

UTAH

Michael Vladeck is an Outward Bound instructor who had an encounter on the night of July 5, 1999, a half hour west of Salt Lake City en route to an Outward Bound retreat. Researcher Thane Mathis put me in touch with the witness, who subsequently sent me his report.

"I pulled off westbound I-80 in Utah onto a ranch exit to put my sleeping bag down and get some sleep," Vladeck wrote. "The view from where I stopped for the night, about three quarters of a mile north of the highway, had a 360-degree panorama of the juniper- and sage-covered plains. There was a consistently present breeze, about twelve to twenty miles an hour, and the sky was covered in a thick, low-lying blanket of stratus clouds. I could see the lights of Salt Lake City bouncing off them about forty miles to the east."

As he put down his ground pad and bag and prepared to lie down, he noticed that the clouds to the west were oddly bright—and becoming brighter. At first he thought it might have been the moon, but when the lights continued to brighten even more, he assumed that the "brights" of an eighteen-wheeler truck parked on the off-ramp of the highway were responsible. "Then, as I was about to get into my bag, a bright light cast my shadow on the ground in front of me [and] as I turned around, I saw an enormous non-aerodynamically shaped craft finish coming through the clouds. My guess was that it was seven hundred feet away from me (although I could be off by an additional three hundred feet, at most).

"It was huge—a 747 airplane could fit inside of it. It seemed to be about 300 to 350 feet long, 110 to 150 feet wide, and 60-plus feet high. It had a rectangular base, and from the super-bright lights (I'll explain those in a moment) shining off the desert floor and reflecting back upward, it appeared as if the side was prowed-out in an arching angle—on the side that I saw, as well as the back. The front of the craft was just past me and I couldn't see its shape.

"All of the craft was dark except for one strip of rectangular lights—about thirty of them pressed together near the front of the underside, spanning about 100 to 130 feet or so [see sketch below]. The lights were very full-spectrum-looking, as the juniper and the desert floor were lit up intensely as if they were under very bright daylight."

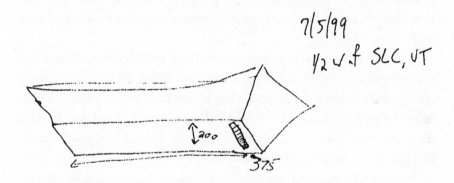

7/5/99
½ v. f SLC, UT
200
375

"The craft was moving about twenty to thirty miles an hour, heading north-northwest, and its elevation remained constant (around five to six hundred feet), and it seemed to stay with the contours of the desert floor—when the land dropped away in the distance, its elevation above the land directly below it stayed the same. It also made no sound that I could hear at all (while there was a breeze, it was still rather quiet out). There seemed to be no kind of propulsion system on it that I could discern.

"When it went out of view, I could still see the clouds above it glowing from the craft's lights off the land and bouncing upward. Then, all told about two minutes from my turning around to see it, the lights in the distance faded out of sight. That was it. I was so blown away by it all. It seemed like I imagined it or dreamed it—even five minutes later. I think this was because it was so out of context with anything else I've ever seen that I had nothing to ground the experience to. . . ."[24]

BIRMINGHAM, U.K.

Another witness profoundly shocked by his experience was Edward Bradley of Birmingham. At 20:30 on the evening of Thursday, March 28, 2002, he was returning on foot from a friend's former flat in High-field Road, having collected mail to forward to him. "As I was walking down Sherwood Road," Edward reported to me, "to the left I saw in the distance three points of light approaching. The only thing that appeared odd was that the lights were not flashing on and off, as you would normally expect to see on an aircraft [apart from the navigation lights, that is—Author], and they were very, very bright red. As I carried on walking, the shape of the craft appeared in full view—and what I saw wasn't a plane.

"The object was a long triangular craft and at each corner there was a red light—three lights in total. It looked red but it didn't look a natural red. It was the same color as blood. The object itself was jet black, the same color as a polished lump of coal, and I was standing not underneath it but diagonally opposite to it, on the left-hand side of it and less than a quarter of a mile away from it. [See photo section.]

"It made no sound and was moving very slowly and steadily. When I say 'moving,' flying is not the word: I think the word is gliding, but it was just on a perfect straight course. The part that made my blood run cold was that it was as if the sky behind it had suddenly gone flat and was sort of shimmering. Imagine a flat black wall and it was affecting what was going on behind it. The sky behind it was like black mercury. That shimmering effect was very odd. There were no clouds that night. Stars were in the sky but not behind the craft—around it, but not behind it. It was having an effect on the sky the other side of it.

"It was a huge craft and very, very low indeed. Lengthwise I would say it would have fit comfortably into a reasonably-sized football ground. It was very close to the tops of the houses in the street and in fact flying in the same line as they were in. From the ground, I would say it was at a height of a twenty-story block of flats. I watched it go in the direction of the Stratford Road toward Solihull and then it just carried on. It didn't shoot away; it carried on at a set speed and a straight course.

"I had a mobile phone with me, but I was so shocked that I never thought to film it—I was mentally taking it in. What surprised me was that I have often read stories about people who see lights in the distance. But this passed me in the street: it was a real object, as clear as seeing a car pass you in the street. And it was passing through a heavily built-up part of a Birmingham suburb. There wasn't a soul about in the street at all, and no one to speak to or say 'Did you see that?' I have no proof whatsoever. My only hope is that someone else saw it that night in the U.K., in another location. . . ."[25]

Edward Bradley—whom I have now met—strikes me as an exceptionally reliable witness. His background includes positions with the Civil Service, the Department of Trade and Industry, Lloyds TSB, and Virgin Trains. He currently holds a responsible position in another company.

NOVA SCOTIA

Don Ledger is a Canadian author, pilot, and UFO researcher who lives in Labelle, Nova Scotia. I have long respected his integrity and previously cited his investigations—and those of Chris Styles—into the Shag Harbour incident of 1967, involving an unidentified submergible object (USO).[26] In a lecture on flying triangles presented at the Halifax UFO International Symposium in 1993, Don included the report of a giant craft seen by Helen M., an experienced amateur astronomer living in Cow Bay, about five miles northeast of the City of Halifax/Dartmouth, on the night of August 13, 2002.

Helen had been watching a few meteors when one, larger than the others, appeared out of the constellation of Ursa Major. "It had a long tail and rather than winking out immediately, it arced across the sky and over her head to the southeast," Don reports. Instead of gradually fading out, however, its progress across the sky was suddenly terminated, "as if it had passed behind something . . . there seemed to be a black curtain being drawn across it from slightly behind her, from the southeast, [and she] was surprised to discover a straight black line was crossing the sky and blanking out the stars.

"At intermittent moments she could see what she described as ridiculous and ludicrous tiny white lights at the outer extremities of this black line as they passed over the canopy of trees surrounding her property [and then] noticed that one light was trailing the other two and she realized she was seeing 'a perfect black triangle of gargantuan proportions' [which] was in the process of crossing directly over the clearing around her house."

"If there had been a full moon, I wouldn't have been able to see it," said Helen. "This thing blocked the entire area of sky above me—we're talking football fields in length and breadth. This thing was enormous—too big to be in the air, you would think. It was pitch black, very black. It moved very slowly—ten miles an hour? There was absolutely no sound at all. Everything became very still. And I felt 'tingly,' like when you get pins and needles, [but] the feeling left when the triangle was out of sight." The entire event lasted about five minutes as the craft passed from the southeast and then disappeared over the trees to the northwest.

Helen's next-door neighbor kept pheasants in a cage on the other side of the fence and, atypically, they were not making the usual bird noises and remained quite still during the incident. "When I got up the next morning," she told Don, "I had a headache which remained with me all day, and I felt nauseous and dizzy once in the afternoon." The headache remained with her until the following day.

"I have to tell you I still feel a little weird about it," she explained to Don. "It's hard to wrap my mind around the reality of what I saw. But see it I did, whatever it was. . . ."

Don Ledger's extensive inquiries yielded other reports of the craft, including input from an air traffic controller who informed him that "there *was* an unknown target with a strong [radar] return at the specified time and in the specified area, moving very slowly in the indicated direction.

"He also advised that even though Helen lost it in the treetops, the object moved very slowly about that area before moving in over the city. He watched the object [on radar] for a ten-minute period [and] advised that from time to time while over the Cow Bay area it disappeared, then reappeared in and out of the clutter at 1,800 feet—a known floor for radar reception in that area. The tapes were recorded off primary radar returns at Moncton Center, some eighty nautical miles from Halifax. The computer sensor had applied a 'chicken's foot' to the return . . . a 'Y' symbol which denotes an unknown. There was no transponder code attached to the return, making it a pure primary return.

"With the very real possibility that this object was at 1,800 feet, I re-did the math, coming up with a length—on each side—of [about] 4,600 feet," reports Don. "How thick was it? Even one foot of thickness gives us 6.48 million cubic feet. For every extra foot of thickness, you add an extra 6.48 million cubic feet. Even at a ratio of 20:1, that would make this object 180 feet high, comprising over 1.6 billion cubic feet of volume. . . ."[27]

ALDERMASTON, U.K.

Alien craft have a long history of monitoring our developments in the field of nuclear weaponry. Britain's Atomic Weapons Establishment (AWE) is located on Ministry of Defence (MoD) property in Aldermaston, Berkshire, and it was adjacent to this area that two witnesses—who prefer to remain anonymous—encountered a large craft on September 11, 2004. One of the witnesses (ML) revealed the details of the encounter to veteran investigator Ananda Sirisena, who reports as follows:

"At around 6:30 A.M., ML and his wife were returning home after babysitting at their daughter's house when they saw a huge object hovering over a field, to the right of the road that they were driving on. At the time of the sighting, it was a bright dawn with a clear, blue sky. ML had spotted the object first through the trees and, while trying to keep it in sight, nearly drove into the ditch on the left-hand side of the road. His wife [queried] why he was driving in such an erratic manner. He stopped the van and told his wife to look out through his window." She then spotted the craft too. "It's a spaceship!" she declared.

"ML informed me that the object was, in his estimation, many hundreds of feet in length, with pastel lights all around that appeared to pulsate softly [and] described it as 'cloud-like,' saying that the colors around the [central rim of the] object were like 'moving clouds.' . . . The couple observed the object for a short while, which ML estimated to be a few minutes. He had gotten out of the van and climbed up on the hood to get a better look. I asked ML to sketch the object, [which] shows a classic 'flying saucer' shape. . . .

"The couple were just past Church Lane, located on Burghfield Road as it approached the M4 motorway, near the town of Reading. The massive object was hovering over a field adjacent to AWE. . . . Suddenly, from a hovering position, the UFO started to move directly over the MoD site, then rapidly toward the M4 motorway [and] was out of sight.

"ML is convinced there must have been many other witnesses because of the sheer size of the [object] and its proximity to AWE. He is certain that the object must have been captured on the innumerable security cameras surrounding the site [and] by drivers on the M4 motorway and possibly even picked up by the cameras that monitor traffic on that busy link between South Wales and London. . . ."[28]

TENNESSEE

Some encounters with flying triangles have disturbing consequences. In the early morning hours of Saturday, October 2, 2004, Sidney, a country and western singer, was driving home from work on a rural road in Bristol, Tennessee, when he noticed what appeared to be a fire between the trees some distance away. "As he drove," reported MUFON Tennessee state section director Kim Shaffer, "he again noticed the 'fire,' which seemed somewhat brighter and appeared to be moving. He neared an intersection near his home and exited his car [for] a better look. Slowly, from behind trees, emerged a huge triangle-shaped craft. The witness started to run but realized there was nowhere to run to, so he stood in awe and watched.

"The craft slowly came into full view, a perfect triangle which the witness estimated to be some three hundred feet in length and width, and only 100 feet or so high, blocking out all the sky. He noted three large domes, comparing each dome to twice the size of his car, burning brilliantly a reddish orange, lighting the treetops and illuminating the entire bottom of the craft. He also noted 'rib-like' structures evenly spaced and running the width of the craft. [See photo section.]

"As the object passed over the witness's head, he stated that his skin burned, tingled, and felt really strange. He also noted that the sound seemed to [permeate] throughout his body and, being a professional musician, assured me that he could never adequately reproduce the throbbing hum he heard. The object passed over the witness, made a westward turn without banking, and was gone from his sight.

"The witness went home and tried to sleep but could not get the object off his mind. He had managed to get some sleep early that morning and awoke to a nosebleed, a metallic taste in his mouth, and his skin feeling sunburned on his back and face. He also noted that when he brushed his hair, strands of it were coming out in the brush. He also has been weak and nauseated since this encounter."[29]

I asked Kim Shaffer for his evaluation of the case. "He is a devout Christian and would not dare to elaborate anything which took place that early morning," he responded. "Sidney had lost fifteen minutes on his electric watch. He has monitored it closely (with the same battery) since and it has lost no time whatsoever. He has also been having recurring nightmares and been awakened several times by beams of light coming in his bedroom and strange noises (humming and buzzing) outside.

"I might add that he was diagnosed with an inoperable brain tumor (very small—three millimeters) in his frontal lobe just prior to the encounter . . . subsequent medical tests (MRI and ultrasound) revealed the tumor was gone—I think this was sometime in January 2005.

"I am shocked as well by the extreme interest shown by Lockheed Martin, Boeing, and the U.S. government to the report on the Web site immediately after the encounter. As webmaster, I am able to see the domains which visit the site. There were hundreds of visits from the aforementioned domains, which have never visited before or since."[30]

CAMBRIDGE, U.K.

"Why don't UFOs appear over major cities?" I am frequently asked. To which my response is that they have done so, on numerous occasions, such as over Aberdeen in 1956 and Phoenix in 1997.

Cambridge may not be a major city in terms of size, but for centuries it has remained one of the world's leading centers of academic excellence. In his column in *The Independent on Sunday* in December 2004, journalist Andy Martin reported that while cycling back from a concert on a Friday night in Newton Road, Cambridge—he neglects to give a date—for a couple of hundred yards he "had a clear view of a trio of radiant white lights in the sky, garnered with a few blinking blue and red lights underneath them. What I couldn't work out was what they were doing there. I was pedaling while they remained perfectly still. . . . Obviously, they were nothing to do with an aeroplane.

"As I approached the end of Newton Road (where I live), I got off my bike and I was looking—slack-jawed—almost straight up. Had the guiding star turned up early? In fact, it was more of a starship, the bright lights just hanging there in the sky, I would estimate at a height of around four or five hundred feet. There was no noise, not a whisper.

"As I looked more closely, I could see the dark outline of a craft that was nothing like a plane. There was no central tube and a couple of wings poking out at the sides; it was more rounded or at least bulkier. But it was big, definitely Jumbo-sized. And it wasn't going up and it wasn't coming down. It was going neither right nor left. . . .

"A couple of minutes passed by in which nothing—except for this great miraculous nothing in the sky—happened. Then, smoothly, gently, quietly, the UFO—for it was certainly unidentified and it was a flying object—tired of immobility and pulled away from its parking spot, picking up speed as it went over my head and over the house in the rough direction of Girton. There was a faint rumble—a kind of deep purring noise—as it went by. The way it moved had a silky, dancing quality. . . . I raced around into the back garden, but it had already vanished.

"I should add, by way of confirmation, that my wife and fourteen-year-old son (who had been playing in the concert) were with me at the time. I said to them, 'Was that a UFO?' 'Yes,' said my son. 'Is there any chocolate going?' . . .

"For at least twenty-four hours I was mentally paralyzed by the conviction that there is, indeed, extra-terrestrial life, and some of it had been visiting Cambridge. . . . Saturday night found me telling an old friend about my ET experience. A blond woman at a neighboring table leaned over and apologized for butting in to our conversation, but she couldn't help overhearing. . . . She told us that there is an experimental aircraft facility at Bassingbourn, only a few miles away as the UFO flies, probably run by the Americans.[31]

"She had heard that they were experimenting precisely with noise reduction and they tended to fly at night, to keep things hush-hush. But even she, she had to admit, was uncertain about the ability of an extremely large object to anchor itself in the sky for long periods. . . ."[32]

My attempts at communicating with Andy Martin to learn more unfortunately drew a blank. Of related interest, another journalist had an encounter that month. Ian Murray, editor of the *Southern Daily Echo*, was driving along the A31 road toward Ringwood, Hampshire, on December 7, when at about 16:30 traffic slowed down to watch a strange craft as it passed overhead.

"Hovering above us was a triangular-shaped aircraft with a spotlight," Murray describes. "It was slow enough to be a helicopter but dissimilar. I mentioned it to the news desk here at the paper. But, I was informed by colleagues barely concealing their smirks, checks with Southampton Airport and Hampshire Police brought no reports of 'strange aircraft' that late afternoon. . . ."[33]

THE CHANNEL ISLANDS

Located in the English Channel between the south coast of the United Kingdom and northern France, the Channel Islands are an archipelago of British Crown Dependencies. In the spring of 2007, two airliners encountered two huge craft of unknown origin. The report was first published as a front-page exclusive in the *Guernsey Press & Star* on April 26, but the story made more of an impact two months later, following publication of an official report by the Civil Aviation Authority (CAA) confirming the incident.

On April 23, 2007, Captain Ray Bowyer was flying an eighteen-seat, three-engine Britten-Norman BN-2a Trislander of Aurigny Air Services from Southampton to Alderney, with passengers on board. The flight deck on this aircraft is not separated from the passengers. At four thousand feet, visibility was very good for a hundred miles, with low-level haze up to two thousand feet, Bowyer reported. He first spotted a brilliant yellow light which he thought was about five or six miles away, but changed his mind after another twenty miles, as the object still seemed at a distance.

"I reached for my binoculars while flying on autopilot," he reports in Leslie Kean's book *UFOs*, "and, viewing it magnified ten times, found that this light-emitting object had a definite shape: that of a thin cigar . . .

sharply defined, and pointed on both ends. The aspect ratio was approximately 15:1 and I could clearly see a dark band two-thirds of the way along from left to right. . . .

"As I drew nearer to the object, a second identical shape appeared beyond the first. Both objects were of a flattened disc shape with the same dark area to the right side. They were brilliant yellow with light emanating from them. I passed the information to Jersey air traffic control (ATC) and they initially said they had no contact. I pressed the point over the next few miles and the controller at Jersey, Paul Kelly, then said he had primary contacts south of Alderney. . . .

"At this point, the passengers began to notice the unusual things and to ask about them. I decided not to make any announcement over the intercom so as not to alarm anyone, but it was obvious that some were getting concerned. By now the two identical objects were easily visible without binoculars. . . .

"ATC then informed me that there were two reflections from primary radar, both to the southwest of Alderney. This was beyond my destination, for which I was glad as the objects were becoming uncomfortably close. Their brilliance is difficult to describe. . . . They both seemed to be stationary, but the radar traces proved otherwise: they were actually moving away from each other at about six knots. . . .

"Approaching the point to begin descent, twenty miles north-northeast of Alderney, I maintained an altitude of four thousand feet to remain in good view of the objects. If they started to move off, I wanted to be able to take action to avoid them if at all possible.

"Due to my close proximity, the dark area on the right of the nearest one took on a different appearance at the boundary between the brilliant yellow and the dark vertical band. There appeared to be a pulsating boundary layer between the two differences in color, some sort of interface with sparkling blues, greens, and other hues strobing up and down about once every second or so. . . .

"The safety of the passengers is paramount [and] so to land was the priority. . . . If the aircraft had been empty, I would have gone a lot closer, perhaps overflown the nearer object to gather further information and satisfy my curiosity. . . ."

On landing, Captain Bowyer asked if any of the passengers had seen anything unusual and, should they want to report it, to leave their name and number at the check-in desk. At least six passengers saw the objects, two of whom—Kate and John Russell—went public. Bowyer's official report, together with a sketch of one object, was sent to Jersey ATC and to the Ministry of Defence and the CAA. While in Alderney, he received confirmation for the radar traces, from which he deduced that he had been about fifty-five miles away from the first object. "It was at this point," he said, "that its massive size became clear, and I estimated it to be up to a mile long."

While inbound to Jersey from the Isle of Man, Captain Patrick Patterson, piloting a BAe Jetstream of Blue Islands airways, witnessed one of the objects, matching Captain Bowyer's description.[34]

My several communications with Captain Bowyer reinforced a conviction in the validity of this remarkable encounter.

In an interview with an American reporter in 2011, Nick Pope, former head of the U.K. Ministry of Defence (MoD) UFO project, commented on the Channel Islands incident, which was included in the release of about nine thousand declassified pages of MoD documents dating from 1985 to 2007:

"The pilot and several of his passengers saw a UFO, which they said was essentially a mile long. And several other pilots saw it, but said, 'We're not going to report this.' And here's the great little get-out-of-jail-free card for the MoD: Just by a matter of maybe a few hundred meters, it turned out that this was in French air space, so MoD was given this little get-out to say, 'Well, it happened in French air space, so it's not an issue for us.' Clearly, that was an absolutely outrageous abrogation of responsibility."[35]

STEPHENVILLE, TEXAS

Steve Allen and two friends were in their home town of Stephenville on the evening of January 8, 2008, when they noticed flashing lights about 3,500 feet above ground level. "The ship wasn't really visible and was totally silent, but the lights spanned about a mile long and a half mile wide," Allen told Angelia Joiner of the *Stephenville Empire-Tribune* (a first-rate journalist with whom I have discussed the case in person). "The lights went from corner to corner. It was directly above Highway 67 traveling toward Stephenville at a high rate of speed—about three thousand miles per hour is what I would estimate."

As they watched, the lights reconfigured themselves from a single horizontal line into two sets of vertical lights, about a quarter of a mile apart. Then they turned into what looked like white flames. Some kind of fireball, perhaps? This was discounted when about ten minutes later the object or objects returned and flew overhead. "Two military jets, possibly F-16s, were in pursuit," said Allen, a private pilot,[36] who later appeared on CNN's *Larry King Live* show, together with others.

Major Karl Lewis, a spokesman for the 301st Fighter Wing at the Joint Reserve Base Naval Air Station, Fort Worth, denied that F-16s or any other aircraft were in the area on the night of January 8.[37] Later that month, however, he admitted that ten F-16s *had* been in the area at the time "on training missions," and eventually the Mutual UFO Network was able successfully to requisition the relevant radar data.

One afternoon in early January—prior to any publicity about the sightings—Ricky Sorrells, a machinist, was hunting on his sixteen-acre property, three miles outside of Dublin, Texas, about ten miles from Stephenville, where he lives with his wife and children. While easing through a stand of trees some distance behind his home, he casually glanced upward, continued on, then froze in his tracks. "I took a step or two, and then I realized what my eyes had seen," he told journalist Ronald Erdrich. "I look back up, and there it is. It's covered the sky, as far as you can see."

Viewed through his rifle's telescopic sight, the object appeared as very large, without seams, nuts, or bolts. "The only distinct characteristics were cone-like protrusions on the bottom that he surmised had something to do with keeping it airborne, and a subtle wavering in the atmosphere beneath it, like heat rising off pavement in the summertime," Erdrich reported. "The object lingered for a moment, and then quickly took off to the north, though it didn't seem to disturb the air when it did so."[38]

Following media publicity, Sorrells came to regret having spoken about it. "Sorrells believes military officials have been harassing him by flying military aircraft over his property at low altitudes, at all hours," wrote

Angelia Joiner. "Not just once, but four times, he claims to have seen the massive flying object he estimates to be the length of 'three or four football fields.' . . ."

The day after speaking with the Associated Press, Sorrells was contacted by a man who implied he was an Air Force lieutenant colonel, and whose behavior became threatening. The colonel also seemed responsible for an ensuing spate of harassment by low-flying military helicopters (often in the small hours) as well as by F-16s over Sorrell's property.[39]

The Stephenville events generated worldwide media interest for many weeks, leading many researchers to believe that finally—perhaps—disclosure was just around the corner. It was not to be.

MONMOUTH, U.K.

In September 2008, the historic border town of Monmouth, South East Wales, was visited by flying triangles. One of the witnesses, Finian Handley, contacted me early in 2010 after hearing an interview on Radio Wyvern in which I discussed the incidents. Finian asked if I had known his late father, the conductor Vernon "Tod" Handley, who died on September 10, 2008. I was delighted to tell him that I had indeed worked with Tod in various orchestras and that, in company with my colleagues, held him in high regard for his fine musicianship and "stick" technique. Unlike many conductors, he was genuinely modest, devoid of superficial showmanship—and always cheerful.

Finian is a taxi driver. At around 21:30 on September 26, while driving with a passenger through Whitchurch, a few miles from Monmouth, two black triangles appeared "almost directly over the car, going slowly in the opposite direction," he related to me. Four blue lights could be seen along the back of each craft. "The triangles were only a meter or two apart. This seemed very strange for two craft to be so close together." The passenger also witnessed the craft, which then disappeared from view. But more was to follow, at around 22:00.

"As I came back into Monmouth, now alone, I saw two 'orbs,' one above the other, hovering just above the trees in Chippenham Park, right next to the A40 dual carriageway. I continued through the traffic lights and directly past the orbs, which were only four lanes away from me and a few meters above the trees at most. I was so close to them as I passed them—less than fifteen meters.

"I noticed that the bottom orb had what I can only describe as a chink or splinter of light coming out of the bottom right side, as if the orb was beginning to change shape. I pulled over (on the slip road over the River Wye that leads to Beech Road) as quickly as possible. In this short period—ten seconds at most—they must have completely changed into black triangles, because by the time I'd got out of the car and turned to look at the orbs, there were triangles in the same spot, one beside the other."[40]

"They were low enough to hit with a stone, about the height of two and a half lamp posts stacked on top of each other," Finian told a local reporter.

"There were several lights on them, arranged symmetrically on the underside (represented by black dots in the drawing) and there were white lights on the three points of each triangle. I can't remember the exact layout of the lights on the underside except that there were at least three different colors, including white and red, and definitely a row of four blue lights along the back end.

"Each triangle was a bit larger than a small passenger jet. They hovered for a second over Chippenham Park [see photo section], then started to slowly move toward me but slightly to my right. Both objects were clearly identical in every way and were moving slower than five miles an hour, taking at least fifteen seconds just to pass over the dual carriageway. They were absolutely silent and there were no other cars on the road at the time. . . ."[41]

"As they slowly and silently crossed the dual carriageway, they elongated slightly," Finian recounted for me. "They momentarily also shimmered, as if becoming partially transparent, but literally for only a second. Then they made a decisive turn away from me—about ninety degrees—and as they departed, all of the different colored lights on the underside, including the flat oval blue lights, faded to white.[42]

"After passing over the dual carriageway, they both turned slightly left, keeping perfect formation, now traveling toward the Kymin [a wooded hill overlooking the Wye Valley and Monmouth]; then a few seconds later they split up, one continuing toward the Kymin and the other departing straight up the dual carriageway, maintaining the same speed and height. . . ."[43]

"I saw exactly the same thing over Wyesham (above Monmouth) on the same evening," wrote one anonymous witness, "the only difference being that what I saw, I believe, was earlier in the evening and the direction was slightly different. But his description of the two 'craft,' the lights, etc., everything was eerily the same . . . these two objects came from a northerly direction, just below the Kymin. But the really bizarre thing that occurred to me as they drew closer and eventually passed over my house was that they were hardly moving—traveling really slowly."[44]

About a year earlier, Finian told me, he had seen similar craft in Monmouth, approximately a mile away from those observed in September 2008. "As I pulled up to my sister's house around seven or eight P.M.," he recounted, "I saw two 'orbs' descend out of the sky. I lost sight of them as I drove up to the house and parked. As I got out of the car and looked to where the orbs had been, I now saw two equilateral black triangles flying almost directly above my head, roughly the size of Big Ben, each with a central white flashing strobe. . . ."[45]

DORSET, U.K.

Similar flying triangles were encountered by a couple in Dorset on October 23 or 24, 2008. "My husband and I were overwhelmed by the sight of three 'roundly' triangular, large objects, which moved through the sky at a low level toward us/our car and then hovered above us on a country lane between Corfe Castle and Langton House (a Holiday Property Bond site) on the Isle of Purbeck," Judith Relf wrote to me. "This was one weekday evening as we drove home after dinner.

"We were 100% sober, we both saw the same gently moving objects, we stopped the car and agreed to get out of the car to see if we could decide what the objects were—perhaps the sound of them would give us a clue (helicopter/microlite?)—but there was no sound. The objects were too large to be Chinese lanterns and there were three distinct colors—red, green, and white lights—on what looked like the underside of the object. They hovered for a full two or three minutes: surely an aeroplane doesn't silently hover? We watched outside the car and then felt 'spooked' and decided to get back inside. The objects didn't move away before we did. We started the engine and my husband 'put his foot down' and focused ahead on getting back to our holiday apartment. The objects then just faded off/away and we couldn't see them anywhere.

"Afterwards, when we came home we told my mother and one of our two friends, one of whom was a 'top dog' in the Ministry of Defence, about our sightings but, afraid of being labeled 'mad,' we have kept this experience to ourselves. . . . Our MoD friend said that there's a military base near to Purbeck, and it was probable that experiments being conducted there would be the explanation. We accepted this—and who were we to argue?"[46]

———

Leviathans of the skies continue to be reported around the world. With the inexorable and exponential advances in alien-derived technology, it is more than likely that quite a number of these vehicles are manufactured on Earth. Yet it is hard to reconcile the majority of reports with such an assumption. . . .

CHAPTER SEVENTEEN
EXPLOITATION

Marius Boirayon, a former Royal Australian Air Force engineer, had recently returned with his wife Miriam from the New Georgia group, part of the Solomon Islands in the Pacific Ocean, where they had acquired a beautiful island. Since they required new rental accommodation on Guadalcanal, Marius sought the assistance of his native friend Joseph, who selected a three-bedroom timber property at Cape Esperance. Marius thus became the first white man to live in that area.

No dates are given for the following incidents, possibly owing to the natives' reluctance to discuss their many disturbing incidents with outsiders. All we are told in this narrative by Marius—which he wrote in 2003—is that his later investigations in the Islands took place in 1996, 1997, and 2002.

"That night," Marius reports, "I started up the generator and sat back with Joseph and a few new friends to relax and have a beer. Later that night, when I was finding out a little bit more about the area, Joseph told me that I had to watch out for the 'Dragon Snake.' . . . They told me that it comes out of the mountains at night and flies around, [and,] with its piercing red eyes, has been feared for generations. It was responsible for people going missing and for killing people."

A few days later, Marius was fishing with another friend, Ci-Ci, when Joseph—who had been spearfishing—suddenly shouted for his friends' attention, pointing down to the beach. "There! There!" he cried. "The Dragon Snake!"

"As I looked down the beach," Marius continued, "I couldn't believe what I was seeing. About a kilometer away, there was a very bright, luminous white object flying slowly over the water. I remember asking myself whether I was really seeing it. I called out for my wife Miriam to bring my binoculars.

"After focusing in on the star-like, brilliantly lit object, I noticed that it was about sixty feet around and seemed to make no noise. We watched it for a couple of minutes until it submerged itself into the sea. Joseph told me to wait about ten minutes and I'd see it come back out again, which it did! When it came back out of the water, it was glowing twice as brightly as when it went in. We continued to watch it with my binoculars as it returned to the coast in the direction whence it had come, until it disappeared out of sight over the top of the coconut trees.

"Somewhat startled by this experience, we went back into the house and sat talking about this 'Dragon Snake' until the early hours of the morning. They told me that if you didn't see it one night, you were quite likely to see it the next. They were right. In fact, over a seven-month period, I lost count of these sightings when they reached the sixty mark. So while we sat talking about this object, I explained the structure of the universe to Joseph and Ci-Ci. I showed them my copy of a Time-Life book, *The Universe*, with its space-type pictures, and said that these so-called 'Dragon Snakes' were what white men call 'Unidentified Flying Objects.' They were absolutely amazed, as they had spent their whole life fearing this thing with superstition and having no real understanding of it. Yet, for that matter, I was also a little fearful.

"This sighting was the first of well over sixty more to follow, during which time I investigated the UFO waterfall lake base of northwest Guadalcanal and later the UFO bases of the central east coast of Malaita and central Small Malaita [also known as South Malaita or Maramasike]. This first sighting, though, had completely changed my mind about the existence of extraterrestrials, and a little investigation revealed that this so-called Dragon Snake had been in the area for well over a century. I realistically began thinking in terms of extraterrestrials inhabiting our planet."

A SERIOUS THREAT

Extensive investigations by Marius revealed that the aliens had displayed contemptible behavior toward the natives of Guadalcanal and Malaita. "Indeed," he adds, "there have been several outright abductions and murders. For example, the grandfather of a good friend of mine was incinerated by one of these UFOs around the early 1900s. Several independent sources have verified this. Countless horrific stories can be heard throughout these islands."

One theory that Marius came up with was that these craft—which I classify as "unidentified submergible objects" (USOs)—seemed to display an interest in the numerous wrecked Allied naval ships, such as the HMAS *Canberra* and USS *Chicago*, destroyed by the Japanese Navy in World War II during the huge naval battles around Guadalcanal in late 1942 and early 1943. "Why the UFOs had so much of an interest in these old warships became a somewhat baffling problem for me at the time," he says.

Determined to learn more, Marius approached two tribal chiefs for further information about the Dragon Snake. "My suspicions were right: the chiefs knew a lot about it. One of the chief's brothers had been killed by it when he was only a little boy. They told me several stories of deaths and abductions, all of which confirmed to me that these UFOs are definitely not friendly. They may be friendly in other places in the world, but certainly not here."

The tribal chiefs pointed Marius in the direction of the Dragon Snake's "house," which they said lay in an unnamed mountain, which for convenience Marius named "Mount Dragon," part of the mountain range which includes Mt. Poporia, about eight kilometers inland. "They told me of a big waterfall high up in the mountain with a lake beneath, into which the water falls . . . inside that lake is where the Dragon Snake lives. A further study of Mount Dragon revealed that there is a small lake in the mountain that is the beginning of a river. . . . What was at the bottom of this waterfall lake, and how many UFOs were there? I had to stop speculating on answers to these questions, as all of this was starting to sound a lot like a science-fiction movie. . . ."

One morning shortly afterward, Joseph informed Marius that a fisherman he knew had been taken to hospital with burns to most of his body sustained from a UFO two nights previously. The two visited the injured man. "He was covered in bandages from head to toe," said Marius, "and was in a great deal of pain, but doped up with pethidine. Joseph began to speak to him in the Guadalcanal language to try and find out exactly what had happened to him. . . .

"He had been out fishing in his fiberglass boat at about 3:00 A.M. when he saw the Dragon Snake flying along [and] started flashing his torch at it. That was when it flew over to him in an instant and hovered overhead. Panicking, he started the motor and took off to get away from the Dragon Snake, but it followed him as he 'zigzagged' his way back to shore. It was during this short pursuit to the beach that it fired some form of light at him, but it only partially hit him. A later inspection of his nineteen-foot boat showed traces of scorching upon some of the boat's interior paint.

"He said that when he drove his boat up the beach and ran into the bush, the Dragon Snake followed him to where he was hiding behind a tree and hovered above. When he moved around to the other side of the tree, it also went around to the other side. It was then that he literally got down on his knees and prayed to God with his hands clasped in front of him. With that, the Dragon Snake moved on. After that, he stumbled his way back to his village and was taken to hospital.

"It was an incredible story, but true," Marius stresses. "He definitely had no reason to be lying. These kinds of UFO encounters have happened on numerous occasions over the past century but, strangely enough, the Solomons being the way they are, reports have not been taken seriously."

In discussions about these aliens with his father-in-law John, Marius explained how some white men believe they are about four feet tall with a large head, big eyes, four fingers, and so on. John said there was a book in the Solomon Islands Cultural Museum with pictures describing just this sort of being. They decided to visit the museum.

"There it was," said Marius. "This fifteen-page book had fourteen detailed hand-drawn sketches of aliens just like the ones we are all used to seeing on television. An islander had compiled this short collection of drawings for the museum from different eyewitness accounts. . . . What I wanted to know was, how could the Solomon Islanders know anything about these kinds of aliens, when 99.99 percent of them had never had any significant type of exposure to white man's media? Most of the old tribal people still thought that the stars were caused by pinpricks in the sky and that the Earth was flat. . . ."

FURTHER EXPERIENCES

Marius pondered on the possible consequences of pursuing the matter any further. "I had initially gone out to the Solomons to enjoy an early, youthful retirement and certainly had not expected to be chasing UFOs," he explains. "But as a former military man, I couldn't stop thinking about the fact that this UFO was continually going near ships that had been involved in a great battle where thousands of men had lost their lives in the cause of freedom. It seemed as if this UFO was robbing graves. This weighed heavily on my mind for weeks."

One night while fishing, Marius watched the UFO submerge near the wreck of the USS *Chicago*[1] and then resurface, shining more brightly. As he peered through his binoculars, he noticed a ship heading in his direction. "From the trigonometric perspective, the UFO couldn't see the ship because of the point that was shielding its view," he assumed. "However, I had both the UFO and the ship in my field of view. After about thirty seconds, when the UFO did see the ship it instantly vanished . . . as if it had turned off its lights. I took my binoculars from my eyes. I was not sure if the craft had instantly accelerated or had somehow cloaked itself. Yet it seemed that the UFO didn't mind the indigenous people seeing it, but it did mind when someone saw it who would possibly know of its real identity."

Marius and Joseph planned an expedition to Mount Dragon, having worked out that the "Dragon Snake" most likely would travel to and from its base via a five-kilometer-long valley that runs in a northward direction past Mt. Dragon. "After searching the area for a suitable position," Marius reports, "we chose an accessible eight-hundred-foot mountain that had all the requirements we needed."

The following day, the men gathered all the equipment they needed, including Marius's 30-shot 7.62mm gun and a shotgun, in the event of an attack by wild pigs. "We knew that the UFO had the habit of appearing at around 10:00 P.M. or 3:00 A.M." After parking their car in the bush, they climbed to the top of the mountain with the aid of torchlights. This gave them a commanding 270-degree view. "With a clear view of the sea to the left of us and the valley's entrance to the right, there was no way that we were going to miss seeing the UFO when it made its appearance—and we didn't.

"Having sat up half the night, watching and waiting and having a few beers to pass the time, at 2:35 A.M. we saw the first glimmer of the UFO's light leaving the valley's entrance. There was an air of excitement. . . . While training my binoculars on the UFO, I noticed that it was traveling toward our direction at a fair rate of speed, which we estimated later to be about a hundred knots. We had been watching it approach us for close on a minute when it came past at an estimated height of three hundred feet, half a kilometer away. No sooner had this UFO passed by than it took an instantaneous 45-degree turn to the left and then accelerated away at phenomenal speed . . . and we watched the UFO's light diminishing over the horizon within seconds while still traveling at near sea level."

Marius determined to make an expedition up the valley sometime to film the UFO. But he only had a Kodak Instamatic which was of no use at night, and video cameras were neither cheap to buy nor available to borrow from anyone he knew. Weeks went by. And the craft continued to appear regularly.

"One morning at 3:00 A.M. a couple of weeks later," Marius reports, "Joseph and I were on the grass outside the house, husking coconuts around a fire, when we noticed the UFO. We observed that it was slowly moving in our direction. It started to get closer and closer, and it seemed to us that if it continued on the path it was on, it would overfly us.

"As it came progressively even closer, we started to move to the door of the house. Both Joseph and I were standing at the door when it flew over the nearby trees and over the top of the house. The brilliance of its white light radiated the whole area as if we were standing amidst the light of a dozen arc welders at once. This was the first time that I could clearly see the vehicle's sphere [shape] with my naked eye. It made no noise as it eerily passed over us. In fact, at the time we made audible comments to each other about what was happening. After it went by, we both ran out to see it disappearing over the trees further on. Joseph had experienced this sort of thing before—but I hadn't."

Marius became partly overcome by a feeling of helplessness and inadequacy around that time, due to his constantly "questioning the reality of it all."

MALAITA BASES

In 1996, 1997, and 2002, Marius made further research trips to the island of Malaita, which is separated from Guadalcanal by the Indispensable Strait. According to members of his wife's family, NASA first made contact with the occupants of a subterranean alien base in central east Malaita in 1961. "This is how they began to gain what partial technology they have today," he claims. "It was through blackmail. This happened because when the great [British] geologist Mr. Gropher was doing his few expeditions in the area in between 1958 and 1960, he saw these UFOs, then reported back to the U.K. (the ruling colonial power at the time) about them.

"Apparently, in 1961, a white man who claimed to be from NASA came to that part of the island and asked for assistance from my wife's relatives to take him to the UFO subterranean base entrances, which they did. I am the only white man ever to have married a woman from the Kwaio, who live in that area. This NASA guy was gone a week and then returned, asking my wife's relatives for further assistance to take him back to these places.

"There is a fifty-meter-diameter bottomless circular reef in amongst the surrounding ten-meter-deep coral reef a few miles north of Kwoi Island (on the border of the Kwaio and Kwara'ae tribes) and south of Namo'ere'ere in central east Malaita. Singalanggu Harbor is slightly further south. UFOs can be seen going in and out of that reef virtually every night. . . . On mainland Malaita, about three to four miles directly inland from that circular reef entrance is a lake which has two connected entrances/exits. When the boys are out fishing at night, they see the UFOs going in one entrance and coming out the other. A UFO coming out of this lake at dusk incinerated my good friend's grandfather, and everyone in the area knows about it.

"The aliens have instilled fear in these people for generations, and many people have gone missing. In the Kwaio and Kwara're areas, there are three entrances in their jungle mountains that I know of where these 'balls of light'-type UFO vehicles can be seen entering and exiting. It is my belief that these entrances are not individual bases but are all connected, making up one big UFO base under the island. I may be wrong, but I also believe that one of the many reasons why they are here is that, for reasons of their own, they are mining a very rare type of gemstone under this kimberlite rock volcanic island.

"The gemstones that my wife's relatives possess have a far higher specific gravity than that of diamonds, and a refractive index such that when you put the stone in light, you see your mirror image in the center of the stone. I once had a 32.4 carat 'ET stone' with these characteristics. There are some old folklore stories supporting the interest in these unique stones. Furthermore, as there are many remnants of the Ramo civilization that can be found on top of the island and the aliens underneath, there is every chance there is a connection. And that goes for on Guadalcanal, too."

Marius also describes a "waterfall lake UFO base" in south Malaita where he has also witnessed activity. This base, he says, is located some three kilometers from Affiou, the main town. "About a kilometer up the jungle mountain is their base entrance," he asserts, "where they can be seen entering and exiting nearly every night, and also brazenly and casually flying along the passage.

"Many Solomon Islanders have told me of flat stingray-type UFOs[2] with big round lights underneath them that hum as they go along. They sometimes see them flying low over the jungle and surfacing out of the sea near where they are fishing. The UFOs have landed near villages, and (white or black) people who get out of them have strange gray uniforms, not seen anywhere else in the world. You can make your own deductions there.

"If there were ever a place that one could call 'UFO Headquarters,' it would have to be central Malaita. Mind you, these are the only ones I know of. Goodness knows what else there is in the rest of the Solomon Islands. . . ."[3] And, I dare say, in the rest of "our" planet.[4]

THE ENCHANTED ISLE

In the U.S. Commonwealth of Puerto Rico—the so-called "enchanted isle"—sightings of alien craft and their occupants are commonplace. Having made seven research trips there, I formed the unequivocal conviction, in company with leading investigator Jorge Martín and others, that the island and its surrounding waters are used as an alien base. Since I have published numerous reports of encounters in previous books, I shall restrict the information in this chapter to some important and more recent further events—mostly from 2005 to 2010.

Around midnight on May 15, 2005, a large triangular craft was reported by a number of witnesses in San Juan. One of the witnesses, "Wilfredo," was driving near Luis Muñoz Marín International airport where he worked. "I was in the town of Carolina near the Los Angeles development, on an avenue exactly facing the airport," he told researchers Willie Durand Urbina and José A. Martínez Echevarria. "Then I saw a glow that came from behind a hill. That's when I heard dogs barking and birds singing [as if] desperate. I was frightened. Then, when I looked behind me, I saw a very large glow. But I couldn't see the craft because I was inside the van. I pulled the van over and got out. That's when I saw an immense triangular object.

"I can't give you the exact measurements, but I can tell you [and compare it] to the size of a ball park—or two enormous ball parks. It was going very slowly and passed directly over me. There was no sound, just a light coming out of the middle. It seemed that the light emitted some sort of heat. It made no noise whatsoever and was going slowly, very slowly, and that's when the van's engine and lights went out.

"I took my camera phone and tried to take photos of the object, but I had to remove the filter to lower the light intensity, because it couldn't be seen in the photos I had taken. That's how I managed to photograph the craft. Then I took another photo from inside my vehicle. And that's strange, because nothing electrical worked—yet my cell phone worked. I tried to turn the engine over—but nothing. It's as if they wanted me to take a picture. The streetlights went out as it flew overhead, flying over the parking lot and away. I also found it strange that the airport lights also went out. And the clouds were lit up by the object as it departed."

Two weeks after the encounter, Wilfredo noticed that the paint on his van began to show little spots, blood-red or mud-colored, throughout the entire vehicle, which could not be removed. Another two weeks later he became ill. "I've never been so sick," he said. "I'm a very healthy person. I don't know if it had anything to do with the experience." Blood tests proved negative.

Shortly after, Wilfredo's car was stolen. "That happened after I spoke to a female co-worker who claimed to have been abducted by aliens. She told me about her experiences, and two days later I felt as though I was being watched."[5]

Since early 2007, Wilfredo observed the same, or similar, huge craft over the airport control tower on many occasions, typically between 20:20 and 20:30. This time using the pseudonym "Mr. Rodriguez" (owing to his work at the airport), he decided to board a scheduled American Eagle flight departing at 20:30 for Vieques, an island off the east coast of Puerto Rico, together with a skeptical friend, to see the object more closely and gain the support of another witness. As Lucy Guzman reports:

"Rodriguez says that as the American Eagle flight gained altitude, it was necessary to look toward Route #3, as this was where the light appears to emerge from, toward the beach area. The UFO approached the plane sufficiently [for him to realize] that it was larger than the airliner. It then made a U-turn, heading toward Fajardo, and then Vieques, as though heading for the nearby islands. He says that he alerted all of the passengers and asked the co-pilot about the strange light, who replied [in English]: 'Forget about it,' which led Rodriguez to believe that pilots are forbidden to discuss what is going on, or else did not want to alarm them. The same event happened on the return trip from Vieques to San Juan."[6]

REPEATED ENCOUNTERS

In 2005, Maria M. Rivera and her family began to experience a series of alarming encounters with alien beings in Aguada, northwest Puerto Rico. At about 03:00 on November 10, Maria and her daughter heard a weird humming sound, like a hurricane wind, going by the house. "The sound was so strange that it penetrated our ears," the report she sent me begins. "When my daughter Barbie and I looked outside, we observed what appeared to be a disc-shaped object moving westward toward the rear of the house where woodland and a huge antenna are located, and which leads all the way to the Atlantic Ocean.

"The disc was silver in color with a row of windows around it and had a greenish haze or aura covering the craft. All the windows appeared to be a darker greenish color. The craft appeared to be descending as though it was about to land somewhere behind the house. We lived in Brooklyn, New York, near Kennedy Airport for over 20 years [so] I know what we have seen, and the sounds it made were very unusual, something we've never heard and seen before. After that, my daughter and I heard the same sound at least twice a week."

On April 28, 2006, at about 03:00, Maria again heard the same sound. "Ten or fifteen minutes later, I heard my dog Dora barking continuously in the backyard. When I went to investigate, turning on the backyard light, I observed my dog lying on her back with her four legs up, apparently unconscious. The dog was chained to a metal pole next to the back fence which separates my property from the rain forest in the back (owned by the U.S. government). I called her name, but she did not respond. When I lifted my eyes and looked at the fence, about twenty-five feet from where I was standing, I observed two creatures standing close to and behind the chain-link fence, looking at me.

"One of the aliens was about three feet from the dog, and about five feet from the other. They were about three and a half feet tall with a large oval head and big black slanted eyes. They had pale grayish skin, a barely visible slit for a mouth, and two little holes for a nose. They also had very skinny arms and seemed not to have any clothes on. Their legs were not showing because under the fence was a cinder-block wall about one and a half feet high. I could only see them from the waist up." [Maria's sketch appears on the next page.]

clothesline→
Metal Pole

"The aliens were staring at me and I was staring at them. I think that they were reading my mind when I said mentally, 'I'm going to wake up my husband, Nelson,' because when I left the window and walked through the hallway leading through to the bedrooms to wake him up, they detoured me to the other bedroom to wake up my seventeen-year-old daughter instead. I woke her up and both of us went to the dining room window where we observed the creatures still standing in the same place.

"Again, they stared at us and we stared straight into their large black eyes for a while. My daughter said to me, 'Mommy, I'm going back to bed because I'm scared, and I won't be able to sleep.' I then followed her to the bedroom because she was afraid to go by herself. Approximately ten minutes later, I returned to the dining room window, and the aliens were still in the same location.

"While staring straight into their black eyes, the one closest to the dog was telling me in my mind to open the door leading to the back yard. I said in my mind, 'I'm not going to open the door.' He demanded telepathically,

'You're going to open the door.' I then felt myself moving toward the door and was getting drowsy.

"I don't remember what happened after that. I woke up in my bed [and] asked my daughter if she had seen the same thing, in case I was imagining things. She described the incident and the creatures in the same way and manner I described them. We then told my husband, who slept in a separate bedroom facing the back yard, because my daughter was afraid to sleep by herself, so I had to sleep with her."

Nelson confirmed having heard the dog barking furiously in the direction of the rain forest at about 03:00. He looked outside without getting out of bed and assumed she was barking at a cat, and did not look in the direction of the rain forest and fence. He then fell back to sleep.

"What concerns me the most," Maria stressed to me, "is that my husband informed me that he discovered the back door open when he got up at about 8:00 in the morning, but did not know what had happened. My daughter informed me she opened her eyes about 5:00 in the morning and did not find me next to her in bed. She thought I was in the bathroom or somewhere around the house and went back to sleep. And the dog did not want to eat or drink anything for days and was lying down, apparently sick. . . . We did take Dora to the vet, but did not dare to mention that some 'aliens' were seen next her. She was just given an antibiotic injection."

On May 1, 2006, at about 00:50, while sitting in the living room talking on the phone, Maria noticed a large bright light moving through the woods. "The light was so bright that it illuminated the inside of the house. I informed my husband and we immediately closed all the louver windows in the kitchen and dining room. I became hysterical and began to cry because I thought they were after me, and my husband had to calm me down.

"At approximately 2:00 A.M. the same night, I heard the same sound again over the house like something hitting the flat concrete roof which shook the house as if something had landed there. We were afraid, but did not call the police for fear of being ridiculed. It was such a terrifying experience that we didn't even consider going outside to check it out. Instead, the three of us huddled in one bed. . . . Could it be possible that I did open the backyard door and was abducted by aliens? I don't know, [but]

I have dotted puncture marks on my left hand [in a circular pattern] and had a slight burning pain which gradually diminished as time went by. . . ."

A week or so later, Maria and her family went to visit the mayor of Aguada, Luís A. Echevarria, at City Hall, but he was unavailable. Instead, they notified Martín Concepción of Puerto Rico's Civil Defense Agency and handed him their written testimony. He said he would investigate and ask the Municipal Police to patrol the area, copying in the mayor. Nothing more was heard.

On May 11, Maria and Nelson were interviewed on Channel 5, but the interviewer tried to debunk their experiences, citing Puerto Rican superstitions and hoaxed claims. "My husband and I were so upset," said Maria. "We told him that we are honest people, not superstitious, and just because someone lied, it does not mean that we are liars.

"We even sent e-mails to several Puerto Rican UFO investigative organizations, but they did not e-mail us back. We did not know who to turn to since we were not getting help from anyone here on the island. So my husband and I started sending e-mails to the U.S. mainland and to other countries to see whether someone or some organization would help us."

FURTHER INCIDENTS

Maria compiled a list of further incidents, which I summarize as follows:

JUNE 5, 2006, CA. 03:00—After watching television, Maria went to get a glass of milk before retiring for the night. As she walked through the living room on her way to the bedroom, she observed a creature peeping through the glass-pane window on the main entrance door. She surmised that "he" was standing on top of a patio chair, assuming it was the same height as the previous creatures. She also said it scared her as it looked "older, meaner" with a sinister look on its face. She woke her husband, who grabbed a machete and went out on the balcony. But the creature had disappeared.

OCTOBER 22, 2006, CA. 23:00—A blackout affected Aguada for three hours. At about midnight, Maria awoke her husband so he could hear a weird humming sound emanating from behind the house in the rain forest.

FEBRUARY 25, 2007, CA. 04:00—Maria observed a disc-shaped craft, similar to the one she had seen before, from her bedroom window. About thirty feet in diameter, it was hovering motionless some 130 feet from the house and the same distance from the ground. She was able to observe aliens, who in turn were observing her through viewing ports, silhouetted against a bright greenish-blue background. No sounds could be detected. By the time she had woken her husband, who picked up a camcorder, the craft had gone.

MAY 21, 2007, CA. 01:00—Maria's daughter Barbie was talking on her cell phone in the living room when she suddenly heard the humming sound again and a greenish-blue light flashed through all the windows, flashing in sequence from the front to the back windows.

JUNE 2, 2007, CA. 02:00—Maria's 21-year-old son, Jonathan, who had come to visit from New York, noticed a very bright beam of green light shining through the windows in his bedroom. "He was so frightened," reports Maria, "that after the light vanished he hysterically ran upstairs in his pajamas to inform us."

AUGUST 14, 2007—Early in the morning, the family's dog Dora was nowhere to be found. A search all over the neighbourhood proved fruitless. "I do not know if it had something to do with those aliens," said Maria, "but after what happened to me and my family in that house, anything is possible." After the disappearance of Dora, the family moved to another house in Aguada, further from the beach and the rain forest. To no avail.

NOVEMBER 3, 2007, CA. 02:00—Maria's most traumatic experience occurred just prior to falling asleep, when she saw a small blueish-green neon light, about the size of a penny, coming from the window and moving round the bedroom in the dark. Maria became paralyzed.

"Suddenly my bed was being surrounded by those creatures. Obviously, I was made unconscious because when I opened my eyes I found myself naked, in a different, cold room, and lying face up on a very cold 'stainless steel' platform."

"This platform," Maria continued, "seemed to be floating on the air without legs or anything supporting it. It was narrow enough that my arms hung over the sides. Still feeling paralyzed but conscious, they commenced injecting me with a long needle or something. I begged them with my thoughts to please not do it, but they ignored me. I also felt that they put something metallic, like a round suction cap about five inches in diameter, on the right side of my abdomen. It felt as if my flesh was being stretched and my inside was being sucked out like a powerful vacuum. I was in excruciating pain when they did that, but I was unable to scream or move. About five or six creatures surrounded the platform, one being taller than the others, and the rest were the short 'grays' I previously saw in my back yard.

"This time they were not communicating telepathically among themselves, because I heard a weird incoherent mumbling sound coming from them. However, I didn't see their mouths move. I remember calling them *'marcianos'* (Martians). They revealed, telepathically, in Spanish, that they don't like being called Martians but prefer to be called 'creatures.'

"When I got up the next morning, I still had pain on the right side of my abdomen, but no mark was visible."

Since Maria's daughter had moved to Pennsylvania, Maria again shared a bedroom with her husband. "He keeps telling me to wake him up when it happens, but I could not move or speak. Many times he stays awake at night, but nothing happens so he falls asleep. I do, however, feel or have a sense when they're around.

"It is important to be noted here that I've had ovarian cancer, and have had several operations to remove parts of my intestine. I also had several operations for breast cancer. I flew occasionally to New York City to see my private doctors, since here on the island private doctors are reluctant to accept Blue Cross, GHI, and Blue Shield, which I got from my husband's retirement. I was informed by my doctors in New

York that the cancer had returned and that I urgently need another operation. I used to be in constant stomach pain and noticed blood in my stool and urine when I went to the bathroom. It was not the first time: the cancer has recurred before and they operated on me after each recurrence. But after the encounter with those creatures on April 28, 2006, I returned to New York, several tests were performed, and no cancer was detected. The pain and bleeding had stopped. I truly feel that those creatures had cured me.

"What is my opinion of those creatures? They could be benevolent and compassionate creatures, but I'm afraid of them. They do not have my permission to do with my body whatever they please. Although I believe they had cured me, I am not their guinea-pig.

"I have something in my right lower back that has been bugging me for a long time. It moves when I touch it and I know it wasn't there before. I saw on the History Channel the program called *UFO Hunters*, when Mr. Bill Birnes took a man who was abducted by a UFO to Dr. Roger Leir. The man had an alien implant in his leg. When Dr. Leir put a powerful magnet where the man had the implant, to our amazement the object inside his flesh moved toward the magnet and the skin bulged. Like that man, I don't have an entry wound or scar where the object is. That prompted me and my husband to do the same experiment. Unfortunately, we do not have a powerful magnet. . . . The mark on my left hand and the object embedded in my back have been noticed by me since my encounter with those aliens on April 28, 2005."

On June 11, 2008, at 02:52, Maria was alone in her living room when she suddenly had a presentiment that she should go outside onto the balcony. "There it was again," she reports. "My camcorder was not in the immediate area, but luckily I had my cell phone with me. It appeared to be a saucer-shaped object, similar to the ones I've seen previously, but with lights around it. You can hear the crickets and the *coquis* (small frogs) chirping, mixed with the sound that the object is making. The sound is similar to the humming of other UFOs I've heard and seen before. It was over the wooded mountains near the other house I moved to in Aguada. . . .

"What happened to me and my family is no hoax," Maria concludes in the report she sent me. "It was a terrifying experience. To prove this, I am willing to submit to a polygraph test, go under hypnosis, be under oath, or whatever."[7]

In September 2009 I received a personal communication from Maria which provides some additional information.

"We do not live in Aguada anymore; we moved to Aguadilla, nearby. We moved from one house to another house in Aguada, but they followed me," Maria began. "This is the third house that we've moved to on the island since we came here from New York City in 2005. At first, I was so afraid that I wanted to return to New York, but now I know that no matter where I move to, they'll find me, so I've decided to remain on the island. However, my daughter was so traumatized that she refuses to come to Puerto Rico, even on vacation."[8]

In 2011, at my request, Maria and Nelson sent me an update on the family's experiences. "Even with neighbors nearby in a nice community and my husband sleeping beside me, on April 3, 2009, at approximately 3:30 A.M., I found myself in the same room I was in when abducted on November 3, 2007," Maria wrote. "The room I entered was almost dark.

"They showed me a little girl who appeared to be about one and a half years old [and] informed me that the little girl sitting there in the corner was my child. When I looked at her, she did look a lot like my daughter, Barbie, with long, dark, curly hair and her face shaped like my daughter's face. The only difference was the eyes that were tilted upwards, slanted like the creatures'.

"It appeared as though they did not want me to get close to her. I could only see her physique. . . . She was skinny, very thin [and] kneeling in a corner, and her eyes looked sad.

"Is it possible that on November 3, 2007, a fetus was being ejected from my womb, then one year and five months later they had shown me the child? I don't know, [but] before I was abducted on that date, I did feel something moving in my abdomen from side to side. . . ."

On March 16, 2010, Maria drove her 27-year-old-niece, Carmen J. Velez, who was visiting from New York, to her sister's house in Aguada. "That night, at about 12:10 A.M., we took a shortcut back home through an isolated wooded road," Maria recounted. Suddenly, the car began shaking, though there was no wind. "I told my niece that we wouldn't be able to make it home and that we would have to turn back. I turned around and parked not far from a house to check on the tires. When I exited the car, to my surprise the front tires looked as if they were torn into a hundred pieces, as if they had been sliced with a razor blade. The tires were about four months old and were not worn.

"I then tried to call my sister's house for help on my cell phone. The signal was good but I couldn't get through. I'm used to calling my sister from that location and I've never had any problems, but that night I couldn't get through. I entered the vehicle, told my niece to lock all the doors, and told her that we had to do whatever it takes to move from there. . . . When I turned on the car, it started okay, but when I put it in DRIVE it didn't move forward.

"Suddenly, we heard a loud humming sound coming from above the car. My niece was terrified and became hysterical, yelling, 'Auntie, it's above us, please don't get out of the car!' I was also scared, but wanted to calm her down. Just when I told her not to worry, we suddenly heard a loud roar, like a wild animal or something, coming from across a field. That really frightened us.

"In desperation, I had no choice but to put the vehicle in DRIVE again—and this time it moved forward. We proceeded at five miles an hour to my sister's house, running on three tires and one front metal rim. . . ."

Further events ensued. "My daughter-in-law, Leslie Miranda-Rivera, and my daughter Barbie wanted to spend the holidays with us here in Puerto Rico since my son is in the Army, stationed in Afghanistan. My husband and I let them both sleep in our bedroom. . . . On November 22, 2010, at approximately 1:00 A.M., my daughter entered the bathroom to take a bath first, while Leslie sat on the bed. While watching television, she saw with the corner of her eyes something or someone behind the balcony doors [which] appeared to be an entity, similar in appearance to the gray aliens but about five to six feet tall. The alien was on the balcony looking inside the bedroom through the glass panels. Leslie just sat there mesmerized.

"She couldn't move or yell—it was like being hypnotized. When Barbie came out of the bathroom, Leslie snapped out of it and explained what she had seen. Barbie said that she thought she had seen something standing there on her way to the bathroom. Suddenly, during their conversation, the curtains on the window, which also faces the balcony, began to curl upward, twisting and tying themselves into a knot, tucking themselves into the blinds. The window was closed and there was no wind. The girls became hysterical. Leslie called me on a cell phone, waking me up, and told me to come over quickly. . . . I banged on my husband's room door. He opened the balcony door, proceeded outside onto the balcony, but nothing was seen."

"When we awoke the following morning," said Leslie, "we found we had bruises on our bodies, mainly on our legs. Maria had pointed them out to us, but we had not even realized they were there, but they were black-and-blue and about two to three inches in size, mainly on our thighs, and I had one that had a lump right on my knee. We were curious as to how they got there. . . ."[9]

"I think it is fair to say that those beings have tagged, branded, and are actively tracking abductees like myself," concludes Maria in an earlier report. "They're quite awful creatures and have no regard for humanity and animals living on Earth. To them, we're just a science project. I could be wrong, but I think the creatures cured my cancer because they need a healthy specimen for their experiments.

"I don't know if they come from another planet and flew here in space-ships, but what we saw and heard were something we've never experienced before, until we moved to Puerto Rico. I am a Christian, and I do believe in our Lord Jesus Christ. Like most Hispanics, I am also Catholic. However, my family and I feel that what occurred in that house is nothing spiritual, religious, occult, voodoo, Santeria, etc. Moreover, we are not superstitious. The whole family confronted a terrifying experience in that house. We know what we saw and heard is the truth and I could swear on the Holy Bible that it's true. . . ."[10]

EVIDENCE

Although Maria Rivera has produced evidence to support her abduction claims, none of this will satisfy the skeptics. What proof is there that any of the abductees have actually been abducted? One witnessed case of a person being abducted took place in Puerto Rico in 1979, and was investigated by Jorge Martín and a colleague.

At about 09:00 one November morning, Héctor Maldonado, a resident of Ponce on the southwest coast, was jogging near the saltings and mangrove thickets of Ponce Salt, close to the sea. Suddenly he noticed five or six strange, thin creatures, varying from five to six feet in height, with large, bald heads. Their big almond-shaped eyes appeared to be illuminated with bright lights. "They had thin necks and long arms, and long hands and fingers," Maldonado told the investigators. "I didn't note how many fingers—I was too shaken to notice. Their skin was a grayish-blue color. I couldn't see any clothing on them [and] to me they looked naked, though I spotted no sign of genitals. The astonishing thing was that they had gotten hold of a man and were taking him away.

"He was a human, olive-skinned, about five feet, nine inches in height, with lank black hair, and apparently unconscious. He looked as if he was petrified, with his eyes closed, and they had gotten hold of him by the armpits. They appeared to be very strong, because two of them were lifting him off the ground with ease: he wasn't even dragging his feet. I didn't get a clear view of his face. . . . I don't think he would have been more than thirty. He was slim, and wearing a two-piece suit with a check pattern. The man was unconscious or dead. I imagine unconscious. . . .

"Behind the beings, above the sea, a bit beyond the mangroves, there was a machine hanging stationary in the air. It looked more or less oval in shape, with a cupola on top, its sides sort of fluted or grooved, and on the top it had a narrow, curved projection with lots of lights. . . . The thing was of a silvery metallic color, and really big, just hanging there in the air, not making a sound."

Suddenly one of the creatures, who had been kneeling on the ground, got up and made a sign to Maldonado, who had continued jogging. "And then I felt something as if it were inside my mind, like a voice [and] coming seemingly from that being. I 'heard' him say jestingly to the others, 'Look at that one—how he's running.' And then the being himself started running, making fun of me. I got the impression that he said, 'Now—just look how *I* run,' and started moving at a fantastic speed. Then he halted beside the others, and I 'heard' him say to them, 'We'll take him *too*.' The others replied something like, 'Not him—leave him alone.' When he was mocking me [I noticed that] he had great big, pointed teeth, like a shark's."

The creature then threw some sort of cold liquid at Maldonado, hitting him in the chest, which induced a feeling as though his body was swelling up, like a type of cramp. He managed to force himself to escape. "I just carried on running, and didn't want to look back." When he finally did look back, the craft, the creatures, and the man were nowhere to be seen.

"Didn't you notify the Police?" asked the investigators. "No! As I've already told you, I was very scared. I didn't think they would believe me. For a long time I felt bad about what might have happened to that chap they were taking, because I have no doubt whatsoever that they were indeed taking him. . . ."[11]

"HAIR OF THE ALIEN"

In his remarkable book of the above title, leading Australian researcher Bill Chalker, who has a background in chemistry and mathematics, describes his exemplary investigations into what has turned out to be arguably the most convincing case for alien abduction. The witness was Peter Khoury, whose experiences apparently began in 1988, when he was living with his Lebanese parents in a suburb of Sydney, Australia.

On the night of July 12, Peter experienced the first instance of being paralyzed by something of unknown origin, becoming aware of "three or four ugly figures only about three to four feet tall" beside his bed. He felt a "tingling and churning" sensation of something that gradually enveloped him, rendering him totally paralyzed. At one stage, two other, different beings appeared, thin, tall, with big black eyes and a narrow chin. Various communications were received telepathically, and Peter sensed warm emotion emanating from them. Finally, a long, flexible crystal tube was inserted into his head and he blacked out. Later, it transpired that he had also had a number of other strange experiences. And in 1992, the most extraordinary—and productive—encounter took place, which did not come to light until much later. As Bill noted in his diary in 1996:

"Peter described a highly personal experience he had at home about two to three years ago—sexual—being forced onto a strange female being— onto its breast. He resisted; then a very strong force pushed him against the breast—he bit a nipple—felt something like a piece of rubber caught in his throat for days—he discovered some very fine wispy hair under his foreskin—he still has one small strand, which he keeps in a plastic bag. He showed this to the two media people and me."

The incident had occurred at about 07:30—when he was awake. "All of a sudden two naked females appeared from nowhere. A blond and a Chinese girl. Very weird-looking eyes and color of blonde," as Peter noted in his diary on July 23, 1992. "Blonde pushed me to her breast a few times, then I bit her nipple and started coughing. She showed no emotion, blood, or screamed in pain. I went to the toilet and found two hairs under my foreskin. . . ."

Peter explained to Bill that the women felt uncannily light. The one sitting opposite him sat with her legs tucked under her backside, the other one halfway kneeling, sitting partially upright. The blond woman appeared to be quite tall and in her mid-thirties. "Her hair was done up like the wind was hitting it, like it was blown back. She had protruding, very high cheek[bones]. The nose was long [and] a longer face than I was accustomed to in females I know. Her eyes were two to three times bigger than our eyes. . . . I knew I wasn't looking at a human female. Her mouth, her lips were normal in size [but] the chin was pointier. . . . She had average-sized breasts, well proportioned [and] her hair came down to about halfway down her back, and like really high up. It was flimsy. . . ." He did not observe any underarm hair, nor did he have an opportunity to notice if there was any pubic hair.

The dark-haired woman looked Asian, though her cheekbones were too extreme. The eyes were dark black. "When I looked at her," said Peter, "I got the impression that she was watching the blond one and learning how to interact. . . . The Asian woman's face looked more human than the other one, except for the eyes and cheekbones." He noticed that both women had expressionless faces. "It was just like looking at someone with glass eyes."

Peter told Bill that he didn't know why he had bitten and taken a chunk out of the blond woman's nipple, other than that it might have been a defensive reaction. "There was no blood, there was nothing, no trace whatsoever." He says he swallowed it and it became stuck in his throat for three days. Had a sexual act taken place? "I don't know what sort of interaction we had," Peter responded. However, given the positioning of the recovered hairs, it would seem likely that some kind of sexual act occurred. The women disappeared as soon as Peter started the coughing fit. One minute they were there, the next minute gone.

Hypnotic regression sessions were held which yielded further information, tending to reinforce the idea that a genetic agenda lay behind the women's visit. I have only touched on some of the many aspects discussed in Bill Chalker's unique book. Most impressive are the results of the "Mitochondrial DNA Sequence Analysis of a Shed Hair from an Alien Abduction Case" by the Anomaly Physical Evidence Group (APEG) in April 1999, a lengthy report which yielded a considerable amount of surprising data. As the biochemistry team leader, Dr. Horace Drew, concluded:

"This genetic analysis of a reportedly-alien, thin blond hair has raised a number of important questions for further work. It generally supports the reality of such extraterrestrial contacts, in a Sydney suburb in 1992 and perhaps elsewhere, owing to rare morphology of such a hair, plus the rare nature of DNA sequences obtained.

"Had that hair been a common Earth artefact, it would have shown up early in the investigation. We cannot prove it is an alien hair, yet Occam's razor supports that notion. Where else in Sydney could Peter Khoury have obtained a long, clear, exceptionally thin head hair that shows Basque-Gaelic DNA in its root, but Chinese DNA in two parts of its shaft?

". . . the most logical scenario would seem to be that higher creatures not from Earth have been following Peter's genetics for many years, or perhaps many generations; and that the almost-human females he met in 1992 may have taken advantage of such information (e.g., a planetary database of human genetics), to select for certain favorable traits in their own reproduction. We have no reliable information about where the non-human or almost-human aliens come from, nor how they entered Peter's house. . . . Yet the clear implication is that humanoid or near-human life forms can be found elsewhere in our galaxy; and that at least some of them are close enough to us genetically to interbreed without any fertility barrier. Indeed, the tall blond alien reported by Peter Khoury in 1992 bears a close resemblance to the short blond alien reported by Antônio Villas Boas in 1957. . . ."[12]

A FULLY RECOLLECTED ABDUCTION

With regard to the aforementioned iconic abduction in Brazil—the first such case to come to public attention[13]—a résumé is warranted here, based largely on the detailed, and lesser-known, deposition provided by the witness to Dr. Olavo Fontes (a medical doctor and internationally respected researcher) four months after the event. Unlike the majority of abductions that began to proliferate on a vast scale at this time, the abductee in this case had total recall of the event.

On the night of October 15/16, 1957, near São Francisco de Sales in the state of Minais Gerais, Brazil, 23-year-old Antônio Villas Boas was plowing a field when a bizarre-looking machine with blinding lights landed nearby, stalling his tractor. Four five-foot-tall humanoids emerged from the craft, dressed in tight-fitting overalls and helmets, from the top of which three silvery tubes ran backwards. Only their light-colored eyes could be seen through the goggles they were wearing. They grabbed Antônio and dragged him, struggling, aboard the craft via a "ladder," communicating with each other in peculiar "slow barks and yelps." Another male humanoid was on board.

Prior to being introduced to the woman, Antônio was divested of his clothes, sponged down with a thick, clear liquid, then led to a room where he remained alone for half an hour or so, after which a grayish smoke exuded from small metallic tubes in the wall, causing him to vomit. A naked woman, about 4.5 feet tall, then entered. She had very fair, almost bleached hair reaching halfway down her neck; vivid blue "Chinese-type" eyes; high cheekbones, making the face look wide but narrowing sharply and terminating in a pointed chin; thin, barely visible lips and rather small ears; "high and well-separated breasts, a thin waist and small stomach, wide hips and large thighs," with very red underarm and pubic hair. A sexual act took place twice during the over-four-hour period spent on board. (Finding her "ugly," Antônio was later at a loss to understand how he could have gone through with it.)

At one stage, he attempted to purloin a heavy, clock-like instrument to furnish proof of his experience, as the men sat on swivel chairs in the cabin, their attention momentarily engaged elsewhere. "As quick as lightning," he said, "one of the men jumped up and, pushing me aside, snatched it from me angrily." Finally, he was taken by one of the men on a guided tour around the exterior of the craft, along a sort of catwalk that encircled it, terminating in "front" near "a large semi-projecting thick sheet of glass elongated toward the sides and stoutly embedded in the metal work." The craft appeared to be about thirty-five feet long and twenty-three feet wide. Ten-foot-long metal shafts functioned as undercarriage. Two square projections protruded from each side and three large metal "spurs" were fixed horizontally (see sketch below). Set vertically in the rear platform was a rectangular piece of metal, which he thought might have acted as a rudder, and what looked like a huge cupola could be seen rotating slowly, illuminated by greenish fluorescent light.

"Even with that slow movement," Antônio reported, "you could hear a noise like the sound of air being drawn in by a vacuum cleaner, a sort of whistle." Pointing to a ladder near the entrance, the guide indicated to him that he should descend it. "When I was down on the ground, I looked up. He was still there. Then he pointed to himself and then pointed to the ground, and finally to the sky toward the south. Then he made a sign for me to step back and disappeared into the machine."

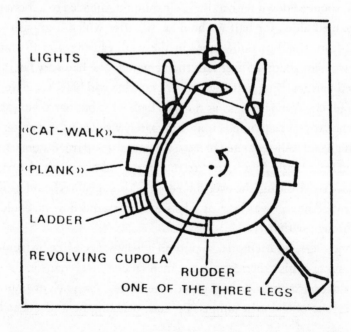

LIGHTS

"CAT-WALK"

'PLANK'

LADDER

REVOLVING CUPOLA

RUDDER

ONE OF THE THREE LEGS

"The metal ladder now began to get shorter, the steps arranging themselves one above the other. . . . The lights of the metal spurs and of the headlamps and of the revolving dish all became brighter, while the dish was spinning faster and faster. Slowly the craft began to rise, vertically. . . . At that moment the sound also increased [and] turned into a veritable hum or loud whine . . . the three shafts of the tripod on which it had been standing rose toward the sides, the lower part of each leg (narrower, rounded, and ending in an enlarged foot) began to enter the upper part (which was much thicker and square), and when that was finished, the top parts began to enter the base of the machine. Finally there was no longer anything to be seen there; the base was smooth and polished as though that tripod had never existed. . . .

"The craft continued to rise slowly in the air until it had reached a height of some thirty to fifty meters. There it stopped for a few seconds, and at the same time its luminosity began to get still greater. The whirring noise of the air being displaced became much more intense and the revolving dish began to turn at a fearful speed, while the light changed through various colors until it was vivid red. At that moment the machine suddenly changed direction, with an abrupt movement, making a louder noise, a sort of 'beat.' . . . Then, listing slightly to one side, [it] shot off like a bullet toward the south [and] was gone from sight in a few seconds."

In the days following the encounter, Antônio suffered from a variety of aftereffects, including excessive drowsiness (though he was unable to sleep for the first two nights), nausea, a pounding headache, loss of appetite, irritation of the eyes, itchy lesions on the arms and legs, and two yellowish patches, one on each side of his nose. In February 1958 he was given a complete medical examination by Dr. Fontes in Rio de Janeiro. Among his findings were "two small hyperchromatic patches," one on each side of his chin, from where the blood samples had been taken, and various "cutaneous lesions and scars." These physical symptoms, stated Fontes, "suggest radiation poisoning or exposure to radiation, but unfortunately he came to me too late for the blood examination that could have confirmed such a possibility beyond doubt."[14]

During his first public appearance, on a Brazilian television show in 1978, Villas Boas recapitulated his experience and added a significant new detail. During his second sexual encounter on board the craft, he said, the woman put a sample of his semen into a container.[15]

Pablo Villarrubia Mauso, a Brazilian journalist and researcher, learned from Antônio's closest sister, Odercia Villas Boas, that five Americans dressed in green uniforms, who she thought were from NASA, took Antônio to the United States for interrogation. Some spoke Portuguese. "They kept visiting several times over eight or ten years," she claimed. "They would always give my brother books written in English as gifts.

"He was subjected to questioning and the lie detector in California [and] taken to an open area where the remains of a flying saucer [had been] found. Then they showed him another, in good condition, inside an enclosed area like a museum, asking him if it was identical to the one he had seen. He told me that it was very similar. He was always accompanied by a [bilingual journalist] who had a foreign name and acted as an interpreter, and was always surrounded by uniformed American personnel. He was in the United States for three days.

"They later gave him two properties near San Francisco and San Rafael. I managed to see the deeds. They sent him back to Rio, where he spent between fifteen and twenty days in a hospital, undergoing new examinations and tests. . . ."[16]

Antônio Villas Boas later graduated with a law degree in Brasilia, married, and had four children, practicing with the title of "Honorable Magistrate." He died in 1992, standing by the validity of his experience to the end.

———

I am often asked if I have been abducted, to which my reply is that I simply don't know: if it has happened, it could only have been while I was asleep. However, on multiple occasions I have experienced the process commonly referred to as "night paralysis," often associated with the abduction scenario, in my case accompanied by intensifying vibrations in the solar plexus. In most cases, although such episodes seem to have been engendered during sleep, they have continued after I have awoken. Whatever source causes such intrusions, I have never sensed anything benevolent about it.

Termination is eventually achieved by shouting at the "entity" to "get out" (using somewhat stronger terminology).

There were two occasions that made me think I *might* have been abducted, the second of which may be worth recounting here. In the small hours of March 27, 2006, I had been reading late in bed until 00:55. Just after falling asleep, I suddenly found myself lying on my back on the side of a country lane lined with hedgerows. I could feel the cold air. As I began to raise myself on one arm, I noticed a dark gray triangular craft with sharply defined apexes, "transfixed" in the dark blue sky, with numerous white lights inset along the inside of each side. I then felt vibrations intensifying in my solar plexus[17] and sensed that I was being "pulled" toward the craft. I resisted mentally, asking for help from who- or whatever. Immediately, I found myself "back" in my bedroom, fully conscious. I checked the time. It was 01:05. Ten minutes had elapsed.

Was I abducted? All I can say is that it *felt* very real. And if it wasn't an actual abduction, I can hazard a guess that it might well have been a so-called "astral projection," which I have experienced previously: as a student, while dozing in bed one sunny morning, I had been "taken" for a low-level "flight" in a Royal Air Force Meteor NF Mk 11 (or later mark) jet fighter, in camouflage livery. Again, it felt very real, but, as with the more recent event, I do not believe it was physical. Which poses profound questions about the nature of abductions. While the evidence suggests that many are physical—as will have been noted in some of the preceding cases—I believe it likely that some involve abduction of the astral body. Which implies a more sinister agenda.

We have seen how the agenda of certain alien species involves, or has involved, the genetic engineering of numerous human beings. To what end? David M. Jacobs, Ph.D., a tenured Associate Professor of History at Temple University, Philadelphia, has made a special study of this aspect of the subject. His perspective is disturbing. "For the first time in over thirty years of researching the UFO phenomenon, I am frightened of it," he writes in his book, *The Threat* (1998). "The abduction phenomenon is far more ominous than I had thought. Optimism is not the appropriate response to the evidence, all of which strongly suggests that the alien agenda is primarily beneficial for them and not for us. . . ."[18]

CHAPTER EIGHTEEN
SPECIAL FORCES

In November 1999, the Center for UFO Studies (CUFOS) received a remarkable letter from a Mrs. Lucile Andrew of Ashland, Ohio. "Today," she began, "I want to share some knowledge that has been, by request, kept secret in our family since sometime in World War II.

"This concerns something that my father was shown by Cordell Hull, who was Secretary of State under Franklin Roosevelt. Sumner Wells was his Under-Secretary of State. Hull was a cousin to my father [who] was on some kind of advisory committee, and made several trips to Washington, D.C. in that capacity. My father, who was young, brilliant, and sound of mind, [told] this story because he didn't want the information to be lost.

"One day when my father was in D.C. with Cordell, Cordell swore him to secrecy and took him to a sub-basement in the U.S. Capitol building and showed him an amazing sight: (1) Four large glass jars holding four creatures unknown to my father or Cordell, [and] (2) A wrecked round craft of some kind nearby.

"My father wanted my sister and myself to make this information known long after he and Cordell were dead, because he felt it was a very important bit of information. . . . Please don't disregard this, because what I have written is true. The jars with creatures in formaldehyde and the wrecked craft are *somewhere*!

"Cordell said they were afraid they would start a panic if the public found out about it. . . ."[1]

After several telephone calls and two visits to Ashland, William "Bill" Jones, a director of CUFOS, reports, the family became comfortable with releasing the name of Mrs. Andrew's father—the Reverend Turner Hamilton Holt—and allowing the story to be told. "Here we have a tale that directly involves one of the greatest statesmen of the 20th century and a conservative man of the cloth," Bill emphasizes, "who would have absolutely no apparent reason to tell a story such as this one if it weren't true, especially at a time when stories of flying saucers and their occupants had not yet become part of our culture."

In an interview conducted in April 2000 by Bill Jones and Irena Scott with Mrs. Andrew and one of her sisters, Allene (who had also heard the story from her father, though too young to recall details), it was learned that Reverend Holt had described the entities in the glass jars as "creatures," not "aliens" or "extraterrestrials," as one would nowadays. They were less than four feet tall, and the incident is said to have occurred in the "late 1930s"—probably 1939. The remains of the wrecked craft were described as "silver-metallic."

Skeptical of such remains being stored in the "sub-basement" of the U.S. Capitol building, Bill contacted the Office of the Architect of the Capitol to determine if there is or was a sub-basement in the building, at least in the late 1930s. He met with Barbara A. Wolanin, curator of the U.S. Capitol, and related details of the story to her. She confirmed the existence of a sub-basement at that time.

"What if we learn that this pre-World War II alien technology wasn't retrieved in the United States but came from somewhere else in Europe or the Far East," asks Bill, "transferred to the United States for protection until after the war that most people knew was coming? What if we learn that this technology was given back to France, China, or Russia after the war? How would this re-transfer of technology change our view of history?"[2]

The U.S. Capitol report is significant, yet another to add to an ever-increasing number of such events. For example, in *Need to Know* I related accounts of other crashed alien vehicles predating the Roswell events: Milan, Italy (1933); Cape Girardeau, Missouri, and Sonoran Desert, Mexico (1941); Gdynia, Poland (1943); Hawaii (1944); San Antonio, New Mexico (1945); Sweden (1946); and Juarez, Mexico (1947).

Marina Popovich is a retired Soviet air force colonel, engineer, and legendary test pilot. Holding 107 aviation world records set in over forty types of aircraft, she is widely regarded as one of the most famous pilots in Russian history. Regarding the alien subject, she has been outspoken and is the author of a book titled *UFO Glasnost*. She confirms that over three thousand sightings have been reported by Soviet military and civilian pilots. She also confirms—unofficially—that the Soviet air force and KGB have fragments of five crashed UFOs in their possession. She gives the crash sites as Tunguska (the famous event in 1908), Novosibirsk, Tallinn/Estonia, Ordzhonikidze/Caucasus, and Dalnegorsk, and states that the analyzed debris revealed that it was not manufactured on Earth with terrestrial technology.[3]

RAND

The Rand (Research and Development) Corporation is a non-profit global policy think tank, initially established in 1946 by the U.S. Army Air Forces as Project RAND, under contract to the Douglas Aircraft Company. It is currently financed by the U.S. government, various corporations, and private endowment. In 1969, a researcher requested a copy of a certain document on UFOs. "Rand has done very little research on the subject," came the reply; "therefore, no publications have been written." A similar request from another researcher was met with a rather different response: "We are unable to identify any Rand publications on UFOs available for external distribution." In March 1970, the actual Rand document was requested by number and title—*UFOs: What To Do?* Rand responded that, as an internal document, it was not releasable. But eventually it leaked out. As researchers C. E. Frey and Earl J. Neff reported, the document was not to be quoted in any publication or company correspondence. "Inquiries by ufologists, NASA personnel, and interested citizens all received a courteous refusal to share the information contained in this study," they note.[4]

In retrospect, it is difficult to understand why. Could the reasons for such reluctance simply stem from the fact that the author, George Kocher, gives an unbiased and intelligent overview of the subject, which could have been interpreted as an acknowledgement of the realities involved? Or, perhaps more likely, that the corporation simply feared internal and external ridicule? In any event, the document, originally published in November 1968, is currently available online from Rand. "This paper was originally produced as an internal document; it was not prepared for or delivered to any of Rand's clients," a short added preface emphasizes. "Peer review has not been undertaken, nor has it been edited or prepared for publication. It is being released at this time as a matter of public interest."

HENRY KISSINGER AND THE OFFICE OF SPECIAL STUDIES

In his ground-breaking book *UFO Crash at Aztec*, Californian researcher William Steinman covers for the first time some related information about Dr. Eric Henry Wang, who seems to have been a crucial link in the study of crashed alien vehicles. Raymond Fowler (another first-class researcher with whom I have also previously communicated extensively) was the first to reveal that Dr. Wang headed the Office of Special Studies at Wright Air Development Center (Wright-Patterson Air Force Base), Dayton, Ohio. That office dealt largely with recovered alien craft and their crews, such as an incident near Kingman, Arizona, in May 1953, involving a number of witnesses, including "Fritz Werner," the pseudonym for Arthur Stansel, part of whose impressive résumé I published in a previous book. Stansel held a number of engineering and management positions at Wright-Patterson Air Force Base from 1949 to 1960, during which period he worked in the Office of Special Studies.[5]

"I personally checked out his résumé by calling former employers during a careful character check," wrote Fowler in 1976. "Neither of the two former 'Bluebook' officers with whom I talked would confirm the Kingman incident. One asked 'Where is the object now?' The other became nervous when I mentioned Dr. Eric Wang's Office of Special Studies and asked me to leave him alone as he wanted to live out his life in privacy."[6]

"The work that Dr. Wang was involved in was so classified that there were no more levels of secrecy left above that," asserts Steinman. Born in Vienna in 1906, Wang taught engineering at the University of Cincinnati before working on government projects at the Wright Air Development Center from 1949 until 1956, when the department was transferred to the Sandia Laboratories complex at Kirtland Air Force Base, New Mexico. He died in 1960, aged fifty-four. A telephone interview by Bill Steinman with Wang's widow, Maria (Steinman does not give her name in his book), is revealing:

ws: I wrote a letter to you on the 23rd March in regards to Dr. Eric Henry Wang and his work involving analyses on recovered flying saucers, and the attempted duplication of them.

mw: Yes, I do remember the letter, but I no longer have it [and] turned it over to the authorities. . . . Military intelligence at Kirtland Air Force Base.

ws: Can you tell me something about Dr. Wang's involvement in the flying saucer project?

mw: How did you know that Dr. Wang was involved in that kind of work? Why do you want to know about that? Who are you? How do I know that I can trust you?

ws: I am a freelance private investigator. I want to know the truth pertaining to the Flying Saucer Project. . . . I believe that the entire scientific community, the public, and mankind in general could greatly benefit from it.

mw: How can I help you? Dr. Wang's papers were all confiscated by military intelligence when he died. His notes were written in his own unique version of German scientific shorthand. Those papers were placed behind lock and key within a special sealed-off section of a highly secret section of the library at Kirtland Air Force Base.

ws: Can you please describe exactly what kind of work Dr. Wang was doing on the saucers?

MW: I can't tell you over the phone. I don't know you at all, and besides, the entire subject *is* classified above Top Secret.

WS: Were the saucers made on Earth? And if so, were they of German technology?

MW: No! To both questions. The person you should write to in Government is Dr. H.A.K. [Henry Kissinger]. He is deeply involved in the flying saucer program. In fact, he was completely in charge of it at the time that Dr. Wang was still alive and involved in it.

"Within two days of talking with [Maria] about Dr. Wang," Steinman reports, "I received a call from a well-known ufologist. He said, 'What did you discuss with M.W.? I understand that you discussed the library at Kirtland Air Force Base. . . .' I asked, 'How did you know about any of this?' He said that he had his intelligence connections, and that I was now being watched very closely."[7]

The reference to Dr. Henry Kissinger is significant. From 1943 to 1946, he had served in the U.S. Army Counter-Intelligence Corps (CIC) and from 1946 to 1949 as a captain in the Military Intelligence Reserve.[8] In some previous books, I have alluded to the Army's Interplanetary Phenomenon Unit (IPU) of the Scientific and Technical Branch, Counter-Intelligence Directorate, an elite investigation group reportedly set up by General George C. Marshall in 1947 to deal with the then-burgeoning reports of "flying discs." The existence of the IPU was confirmed for me in 1987 by Colonel Antony J. Gallo, Jr., General Staff, Director of Counterintelligence. "Please be advised," he added, "that the aforementioned Army unit was disestablished during the late 1950s and never reactivated. All records pertaining to this unit were turned over to the U.S. Air Force, Office of Special Investigations, in conjunction with Operation 'BLUE-BOOK.' . . ."[9] General Douglas MacArthur is also believed to have been involved with the IPU. During a meeting with Mayor Achille of Naples in New York in 1955, MacArthur is reported as having stated his belief that "all the countries on Earth will have to unite to survive and to make a common front against attack by people from other planets."[10]

Kissinger served (in 1952) as a consultant to the Psychological Strategy Board, a covert arm of the National Security Council established in 1951, comprising the Under-Secretary of State, the Deputy Secretary of Defense, and the Director of Central Intelligence. He also acted as a consultant on the Operations Coordination Board. Thus, in that period he would have had access to the most sensitive intelligence on the alien problem. Later, he became a consultant for a number of other organizations, including the Rand Corporation, the National Security Council, and the Council on Foreign Relations, and he served as Director of the Special Studies Project for the Rockefeller Brothers Fund. By 1973 he had become Secretary of State, continuing to hold the position of Assistant to the President on National Security Affairs. He is also a holder of the Nobel Peace Prize.[11]

L. Fletcher Prouty, a former U.S. Air Force colonel who spent his last nine years of service in the Pentagon as the official Focal Point Officer, first for the USAF and then for the entire Defense Department with the CIA (clandestine operations), makes reference in one of his books to the power held by Kissinger, describing him as "the titular head of the intelligence community's clandestine operations reaction faction," as he wrote in *The Secret Team* (1973). "His appearance as a one-man power center is simply due to the fact that he fronts for the Secret Team [discussed later] and the secret intelligence community."[12] I surmise that Kissinger retains a close association with the alien situation to this day, even at the age of almost ninety.

MILITARY INDOCTRINATION

In 2008, an unusual report appeared in a British newspaper in response to an article on UFOs. "The township of Roswell was the scene of probably the most famous alien encounter in history," wrote retired British Army veteran Harold Varnam. "While serving on a NATO attachment to the U.S. Fifth Army, we were shown classified film taken at the time of the Roswell crash that purported to show that one of the alien creatures survived the impact and lived for several hours afterwards." Varnam went on to mention, somewhat cynically, Roswell's current popularity and its annual festival.[13] Determined to learn more, I contacted him.

"I am not absolutely sure of the date when we saw this film but I do remember that it was around the time of the Cuban missile crisis, and the place was the huge airbase at Karlsruhe [Germany]," he replied. "The gigantic Karlsruhe base had all the usual luxuries, including a full-scale plush cinema which not only showed the latest Hollywood releases but doubled up as a lecture theater for the showing of training films. The Americans were exceptionally keen on these films, and it was not unusual for us to see anything up to half a dozen or so during our visit. So when we settled down in the cinema, we were not expecting to see anything extraordinary. As it's almost fifty years ago, I will try to recall as best I can what we were actually shown.

"Strangely enough, we were not briefed in advance and the film itself was unusual in that it was not preceded by the 'over-the-top' rhetoric that usually introduced these training films. There was only a sparse commentary, but what was surprising was that the first part of the film was in color; not the garish Technicolor version, but a kind of subdued soft-focus look.

"The opening scenes were of the New Mexico desert and what was obviously the crash site. It was plainly obvious that the movie was an amateur affair probably shot by a local, and several people appeared in it holding up what looked like pieces of metal and grinning at the camera. The wreckage was apparently spread over a vast area and was reduced to just small pieces, nothing resembling an aircraft, and whatever had impacted there must have done so at colossal speed and force.

"It was obvious that this footage had been shot before the area had been secured. This part of the film had no commentary at all. Then there were scenes of the wreckage being taken away by the military and mention of a secure airbase somewhere which was only identified by a number. Then surprisingly the film reverted to black and white and became much slicker and professional.

"The scenes at the airbase showed the unloading of the recovered material and only then did the commentary mention strange 'creatures' found with the wreckage and the startling admission that one of them was still 'alive,' whatever that meant. There were shots of military ambulances and something being off-loaded onto wheeled stretchers.

"Then the scene switched to what looked like a hospital operating theatre. I must explain that this section of the film was scratched and grainy as if it had been shown many times, as it probably had. The camera shots were angled so that you didn't really get a clear shot of the 'alien' body, but there was just one brief moment when it came into focus. The tiny creature was obviously mangled badly but I can only describe it as being like those aliens shown in sci-fi movies, with an oversized head and small body and limbs.

"Once again, the commentary was sparse and there was no attempt to explain or tell what happened to the alien. I would estimate that the entire film did not last more than fifteen minutes or so, but then at the very end it reverted to type and there was some blurb about being constantly vigilant and keep watching the skies, etc.

"Naturally the British lads reviewed all of these films with a healthy skepticism and their usual brand of deprecating humor. I don't remember anybody at the time being particularly impressed, as we all considered the Americans to be guilty of over-nervousness bordering on paranoia about their attitude to the Soviet threat. This was, after all, the height of the Cold War [with] the hysteria that was prevalent at that period in our history. . . ."[14]

According to a military officer stationed at the U.S. Army Reserve base at Fort Allen, Juana Díaz, Puerto Rico, in 1990 (following a period involving an alarming increase of alien activity on the island, including the capture of U.S. Navy F-14 Tomcat jets), a video film was shown to the men as part of an indoctrination. "They showed us an old black-and-white film about a UFO crash that supposedly happened in New Mexico many years ago," the officer related to investigator Jorge Martín. "We all saw the craft, which was semi-buried in the ground at a 45-degree angle, and there were several bodies of the crew. According to what we were shown, these bodies were about five feet tall, thin, very pale, and had large bald heads. They had big round eyes and a small nose, but I don't recall any mouths or ears.

"They also showed us another video of UFOs filmed by them around the island. They wanted us to know that UFOs are real, but they wouldn't elaborate when asked for details. It seemed to me that they wanted us to know this was real and that the beings were not perfect: they are fallible, their crafts crash, and they also die—they are not invulnerable. Apparently, they wanted to condition us to the idea that they exist, and to accept the possibility of someday having to liaise with them."[15]

SURVIVORS

At the time of writing, the most recent report relating to the New Mexico incidents was sent to me by the American researcher Ted Oliphant, a former police officer. He had acquired the information from a confidential source whose father had developed the film of the Roswell incident.

"The whole thing was documented," Ted revealed. "He was in the service, then went to work for 'Uncle Sugar' as a civilian. He said there was one surviving creature. Everything went to Wright-Pat [Wright-Patterson AFB]. He also said many of those involved in the retrieval later died of cancer.[16] I just learned this today; I'd known him for years but this is the first time it ever came up in conversation. Nathan Twining Jr., the son of General Twining [Commanding General of Air Materiel Command at the time], says that years later, his dad told him that he'd seen the survivor himself, and that they communicated telepathically."[17]

There are remarkable parallels in this report with another, which I first learned of in 1995 from Sir Mark Thomson, a friend who had served as a jet pilot with the Royal Navy's Fleet Air Arm (then holding Top Secret Atomic clearance). He related to me that during a flight on an airliner in the United States in 1995 he had met a lady, Linda Pitchersky, who asserted that her father, Robert R. Largent, a former U.S. Army Air Corps flying instructor, had spoken with a fellow officer who claimed to have cared for "the only living, remaining being" who had survived the Roswell incident. Sir Mark shortly thereafter interviewed Largent by telephone and provided me with the following report:

"This elderly man had been a B-29 pilot [during] the war. As his Squadron had a nuclear capability, he had a very high security clearance. Since his retirement [as a major in the Reserves], his civilian job had involved a high amount of commercial flying. On one of these trips in the 1960s, [Robert] happened to sit next to a man who was a colonel in the Air Force, and their conversation centered on Air Force and flying matters.

"After Robert had explained his previous very high security clearance, he asked the colonel what he was presently doing. He told Robert that he had been looking after an alien for the past two and a half years at a base (presumably U.S. Air Force) near Dayton, Ohio. He went on to say that they had had the most terrible time feeding the alien. They had tried everything, but nothing satisfied his nutrition and dietary requirements, and as a result of this he had recently died. The colonel went on to say that he so cared for the alien that when he died, he nearly cried. He did not give Robert his name and continually stressed that if he ever disclosed this to anyone, he would be in the gravest difficulty.

"At this point in our conversation, I asked Robert various questions. Why did Robert think a complete stranger, a U.S. Air Force colonel, chose to reveal this great secret to him? He replied that firstly they shared a great bond, both being pilots (I can certainly confirm this unique, strong bond between military pilots all over the world!). It was clear to Robert that the alien had recently died and the colonel really wanted to talk to somebody about his grief and feelings of loss, and that Robert's high security clearance made him comfortable in discussing it.

"This is the total of Robert's knowledge from this chance meeting with the colonel," Mark concluded. "Of course, I am not to know whether the colonel told Robert other things that Robert is declining to tell me, but I certainly got no indication of this. Robert struck me as an extremely sincere and intelligent older man. . . ."[18] Both men felt that their lives were threatened if they revealed what they knew.

In 2005, Robert's daughter Linda contacted me, reminding me that, coincidentally, we had met briefly at a UFO presentation I gave in North Carolina in 1993. I asked her what she had learned from her father (now deceased):

"My memory of what Dad had to say was that he had met the gentleman who cared for the only remaining living being on the spaceship that crashed [near] Roswell. Dad said that the fellow cried as he told him, because he missed the little one so much. He told Dad that it was like living with Jesus Christ. And he recounted that they didn't speak verbally, but telepathically, mind to mind. Dad remembered that he told him that the little man was so gentle and kind.

"Dad also remembered that he said the alien had only lived for eighteen months, due to the atmospheric conditions and unacceptable food. Dad and this other Air Force officer (perhaps a lieutenant) met on an Air Force transport sometime during his stay in the service. Dad would have been in the Air Force Reserves."[19]

"Assuming the U.S. personnel were able to communicate with this alien," Mark pointed out to me, "why couldn't he tell them about their dietary needs? In view of their superior intelligence and as they had already been here for some time, they must have known what foodstuffs were available on Earth. My clear understanding from Robert was that it was a feeding problem as opposed to a disease or illness problem." A good question. I have learned a great deal, for instance, from "Thomas," one of the hand-picked team that took care of *two* survivors from the Roswell incident for a considerable period of time, as part of an Anglo-American-Alien "arrangement" (Chapter 10). The injured aliens they cared for and communicated with extensively (via a type of telepathy, as in the two previous cases) seemed mostly capable of consuming their own liquid-based nutriments.

Although some of Linda's information is at variance with that supplied to Sir Mark by her father, it does not, in my view, negate the essentials of the story. When dealing with sensitive information, it is as common for informants to deliberately alter some of the facts as it is for recipients sometimes to get their facts wrong.

ANGLO/AMERICAN INCIDENTS

The village of Tarland lies some twenty-five miles west of Aberdeen, Scotland. In the summer of 1957, the Aberdeen Division of the Territorial Army (TA) had chosen this area, which included much densely wooded terrain, for an exercise. The following report was supplied to me by researcher Ian Taylor.

At around 04:00, two young recruits from the main force heard what they thought were the advancing "enemy" coming toward their position through the trees. Armed and ready in their trench for a surprise attack, they suddenly heard strange, guttural-like voices and the cracking of twigs as though people were breaking them underfoot. What happened next threw the men into a state of abject panic:

"They saw two human-like figures coming toward them that seemed to be around seven to eight feet in height, wearing what they described to be very tight-fitting, one-piece silvery-colored garments. The guttural-like sounds they first heard were in fact some form of dialogue between these entities.

"The soldiers jumped up from their positions and took off in the opposite direction toward the roadway. They continued to run, still in a state of panic. Then, just above the tree-line close to the Tarland roadway, a large and glowing disc-like object of intense brightness appeared overhead, showering down what looked like sparks. The object appeared to follow them as they ran, and then rapidly overtook them and shot skyward.

"One of the men collapsed from exhaustion and lay at the side of the road while his colleague continued to run, eventually reaching a Post Office line engineer in a roadside trailer. The soldier apparently hammered on the door for help. Eventually the two men returned to fetch the other soldier and brought him to the trailer to recover. . . .

"The press carried an article a couple of days later, but in no great detail. Following the article, the two young TA recruits had been interviewed by personnel who had traveled up from Whitehall in London. I can recall years later someone who claimed he knew one of the soldiers, who said they had been given instructions to maintain a vow of silence over the event. . . ."[20]

Harold Varnam, the British Army veteran cited earlier in connection with the indoctrination film shown at the Karlsruhe air base, Germany, also sent me his report of an encounter with a "definite foreign object," an incident which occurred in June of either 1971 or '72 while he was participating in an exercise at the Stanford Battle Area—better known as the Stanford Training Area (STANTA)—located in the county of Norfolk.

"Our small unit of the Army Emergency Reserve (AER) was under the auspices of NATO, and we usually did our annual fifteen-day main exercise on the Lüneberg Heide [a large area of heath and woodland in northern Germany] attached to the 4th Armoured Division," his narrative begins. "Sometimes we went further afield to Canada, Cyprus, or Kenya, etc. But for some reason, on this particular year we joined the scheme in Norfolk.

"It was an extended NATO exercise covering most of the European Theater and had been going for some time when we joined it. I believe the exercise was coded 'Greensward,' which was conducted in two phases—Greensward I and Greensward II. Our phase, Greensward I, was more of a search and evasion exercise and was infantry-based, although there was artillery and aircraft support. At the first briefing there were groans of dismay when we were told that it would be a live-firing exercise and then sighs of relief when we were told that although the scheme was being run by the U.S. Fifth Army, the live-firing would be the responsibility of 2nd Coldstreams, whose motto was *Nulli Secundus* ['Second to None']. We knew that the disciplined Guards would ensure that accidents, always inevitable, would be kept to a minimum.

"Our unit's four-man night patrols were tasked with our usual role of observation and reconnaissance, but we were given free rein to harass the 'enemy' whenever targets of opportunity arose. The weather was splendid, and to tell the truth it never really got properly dark. . . . On the night of the incident, which we think was a Thursday/Friday, our own patrol had split into two pairs as we approached our designated target. My partner, a man who I will refer to as 'Lange Jan' [named after a church steeple on the island of Walcheren, one of the highest points in Holland], was very popular with the Dutch Kriegsmarine Kommando who we trained with, and they had bestowed that nickname on him.

"As we approached our target area, a very bright light appeared on the horizon.

"It looked at first like huge car headlights, but this was very unusual as, apart from the odd tracers and flares, the battlefield was almost always in darkness. Then suddenly, and I do mean instantaneously, the light was immediately to our front, probably some three miles away. The only way I can describe this light is to call it 'blue-white,' rather like that given off by the new LED bulbs—only very much brighter. Then we realized a peculiar thing: the light did not radiate, it simply seemed to be self-contained [and] appeared to either be hovering over, or in, a wooded area in our target zone. We decided to take a closer look.

"Lange Jan, originally out of 1 PARA [1st Battalion of the Parachute Regiment], was the best field soldier I ever knew, and he had the ability to almost merge with any terrain, but nevertheless after a stealthy thousand yards or so we were bumped by an American patrol who told us that this area was now out of bounds. Undeterred, we tried again, but when we were stopped a second time by a very jumpy officer, extremely nervous, and told in no uncertain terms that we had to leave, we decided to let it go.

"As it was already becoming daylight in the east, we started to head back to our lines when instantly the light went out, just as if someone had thrown a switch. But we could clearly see fires burning in the wooded area and what looked like considerable damage to the trees and undergrowth, although there was no sign of debris.

"At the next morning's 'O' Group debriefing session, we learned that only two of our patrols had seen the strange light, but when we brought it up an intel [intelligence] officer said that a Phantom [jet] had crashed and the area was now off-limits for the rest of the exercise. The Phantoms, operating out of Lakenheath, had indeed been taking part in the scheme, doing low-level mock strafing and bombing runs (and terrifying they were too). But I had previously served in the Royal Air Force in Air/Surface Movements (what would now be called a 'dispatcher') and had seen first-hand some plane crashes, and the incident in the woods did not resemble in any way a 'normal' air crash. But that was the end of the matter: it never came up again.

"Generous as ever, the Americans allowed us the use of the facilities at [RAF] Alconbury: the PX stores (hypermarkets where one could purchase an almost unbelievable range of goods at very competitive prices) and the Rod and Gun Club lounge, when we were on stand-down. In the club the following day, we brought up the subject of the downed plane, but no one seemed to know anything about it, or if they did, they were playing tight-lipped.

"After de-briefing and release on the Saturday, we decided once more to take a look for ourselves at the site. At the time, Lange Jan had a long-wheel-base Land Rover, [and] so six of us got aboard and we headed for the crash site. But this time it was heavily cordoned off and we could not get really close, but we did have field glasses and we could clearly see the scorched area of the wood, which looked as though a road had been carved through it, maybe some seventy or eighty yards wide. Since we were attracting unwarranted attention, we decided to scoot. Since that day, I had never really thought about it. Only some local interest in a UFO incident brought back the memories of that night in Norfolk. . . ."[21]

On the night of May 23/24, 1974, men of the U.S. Army's 4th Platoon, Bravo Company, B Battalion, 2nd Regiment of the 32nd Air Defense Command were deployed in a mountain pass northeast of Ramstein Air Force Base, Germany. First Lieutenant Robert Cardeni was the 4th

Platoon leader and Captain Michael J. Shestak was commanding Bravo Company. The soldiers had been told they were on special duty owing to Russian and/or Warsaw Pact forces testing American radar defenses. The men were surprised that live ammunition for the Vulcan 20mm cannons and live Chaparral antiaircraft missiles was to be utilized. Lt. Cardeni gave orders to the crews of the cannons to load canisters of live high-explosive phosphorus rounds and to maintain high alert.

At about 00:45, Lt. Cardeni gave orders that something hostile was incoming and that the gunners were to shoot down anything coming though the pass, stating that since "no friendlies" would be flying below 2,700 feet, anything else was to be shot down. At around 01:00, a Sergeant Yonts noticed a fast-approaching, zigzagging, flattened ellipsoid-shaped craft with rounded edges, about thirty feet long and glowing with a silvery iridescence. "It took a few seconds for Sgt. Yonts's cannon's computer and Doppler radar to calculate a precise speed, range, and direction of travel and to achieve a lock-on," reports Ed Komarek, an American researcher who received the report anonymously, via mail. "When the cannon locked on to the object through the [reticulated] gunsights, he began firing, first a few rounds for effect and then three four-second bursts of 110 rounds each into the side of the object. . . ."

"Sgt. Yonts was almost at eye level with the object as he watched his rounds pouring into its sides. He was expecting to see the 'blooming flower' effect of the phosphorus rounds exploding, but he did not. . . . 'It was as if the shells were being absorbed or being vaporized by some sort of 'force field,' Yonts said, [which] was quite a remarkable containment of shells having a 35-meter kill radius."

Meanwhile, on the mountainside, Sgt. William McCracken, inside the launch-control console of a Chaparral battery, locked on to a target and fired a missile, which climbed to about nine hundred feet, located the object, moved close ahead of the target, and detonated. Gunners and observers watched as the target started wobbling, "then stop[ped] forward motion and finally wobble[d] downward to the valley floor in what the observers believed was a controlled descent."

U.S. Air Force personnel later secured this crash/landing site. According to Komarek's source, various Air Force personnel, including a Major Mike

Andrews (pseudonym?) and three Army officers from the Army Vulnerability Assessment Laboratory in Alamogordo, New Mexico, were flown in a C-141 Starlifter transport to Ramstein. "The soldiers who had had a direct active part in the mission less than twelve hours earlier met individually with the debriefers," Komarek's report continues. The three Army officers handled the first debriefing, followed by groups of Air Force officers, who warned the men that "if they ever told anyone about what they had imagined had happened, they would never work for the government [and] warned of unspecified dire things that would happen to them should they ever talk . . . the men were required to sign a security oath to never divulge the details of that night [and] if questioned in the future, to deny that it ever happened."

On the afternoon of May 25, Major Andrews and his crew were told to report to their aircraft, parked at a remote location on the Ramstein air base, and he was shocked to note that a set of metal supports had been constructed on the wings and fuselage of his C-141, attached to which was "something large and ellipsoid," covered with olive drab green canvas tarpaulins. During preparations for takeoff, Andrews noted the minimal fuel load, due to the weight of the additional craft. On reaching its cruise altitude, the C-141 was refuelled by a KC-135 tanker.

"Major Andrews's orders were that he was not to land until he reached Wright-Patterson AFB, and that he would be met by refuelling tankers at strategic points across the Atlantic," Ed Komarek learned. "It was dark in Ohio when Major Andrews landed to disembark the airmen—all but four who were to remain aboard and who then were carrying M16 rifles in addition to their sidearms. The pilots and crew of the C-141 were not allowed out of the plane and they did not refuel.

"Taking off again with a minimal fuel load, they were once again met at altitude by another KC-135 tanker and flew on direct to Nellis AFB, Nevada, where the crew was once again not allowed outside the aircraft as their wing-top cargo was offloaded and taken away, again covered completely." On returning to McGuire AFB, New Jersey, Andrews and his crew were debriefed by an Air Force colonel who warned them never to discuss the mission with anyone.

Another source present during the downing of the craft pointed out to Komarek that, although he had observed the incident, there were no mountains northeast of Ramstein, only hills. However, although this informant did not witness the May 23/24 attack per se, he believes he did see the crashing object "looking like it was dripping iridescent white fire." He also claims that a couple of weeks earlier another unknown craft was almost hit by a Nike missile, whereupon it "started flying erratically, then two F-4s [Phantom jets] came and gave chase, disappearing beyond the ridges. Don't know if they got that one, but the base went on full alert. We were anticipating the Russians to be coming, not the spacemen. . . ."[22]

THE SECRET TEAM

In 1994 I had the privilege on two occasions of interviewing L. Fletcher Prouty, a retired U.S. Air Force colonel—cited earlier—in Washington, D.C. A former fighter pilot and professor of air science and tactics at Yale University, he was also directly in charge of the global system designed to provide military support for the clandestine activities of the CIA.

Regarding the UFO subject, Prouty revealed a hitherto Top Secret report he had investigated in 1953–54 relating to the observation of a large unknown craft which paced a C-54 military transport plane over the Pacific Ocean for over an hour, witnessed by the entire crew and passengers. His report appears in two of my books.[23]

All CIA military activities were channeled through Prouty. Not being a CIA man, per se, he was exempt from taking the oath of secrecy. And being the Focal Point Officer placed him in a very privileged position. "In effect," states the publisher's blurb to *The Secret Team*, one of two of his books he gave me, "Prouty has far more knowledge of CIA activities than almost all members of that organization." The subtitle does not mince its words: *The CIA and its Allies in Control of the United States and the World.* "Like it or not," he wrote in a preface to the second edition in 1990, "we now live in a new age of 'One World.' This is the age of global companies, of global communications and transport, of global finance and—just around the corner—global accommodation of political systems. . . . It is time to face the fact that true national sovereignty no longer exists. We live in a world of big business, big lawyers, big bankers, even bigger moneymen and big politics. It is the world of 'The Secret Team.'

"In such a world, the Secret Team is a dominant power. It is neither military nor police. It is covert, and the best (or worst) of both. It gets the job done whether it has political authorization and direction or not. It is independent. It is lawless. [This book] is based upon personal experience generally derived from work in the Pentagon from 1955 to 1964. At retirement, I was Chief of Special Operations (clandestine activities) with the U.S. Joint Chiefs of Staff. These duties involved the military support of the clandestine activities of the CIA and were performed under the provisions of National Security Council Directive No. 5412/2."

He continues: "I was the first author to point out that the CIA's most important 'Cover Story' is that of an 'Intelligence' agency. Of course the CIA does make use of 'intelligence' and 'intelligence gathering,' but that is largely a front for its primary interest, 'Fun and Games.' The CIA is the center of a vast mechanism that specializes in Covert Operations. . . . In this sense, the CIA is the willing tool of a higher level Secret Team, or High Cabal, that usually includes representatives of the CIA and other instrumentalities of the government, certain cells of the business and professional world and, almost always, foreign participation. It is this Secret Team. . . ."[24]

"At the heart of the Team, of course, are a handful of top executives of the CIA and of the National Security Council (NSC), most notably the chief White House adviser to the president regarding foreign policy affairs. Around them revolves a sort of inner ring of presidential officials, civilians, and military men from the Pentagon, and career professionals in the intelligence community. It is often quite difficult to tell exactly who many of these men really are, because some may wear a uniform and the rank of general and really be with the CIA and others may be as inconspicuous as the executive assistant to some Cabinet officer's chief deputy.

"Out beyond this ring is an extensive and intricate network of government officials with responsibility for, or expertise in, some specific field that touches on national security or foreign affairs: 'Think Tank' analysts, businessmen who travel a lot or whose businesses (e.g., import-export or cargo airline operations) are useful, academic experts in this or that technical subject or geographic region, and quite importantly, alumni of the intelligence community—a service from which there are no unconditional resignations. . . ."[25]

"Sponsored by President Truman and established by an act of Congress," summarizes the publisher's blurb for *The Secret Team*, "the CIA was initially founded as a data-coordinating, intelligence-gathering agency to help fight the Cold War, [but] its profile today is unrecognizable, and its power is unstoppable. . . . The President of the United States is impotent against it, Congress cannot legislate it, the military cannot corral it, and the public doesn't even know about it."

Regarding the CIA UFO-debunking program, in October 1994 I had the pleasure of spending a day in the delightful company of Frederick C. Durant III, a former U.S. Naval Reserve pilot who was on the CIA's Office of Scientific Intelligence advisory panel convened in January 1953 to discuss methods of debunking the subject. Its final report is commonly known as "The Durant Report." We subsequently corresponded regularly. While continuing to "toe the line," a note he sent me in March 2007 was encouraging: "Hi, good friend! Never, never, ever give up. . . ."

A TIGHT LID

"The U.S. government and the British have made secret treaty agreements with the aliens in exchange for technology and so-called 'recon' missions during times of human conflict," claims an anonymous three-star general. "The aliens have basically agreed not to concern themselves with the wars or conflicts of humans—'not to interfere' in society. Let the governments rule and decide. Exactly what the aliens get in return was not exactly made clear or available. Also, there are special 'teams' which eradicate, discredit, harass, and 'trump up charges' to control humans who experience any visitations from aliens, or make verifiable UFO sightings. This is one of the reasons I retired. . . ."[26]

William J. Pawelec, the former U.S. Air Force computer operations and programing specialist cited in Chapter 14, confirms some of the above. "I would say this is international in scope," he told Steven Greer of the Disclosure Project, in an interview that Pawelec had specified not to be released until December 2010:

"The projects that we have are closely tied in with other allies' governments. In fact, I have been told back in the late 1970s, on one of the early classified projects I worked on . . . that there was a secret agreement between us and the Brits, so whatever we invent, they get. And there is no limitation as to what it is. The Brits can make their duplicates, and we don't hold back on any of the technology, because of that secret agreement that was cut during World War II. And we have other allies like that. I believe that what we see also is a lot of cross-pollination of scientists from different countries working on projects even in the most classified arenas in the United States."

Pawelec also hinted that certain British commando units liaise with their American counterparts on the problem (as for example in the 1971/72 incident described earlier by Harold Varnam). All these "black" projects were highly classified. "What concerns me," he continued, "is when these projects go 'beyond black'; people with ulterior motives that have gotten in control of these projects and/or the funding for them, and/or the ability of what *really* is scary, to write their own unlimited checks with no recourse to anybody. They're not even a budget item any more. They literally authorize the Treasury to cut them checks [and] it becomes evident that they have agendas that are independent of the goals of the United States. And the attitude is seemingly one of control—power and control.

"The ability of certain forces out there to use force whenever absolutely necessary, or other controlling mechanism to ameliorate the danger of a leak, or maintain secrecy with fear, is always there. If they can do one high-profile hit on somebody in a specific way, what it does is put the fear of God into those that they want to continue to control, so that they don't say anything out of turn—they don't probe where they shouldn't probe, like Congressman Steven Schiff was doing. . . ."[27]

"My concerns are for the freedom of our country—and of the free world. It sounds rather simplistic, but we have a philosophy upon which we base our lives, and my philosophy is the republican form of government—if we can get back to it in some way, shape or form—[which] is the strongest form of government developed by man. If we don't find ways to neutralize these negative forces, we're going to find our lifestyles—our concepts of life as a species—nullified."[28]

As Dwight D. Eisenhower had warned in his farewell speech as president in January 1961: "In the councils of government, we must guard against the acquisition of unwarranted influence, whether sought or unsought, by the military-industrial complex. The potential for the disastrous rise of misplaced power exists and will persist. We must never let the weight of this combination endanger our liberties or democratic processes. . . ."[29]

That scenario of a satellite government has long since arrived. In their book *A.D. After Disclosure*, Richard Dolan and Bryce Zabel refer to it as "The Breakaway Group." "Bolstered by tremendous co-opted assets worldwide," they claim, "they have over the years gained tremendous independence from the established political and military authorities. For it is likely that this Breakaway Group answers not so much to the president of the United States as it does toward powerful, private, internationally based individuals and groups. . . ."[30]

Dolan and Zabel also cite the research by Dr. Richard Sauder into massive, deep, clandestine bases and tunnels—including those beneath our seabeds—plans of which were initiated by the U.S. national security establishment in the 1960s.[31] And according to Dolan and Zabel, an assistant secretary to a branch of the armed forces "told a family friend that he had been 'briefed' for some eight weeks at an underground facility outside of Washington. Asked the purpose of the briefing, this highly placed man, who went on to become a cabinet secretary, said, 'There is intelligent life in the universe. It's here. And I've seen it. . . .' The cabinet secretary told the family friend that aliens were just the 'tip of the iceberg' in terms of mind-blowing revelations. . . ."[32]

CHAPTER NINETEEN
WHAT ON EARTH?

E arlier, I revealed information pertaining to an alien technology transfer program provided for me by a U.S. Army Intelligence veteran, a senior aerospace reporter based in the Washington, D.C. area. He, in turn, acquired that knowledge from a high-ranking source at the Pentagon in the USAF Air Staff and Joint Staff in the 1980s. If what my source has learned about the alien presence on Earth is true, it supports Dr. David Jacobs's contention that a hybridization program poses a serious threat to humankind.

The following scenario is based on some new information relating to "Project Aquarius," acquired more recently from my source relating to a particular species—probably the predominant group—involved in the abduction program. I shall also touch on some of the material first revealed in *Unearthly Disclosure*. As to what is happening currently, I have no idea, apart from the information supplied to me by Maria Rivera.

The creatures have/had a long-term plan to create a race of alien/human hybrids, purportedly to make us more peaceful. Their true purpose, however, is to create a passive human race, incapable of violence, by eradicating the human emotions that enable us to survive—thus laying us open to conquest. However, if this has been a long-term stratagem, I've yet to see much evidence of the human race becoming less violent. In any event, these particular aliens are not omnipotent, and to a certain extent feared us. Although possessing a type of handheld weapon, some of them had been killed by our military.

A number of their bases were guarded by elements of the U.S. military. Compartmentalization within Project Aquarius was extreme. A select cell within the Army, for example, worked with other security cells in the Air Force and Navy. Around a hundred personnel from the Air Force Office of Special Investigations (AFOSI) were involved. During my meeting in 1998 at the Defense Airborne Reconnaissance Office (DARO) in the Pentagon, the director, General Kenneth R. Israel, confirmed for me that AFOSI was involved in investigations, since the phenomenon seemed to him to be more of a policing problem rather than one affecting national security.[1]

Even theater commanders-in-chief (CINCs) were "out of the loop," I learned. Those in the loop were said to include the president (though not always), the Secretary of Defense, the Director of Central Intelligence, and the Chairman of the Joint Chiefs of Staff. The latter was said to be in charge of Project Aquarius, which, given his legal status as the highest ranking military officer in the U.S. Armed Forces and prinicipal adviser to the president, makes sense.

In the event of leaks, dossiers on potential offenders were prepared by security personnel to discredit their reputations in the media. Those few in Congress and the media who expressed an interest and asked too many questions were "dealt with"—as I hinted in the previous chapter.

A president, as well as a chairman of the Joint Chiefs, is alleged to have been abducted. As to who, I haven't a clue. But in this connection, I remain intrigued by an extraordinary and barely known report in 1982 relating to General William C. Westmoreland (1914–2005), a U.S. Army general who commanded military operations in the Vietnam War (1964–68), afterwards serving as U.S. Army Chief of Staff (1968–72):

"UFO KIDNAP" PUTS U.S. ARMY IN A FLAP
Los Angeles, Thursday
A report that America's Vietnam commander, General William

Westmoreland, had been "snatched by a flying saucer" sparked off a full-scale emergency alert.

The report was made by 49-year-old Mrs. Edith Mello. Security police immediately tried to track down the general. They failed. And troops at El Paso Army base in Texas were put on full alert.

"We put out an all-points bulletin," said Army spokesman Ed Starnes. "But four hours later we decided the woman's claim was just too much so we called off the search."

The Army said later that General Westmoreland had been found . . . but refused to say where.[2]

GRAYS' ANATOMY

The alien species described by my source said they lived for several hundreds of years. Anatomically, they had a bi-chambered heart, and a single lung served to oxygenate their blood and tissues and to eliminate bodily wastes in gaseous form. Vegetable-based food was liquefied and its nutrients absorbed through their tissues, not gastronomically. Their genitals were similar to ours, but those of the male were much smaller.

Regarding the *modus operandi* relating to the alien hybridization process, the wombs of their females are much smaller than those of humans, thus unable to accommodate transgenic fetuses for more than two months, hence human wombs were favored. Cross-species copulation was very seldom employed, since the alien male organs were too soft. Thus artificial insemination prevailed. The fetuses, extracted prematurely after the two-month period, were nurtured somehow until reaching term at seven months. In addition to their cross-breeding experiments, these aliens supposedly had experimented with various types of bacteria and viruses, which gave rise to concern.

Though generally thinner and shorter and with somewhat larger heads and eyes, the hybridized men and women appeared human. Some, of both sexes, appeared well-formed, even good-looking. However—at that time anyway—they were unable to vocalize as we do, owing to underdeveloped tongues and larynxes. By way of food, they consumed nothing solid. Some of these hybrids lived in the aliens' bases on Earth, others elsewhere, including their own planet(s). Only a few lived among us. The aliens reckoned it would take around a hundred years for them to infiltrate our planet.

ALIEN BASES

In 2011, a fellow researcher revealed to me that, according to an apparently reliable source, there is "a large area somewhere in Mexico, quarantined by the American military, where three hundred thousand aliens reside. These aliens have also created hybrids that look like us. There is also a technology transfer between this quarantined group and the military." I pressed for further information. "As to this rumor," my friend replied, "it comes from a very special international military source I have promised not to reveal. I don't know if there is any truth to this claim, but I have so many clues to UFO bases in Mexico that I keep an open mind."

The researcher cites a letter from Fred Steckling to Major Hans C. Petersen (George Adamski's Danish representative) in October 1967, in which he reports that Fred and his wife Ingrid, while visiting the area where a base was said to be located not far from San José Perua, where Adamski visited several times, saw a craft disappear into a mountain. Also, contactee Richard Högland describes (in Chapter 11) how in 1967–68 the aliens with whom he was in regular contact moved their Bahamas base to an area outside Mexico City.

Like the Amicizia group, the aliens cited by my Washington source created huge bases in mountainous and undersea locations. To accommodate their smaller craft, mountain locations were favored, but their giant "command ships" were restricted to the undersea bases. Our military expressed concern that these craft contributed to the heating up of the oceans, but this was denied. Lieutenant Colonel Philip J. Corso, the intelligence officer who served on President Eisenhower's National Security Council Staff at the White House and headed the U.S. Army's Foreign Technology desk at the Pentagon, confirms that "USOs" were of considerable concern to military authorities.

"Unidentified Submerged Objects [were] a worry in naval circles, particularly as war planners advanced strategies for protracted submarine warfare in the event of a first strike. [USOs] could plunge right into the ocean . . . and surface halfway around the world without so much as leaving an underwater signature we could pick up. Were these USOs building bases at the bottom of the oceanic basins beyond the dive capacity of our best submarines?"[3]

MASS APPEARANCES

The Joint Chiefs and other insiders fear sightings witnessed by numerous observers. Although this has yet to occur simultaneously on a wide scale, large numbers of people in various parts of the world have sighted—and sometimes filmed—multiple craft. One such incident occurred in Italy—perhaps an early incursion related to the Amicizia group of aliens—on October 27, 1954. A crowd of around ten thousand had gathered to watch a reserve game between Fiorentina and nearby rivals Pistoiese at the Stadio Artemio Franchi.

"I remember clearly seeing this incredible sight," said Gigi Boni, a Fiorentina fan now in his eighties. "They were moving very fast and then they just stopped. It all lasted a couple of minutes. I would like to describe them as being like Cuban cigars. . . . I think they were extraterrestrial." The stadium fell silent as the players and fans stood transfixed, staring at these strange objects.

"I remember everything," said Ardico Magnini, a key player in the Fiorentina side. "Everything came to a stop because everybody was looking up at the sky intently [and] also there was some silver 'glitter' coming down from the sky. We were absolutely shocked from the moment we saw it."[4]

Another incident was reported in Chile, where the Amicizia group are said to have established a base during that period on an island in south Chile (Chapter 13).

On the afternoon of August 17, 1985, an estimated two million people watched two UFOs for four hours in Santiago, the capital of Chile. "The general area where the objects were observed included Santiago's metropolitan area with a population of over three million people, the central coastal region around the main port of Valparaiso, and various other resorts and locations in central Chile," reports Antonio Huneeus. "Across the Andes in Argentina, the UFOs were also observed in the evening hours in Umkai, Mendoza, and other sites near the border with Chile. There was a large number of highly reliable witnesses.

"These include astronomers at the University of Chile's Cerro Calan Observatory in Santiago, engineers at NASA's Satellite Tracking Station in Peldehue, pilots of commercial airliners, military personnel, etc. The UFOs were also filmed by cameramen from the national TV station, Channel 7, the Cerro Calan astronomers, and private individuals.

"An 'unidentified radar target' was detected as well by the radar screens at Santiago's International Airport of Pudahuel [and] published in the official magazine of Chile's General Administration of Civil Aeronautics."[5]

A SINISTER AGENDA

Returning to my Washington source, I learned that, shockingly, many children had gone missing, believed to have been abducted, particularly in the South Carolina area at that time. This was "confirmed" by the anonymous three-star general (cited in the previous chapter) to an American researcher in 1989. "There are over a million missing children every year in the United States alone," he alleged. "The aliens take about 2,200 children a year from the United States and other countries. . . . The rest of the missing children are the result of Mankind's 'dark side.' The children are used in several ways: biological, to educate and return, experimentation, and disease studies. The same as adults."[6]

ALASKA BASE

As briefly mentioned in an earlier chapter, an alien base was sited in Alaska—the nation's largest state. George Adamski, the first to claim that aliens had established bases on Earth, remarked in a private letter to Emma Martinelli that he had learned from a marine engineer in Alaska that spacecraft landed frequently in a certain area "around the Aleutians." "I have seen them, lots of them," the engineer told Adamski in person in early 1952 (prior to Adamski's first contact). "Not only the flying saucers but the cigar-shaped type too. I have a two-year-old daughter who has seen more of them and has even been inside more of them than most people will ever see. . . . They have been landing there. When they come in, we usually drive out to see the ships and visit the crews. My little girl is with me on most of these drives."

"He told me the following, as I asked different questions," Adamski continued. "All space craft are magnetically propelled [and] they vary in size all the way from thirty feet to five miles in length. No greater comfort or beauty could be found anywhere than is inside these ships. . . . They are coming from Mars, Venus, Saturn, and a system beyond ours known as System 359, the Wolf Star.

"The men average from three feet to six and a half feet in height [and] are very handsome. As he said, we are a crude form of humanity alongside of them. . . . The uniform of the tall men is a one-piece garment with an automatic button by which, when they press it, the whole garment opens up and can be dropped off easily and quickly, if desired. The little men wear two-piece uniforms fastened together with the same type fastener."[7]

Patrick Price, a gifted psychic employed by a CIA contractor in the 1970s, "remotely viewed" an alien base in Alaska, which he said lay under Mount Hayes. He described these alien occupants as "looking like *homo sapiens*, except for the lungs, heart, blood, and eyes."[8,9]

According to Preston Dennett, an established Californian researcher, a "friend of a friend," given the pseudonym Tom, had worked for the U.S. government with a top-secret clearance at a base in Alaska, located almost totally underground in an eight-story building. The base, Dennett learned, supposedly financed itself by setting up the world's leading drug smugglers. "Officials would arrest the drug smugglers, confiscate all the money and drugs, and then turn around and sell the drugs back to another smuggler—whom they would then proceed to arrest and confiscate [from]."

Tom claimed that some of the best scientific minds in the country were employed in advanced research, involving the latest technology. The major areas of research and development included biological weapons; electronic sensory and detection devices which allowed telescopic sight through solid objects, such as walls; and electromagnetic propulsion devices, "flying craft which needed no fuel other than the Earth's magnetic field on which to operate. According to Tom, the ships look like UFOs, and are able to hover silently and move at astonishing speeds."

Such was the level of security, it was claimed, that each week Tom was taken to a special room and injected with sodium pentothal, hypnotized, then "interrogated about every aspect of his life for the past week."[10]

Another apocryphal story, of course. But in view of the additional accompanying hearsay evidence, such stories should not be dismissed arbitrarily.

Robert F. Dorr, a former senior diplomat and leading aviation authority who served in the U.S. Air Force, claims that the 49th state was the center of a "UFO war" in the 1970s. He cites, for instance, a case in June 1975 involving a Lockheed T-33 two-seat trainer repeatedly buzzed by a circular craft estimated to be 150 feet in diameter. All attempts at avoiding the craft failed. Indeed, the pilots were convinced the craft was attempting to ram them. Fortunately, the craft suddenly "vanished." Furthermore, bizarre weather conditions were frequently encountered by pilots. "Radios and electronic instruments don't work the way they're supposed to," said an experienced air charter pilot. "Thunderstorms, tornadoes, and lightning appear when there's no meteorological reason to expect them. Even when the weatherman predicts CAVU [ceiling and visibility unlimited], you sometimes get storms. And you get these weird cloud formations where the whole sky suddenly turns a milky, amber color. It's terrifying."[11] Such deliberately induced manipulations of weather by aliens were verified for me by the Washington source—and by the distinguished Brazilian explorer and researcher Dr. Rubens J. Villela (see *Unearthly Disclosure*).

John B. Alexander is a retired U.S. Army colonel who served as a project manager at Los Alamos National Laboratory and worked with the National Research Council, the Council on Foreign Relations, and as a consultant to the National Intelligence Council, the CIA, the U.S. Special Operations Command, and the Army Science Board. In his book *UFOs* he concedes the reality thereof, per se, but dismisses an alien interpretation. In the late 1980s, an unnamed friend in the Inspector General's Office came across a stack of reports that had accumulated in a battalion command center in Alaska. "There were eighteen reports of events in January 1987 near St. Lawrence Island, which lies in the Bering Sea well west of the Alaska mainland," writes Alexander. "This rather large island is home to just more than a thousand people, mostly Yupik, who are among those who hunt for survival purposes." Of the reports described to Alexander, the following is interesting:

"At picture A is a replica of the drawing submitted. . . . The large domed object on the right side of the picture was described as far larger than a

Boeing 747 aircraft. It was followed by two smaller discs. All were very dark on the underside and were traveling toward the north trailing smoke. The observers then noticed that the large craft appeared to generate a cloud that engulfed it. The UFO, shrouded in the cloud, was then seen to fly against [the] direction from which the wind was blowing."[12]

Perhaps of relevance here is the well-known case involving the extraordinary radar-confirmed encounter with a giant craft reported by the crew of a Japan Airlines Boeing 747 on its approach to Anchorage Airport on November 17, 1986, to which I alluded briefly in Chapter 15.

PRESIDENTIAL INVOLVEMENT

A number of U.S. presidents have been exposed to the alien situation. According to Bruno Sammaciccia of the Amicizia W56 group, even George Washington was contacted. No details are provided, other than that in addition to "W56"—referring to the group's starting date in 1956—it was also meant as a form of homage to the nation's first president.[13] Chapter 4 describes several meetings with aliens said to have been arranged with President Eisenhower. And according to the comedian and musician Jackie Gleason, who had a great interest in the subject, one night in 1973 he was taken by his friend President Richard M. Nixon to a top-secret repository at Homestead Air Force Base, Florida, where bodies of aliens were stored. Beverly McKittrick, Gleason's wife, confirmed that her husband had returned from the trip visibly shaken by the experience.[14]

In Chapter 15, I cited evidence from Captain Bill Uhouse, a former U.S. Marine Corps fighter pilot who claims to have worked on a top-secret program relating to the avionics of simulators built for the reproduction of alien vehicles. In an interview with Glenn Campbell, using the pseudonym "Jarod-2," Uhouse stated that to protect what was found at the disc crash sites, "those in charge at the time scrambled for a position and a decision as to whom in the government would carry the responsibility:

"This included security, material, personnel, documents, and military and civilian intelligence. It was not decided until the Eisenhower administration in the early part of 1953. A group was formed by the president, and the chairman of the group was Vice President Richard Nixon. Around June of 1953, the final decision was made to set up a 'satellite government.'

This separate government would interface with the U.S. government for support only."

Personnel involved in any part of the disc retrievals were reassigned to this satellite government, new security requirements were established, and new clearances were assigned. "Think what you would do to maintain a level of secrecy of something inherently totally bizarre in nature," Uhouse explained. "Nixon did it right by establishing the satellite government. This provided cover for the visitors plus a totally new concept for protecting all information relating to this subject."[15]

President Ronald Reagan took a considerable interest in the subject of aliens, having had two sightings. One of these occurred in 1974 when he was the governor of California. "We were near Bakersfield when Governor Reagan and [his security personnel] called my attention to a big light flying a bit behind my plane," reported Reagan's pilot, Bill Paynter. "It was a fairly steady light until it began to accelerate, then it appeared to elongate. Then the light took off . . . from a normal cruise speed to a fantastic speed instantly."

Reagan himself described the incident to Norman Miller, then Washington bureau chief for *The Wall Street Journal*. According to Miller, Reagan ordered his pilot to follow the object. "All of a sudden, to our utter amazement it went straight up into the heavens," said Reagan. "When I got off the plane, I told Nancy all about it. And we read up on the long history of UFOs."[16]

On the evening of June 27, 1982, Reagan hosted Steven Spielberg in the White House at a special screening for thirty or so guests of the soon-to-be-released movie, *E.T.—The Extraterrestrial*. In an interview with "Quint" (Eric Vespe of Ain't It Cool News) in 2011, Spielberg finally addressed the question of what Reagan was rumored to have said about the subject matter following the showing.

"The story I heard," began Quint, "is that when Reagan saw it, he started talking about how close to reality it was, and he was quickly ushered out of the room. Is that true?"

"No, he wasn't," replied Spielberg. "He was the President of the United States. Nobody could usher Ronald Reagan out the room! It was in the White House screening room, and Reagan got up to thank me for bringing the film to show the president, the First Lady, and all of their guests, who included Sandra Day O'Connor in her first week as a Justice of the Supreme Court, and it included some astronauts. I think Neil Armstrong was there—I'm not a hundred percent certain. But it was an amazing, amazing evening.

"He just stood up and he looked around the room, almost like he was doing a head count, and he said, 'I wanted to thank you for bringing *E.T.* to the White House. We really enjoyed your movie.' And then he looked around the room and said, 'And there are a number of people in this room who know that everything on that screen is absolutely true.' And he said it without smiling. But everybody laughed—the whole room laughed because he presented it like a joke. But he wasn't smiling as he said it. . . ."[17]

Leading Canadian researcher Grant Cameron points out that, coincidentally, on the morning following the *E.T.* screening, a meeting took place in the Oval Office of the White House between President Reagan and James A. Baker III, Chief of Staff; Edwin Meese III, Counselor; and Michael K. Deaver, Deputy Chief of Staff. "From there," reports Grant, "the four men went to the highly secure White House Situation Room, where the president participated in a briefing of the U.S. Space Program. Participants included six members of the National Security Council or National Security Affairs and *no one from NASA*.

"The absence of anyone from NASA for a briefing of the U.S. Space Program is unheard of. The absence of any NASA people is even more unusual, in light of the fact that a couple of days later, President Reagan attended the landing of the U.S. Space Shuttle at Edwards Air Force Base."[18]

President Mikhail Gorbachev has confirmed officially that during the Geneva Summit in 1985 with Reagan, the question of collaboration on the alien problem was discussed. "The U.S. President said that, if the Earth faced an invasion by extraterrestrials," he stated at the Kremlin in 1987, "the United States and the Soviet Union would join forces to repel such an invasion. I shall not dispute the hypothesis, though I think it's early yet to worry about such an intrusion."[19] During an interview by Fabio Fazio with Gorbachev on Italian television in 2006, the former Russian president confirmed his discussion with Reagan:

". . . At that time it was a very difficult dialogue because we could not meet each other halfway. And I remember during a walk by the villa garden where we met, President Reagan stopped and said, 'But listen to me, President Gorbachev: If we were attacked from space, would we come together? Would we unite?' I answered him, 'I do not know what you think about it but I propose to come together, that we join forces. . . .'"[20]

Was an alien responsible for Reagan's presidency? According to *I Love Lucy* star Lucille Ball, Reagan confided in her that in the 1950s, while still an actor, he had a close encounter of the third kind. Ball told screen legend Shirley MacLaine about the encounter, which supposedly took place when Reagan and his wife Nancy were on their way to a party in Los Angeles. Apparently a UFO landed and the alien emerged, telling Reagan to quit acting and take up politics![21]

In *Need to Know*, I referenced a leak of information provided to Anthony L. Kimery, an award-winning editor and journalist specializing in global security, defense, and intelligence issues. In 1989, an Executive Branch employer revealed to Kimery that he had seen a top-secret National Security Council report prepared as a briefing paper for the new administration of President George H. W. Bush. The report referenced the operation of a deep underground government facility dealing specifically with the alien situation somewhere along the northern New Mexico border.[22] As mentioned in Chapter 15, I learned that the facility was located in the nuclear-weapons storage area within the Manzano Mountains, which are actually in central New Mexico.

In 2003 I wrote to former president George H. W. Bush (a former U.S. Navy pilot and Director of Central Intelligence), requesting a dialogue to discuss "these delicate matters." "Mr. Bush appreciated hearing from you," responded his assistant, "and while he appreciates the spirit of your request, he must respectfully decline [owing to] the many requests he receives for personal appointments. . . ."[23]

As for President George W. Bush (a former Air National Guard jet pilot who flew the F-102 Delta Dagger jet among others, on several occasions), a friend of mine who had known President Bush Jr. for many years queried him about the subject during a visit to the White House. "Ask Cheney," came the terse reply, referring to Vice-President Dick Cheney.

THE KENNEDY CONNECTION

In *Need to Know*, I revealed for the first time that in 1961/62, President John F. Kennedy requested to be shown the alien bodies associated with a certain crash site. A former White House Staff source told me that the request had been granted, and JFK, along with "top brass" headed by General Godfrey T. McHugh, was flown in Air Force One to Tyndall Air Force Base, Florida, where the bodies had been preserved at a medical facility. The visit remains highly classified.[24]

As a military aide, McHugh also accompanied JFK during the trip to Dallas on November 22, 1963, and was present at Bethesda Naval Hospital, Maryland, during Kennedy's autopsy, as Colonel Fletcher Prouty reports.[25]

In *George Adamski: The Untold Story* and in *Alien Base*, Lou Zinsstag described the sometimes difficult period she spent with Adamski as one of his co-workers: my section analyzed critically the numerous claims he made over the years. Some of these claims seem ludicrous. However, despite his reputation among many researchers as a charlatan, it is a fact that Adamski was consulted by a number of people at high levels of the U.S. government. According to Dr. Jacques Vallee, Adamski carried a passport bearing special privileges, and several of his associates assured me that he also possessed a U.S. Government Ordnance pass which gave him access to all U.S. military bases and to certain restricted areas—including the White House.

In 1963, President Kennedy met Adamski at the Willard Hotel in Washington, close to the White House, according to my late friend Madeleine Rodeffer, who looked after Adamski at her house in Silver Spring, Maryland, a Washington suburb, for several months prior to his death in 1965. (On February 26 that year, Adamski had taken color movie footage of a classic "scoutcraft" describing maneuvers outside the house, in the presence of Madeleine and some U.S. government personnel. The 8mm film was authenticated by William Sherwood, an optical physicist and former senior project engineer at Eastman-Kodak, Rochester, who also introduced Adamski to other Kodak specialists.)[26]

On May 5, 1963, after arriving in Denmark during his European tour, Adamski revealed to his Danish representative Major Hans C. Petersen, Senior Air Traffic Control Officer in the Royal Danish Air Force (1949–1976), that shortly before leaving for Europe he had had a secret meeting with Kennedy. Adamski also revealed to the press some details of his visit to a "U.S. government office" (without mentioning Kennedy). The following day, reports Ragnvald A. Carlsen, a Danish researcher who, together with Hans Petersen, helped arrange the Adamski visit, a large billboard for the *Fredericia Dagblad* displayed the following headline: *'ADAMSKI: Venus-mand advarede mig om Cuba-krisen"* ("Man from Venus warned me about Cuba crisis").

"Despite his seventy-two years he is still supple and gives the impression of being a well-balanced person," wrote the reporter. "One cannot demand that people believe in flying saucers," Adamski was quoted as saying. "They want proof; it's human nature. But those who have seen these objects have become convinced. . . . I expect even less that people should believe that I have been contacted many times by men from Venus, [but] a year ago I was contacted by [such] a man who said that, before long, there would be a crisis over Cuba, which could perhaps mean a Third World War. That was three months before the Cuba crisis started. At that time I happened to be in Washington, D.C., and I went along to a government office where I passed on the information."

During a visit to Washington in 1995, following a lecture he had given to a group of interested delegates at the United Nations in New York, Major Petersen made some interesting comments, including reference to a trip to another planet claimed by Adamski in early March 1962, specifically in relation to what eventually turned out to be the Cuban missile crisis in October that year. On his return, Adamski called Petersen, explaining that he had to go to Washington to deliver a message for the president. "I cannot tell you what this message is," said Adamski, "but if you follow the political situation on Earth, you will be able to see for yourself what the message contains." Had Kennedy not solved the Cuba crisis the way he did, Petersen pointed out, there would have been a Third World War.[27] As General Anatoly Gribkov, former Soviet Army chief of operations, admitted: "Nuclear catastrophe was hanging by a thread . . . and we weren't counting days or hours—but minutes."[28]

I learned from Lou Zinsstag that, on an unknown date, Adamski had been entrusted with a written invitation for President Kennedy to visit one of the aliens' huge motherships at a secret airbase in Desert Hot Springs,

California, for a few days. In order to keep this visit absolutely secret, Adamski was to take the invitation directly to the White House through a side door, where a man he knew was ready to let him in. Adamski later learned that Kennedy had spent several hours at the airbase, after having canceled an important trip to New York, and that he had had a long talk with the ship's crew, but that he had not been invited for a flight.[29]

Emily Crewe, the British researcher cited in Chapter 16, has related to me that on June 6, 1963, Adamski was invited for a meeting at Desmond Leslie's home in St. John's Wood, London. Those present included Earl Mountbatten of Burma, Supreme Allied Commander in Southeast Asia during World War II and appointed Chief of the Defence Staff in 1965; Lord Dowding, former Commander-in-Chief of RAF Fighter Command during the Battle of Britain in 1940; the Earl of Clancarty (Brinsley Le Poer Trench), and Emily. The group (minus Emily, not in the best of health at the time) was later invited by Mountbatten for discussions at Broadlands, his estate in Hampshire.

During the London meeting, Adamski revealed further details about the Kennedy contact. The alien craft had landed in the small hours on the tarmac at the end of one of the airbase runways. "When Kennedy arrived," Emily reports, "his car was stopped and he was advised to get out and walk to the ship that awaited him. He was to come alone. JFK obeyed the summons and he was seen entering the alien vessel and stayed for some time before he came out at last, later refusing to speak about the incident."[30]

According to Henry Dohan, previously referenced in Chapter 7, many years prior to becoming president, Kennedy met with Adamski on several occasions at the latter's home in Vista, California, where he was introduced to several of the aliens living among us. "Since the space people know the past, present, and future of every one of us," claimed Dohan, "they told Kennedy that he would become the president of the U.S. Kennedy thought it was ludicrous, since he was Catholic, and the space [people] told him, 'No, you go for it and you will get it.' Kennedy kept in touch with Adamski and had clandestine meetings with him, even when he was president.

"Kennedy had one weakness, and that was that he loved too many women. I believe he was intimate with Marilyn Monroe and confided in her about his extraterrestrial knowledge. Also, he was the first U.S.

president to invest one billion dollars of the U.S. budget in space research. He became a threat to our oil and industrial magnates, which led to his Mafia assassination and that of Marilyn Monroe."[31] If there's any truth in the Lucille Ball/Reagan story mentioned earlier, it seems Kennedy wasn't alone in being encouraged to push for the presidency.

Regarding Monroe, a putative CIA document dated August 3, 1962, is possibly revealing.[32] Classified Top Secret, it references the FBI wiretapping of a conversation between the noted reporter Dorothy Kilgallen and Monroe's friend Howard Rothberg, in which the latter reveals to the reporter that Monroe kept a "diary of secrets" relating to her trysts with President Kennedy and his brother, Attorney General Robert Kennedy.

The memo also cites Rothberg as saying that Marilyn had "secrets to tell," including "the visit by the president at a secret air base for the purpose of inspecting things from outer space. . . . In the mid-fifties, Kilgallen learned of secret efforts by the U.S. and U.K. governments to identify the origin of crashed spacecraft and dead bodies, from a British government official." (Almost certainly, the visit cited was the one JFK made to Tyndall Air Force Base, described earlier.) The CIA memorandum goes on to cite a number of threats made by Monroe, including holding a press conference in which she would "tell all."[33]

PRESIDENT CARTER

In 1969, President-to-be Jimmy Carter had a UFO sighting in Georgia, which he spoke about publicly on several occasions. Skeptics claimed he had merely spotted the planet Venus, a ridiculous explanation given Carter's background as a U.S. Navy submarine line officer—thus familiar with planets and stars. Harvey Jack McGeorge II, formerly in the Special Forces Reserve, Green Berets, at Fort Bragg, North Carolina, later worked in the U.S. Secret Service (Technical Security Division) at the White House as adviser on national and international terrorism. Having struck up a friendship with Carter, he is said to have been the first member of the Secret Service, outside of its chief, to have witnessed a presidential briefing on UFOs. The following report originates from an account which McGeorge gave to a friend in the 1980s, which was then passed on to Harry Lebelson of *OMNI* magazine.

"Upon Carter's insistence, and in spite of protestations from the National Security Agency," states a transcript of the report, "McGeorge was allowed to attend [a] briefing session. . . . There were two briefings given to Carter. McGeorge attended at least the initial briefing.

"Once the president was in the room, seated at a table, Jack McGeorge at another table, a member of the NSA gave an overall briefing on the phenomenon, stating its historical characteristics and bringing it up to the present time. At that point, a number of documents describing the evolutionary habits of the beings, the reasons they were here, and other matters of that consequence were shown. . . . The next thing to be shown to Jimmy Carter was a fifteen-minute [color] film taken at Holloman AFB in which UFO inhabitants and military personnel made physical contact. . . .

"After that there were more briefings by national security people—and basically that was the end of the briefing. McGeorge, being a very observant person, noticed that on re-entering Carter's office about half an hour after the briefing—and I know this is going to be hard to believe—but he stated that Carter had tears in his eyes. . . ."[34]

PRESIDENT KIRSAN ILYUMZHINOV

Kirsan Ilyumzhinov, former president (1993–2010) of the southwestern Russian region of Kalmykia (the only Buddhist region in Europe)—a multimillionaire businessman and current president of the World Chess Federation (FIDE)—made the newswires in 2006 when he claimed to have been taken on board an alien spacecraft while on a business trip in 1997. "It happened on the 17th of September," he told a British journalist. "I was taken from my apartment in Moscow and taken to this spaceship, and we went to some star. I asked, 'Please bring me back,' because the next day I had to be back in Kalmykia—in Elista—to go to the Ukraine. 'No problem,' they said, 'you have time.'"

"How much of that experience do you recall?" asked the journalist.

Ilyumzhinov's responses were somewhat brief. "They are people like us," he replied. "They have the same mind, the same vision, and so on. I talked with them. I understood that we are not alone—we are not unique. I am not a crazy man. But after that, when I gave the first interview to Radio Freedom in Russia five years ago, thousands of people wrote me letters or called by phone, saying, 'Kirsan, you are a politician and you are not afraid to talk about it.'" Which, at least, is more than can be said for any other president or national leader—apart, perhaps, from the current Russian Prime Minister and former President Dmitry Medvedev (see later).

In another interview, on a Russian talk show on April 26, 2010, Ilyumzhinov revealed that the experience had begun with the appearance of a "semi-transparent half tube" on the balcony of his apartment. He then entered it and met "human-like creatures in yellow spacesuits," the *Moscow Times* reported. "I am often asked which language I used to talk to them. Perhaps it was on a level of the exchange of the ideas," he explained to the program host. "They put a spacesuit on me, told me many things, and showed me around. They wanted to demonstrate that UFOs do exist."

"What has gotten his Russian political peers suddenly agitated after all this time," reports Glenda Kwek, "is whether he let slip any state secrets and whether there is a proper procedure for dealing with aliens. Andrei Lebedev, a State Duma deputy, was apparently moved by 'holy terror' at Mr. Ilyumzhinov's claims, and yesterday wrote to Russian President Dmitry Medvedev asking him to launch an investigation, the *Times* said. He was concerned about whether Mr. Ilyumzhinov's brush with the spacemen affected his ruling of Kalmykia and whether they might have tried to get him to divulge state secrets to them."[35]

PRESIDENT OBAMA

During a live interview with Chris Moyles on BBC Radio 1 in May 2012, actor Will Smith (of *Men in Black* fame) said that during a recent private tour of the White House with President Obama, Smith's thirteen-year-old son Jayden (himself a Hollywood star) asked Obama for his view on aliens.

"The aliens, right?" responded Obama. "Okay. I can neither confirm nor deny the existence of extraterrestrials, but I can tell you that if there had been a top-secret meeting and if there would have had to have been a discussion about it, it would have taken place in this room."[36]

The room referred to is the White House Situation Room, a five-thousand-square-foot conference room and intelligence management center in the basement of the West Wing of the White House, created in 1961 by President Kennedy. Run by the National Security Council staff for the use of the president and his advisers, the Situation Room serves to monitor and deal with crises at home and abroad and to conduct secure communications.[37]

Of more interest is an additional comment made by Will Smith on the radio show. "Listen, here's the deal," he claimed to Chris Moyles. "I *have* the top-secret information, I just can't share it. You don't think I've made all these movies and *not* been briefed by the White House?"[38]

In the seemingly unlikely event that a movie star can be briefed on the subject, it is axiomatic that President Obama would have been briefed to a far greater depth prior to, or following, his inauguration. Although indirectly related, according to investigative journalist and former National Security Agency employee Wayne Madsen, government files reveal CIA connections with President Obama's biological father, Barack Obama Sr., and the president's mother, Stanley Ann Dunham, who is said to have conducted espionage activities in 1960s post-coup Indonesia on behalf of a number of CIA front operations, including the East-West Center at the University of Hawaii, the U.S. Agency for International Development (USAID), and the Ford Foundation. Furthermore, Obama's stepfather, Lolo Soetoro, who met Dunham at the East-West Center, was "recalled to Indonesia in 1965 to serve as a senior Army officer and assist General Suharto and the CIA in the bloody overthrow of President Sukarno." Madsen further reveals that President Obama himself worked from 1983 to 1984 for Business International Corporation, "a CIA front that conducted seminars with the world's most powerful leaders and used journalists as agents abroad. . . ."[39]

According to a poll of 1,114 adults conducted across the United States by the National Geographic Channel in May 2012, sixty-five percent of Americans believe President Obama would be more adept than his Republican rival Mitt Romney at dealing with an alien invasion, with women and younger Americans more likely than men and over-65s to agree with that prospect. Eleven percent of respondents were confident they had seen a UFO.[40] National Geographic also claims that eighty million Americans— that's over one quarter—believe in UFOs.

PRIME MINISTER MEDVEDEV

On December 7, 2012, Russian Prime Minister (former President) Dmitry Medvedev gave a television interview to five reporters, following which he continued responding to the reporters, making some off-air comments—supposedly without being aware that his microphone was still on. At one point he was asked if "the president is handed secret files on aliens when he receives the briefcase needed to activate Russia's nuclear arsenal?"

Medvedev responded: "Along with the briefcase with nuclear codes, the president of the country is given a special 'top secret' folder. This folder in its entirety contains information about aliens who visited our planet. . . . Along with this, you are given a report of the absolutely secret special service that exercises control over aliens on the territory of our country. . . . More detailed information on this topic, you can get from a well-known movie called *Men in Black.* . . . I will not tell you how many of them are among us because it may cause panic."

None of the television stations that interviewed Mr. Medvedev broadcast the off-air comments, but they were delivered to Reuters as "a pool signal" and some were shown on YouTube. Was it all a joke? The London *Telegraph* claimed that, in response to the question, Medvedev had "answered playfully."[41] In fact, his demeanour remained serious.

Russian television channels were passing the blame after the unofficial footage was leaked, according to the *Moscow Times*.[42] Readers can be forgiven for assuming that the prime minister was referring to the latest American *Men in Black* science-fiction film. A more accurate translation of what Medvedev actually said (to journalist Marianna Maksimovskaya, I learned from Nikolay Lebedev, a leading researcher) is: "You can receive more detailed information having watched the documentary film of the same name." Among other aspects, this excellent Russian documentary, *The Secret about Men in Black,* examines testimony that extraterrestrial bases have been established on Earth, and that some are in restricted U.S. military areas with the full knowledge of the Pentagon.

THE ROCKEFELLER INITIATIVE

It is not widely known that Laurance S. Rockefeller, the billionaire philanthropist (1910–2004), took a serious interest in aviation and, in later life, the UFO/alien subject, funding a number of projects relating thereto. As Antonio Huneeus, the preeminent researcher, explains: "This has come to be known as the Rockefeller Initiative, since in some cases they went beyond funding and included an actual lobbying effort to the Clinton White House, undertaken by Rockefeller himself and his lawyer Henry Diamond, in the mid-1990s."

Antonio and I were among those involved in one of these projects, resulting in *Unidentified Flying Objects Briefing Document: The Best Available Evidence*, a report authored by the distinguished American aviation journalist Don Berliner, a long-time student of the subject, and Antonio Huneeus.[43] The project was co-ordinated by Marie Galbraith, wife of investment banker Evan Galbraith, who served as U.S. Ambassador to France during the Reagan administration. I never met Rockefeller, but I liaised with Madame Galbraith in London on the project. One thousand copies of the original edition were printed and distributed to selected VIPs in the U.S. and abroad, including President Clinton.

"Unfortunately," Antonio points out, "the success and impact of the UFO Briefing Document was limited in real political terms. Most people and the press seemed far more interested in the fact that Rockefeller had sponsored it and was interested in UFOs than with the contents of the report and its political, military, and scientific implications. One significant exception was France. Because of Marie Galbraith's extensive social and political connections from the time she had lived in Paris as the American ambassador's wife, many copies were distributed there, including President Jacques Chirac and CNES [National Center for Space Studies]. The Briefing Document eventually became the model for a similar report prepared by a number of former high-ranking French military and intelligence officers and scientists, who formed a study group called COMETA (Committee for In-Depth Studies) that led to the release of their own report, *UFOs and Defense: What Should We Prepare For?*"

COMETA stressed its concern with the continuing high level of secrecy surrounding the subject. "For the editors of the book," explained the authors, "this secrecy is essentially military in origin: the nation that is first to produce the exceptional characteristics of UFOs will dominate the world. The secrecy was justified during the Cold War, but it is no longer justified now, given the scientific and technical breakthroughs useful to humanity that one can expect [to obtain] from the study of

UFOs."[44] The knowledgeable French authors, however, sidestepped mentioning their own government's highly classified investigations into the subject.

In February 1996, Laurance Rockefeller sent a copy of the Briefing Document to Dr. John H. Gibbons, Assistant to the President for Science and Technology. In his covering letter (see p. 408), released under the Freedom of Information Act—together with many other documents relating to the Rockefeller UFO Initiative—Rockefeller wrote:

". . . The public interest in UFOs and extraterrestrial intelligence obviously remains very high as evidenced by the recent cover story in *Time* magazine [and] the many television programs including one this week. . . . I sponsored this report because it seemed useful to bring together the most credible evidence about UFO sightings. . . . While I do not necessarily agree with every finding and conclusion, I do believe that the evidence presented indicates that this subject merits serious scientific study. Toward that end, I hope that our government, other governments, and the United Nations will cooperate in making any information they may have available. . . ."[45]

Rockefeller's comment about the subject meriting serious scientific study seems to indicate his unawareness of the fact that numerous scientists worldwide have been studying and dealing with the subject since the 1940s. In the U.S., very high security clearances are required for those involved in the Special Access Programs (SAPs) relating to the matter. As science journalist Terry Hansen points out in his masterly book, *The Missing Times: News Media Complicity in the UFO Cover-up*, "the findings of private science are not available to those who don't have the necessary security clearances [and] the Pentagon has an incentive to ensure that the knowledge acquired by private science is not independently discovered by public science."[46] In China, numerous scientists are likewise involved. However, academic freedom is claimed to prevail. In 1985, for instance, at a scientific conference on UFOs held in Darlian, some forty papers were presented.[47] And by 1992, the China UFO Research Association, affiliated with the China Association for Science and Technology, had 4,600 full members as well as 40,000 research associates, mostly scientists and engineers.[48]

RELIGIOUS RAMIFICATIONS

In *A.D. After Disclosure*, Richard Dolan and Bryce Zabel explore the possible ramifications arising from hypothesized official disclosure of the alien situation. They cover a lot of ground—including the religious aspects. In this respect, the Vatican seems more open-minded than most, some of its astronomers publicly expressing their opinion that life is widespread throughout the cosmos. Citing Paola Harris,[49] Dolan and Zabel report for example that the late Monsignor Corrado Balducci, a long-time friend of Pope John Paul II, stated his conviction in the reality of alien life on many occasions, and more than once attested to his belief that contact between humans and extraterrestrials was real.[50]

Dolan and Zabel also cite a 1994 survey by Victoria Alexander of clergy from Protestant, Catholic, and Jewish congregations. One of the questions asked was if any hypothetical official confirmation of the discovery of an advanced, technologically superior extraterrestrial civilization would have severe negative effects on the country's moral, social, and religious foundations. "In sharp contrast to the 'conventional wisdom' that religion would collapse," Victoria writes in her book *Extraterrestrial Life and Religion*, "ministers surveyed do not feel their faith and the faith of their congregation would be threatened." A 2002 Roper Poll asked a similar question, and received a similar response. "Not only was the answer overwhelmingly 'no,' it actually rose with age," Dolan and Zabel report.[51]

But what if these respondents had been made aware of the negative aspects of the alien scenario such as abductions, as opposed to a naïve set of beliefs based perhaps on films such as *E.T.—The Extraterrestrial*? Reaction to any official disclosure will surely be predicated on what we are told—which is unlikely to reflect the truth.

Earlier I cited the briefing of President Carter on the alien problem, attended by Harvey Jack McGeorge II, among others. "According to McGeorge," a friend of his reveals, "the two main reasons the government is withholding the truth about UFOs are the religious question, and the fact that we do not have control of the situation. 'They' are in charge. According to McGeorge, if the Bible said that God created the Heaven and Earth, then what the hell do the aliens believe in? The thing that the aliens fear the most is that Man would find out that we are not the creation of an omnipotent supreme being, but possibly the creation of these aliens them-selves—that we are a genetic experiment. And they also fear greatly that religion, as a controlling factor on behavior in the world—if the truth was known—that that controlling factor would immediately be destroyed and there might be anarchy. The second reason—that we are not in control—I think is pretty obvious."[52]

But times are changing. In 2008, for example, Pope Benedict XVI let it be known that there is no conflict between believing in God and in the possibility of "extraterrestrial brothers" perhaps more evolved than humans. Journalist Nick Pisa reported that the papal ruling came from Father José Funes, a Jesuit then in charge of the Vatican's Observatory and an expert on galaxies. In an interview with the Vatican's official newspaper, Funes stated (in part) as follows:

"Astronomers believe that the universe is formed of hundreds of millions of galaxies and in these are hundreds of millions of stars. Many of these or all of them could contain planets. So how can we exclude that developed life cannot be elsewhere? It's possible to believe in God and extra-terrestrials without bringing into question our own faith. . . ."[53]

PAPAL CONNECTIONS

On May 31, 1963, George Adamski had a private audience at the Vatican with the ailing Pope John XXIII, to deliver an important package he said had been given him by one of his alien contacts (probably Orthon). Prior to entering the Vatican, he was accompanied by Lou Zinsstag and May Morlet, his Swiss and Belgian representatives respectively. "I expected him to be admitted through the well-known gate where the Swiss Guards were posted," Lou reported. "Yet, without any hesitation, he walked to the left of the Dome where I now noticed a high wooden entrance gate behind the open doorway, with a small built-in door. The door was partly opened and a man was standing inside it, gesturing discreetly to George. On his chest I noticed some kind of material in white, green, and red. . . . May and I returned an hour later.

"There was George already, grinning like a monkey [with] his eyes shining like black topazes. 'We have done it,' he said. 'I was received by the

Pope. He gave me his blessing and I gave him the message.' When later in the day we lunched with George, he told us that the Pope was not lying in the room above St. Peter's Square, as the people had been told, but that his bedroom faced the most beautiful part of the Vatican garden. And he added confidentially, 'If you ask me, the Pope is hardly a dying man. . . . They haven't yet tried to operate on him, but I'm sure that's what they will do soon.' George added that the Pope even had rosy cheeks, and had said that he did not feel so bad.

"George had been helped on with a kind of cassock over his suit before he entered the bedroom. The Pope gave him a nice smile and said: 'I have been expecting you.' When George handed him the sealed package from Copenhagen, he said—also in English: 'My son, this is what I have been waiting for.' He then spoke to his visitor in a very low and soft voice for a few minutes. Adamski had to bend his head down close to the Pope's, whose last words were: 'My son, don't worry, we will make it.' After receiving the Papal blessing, Adamski was ushered out."

Although only in the preliminary stages of cancer, the Pope died two days later.

There is ample evidence that this meeting did take place, such as the gold medallion given to Adamski during the audience, with the Pope's head in profile thereon, dated May 31, 1963. Following the meeting, Adamski showed the medallion to Lou and May, and it was ascertained from banks in Rome that the ecumenical coin had not been available officially until two weeks later. Also of relevance was the small plastic wallet in which the coin was wrapped. "It bore the most singular inscription I have ever seen, protected by a transparent cover," said Lou. "The written characters were of a very unusual kind; certainly neither Roman nor Gothic, nor were they Russian, Chinese, Japanese, Arabic, or Hebrew."[54]

According to Major Petersen, Adamski had had another audience with Pope John XXIII. In confidential talks with Petersen during his trip to Europe in 1959, Adamski revealed that he had to attend an important meeting at the Vatican. "Are you to meet with the Pope?" asked Petersen.

"I don't know, but it is possible," Adamski responded. "Orthon will also be there. He has been there three times before, twice during Pope Pius's time [1939–1958] and once during Pope John's."[55]

WAS CHRIST OF ALIEN ORIGIN?

It will be recalled that in Chapter 7, Henry Dohan implies that Orthon was the reincarnated Christ. My views about religions, per se, are ambivalent. While I am sure that profound truths have been passed down in the world's scriptures, should we not, objectively, acknowledge the numerous contradictions, inconsistencies, and sometimes altered translations over the centuries? Exactly how much is factual? For example, in a letter to a British newspaper, a reader aptly points out that: "We don't have His sermons in the original Aramaic, so must rely on varying, often conflicting, translations via the Koine Greek gospels. Indeed, the use of parables by Jesus was a deliberate unclarity that puzzled the disciples (Matthew 13:10–14). Alas, much schismatic blood has been spilled ever since, arguing over the precise meaning of His far from 'clear and simple' message. How does Peter [another reader] parse: 'Think not that I am come to send peace on Earth; I came not to send peace, but a sword' (Matthew 10:34)?"[56]

Nonetheless, if some of the Biblical references to Jesus are more than apocryphal, such as the following, they support his out-of-this world provenance:

The visit to Mary by Gabriel, the "angel" (derived from *aggelos*, Greek for messenger, transliterated as *angelos*), foretelling the "immaculate conception";[57] An angel announcing the birth of the Christ, followed by the "heavenly host" of angels which afterwards departed "into heaven" (i.e., the sky);[58] The "star" reported by the wise men "which they had seen at its rising" and "went ahead of them until it stopped above the place where the child lay";[59] Jesus's comment to a group of Jews: "You belong to this world below, I to the world above. Your home is in this world, mine is not";[60] The so-called "resurrection" witnessed by the apostles when "as they watched, he was lifted up, and a cloud removed him from their sight [and] as they were gazing intently into the sky, all at once there stood beside them two men in white who said . . . 'This Jesus, who has been taken away from you up to heaven, will come in the same way as you have seen him go'";[61] Paul's experience on the road to Damascus "when suddenly about midday a great light flashed from the sky all around me, and I fell to the ground" and Jesus spoke to him.

Though unable to hear Jesus's voice, Paul's terrified fellow travelers also saw the brilliant light, which left Paul temporarily blinded.[62] Other possible alien factors to be taken into consideration in this context are Jesus's evidently telepathic ability, in addition to his healing and mastery of teleportation.

In one of his two books on Christ, theologian Holger Kersten adduces compelling evidence that Jesus lived in India following his "resuscitation" (as the original Aramaic word implies), dying there in old age and buried in Srinagar, the capital of Jammu and Kashmir. His tomb still exists in Kashmir, and he is said to be revered there to this day.[63] For die-hard Christians who dismiss the possibility, they should ponder on the fact that the New Testament has only one sentence (in Luke) about Jesus's years from the age of thirteen to thirty.

Suppose Jesus had later reincarnated and returned again to Earth "in the same way as you have seen him go": I doubt that such a revelation would be welcomed, or even believed, by the Christian hierarchy. However, assuming any truth to Henry Dohan's implication, I am minded to wonder about the claimed connection between Orthon and the two Popes cited earlier.

OPEN CONTACT?

John L. Petersen served as a flight officer in the U.S. Navy and Navy Reserve and is a decorated veteran of both the Vietnam and Persian Gulf wars. His government and political experience includes stints at the National War College, the Institute for National Security Studies, the Office of the Secretary of Defense, and the National Security Council staff at the White House. Currently he heads the Arlington Institute, a think tank based in Arlington, Virginia. We have met on a number of occasions over the years in Washington. In *The Road to 2015: Profiles of the Future*, one of three of his books he has given me, he invokes a possible scenario when open contact is made with extraterrestrials:

"For many in the majority segment of people in industrial societies who believe that UFOs are real, this event, though disquieting, was seen as opening up the window to a whole new world and reality full of immense questions—but not all necessarily negative. There was wonder and questioning in the context of a desire to solidify relationships and learn more from these strange 'people.'

"At the same time, pockets of people (and some governments) reacted as though acutely threatened. The assumption was that these beings were coming to take over, or unduly influence, the world and that the appropriate response was to quickly build up corporate and individual defenses. . . .

"All societies with access to television are transfixed by this event. Never-before-seen levels of global excitement and anxiety are experienced. The implications of this event cause an ultimate change in most every aspect of life on Earth.

"One of the hardest-hit groups are conservative religious organizations, for whom this event does not fit into their relatively narrow explanation of reality. This, perhaps the biggest event in history, causes religious leaders to scramble to explain (and in some cases, modify) theology to fit this new situation.

"Although some groups see the benefit of the new visitors in terms of new technology that can be made into weapons, many others see it as a hope for solving some of the very serious, intractable problems the world is confronted with at that time. Energy production is of particular interest."[64]

All of which may be true. But is open contact a viable scenario? We have learned that many types of aliens populate the cosmos—including Earth. A number of these races, such as those involved in the hybridization programs, definitely do not have our best interests at heart. And those who are "on our side" in such matters evince an understandable reluctance to engage with us *en masse*. We remain a relatively primitive bunch. As Daniel Fry, a pioneer rocket technician whose first encounter took place in 1949, was informed by his alien contact:

"If we were to appear as members of a superior race, coming from above to lead the people of your world, we would seriously disrupt the ego balance of your civilization. Tens of millions of your people, in their desperate need to avoid being demoted to second place in the universe, would go to any conceivable length to disprove or deny our existence.

"If we took steps to force the realization of our reality upon their consciousness, then about thirty percent of these people would insist upon considering us as gods, and would attempt to place upon us all responsibility for their own welfare. Of the remaining seventy percent, most would consider that we were potential tyrants who were planning to enslave their world, and many would immediately begin to seek means to destroy us.

"If any great and lasting good is to come from our efforts, the actual leaders must be your own people, or it must come from men who are indistinguishable from them."[65]

NON-DISCLOSURE

In November 2011, two petitions with over seventeen thousand signatories were sent to the White House, one demanding immediate disclosure of "the government's knowledge of and communications with extraterrestrial beings." Earlier that month, two petitions with similar aims were able together to garner the required number of signatures to gain a response.

"The U.S. government has no evidence that any life exists outside our planet, or that an extraterrestrial presence has contacted or engaged any member of the human race," responded Phil Larson from the White House Office of Science & Technology Policy. "In addition, there is no credible information to suggest that any evidence is being hidden from the public's eye." While conceding the possibility of aliens and a variety of NASA projects aimed at searching for them, Larson stressed there was "no credible evidence of extraterrestrial presence here on Earth."

"Although it's an official White House statement, the nothing-to-see-here response is not likely to satisfy public interest," reports journalist Conan Milner. "Despite similar statements, one petition cited opinion polls indicating that more than fifty percent of Americans believe there is an extraterrestrial presence, and more than eighty percent believe the government is not telling the truth about this phenomenon."[66]

Nikola Duper's unnamed participant in the Amicizia saga makes some apposite comments regarding disclosure. "The Friends never predicted anything about 'disclosure day.' I never heard them speak about 2012, [which] so many people mention." He added:

"At the end of the 1940s, the Friends offered their collaboration to the head of the U.S. administration. In exchange, they asked that the nuclear weaponry program be given up. But their offer and request were rejected, and other extraterrestrial populations have been collaborating with the USA and other Powers. The results of this have been highly negative. . . . One of the reasons—there are others—which delay disclosure is the fact that the USA administration should assume responsibility before the whole planet for having refused a vital collaboration and for having activated another highly negative one, exclusively for the sake of power and domination, lying to citizens and covering up for decades.

"Following the American politico-military refusal, the Friends undertook the strategy consisting of confidential contacts with small groups of terrestrials, trying to emphasize the quality of human personal relationships. . . ."[67]

THE ROYAL SOCIETY AND ET

In 2011, the *Philosophical Transactions of the Royal Society*—the world's oldest scientific journal—devoted its edition of January 10 to speculation on alien life in the cosmos. American psychology professor Dr. Albert Harrison, for example, suggested that the discovery of extraterrestrial intelligence "may be far less startling for generations that have been brought up with word processors, electronic calculators, avatars, and cell phones, as compared with earlier generations used to typewriters, slide rules, pay phones, and rag dolls." Surveys suggested, he added, that half the population of America and Europe believes aliens exist, and that a "substantial proportion" was convinced alien spacecraft had already visited Earth.

Dr. Harrison also claimed that the discovery of alien life—should it happen any time soon—would be more likely to inspire delight than incite pandemonium here on Earth, he told SPACE.com. He added that, even if an alien civilization had become greedy and imperialistic, there's no guarantee it would be able to run roughshod over its neighbors.

"It's possible to have very acquisitive civilizations out there," Harrison conceded. "Maybe they get to a certain point, but they may collapse or be beaten back." He added a comment with which I concur: "No one civilization is necessarily going to take over, because there will be coalitions of other civilizations that will keep them in check."[68] At least, we hope so.

As for Dr. Harrison's claim that the discovery of aliens would be unlikely to incite pandemonium, in the spring of 2010 a headline on the front page of *Al-Ghad*, a local newspaper in Jordan, stated that flying saucers flown by creatures ten feet tall had landed in the desert town of Jafr. Amid panic, the mayor, Mohammed Mleihan, put the security authorities on full alert. They searched the area, but found nothing. "I almost considered evacuating the town's thirteen thousand residents," said Mleihan. "Students didn't go to school. People were scared the aliens would attack them."

It turned out to have been an April Fool's Day hoax.[69] Panic, however, has featured relatively rarely in actual public landings. Those reported in the U.K. and Australia in 1955 and 1966, respectively, for example (Chapter 5), engendered astonishment and wonder—but little panic. Predicated on cultural differences, perhaps?

"When that truth of alien intervention in our planet's affairs and our ongoing contact with an alien culture is finally revealed," states Col. Philip Corso, "it won't be frightening, even though it will be a shock."[70]

THE PROBLEM

Gary S. Bekkum describes himself as an independent "occasional rogue journalist," whose international network of contacts includes past and present intelligence officials interested, for example, in the application of exotic phenomena ranging from antigravity to mind-to-mind communication. Bekkum shares my conviction that, if the alien presence is real, the odds are against government disclosure—or at least, full disclosure. As he claimed in 2009:

"Among members of the Intelligence Community, the tale of the alien presence is known as the 'core story' of contact between the aliens and the government. The strong rumor is there is a 'disturbing' aspect to this 'core story,' something so dire that it leaves battle-hardened military types shaking in their boots. . . . According to one of the intelligence officials who pursue the UFO topic (and many are at the highest levels of the government), the 'core story' may fall outside of the president of the United States' 'need to know.' . . .

"Dr. Edgar Mitchell, the Apollo astronaut who was the sixth man to walk on the Moon [Apollo 14], remains an outspoken supporter of the 'core story' explanation for government secrecy. Mitchell spoke of his contact with a ranking admiral with the Joint Chiefs who agreed to investigate the 'core story' of alien contact and report back. Some reporters were miffed when Mitchell refused to disclose the name of the admiral, but Mitchell did provide to me confirmation that another report was 'essentially correct.'

"Mitchell requested my help in clarifying why his testimony appeared to be contradicted by the admiral, who had been identified by the *Herald Tribune* as Rear Admiral Thomas R. Wilson. Quoting an article taken from the prestigious *Jane's Defence Weekly*, Mitchell implied that the admiral had discovered that the 'core story' was protected by a Special Access Program [SAP]."[71]

An SAP is "a program imposing 'need-to-know' or access controls beyond those normally provided for access to Confidential, Secret, or Top Secret information."[72] Jane's further defines an SAP as one which must remain unacknowledged when it is "considered so sensitive that the fact of its existence is a 'core secret.' . . ." Bekkum speculates on the disturbing possibility of "the existence of government doomsday survival plans in the event of massive extraterrestrial manipulation of the world's population."[73]

Anthony L. Kimery, a respected American journalist who has covered global security, intelligence, and defense issues, revealed in 1989 that, according to an Army source who worked with the Joint Chiefs of Staff (JCS) at the Pentagon's National Military Command Center (NMCC) in the 1970s, a highly secret, centralized command structure dealing with UFOs has been in operation since the mid to late 1970s, and (in 1989) continued to handle the UFO problem from the ranks of the NMCC. Kimery believes that "military and political leaders have . . . considered the UFO reality serious enough to warrant a consolidated oversight mechanism and planning force, on a par with management for global conflict. . . ."[74]

That NMCC is (or was) the "nerve center" dealing with the UFO problem has been confirmed for me by another knowledgeable source.

ANCIENT RACES

It seems to me that at least some groups of aliens have always been here. In Chapter 13, I allude to reports of possible extraterrestrials described in the *Rigveda*, an ancient Indian sacred collection of Vedic Sanskrit hymns. One of the oldest known texts in any Indo-European language, evidence indicates that it was composed between approximately 1700 and 1100 B.C.

In the early 1900s, Professor Edgar L. Larkin, Director of Mt. Lowe Observatory in Southern California, observed on several occasions through a powerful telescope some odd structures in the environs of Mt. Shasta. These included two domes rising above the treetops near Shasta and part of a third one. "Moving the telescope once again," writes Wishar S. Cervé, "he found visible between the trees a corner of another structure seemingly made of marble. Knowing that there were no such structures in Northern California, and especially in land around Shasta, he left his telescope fixed to see what these things would look like in the setting sun and in darkness. He was surprised to find later in the night that around this dome were great lights, apparently white, which partially illuminated and made them visible even though there was no moon to cast any light at the time."

Others reported encounters with extraordinary beings, said to be descendants from the fabled continent of Lemuria, residing in Mt. Shasta. In the early 1900s, for example, strange tall humans were seen emerging from forests in the vicinity and visiting local stores in Weed to trade gold nuggets in exchange for basic commodities. Described as graceful and agile, with distinctive features such as large foreheads and long curly hair and dressed in unusual clothes, they were said to have spoken English "in a perfect manner with perhaps a tinge of the British accent, and have been reluctant to answer any questions or give any information about themselves." Any intruders approaching them in the vicinity of their hidden residence would invariably be physically removed, or they might encounter some invisible influence, causing temporary paralysis. Also of particular relevance here, cars approaching the area stalled mysteriously and sightings were often made of unusual "flying boats," one of which was described by a group of witnesses as "a peculiar, silver-like vessel [which] was unlike any airship that has ever been seen and there was absolutely no noise emanating from it."

Wishar Cervé also reports knowledge of records pertaining to another group of descendants from Lemuria, found living in the center of an extinct volcano in Mexico, "hidden from all possible worldly observation."[75,76]

In an interview for *Fate* magazine in 2007, a witness, Jason, revealed that on a certain date he had encountered an extraordinary man on the lower slopes of Mt. Shasta. "I knew instantly what he was," he told the reporter. "I've lived around here all my life and I've heard the stories." The stranger had "flowing white hair and piercing blue eyes. He was wearing white robes and no shoes. I was scared. . . . It wasn't that he was doing anything threatening, but his appearance there on the side of the mountain was just so unexpected.

"I jumped up from where I had been lying on the ground, and when I did he looked surprised. It wasn't until I was standing that I realized how tall he was. He had to have been at least eight feet . . . he wasn't acting aggressively, but I was unreasonably scared, for some reason. . . . Then he told me not to be afraid. But it was too late for that. I guess he must have realized I was about to lose it, because just like that, he faded and disappeared."[77]

In the early 1960s Lucius (Lou) Farish, a first-class researcher—who sadly died in January 2012, and until several years ago organized the annual Ozarks UFO Conference held in Eureka Springs, Arkansas—learned an apocryphal but relevant story from an author who claimed to have met a truly remarkable person in the 1930s.

"He was about eighty then, an old sailing boat skipper who had participated in the great grain races around the Horn, who called himself only 'Harmonious,'" wrote the author. "We used to sit around on the beach and listen while he told us, quietly and without affectation, of his meetings with his 'astral' friends high atop Mt. Shasta (many years later, the first UFOs were sighted near that spot) and of his many trips throughout this system and others.

"He was bearded, never seemed to change from one year to the next; a vegetarian, and a gentle soul. His description used for the vehicle of flight very closely resembled certain other descriptions now in common usage—all this long before the huge UFO scare. Harmonious was last seen in the late 1950s—and looking exactly as he had thirty years before. . . . He never attempted to capitalize on his experiences."

Intrigued, Lou wrote back asking for more details. "When he talked of beings on other planets, he was often facetious," the author continued in his reply. "However, he was deeply serious whenever he spoke of the 'Old Ones.'

"Insofar as the Old Ones were concerned, his particular friend used a vehicle that, apparently, was a low-slung gondola, without wheels or any visible means of support or propulsion, for that matter. He'd often pick up a clam-shell or half-shell, that is, and say the vehicle looked almost like that. A low couch, nothing else. No top, or sides, or windshields. When it moved, the atmosphere surrounding the vehicle darkened and became opaque—nothing was visible. Also, no feeling of motion, or gravity. Apparently, his friend (an Old One) utilized applied levitation as a propulsive force. This vehicle was used only to pick him up and take him to the domain of the Old Ones. This was far beneath the earth. Usually he entered via a cavern on Mt. Shasta. There are other entrances: Antarctica, the Andes—in fact, look at the so-called 'circle of fire' on a good geological map and the great faulted areas surrounding the Pacific, and you'll approximate the many areas he mentioned as portals to the old people's world.

"These Old Ones dated back several hundred million years (and yet, taking planet Earth as a criterion, there's been more than enough time for fifty such races to have arisen, achieved godlike eminence, decayed, and fallen into silence). Often, in his joking manner, Harmonious spoke of the many planets that are around our sun and are still undiscovered. He was quite casual about the surface features of the planets, probably because he never spent much time there—he was always in them, not on them. I get the impression that there may be others, not of the Old People, utilizing these planets; apparently, these others are of little interest to Harmonious (and, by extension, to his friends the Old Ones; they are even something of a joke to him—and again, to the Old Ones).

"All the Old Ones are of one race, both here and on the other planets. They carry on intercourse with one another here on Earth, the planets, and their various natural satellites (all of which are inhabited underground). They have a great many artificial satellites around the gravitational nodes of all these bodies, which are used, I assume, solely for docking facilities for their interplanetary craft. (All this was told us by Harmonious long before World War II—and certainly long before the first UFO outcry following the Mt. Rainier sightings.) The Old Ones were naked or wore simple loincloths. (We found this amusing.)

"To extrapolate from Harmonious's stories of the old people: deep within the core of any planet, the temperature would be controllable given an inexhaustible source of power (and knowledge), and such power is inherent in the very force that created this planet. Incidentally, Harmonious anticipated Velikovsky by some years, when he told us of a disaster of unparalleled magnitude that struck the Earth several hundred millions of years ago, and which he saw reproduced by a recording device similar to a moving picture projector, but unlike it in action: a planetoid approached Earth and caused the complete destruction of the existing atmosphere. . . . The only life to survive was that in the depths of the seas and deep underground.

"If this sort of accident occurs in nature as a matter of course, one could well understand why an ancient and immensely intelligent race would choose to modify their environment and live far underground on all the planets, manufacturing all their necessities. . . . So, according to Harmonious, all the planets are inhabited by a long-lived scientifically advanced race, all living deep beneath the surface (at least well down in the crust—here it would be about thirty-five miles down), all humanoid in appearance, and undoubtedly masters of the solar system. There may be others living on the surfaces; undoubtedly, a younger, inferior race (perhaps remnants of other earlier surface races), but far younger than the Old Ones. On this planet, we are the surface dwellers; we have a long way to go yet—and when we get there, the Old Ones will have been there first, and long since moved on.

"Considering the foregoing information," concludes Lou Farish, "perhaps we should reconsider all the various writings on underground civilizations inhabited by advanced cultures (or extraterrestrials), as well as books such as the late M. K. Jessup's *The Case for the UFO*.[78] Jessup's comments on the use of 'gravitational nodes' by alien spacecraft echo the remarks of Harmonious. If it is accepted that there is someone 'out there' who is visiting the Earth, should we then consider that there may also be someone 'down there'?"[79]

I have always been fascinated by the Comte de St. Germain (his most frequently used pseudonym—another of which was the "Count de Well-done"!). Described by Voltaire in his *Oevres* as "a man who never dies, and who knows everything" and capable of astonishing feats, as witnessed for example by Count Alessandro Cagliostro (the occultist Giuseppe Balsamo), St. Germain seems to have lived for an indeterminate period. Held by many to be a charlatan, he nonetheless liaised with, and was respected by, many government ministers and royal families in Europe, such as the court of Louis XIV. He was also an accomplished violinist and composer. In connection with Harmonious, it is perhaps apposite to note that Dr. Anton Mesmer, also an occultist and fine musician (numbering Mozart and Haydn among his friends), founded the "Harmonious Society," a secret group of savants based in Vienna and later Paris, and received a great deal of help from St. Germain.[80]

It seems likely to me that St. Germain and others of his kind were associated with the "ancient races."

I have endeavored in this book to stress the wide diversity of alien beings populating the cosmos, and the diversity of their motives regarding the planet we inhabit.

We treasure the illusion that we alone are indigenous to Earth, and will remain so. But, as one of Leo Dworshak's alien friends reaffirmed as far back as 1936, "this planet was their concern, that Man has his own mind, and that he must learn to take care of his planet if he wants to keep his home. [He] assured me our planet would continue to exist. But I was not assured that Man would continue to exist on it, if he did not learn to take better care of his most valuable possession."

And as "Thomas" and his military team (Chapter 10) were warned: "Our own activities required monitoring by other than human beings, simply because Earth is a vital and necessary planet for others. We could not be permitted to despoil it even though despoliation had begun and we were doubted as to our integrity and genuine concern for the planet and its myriad life forms." The aliens reiterated that the overpopulation of Earth, combined with pollution, would lead to catastrophic consequences during the twenty-first century.

As the Amicizia group informant explained to Nikola Duper in 2009: "The Friends are our elder brothers. They are human. Indeed, in comparison it's we terrestrials who are less than human. Individuals from various other populations are among us, because the Earth is a very particular planet inside the economy of this part of the Universe. . . ."

There is said to be an ongoing conflict between various species regarding the future of our planet. "Other populations in the Universe have chosen Evil," the informant points out. "This dualism between Good and Evil is fundamental in order to understand both the still-ongoing Struggle and why it is so hard for truth to be disclosed to the inhabitants of our planet. . . . Other populations are here for other reasons, and the abduction by extraterrestrials of terrestrials, as well as the creation of hybrids, is a reality that the Friends told us about as far back as the 1960s. . . ."[81]

"The enemies are trying to conquer our planet in a very gradual and seemingly painless way, most of all working over our minds. Unfortunately, this is not science fiction. If only it were so! [And] this is not paranoia. . . . However, just hinting at these subjects leads to the discrediting of the person who says or writes them; and this is a powerful weapon in the hands of those who want to harm us."[82]

As to what the future will bring, I do not pretend to know. But I have been assured—by those who do know—that the alien situation presents the most profound dilemma facing humankind on Earth. . . .

30 ROCKEFELLER PLAZA
NEW YORK, N.Y. 10112

ROOM 5600   (212) 649-5600

February 29, 1996

John H. Gibbons, Ph.D.
Assistant to the President for
  Science and Technology
Old Executive Office Building, Room 424
17th and Pennsylvania Avenue, N.W.
Washington, D.C. 20500

Dear Jack,

I am pleased to send you the enclosed copy of a report
entitled, "Unidentified Flying Objects, the Best Available
Evidence."

The public interest in UFOs and extraterrestrial
intelligence obviously remains very high as evidenced by the
recent cover story in Time Magazine, (which I also enclose)
and the many television programs including one this week on
public television's distinguished NOVA series. I sponsored
this report because it seemed useful to bring together the
most credible evidence about UFO sightings in the form of
eyewitness reports, official statements, and scientific
views.

While I do not necessarily agree with every finding and
conclusion, I do believe that the evidence presented
indicates that this subject merits serious scientific study.
Toward that end, I hope that our government, other
governments, and the United Nations will cooperate in making
any information they may have available.

A new draft of our proposed letter to the President also
is enclosed. As always, your reactions will be helpful. In
particular, we hope you will be able to follow-up on the
pilot amnesty project you suggested.

With warm regard, I am

Sincerely,

Laurance S. Rockefeller

*A letter from Laurance S. Rockefeller (1910-2004) to President Clinton's
Assistant for Science and Technology, referencing a report prepared by
leading researchers on the UFO subject.*

"Don't worry General . . . I don't see them either."
www.americanscientist.org 2009 March–April

A cartoon found in the OSTP package of documents. It was taken from the
January 21, 1994 Albuquerque Tribune, *and included in a collection of*
articles dealing with the Congressman Schiff Roswell investigation.

REFERENCES

INTRODUCTION

1. Harnden, Toby, "Aliens targeted nuclear missiles, say ex-officers," *The Daily Telegraph*, September 28, 2010.
2. Brookes, Trevor, "UFO was inches from car, say elderly couple," *Teesdale Mercury*, January 18, 2012. Mr. Brookes (the newspaper's editor) told me that the couple unfortunately were unable to recall the exact date of the incident, in January 2010.
3. "UFO seen in Phear Park, Exmouth," *Exmouth Journal*, February 11, 2010.
4. "Close encounter had me running home, says Roy," *Exeter Express & Echo*, February 13, 2010.
5. "The Truth is in Here: The human mind, not alien life, is the source of UFOs and much other superstition," *The Times*, in "Leading articles," August 5, 2010.
6. Beabey, Keith, "UFO Lands in Suffolk—and that's Official," *News of the World*, London, October 2, 1983. As described in both *Above Top Secret* and *Beyond Top Secret*, on the afternoon of December 15, 1980, ten days prior to the first of the Rendlesham Forest incidents, an identical craft was observed for well over an hour by numerous witnesses (some with binoculars) over southeast London and northwest Kent. It alternately hovered for lengthy periods, and occasionally seemed to split into up to five separate elements before regrouping into a common element. All this took place in a completely cloudless sky. Thousands of people must have witnessed the display, and a video film was taken from Seal Chart, in the Sevenoaks area. I myself saw the object briefly (as a brilliant, large star-like object) as I was nearing my apartment building after a shopping trip. The time, I noted, was 16:07. Frustratingly, this was one of the rare occasions when I had neither binoculars, camera, nor ciné-camera with me. I dashed the remaining short distance home and opened the windows in preparation for observing the

object through my telescope and taking both movie and still film if it turned out to be unusual. But by now the object was no longer visible. It was 16:15. The next day, a journalist phoned to tell me that at least 40 witnesses in Orpington had observed the object since 15:00, some through 20x binoculars. The main object was described to me by one of the witnesses as of an elongated triangular shape—identical to that of the main object which landed in Rendlesham Forest. At 16:15 (the time I arrived home) it pointed itself toward the west and shot off vertically, seemingly dividing into two distinct objects. Curiously, this supportive evidence has been lacking in books on the Rendlesham Forest incidents, though Nick Pope hopes to include some of it in a new book (see below).

7. For the definitive books on the Rendlesham incident, see *You Can't Tell the People: The Cover-up of Britain's Roswell*, by Georgina Bruni, Sidgwick & Jackson, London, 2000, and *Encounter in Rendlesham Forest*, by Nick Pope, Thomas Dunne Books, 2014 with John Burroughs, USAF, Ret. and Jim Penniston, USAF, Ret.

8. Wheatley, Gemma, "Brit Nuke Base Zapped by UFOs," *Daily Star*, London, September 28, 2010. This remarkable conference at the National Press Club was hosted by Robert L. Hastings, author of *UFOs and Nukes: Extraordinary Encounters at Nuclear Weapons Sites*, AuthorHouse, 2008.

9. Henderson, Neil, "UFO files reveal 'Rendlesham incident' papers missing," bbc.co.uk/news/uk, March 3, 2011.

10. Copping, Jasper, "There isn't something out there," *The Sunday Telegraph*, London, August 7, 2011.

11. Personal communication, August 8, 2011.

12. Personal communication, August 9, 2011.

13. "Charles Halt, Former Air Force Colonel, Accuses U.S. of UFO Cover-Up," huffingtonpost.com, September 9, 2012.

14. Wheeler, Virginia, "UFO closes an airport," *The Sun*, October 5, 2010.

15. BBC Radio Five Live, August 4, 2011.

16. Baker, Jennie, "'Gobsmacked' by UFO sighting," *Cambridge News*, August 4, 2011.

17. Yang Jian, "Flying Saucers . . . or moths?" www.ShanghaiDaily.com, June 20, 2012.

18. Namrata-Malhotra (reporters),"UFO Sightings At Indo-China Border Leave Indian Army Astounded," *International Business Times*, November 7, 2012.

19. "Aliens Among Us? Half of the entire Chinese population believes in UFOs," *Pravda*, Russia, January 2004.

20. Lin, Rosanne, "ETs Live Among Us Says ex-China Foreign Ministry Official," *Shanghai Star*, ChinaDaily.com, July 20, 2002.

21. "As U.K. Releases UFO Files, Former UFO Project Chief Apologizes for 'Spin and Dirty Tricks,'" huffingtonpost.com, August 17, 2011.

22. Pope, Nick, "The Calvine UFO Photo," nickpope.net/calvine-ufo-photo.htm

23. Brown, Craig, news.scotsman.com, November 14, 2012.

24. Riley, Ed, "God? A greater chance of aliens," *Daily Star*, October 13, 2012.

25. For the definitive book on USOs, see *UFOs and Water* by Carl W. Feindt, Xlibris Corporation, 2010.

CHAPTER ONE: ENVIRONMENTAL SURVEY

1. Dworshak, Leo, *UFOs Are With Us—Take My Word*, Dorrance Publishing Co., Inc., Pittsburgh, 2003. See also *Montana UFOs and Extraterrestrials*, by Joan Bird, Ph.D., Riverbend Publishing, Helena, Montana, 2012.

2. Personal communication, December 2010.

3. Former NASA meteorologist Rubens Villela experienced a dramatic example of alien weather manipulation in Brazil, as described in my book *Unearthly Disclosure*.

4. Similar phenomena have been reported. Jean-Gabriel Greslé, a former fighter pilot and Air France captain, related to me how, in November 1990, an enormous structured object flew low over him and other witnesses in a suburb of Paris, carrying what he described as its own "zone of silence" (see p. 290).

5. Personal interview, Helena, June 10, 2004.

6. Personal communication, December 2010.

7. Personal interview, Helena, June 9, 2004.

8. A similar process is reported in much later contacts. In November 1973, for example, when Enrique Castillo Rincón was "beamed" aboard an alien craft in Colombia, he was asked to undress completely. A blue-colored smoke, smelling similar to lemon or lime, issued from a joint between the walls and floor. He was informed that this process disinfected him from whatever microbes he might have brought in. See *Unearthly Disclosure*. See also the 1977 case reported by Barbara Beavers (Chapter 12).

9. Ibid., Helena, June 2004.

10. Ibid.

11. Certificate of Discharge, March 31, 1937, supplied by Barry Potter.

12. Personal communication, December 2010.

13. Information supplied by Barry Potter.

14. Axline, Jon, "UFOs Sighted in Helena," published in *More from the Quarries of Last Chance Gulch*, Helena Independent Record, 1995, pp. 168–9.

15. Personal interview, Helena, June 9, 2004.

16. Testimonial, May 29, 2010, supplied by Barry Potter.

17. Personal interview, Helena, June 9, 2004.

18. Personal communication, November 2010.

19. Good, Timothy, *Need to Know: UFOs, the Military and Intelligence*, Pegasus Books, New York, 2007.

20. Personal communication from Barry Potter, June 14, 2010. Leo also related to Barry that during his naval service he came to know John F. Kennedy, whom he described as "a sort of rich playboy who claimed he never had any money, expecting others to pay for his drinks, food, and entertainment." Of incidental interest, Kennedy joined the staff of the Office of Naval Intelligence in 1941.

CHAPTER TWO: GALACTIC GUARDIANS

1. Monnet, Pierre, *Dossier Contacts et Synthèse*, translated by Anne Smith.

2. Troadec, Jean-Pierre, at rr0.org/personne/m/MonnetPierre.

3. Monnet, op. cit.
4. Monnet, Pierre, *Les Extra-Terrestres m'ont Dit*, Lefebvre, Paris, 1978. (Monnet also wrote *Contacts d'Outre-Espace*, Amrita, 1994.)
5. *Dossier Contacts et Synthèse*.
6. Ibid.
7. Ibid.

CHAPTER THREE: ITALIAN DEVELOPMENTS

1. Broken rocky matter or sediment, formed from boulders down to cobbles, gravel, sand and silt, which has been carried by a river or stream.
2. The apparent "shrinkage" of alien craft—caused perhaps by the effects of a powerful gravitational field—was reported in a number of cases in later years, which adds credibility to Johannis's claim.
3. Creighton, Gordon, "The Villa Santina Case," *Flying Saucer Review*, Vol. 13, No. 1, January–February 1967, pp. 3–8.
4. Johannis, Professor R.L., "Ho visto un disco volante," *Clypeus*, No. 2–5, Centri Studi Clipeologici, Turin, May 1964.
5. Letter from Professor R. L. Johannis to Gianni Settimo, Director, Centri Studi Clipeologici, Turin, March 20, 1964.
6. Johannis, Professor R. L., "I Saw a Flying Saucer," translated by Gordon Creighton from *Clypeus* (see ref. 4) and appearing in "The Villa Santina Case: An important early contact claim" by Creighton, *Flying Saucer Review*, Vol. 13, No. 1, January–February 1967, pp. 3–8.
7. A localized silence usually surrounded Leo and Mike Dworshak during their encounters.
8. Monguzzi used a Kodak Retina 1 (probably the 1A model) with a Schneider-Kreuznach Xenar 50mm f/3.5 lens, set at f/8 and 1/500 second shutter speed, and Ferrania 24mm × 36mm black & white film, 100ASA/21DIN.
9. *Epoca*, November 1952, translated from the Italian by Lou Zinsstag, Basel.
10. Letter to Lou Zinsstag from the Direktion der Militärflugplätze, Betriebs-Gruppe Buochs/Ennetbürgen, June 28, 1958.
11. Zinsstag, Lou, "Monguzzi Takes Saucer Photos of the Century," *Flying Saucer Review*, Vol. 4, No. 5, September–October 1958, pp. 2–4.

CHAPTER FOUR: EISENHOWER AND THE EXTRATERRESTRIALS

1. Stringfield, Leonard, *UFO Crash/Retrievals: Amassing the Evidence—Status Report III*, 1982, p. 34, citing a copy of letter from Antonio Ribera to Richard W. Heiden.
2. Ibid., p. 34.
3. ufocrashbook.com/eisenhower.html
4. Hastings, Max, "The Defence of the Realm," *The Sunday Times*, Culture section, p. 42, July 11, 2010, reviewing *The Secret State: Preparing for the Worst 1945–2010* by Peter Hennessy, Allen Lane, 2010.
5. On June 22, 1965, Godfrey recounted on one of his coast-to-coast programs how

he and his co-pilot, Frank Munciello, had encountered a brilliantly lit object which suddenly appeared off the starboard wing of their twin-engined Convair plane on a night flight from New York to Washington, D.C., forcing Godfrey to take evasive action. He contacted the FAA tower at Philadelphia, who said nothing could be seen on radar. At that instant the object reversed its course and circled the plane, coming up seconds later behind the port wing. Godfrey's continuing evasive maneuvers were met with duplicated moves by the UFO, before it eventually veered upward and disappeared. No date is given for the incident. (From *Flying Saucers—Serious Business* by Frank Edwards, Lyle Stuart, New York, 1966, pp. 130–1.)

6. Kittinger, Jr., Capt. Joseph W., "The Long, Lonely Leap," *National Geographic*, December 1960; Wikipedia. See also *Come Up and Get Me: An Autobiography of Colonel Joseph Kittinger*, by Joe Kittinger and Craig Ryan, with a foreword by Neil Armstrong, University of New Mexico Press, 2010. More recently, Col. Kittinger advised Felix Baumgartner's October 14, 2012 record-breaking free fall from 128,100 feet and served also as capsule commander (CAPCOM).

7. Good, Timothy, *Need to Know: UFOs, the Military and Intelligence*, Pan Books, London, and Pegasus Books, New York, 2007, p. 187.

8. McAndrew, James, *The Roswell Report: Case Closed*, Headquarters United States Air Force, U.S. Government Printing Office, Washington, D.C. 20402, 1997, pp. 176–7.

9. Ibid., pp. 103, 174–7.

10. Clarkson, James E., *Tell My Story: June Crain, The Air Force & UFOs*, Black Triangle Press, P.O. Box 12328, Olympia, WA 98508, 2010, pp. 42–3, 61–2, 121–2.

11. Art Campbell points out that Kittinger's service record indicates that he was at Holloman AFB from the fall of 1954 to the summer of 1955.

12. Search online for "President Eisenhower UFO aliens Henry McElroy."

13. *Valor* magazine, October 9, 1954, and confirmed to the author by Desmond Leslie.

14. Rivas, Juan A. Lorenzo, "President Eisenhower's 'ET' Encounter: What Really Happened at Muroc Base?" *Flying Saucer Review*, Vol. 44, No. 3, 1999, pp. 2–5.

15. Picton, John, "Eisenhower Was Visited by UFO, British Lord Claims," *Toronto Star* (date not available, but the story was confirmed to the author by Lord Clancarty).

16. Rivas, op. cit.

17. Letter from Gerald Light to Meade Layne, received April 16, 1954. Light gave his address as 10545 Scenario Lane, Los Angeles 24. In the 1970s, researcher William Moore tried in vain to trace the witness, though, as he notes in *The Roswell Incident*, a Gerald Light was employed in the early 1950s as director of advertising and sales promotion for CBS Columbia in Los Angeles. As for the other three witnesses, several previous attempts had been made to contact all of them about Light's story, but none would discuss the matter or even acknowledge receipt of letters concerning it.

18. Berlitz, Charles, and Moore, William, *The Roswell Incident*, Granada, 1980, pp. 119–20.

19. McElroy, Henry, "American Renaissance 2012," April 13, 2012, henrymcelroy. wordpress.com
20. Light, Michael, *100 Suns*, Jonathan Cape, London, 2003, chronology section.
21. Personal communication, Woodstock, Virginia, May 8, 1998.
22. ufocrashbook.com/eisenhower.html

CHAPTER FIVE: PUBLIC LANDINGS

1. Fry, Margaret-Ellen, *Link to the Stars*, with a foreword by Desmond Leslie, privately published, 2009, pp. 1–4. I have supplemented this account with periodic updates sent to me by Margaret. She has also authored another book, *Who Are They?* (privately published, 2004). For signed copies, contact The Secretary, WFIU, 5 The Broadway, Abergele, Conwy, Wales, LL22 7DD.
2. Report form to Contact (UK) signed by Steve Fredrick Costello, July 1, 1978.
3. Fry, op. cit., p. 4.
4. Piper, Linda, "UFO kids urged 'phone home,'" *News Shopper*, Bexley (and other local areas), September 4, 2002.
5. Piper, Linda, "Did you spot this 1955 UFO?" *News Shopper*, Bexley, September 18, 2002.
6. Fry, op. cit., pp. 209–10.
7. Hanson, John and Holloway, Dawn, *Haunted Skies: The Encyclopaedia of British UFOs, Volume 1, 1940–1959*, CFZ Press, Bideford, Devon, 2010, pp. 171–4.
8. Information supplied to me by Margaret Fry, who knew Doris Jacques.
9. Hanson and Holloway, op. cit., p. 169.
10. Personal interview, April 5, 2011.
11. Hanson and Holloway, op. cit., pp. 174–5.
12. Fry, op. cit., p. 210.
13. Fry, op. cit., p. 211.
14. Fry, Margaret-Ellen, *Who Are They?* p. 2.
15. Fry, *Link to the Stars*, p. 212.
16. Ibid., pp. 4–5.
17. Luton, Tina, "The Day Westall High Stood Still," *Inspire*, Issue 3, April 2011, pp. 52–5, published by the Communications Division for the Department of Education and Early Childhood Development, Melbourne.
18. Ryan, Shane, "The Forgotten Story of Melbourne's 1966 Westall Flying Saucer Incident," *UFO Matrix*, Vol. 1, Issue 6, 2011, pp. 13–14.
19. Luton, op. cit.
20. Ryan, op. cit., p. 16.

CHAPTER SIX: TALES FROM THE VIENNA WOODS

1. Good, Timothy, *Alien Base: Earth's Encounters with Extraterrestrials*, Century, London, 1998, also published by Avon Books, New York, 1999, pp. 233–8.
2. Wanderka, Josef, *Meine UFO-Kontakt and Sichtungsdokumentation*, 1975, sent to the author in January 1983. Translated by Dorothee Walter.

3. Personal interview, Vienna, September 6, 1996.

4. Creighton, Gordon, "A Weird Tale from the Vienna Woods," *Flying Saucer Review*, Vol. 24, No. 6, April 1979, pp. 20–1.

CHAPTER SEVEN: INFILTRATION

1. Wilkins, Harold T., *Flying Saucers on the Attack*, Ace Books, New York, 1954, p. 46.

2. Anderson, Carl A., *Two Nights to Remember*, New Age Publishing Co., Los Angeles, 1956.

3. Lecture at a conference in Reno, Nevada, July 10, 1966.

4. Ibid.

5. Wilkins, op. cit., p. 261.

6. Lecture, Reno.

7. "Dr. Hermann Oberth discusses UFOs," *Fate*, May 1962, pp. 36–43.

8. Collyns, Robin, *Did Spacemen Colonise the Earth?* Pelham Books, London, 1974, p. 236.

9. Oberth, op. cit.

10. Lecture, Reno.

11. Van Tassel, George, "The Perfect Defense," *Proceedings*, Vol. 6, No. 2, May–June 1958.

12. Lecture, Reno.

13. Good, Timothy, *Alien Base: Earth's Encounters with Extraterrestrials*, Century, London, 1998, and Avon Books, New York, 1999, pp. 30–9. See also *The Shocking Truth* by H. Albert Coe, The Book Fund, Beverly, New Jersey, 1969.

14. Clark, Jerome, *The Emergence of a Phenomenon: UFOs from the Beginning through 1959*, The UFO Encyclopedia, Volume 2, Omnigraphics, Inc., 1992, pp. 295–7.

15. "Centralian Tells Strange Tale of Visiting Venus Space Ship in Eastern Lewis County," *Centralia Daily Chronicle*, April 1, 1950.

16. Clark, op. cit.

17. Personal interview, Mount Palomar, California, August 19, 1976.

18. Freed, David, "Emissary," *Air & Space* (Smithsonian), Vol. 27, No. 3, August 2012, p. 22.

19. quest.nasa.gov/aero/planetary/mars.html

20. Good, op. cit., p. 246.

21. Personal interviews, Ontario, California, 19–20 November, 1979.

22. Sagan, Carl, *The Cosmic Connection: An Extraterrestrial Perspective*, Coronet Books, London, 1975, pp. 151–2.

23. Steckling, Fred, *Why Are They Here? Spaceships from Other Worlds*, Vantage Press, New York, 1969, pp. 71–4. See also adamskifoundation.com or write to GAF International/Adamski Foundation (run by Glenn Steckling) at P.O. Box 1722, Vista, California 92085.

24. "NASA awards CU-Boulder $3.3 million for Venus mission," Metro Denver Economic Development Corporation News Center, metrodenver.org.

25. Kean, Sam, "Forbidden Planet," *Air & Space* (Smithsonian), Vol. 25, No. 5, October/November 2010, pp. 63–7.

26. Interview on the Art Bell Radio Show, Coast to Coast FM, November 2, 2003.

27. Recorded interview with Albert Coe by Dr. Berthold Schwarz, May 17, 1977.

28. Zinsstag, Lou and Good, Timothy, *George Adamski: The Untold Story*, with a foreword by Lady Falkender, Ceti Publications, 1983.

29. Leslie, Desmond and Adamski, George, *Flying Saucers Have Landed*, Wernie Laurie, London, 1953.

30. Adamski, George, *Inside the Space Ships*, Arco Publishers and Neville Spearman Ltd., London, 1956, p. 56.

31. Tolman, Alan G., "My Early Experiences with Flying Saucers and Early Contactee George Adamski," provided for me by Glenn Steckling via Alan Tolman.

32. Wilkins, op. cit., pp. 260–61.

33. Leslie, Desmond and Adamski, George, *Flying Saucers Have Landed* (revised edition), Neville Spearman, London, 1970, pp. 248–9.

34. Dohan, Henry, *The Pawn of His Creator: Early Contactees of Interplanetary Visitations*, edited and published posthumously by David R. Kammerer. Second, revised edition, August 2008, P.O. Box 96701, Las Vegas, Nevada 89193, p. 124.

35. Good, op. cit., p. 105.

36. Dohan, op. cit., pp. 245–6.

37. Speech by Senator the Hon. G. Brown, Appropriation Bill (No. 2) 1962–63 (First Reading), from *Parliamentary Debates*, 14th May, 1963, p. ii, reproduced at the end of Dohan's book.

38. Steckling, op. cit., p. 78.

39. As reported in *Alien Base*, in June 1963 Apolinar Villa witnessed the landing of a large disc from which emerged four men and five women, ranging in height from seven to nine feet. Some had blond hair, some black—and others red.

40. Lecture, Reno.

41. *Neues Europa*, January 1, 1959.

CHAPTER EIGHT: AIRBORNE ENCOUNTERS

1. National Archives, DEFE-24-2013-1, pp. 273–82. If there is any truth to the Churchill/Eisenhower story, it is odd that in an official memo to the Secretary of State for Air and Lord Cherwell on July 28, 1952, Churchill asked: "What does all this stuff about flying saucers amount to? What can it mean? What is the truth? Let me have a report at your convenience." If he already knew enough to insist on a cover-up in the Second World War, why would he have needed to ask such a question?

2. Malvern, Jack, "So, flying saucers—what's the truth, Churchill asked," *The Times*, London, August 5, 2010, pp. 12–13.

3. Kissner, J. Andrew, *Peculiar Phenomenon: Early United States Efforts to Collect and Analyze Flying Discs.* (Currently unpublished.)

4. The Kenny Young Archives and *UFO Frontier* by Kenny Young, edited by S. Patrick Feeney, available via Amazon. (I have corrected details of some of the aircraft types.)

5. Wilkins, Harold T., *Flying Saucers Uncensored*, Arco, London, 1956, p. 137.

6. See *Empire of the Clouds: When Britain's Aircraft Ruled the World* by James Hamilton-Patterson, Faber and Faber, London, 2010.

7. Supplied by Dr. Olavo Fontes, a Brazilian researcher, to Richard H. Hall, an American counterpart, March 15, 1958.

8. Vike, Brian, "Lt. Col. Roy Jack Edwards tells his son of his UFO encounter as a test pilot," americanchronicle.com/articles/50322 (January 26, 2008).

9. Torres, Noe and Uriarte, Ruben, *The Other Roswell: UFO Crash on the Texas-Mexico Border*, RoswellBooks.com, 2008, pp. 23–6.

10. Ibid., pp. 33–5.

11. Ibid., p. 36.

12. Ibid., pp. 45–9.

13. Ibid., pp. 51–8.

14. Personal communication, November 11, 2010.

15. Ibid., pp. 63–7.

16. Ibid., pp. 68–73.

17. Possibly General Thomas D. White, who became assistant chief of staff for intelligence in 1944 and chief of staff for the U.S. Air Force in 1957.

18. Torres and Uriarte, op. cit., pp. 83–4.

19. Good, Timothy, *Need to Know: UFOs, the Military and Intelligence*, Pan Books, London, and Pegasus Books, New York, 2007, p. 55.

20. Torres and Uriarte, op. cit., p. 91.

21. Ibid., pp. 119–21.

22. Good, Timothy, *Beyond Top Secret: The Worldwide UFO Security Threat*, Pan Books, London, 1997, p. 537.

23. Ibid., pp. 121–2.

24. Randle, Kevin D., "Crash Goes the Del Rio Crash," *UFO Magazine*, Vol. 24, No. 1, January 2011, pp, 18–19.

25. Personal communication, January 7, 2011.

26. Letter from Dr. Milton Torres to the Ministry of Defence, London, July 1988, released in October 2008.

27. Cox, Billy, "UFO Chaser to Obama: 'Open the Books!,'" theufochronicles.com/2009/02/ufo-chaser-to-obama-open-books.html

28. Letter to the Ministry of Defence, July 1988.

29. Evans, Michael, "Close Encounter: the airman who tried to shoot down a UFO," *The Times*, London, October 20, 2008.

30. Letter to the Ministry of Defence, July 1988.

31. Hoffman, Michael, "Retired Air Force pilot recalls attempt to shoot down UFO," *Air Force Times*, October 20, 2008.

32. Letter to the Ministry of Defence, July 2008.

33. military-writers.com/airforce/milton_torres.html

34. Spangler, David, "Retired Air Force pilot tells of close encounter 50 years ago," *Miami Herald*, October 22, 2008.

35. O'Brien, Miles, in a transcript of *American Morning*, November 24, 2008.

36. Letter to the Ministry of Defence, July 1988.

CHAPTER NINE: "A NEW WORLD—IF YOU CAN TAKE IT"

1. Corso, Col. Philip J., with Birnes, William J., *The Day After Roswell*, Pocket Books, New York, 1997.

2. This information was revealed in a videotaped interview with Corso by the Italian investigator Maurizio Baiata.

3. Corso, Philip J., USA Ret., *Dawn of a New Age*, kindly supplied to me by the researcher Paola Harris, a friend of Corso. This section of Corso's manuscript for *The Day After Roswell* was not included in the book.

4. Ibid., p. 156.

5. Ibid., pp. 166–8.

6. Ibid., pp. 157–8.

7. Ibid., pp. 159–61.

8. This brings to mind an interesting parallel. In July 1949, at White Sands, Daniel Fry, a rocket engineer for Aerojet General Corporation, encountered a landed craft and was invited aboard by its humanoid pilot, "A-lan." At one point, Fry was astonished to notice the caduceus symbol in the craft. "You are perfectly correct when you point out that the symbol of the tree and the serpent is a common one in the history and the legends of your planet," said A-lan. "The explanation is that we have, at least in part, a common ancestry. Tens of thousands of years ago, some of our ancestors lived on this planet, Earth. . . ." (*The White Sands Incident* by Dr. Daniel Fry, Best Books Inc., Louisville, Kentucky 40218, 1966. See also my book *Alien Base*.)

9. Corso, op. cit., pp. 162–4.

10. Keller, Tom L., *The Total Novice's Guide to UFOs: What You Need to Know*, 2FS (publishing) LLC, P.O. Box 5481, Palm Springs, California 92263-5481, 2010, pp. 165–8.

11. Presentation for Steven Greer's Disclosure Project at the National Press Club, Washington, D.C., May 9, 2001.

12. Keller, op. cit., p. 168.

CHAPTER TEN: GRAY LIAISON

1. Personal communication, July 14, 2009.

2. *Code Orange* is due for publication in 2015 (with the author's real name).

3. Wikipedia.

4. *Flying Saucer Review*, Vol. 48, No. 2, Summer 2003, p. 23.

5. Corso, Col. Philip J., with Birnes, William J., *The Day After Roswell*, Pocket Books, Simon & Schuster Inc., New York, 1997, pp. 182–3.

6. Ibid., p. 183.

CHAPTER ELEVEN: THE OVERLORDS

1. Blomqvist, Håkan, "The Helge File—Men in Black in Sweden?," *AFU Newsletter*, No. 20, October/December 1980, Archives for UFO Research, Norrköping, Sweden, and updated material supplied to the author. ("Helge" was the pseudonym used for Höglund prior to his death.)

2. Blomqvist, Håkan, "Some further notes from the Helge File" (1984), supplied to the author, including subsequent updates.

3. Blomqvist, Håkan, *Främlingar på vår jord: Ufokontakter i Sverige*, Parthenon, Nyköping, 2009.

4. *Folket*, June 1, 1968.

5. Personal communication, April 12, 2012.

6. Letter to Gösta Johansson, January 16, 1969.

7. Interview with Gunvor Höglund by Håkan Blomqvist, June 1, 1984.

8. *Dagens Nyheter*, Stockholm, October 21, 1971, as cited in *KGB: The Secret Work of Soviet Secret Agents* by John Barron, Corgi Books, London, 1975, p. 28.

9. Keel, John A., *The Eighth Tower*, Saturday Review Press, E.P. Dutton & Co., Inc., New York, 1975, p. 141.

10. Menger, Howard, *From Outer Space to You*, Saucerian Books, Clarksburg, Virginia, 1959, pp. 143–4.

11. Good, Timothy, *Alien Base: Earth's Encounters with Extraterrestrials*, Century, London, 1998, pp. 192–3.

12. Keel, John A., *Operation Trojan Horse*, Souvenir Press, London, 1971, p. 296.

13. Good, op. cit., pp. 54–5.

14. Blomqvist, Håkan, "The Helge File—Men in Black in Sweden?"

CHAPTER TWELVE: RELUCTANT GUINEA PIGS

1. Photochromic glass is used, for example, in eyeglasses which darken on exposure to ultraviolet radiation, but once indoors revert to their clear state (often referred to as "photo-gray").

2. "Kirlian auras" are a form of contact-print photography named after Semyon Kirlian, who in 1929 inadvertently discovered that if an object on a photographic plate is subjected to a strong electrical field, an image is created on the plate. He claimed the resulting images were proof of the "life force" or "aura" surrounding living beings. It is most likely, in my opinion, that alien technology in this regard is a great deal more advanced than that of the Kirlian system, as evidenced by its ability to display chakras.

3. Good, Timothy, *Unearthly Disclosure: Conflicting Interests in the Control of Extraterrestrial Intelligence*, Arrow Books, London, 2001, p. 137.

4. Atlanti, Shawn, "Narrative of Barbara Beavers" (transcribed from notes). Shawn wishes to point out that this narrative had not been checked with the witness as to accuracy or completeness. I have no further information on the witness from Shawn, other than that she had a previous experience with UFOs in Tennessee in 1968 and did two years of college training as a dental technician, but took no science courses.

CHAPTER THIRTEEN: AMICIZIA

1. Breccia, Stefano, *Mass Contacts*, AuthorHouse, 2009, pp. 156–7. The Italian edition is *Contattismi di massa*, published by Nexus Edizioni, Roma, 2006.
2. Duper, Nikola, "The Story of 'Friendship.'"
3. Breccia, op. cit., p. 316.
4. Di Girolamo, Paolo, *Noi E Loro: T & ET,* Nexus Edizioni, 2009.
5. Breccia, op. cit., pp. 166–74.
6. Ibid., pp. 184–6.
7. Ibid., pp. 187–8.
8. Personal interview, Chieti, April 6, 2010.
9. Breccia, op. cit., pp. 188–92.
10. Ibid., p. 239.
11. Personal interview, April 6, 2010.
12. Breccia, op. cit., pp. 284–5.
13. Personal communication, December 22, 2010.
14. Breccia, op. cit., p. 221.
15. Personal interview, April 7, 2010.
16. Breccia, op. cit., pp. 197–8.
17. Personal interview, April 7, 2010.
18. Breccia, op. cit., p. 225.
19. Personal interview, April 7, 2010.
20. Breccia, op. cit., p. 239
21. Breccia, Stefano, *Amicizia: Fifty Years Later*, Nexus Publishing, 2012.
22. Described by Bill Gunston as comprising a fixed beacon emitting a fixed circular horizontal radiation pattern at 108–118 MHz, on which is superimposed a rotating directional pattern at 30 Hz, giving output whose phase modulation is unique for each bearing from the beacon. "Thus airborne station can read from panel instrument bearing of aircraft from station, called inbound or outbound radial . . ." *The Cambridge Aerospace Dictionary* (Second Edition), by Bill Gunston, Cambridge University Press, New York, 2009, p. 760.
23. Personal interview, June 22, 2010.
24. Breccia, op. cit., pp. 288–90.
25. Personal interview, June 24, 2010.
26. Personal communication, November 9, 2011.
27. Personal interview, April 7, 2010.
28. Breccia, *Mass Contacts*, p. 290.
29. Uriarte, Ruben and Reichmuth, Steven, "UFHs—Mexico's Flying Humanoids," *MUFON UFO Journal*, No. 467, March 2007, pp. 3–5.
30. Breccia, op. cit., p. 183.
31. Ibid., pp. 178–81.
32. Barbatelli, Teresa, "A tentative study of the strange picture at the end of *Contattismi di massa*," 2009.
33. *Fortean Times*, No. 204, December 2005.

34. Genesis 6:4, *The Holy Bible*. Scripture taken from the New King James Version. Copyright © 1979, 1980, 1982 by Thomas Nelson, Inc.

35. Good, Timothy, *Above Top Secret: The Worldwide UFO Cover-up*, William Morrow, New York, 1988, pp. 400–1, citing *Preuves Scientifiques OVNI* by Jean-Charles Fumoux, (Monaco, 1981).

36. Personal communication, May 7, 2008.

37. Personal communication, December 21, 2007.

38. Good, Timothy, *Need to Know: UFOs, the Military and Intelligence*, Pan Books, London, 2007; Pegasus Books, New York, 2007, pp. 426–7.

39. Personal communication, July 6, 2012.

40. Breccia, op. cit., 272–3.

41. Personal interview, June 22, 2010.

42. Breccia, op. cit., p. 223.

43. Personal interview, June 8, 2010.

44. Breccia, op. cit., pp. 309–13.

45. Ibid., pp. 153–4.

46. Personal interview, April 7, 2010.

47. Good, op. cit., pp. 406–11.

48. Personal interview, April 7, 2010.

49. Breccia, *Mass Contacts*, pp. 381–2.

50. Ibid., pp. 231–3.

51. Ibid., p. 230.

52. Ibid., p. 235.

53. Ibid., p. 230.

54. Ibid., pp. 233–4.

55. Ibid., p. 228.

56. Ibid., p. 296.

57. Ibid., p. 237.

58. I am particularly drawn to the works of William Walker Atkinson. Probably owing to his status as a barrister (Pennsylvania Bar), he used a number of pseudonyms for some of his books, e.g. "Yogi Ramacharaka" and "Theron Q. Dumont." First published by the Psychic Research Company (New York) and Yogi Publication Society (Chicago) at the start of the 20th century, many of these books are still in print. As an introduction, I recommend *Fourteen Lessons in Yogi Philosophy* (1903).

59. Breccia, *Mass Contacts*, p. 297.

60. Ibid., p. 266.

61. *Ṛgveda Saṃhitā*, Book 1, Hymn 139, p. 619. English translation by Svami Satya Prakash Sarasvati and Satyakam Vidyalankar, Veda Pratishthana, New Delhi.

62. Personal interview, April 8, 2010.

63. Breccia, op. cit., p. 7.

64. Ibid., pp. 256–7.

65. Ibid., p. 315.

66. Good, Timothy, *Alien Base: Earth's Encounters with Extraterrestrials*, Century, London, 1998, pp. 215–17, citing an article from *Le Ore*, 24/31 January 1963, translated by Gordon Creighton in *Flying Saucer Review*, Vol. 9, No. 3, May–June 1963, pp. 18–20.

CHAPTER FOURTEEN: ALTERNATIVE SPACECRAFT

1. Cox, Billy, "Locals tell tales of UFO sightings," *Florida Today*, Melbourne, Florida, July 6, 1997.
2. Lethbridge, Cliff, "Launch Pad 3 Supports the First Rocket Launch from Cape Canaveral," spaceline.org.
3. Good, Timothy, *Alien Base: The Evidence for the Extraterrestrial Colonization of Earth*, Avon Books, New York, 1999, p. 243.
4. Cox, op. cit.
5. Debus, Kurt H., "John F. Kennedy Space Center Management Instruction, KMI-8610.4," June 28, 1967.
6. Oglesby, J. E., *Proof of Extraterrestrial Intelligence: The Cape Canaveral Apollo Program Chronicles*, LuLu.com, 860 Aviation Parkway, Suite 300, Morrisville, NC 27560, 2008, pp. 17–26.
7. Ibid., pp. 28–9.
8. Ibid., pp. 128–9.
9. Ibid., pp. 62–4.
10. Ibid., pp. 69–70.
11. Ibid., p. 73.
12. Ibid., pp. 75–8.
13. Ibid., p. 115.
14. Ibid., pp. 120–2.
15. Ibid., pp. 132–40.
16. *Apollo II: The Untold Story*, a British One-hour Special for the Discovery Channel, first shown on Channel Five (UK), July 24, 2006.
17. *San Bernardino Sun-Telegram*, July 20, 1969.
18. Good, Timothy, *Above Top Secret: The Worldwide UFO Cover-up*, William Morrow, New York, 1988, pp. 383–4, citing *Saga UFO Special*, No. 3.
19. Faucher, Eric; Goodstein, Ellen; and Gris, Henry: "Alien UFOs Watched Our First Astronauts on Moon," *National Enquirer*, September 11, 1979. I am well aware of the *Enquirer*'s reputation for unsubstantiated tabloid stories, but the late Bob Pratt, who investigated numerous UFO cases for the paper—in the USA and abroad—assured me that (to his own bemusement as well) such stories were published accurately.
20. Greer, Dr. Steven M., *Disclosure: Military and Government Witnesses Reveal the Greatest Secrets in Modern History*, pre-publication edition, Crossing Point, Inc., PO Box 265, Crozet, VA 22932, 2001, pp. 419–21.
21. Adamski, George, *Inside the Space Ships*, Neville Spearman, London, 1966, p. 143.
22. Ibid., p. 204.

23. Personal communication, January 31, 1995.

24. Letter to the author from Neil. A. Armstrong, December 29, 1986.

25. Personal communication, January 31, 1995.

26. I.H.Ph. Diederiks-Verschoor, "International Symposium on Space Lab held in Naples and Capri from 11-16 June 1984," *Journal of Space Law*, Vol. 12, No. 2, pp. 193–4.

27. "Spacelab to Space Station," *Earth-oriented Applications of Space Technology*, Vol. 5, Nos. 1/2, Pergamon Press, 1985.

28. Corso, Col. Philip J., *The Day After Roswell*, Pocket Books, New York, 1997, pp. 128–9.

29. Hellyer, Paul, *Light at the End of the Tunnel: A Survival Plan for the Human Species*, AuthorHouse, Bloomington, IN 47403, 2010, pp. 11–12.

30. Buncombe, Andrew, 'Space: America's new war zone,' *The Independent*, October 19, 2006, pp. 1–2.

31. Dowling, Kevin, "Wanted: volunteer martyrs for one-way trip to Mars," *The Sunday Times*, April 24, 2011.

32. Buncombe, op. cit.

33. NASA Information Sheet Number 78/1, prepared by Public Services Branch, Office of External Relations, NASA Headquarters, Washington, D.C. 20546, February 1, 1978.

34. Cooper, Gordon, with Henderson, Bruce, *Leap of Faith: An Astronaut's Journey into the Unknown*, HarperCollins, New York, New York, 2000, pp. 82–6.

35. Letter to Ambassador Griffith from L. Gordon Cooper, Col. USAF (Ret.), Astronaut, November 9, 1978.

36. Part of an article by J. L. Ferrando in an unknown French newspaper, translated by Louise Zinsstag, based on a taped interview with Gordon Cooper by Benny Manocchia during an international congress in New York, 1973.

37. Good, Timothy, *Alien Contact: Top-Secret UFO Files Revealed*, William Morrow, New York, (revised edition), 1993, pp. 224–6.

38. www.jsc.nasa.gov/Bios/htmlbios/stafford-tp.html

39. Good, op. cit., pp. 226–8.

40. Personal interview, Grosvenor House Hotel, London, November 24, 1996.

41. Larson, George C., "Moments & Milestones," *Air & Space/Smithsonian*, Vol. 26, No. 2, June/July 2011, p. 80.

42. Good, op. cit., 230–4.

43. Personal communication, April 8, 1992.

44. kurzweilai.net/nasa-ames-worden-reveals-darpa-funded-hundred-year-starship

45. Keller, T.L., *The Total Novices Guide to UFOs*, 2FS (publishing), LLC, PO Box 5481, Palm Springs, CA 92263-5481, 2010, p. 167.

46. *Jane's Defence Weekly*, June 12, 1993.

47. LaViolette, Paul A., *Secrets of Antigravity Propulsion*, Bear & Company, Rochester, Vermont, 2008, pp. 395–6.

48. Interview on the Art Bell Radio Show, Coast to Coast FM, November 2, 2003.

49. LaViolette, op. cit, p. 396–7.

50. Reagan, Ronald, *The Reagan Diaries*, edited by Douglas Brinkley, HarperCollins, New York, 2007, p. 334.

51. Sheridan, Michael, "China's £30bn space gallop leaves US on launchpad," *The Sunday Times*, November 6, 2011.

52. *Aerospace & Defense News*, May 22, 2012.

53. Ibid., May 25, 2012.

54. Ronson, Jon, "Game Over," *The Guardian/Guardian Unlimited*, London, July 9, 2005. In May 2011, despite a lengthy and intensive campaign mounted by the *Daily Mail* and the support of numerous politicians (including Prime Minister David Cameron), President Obama's top law officer, Eric Holder, the U.S. Attorney General, vowed to "take all of the necessary steps" to have Gary—who suffers from Asperger's syndrome—extradited and "held accountable for the crimes that he committed." Previously, in conversation with Mr. Cameron at the White House, Mr. Obama had promised to find an "appropriate solution" *(Daily Mail*, London, May 13, 2011). The matter was raised again by the Prime Minister during President Obama's visit to Britain in late May 2011. "We have proceeded through all the processes required under our extradition agreements," the president stated. "It's now in the hands of the British legal system." (*Daily Mail*, May 26, 2011.) In October 2012, Britain's Home Secretary Theresa May vetoed the extradition.

The Americans were furious. The U.S. Department of Justice expressed disappointment at the Home Secretary's decision, "particularly given the past decisions of the U.K. courts and prior Home Secretaries that he should face trial in the United States." It did not, however, view the ruling as a precedent for other cases. U.S. lawyer David Rivkin criticised Ms. May's decision, saying that to deny the extradition on health grounds was "laughable." (Kumar, Nikhil, "U.S. disappointed by 'laughable' decision," *The Independent*, London, October 17, 2012). For a lengthy period, it was likely that Gary would face prosecution in a British court of law. No longer.

"On the 14th December, 2012," Gary wrote to me in March 2013, "we were awaiting a decision from the United Kingdom Crown Prosecution Service as to whether or not I would have to face a UK trial . . . with some trepidation, we awaited the outcome of this decision, having been told it would be on this day. To our huge relief, the CPS, having formed a special panel with the Metropolitan Police (which is highly unusual in these circumstances) decided that a UK prosecution would be of no use and that they probably wouldn't be able to get a conviction."

CHAPTER FIFTEEN: TECHNOLOGY TRANSFER

1. *Filer's Files* #9-2012, edited by Maj. George A. Filer, USAF (Ret.), Majorstar@verizon.net

2. Arthur Stansel, a supervisory engineer who worked at Wright Air Development

Center (Aircraft Laboratory) during this period, was the first to publicly release information on the Kingman, Arizona, incident of May 1953. In his sworn 1973 affidavit, Stansel described that craft as "oval and about 30 feet in diameter," as opposed to Bill Uhouse's 30-meter-diameter claim. (See my book *Need to Know*.)

3. Greer, Steven M., *Disclosure: Military and Government Witnesses Reveal the Greatest Secrets in Modern History*, pre-publication edition [etc.], Crossing Point, Inc., PO Box 265, Crozet, VA 22932, pp. 384–7.
4. Dohan, Henry, *UFOs: The Pawn of His Creator*, published by David R. Kammerer, PO Box 96701, Las Vegas, Nevada 89193, second, revised edition, 2008, pp. 253–4.
5. LaViolette, Paul A., *Secrets of Antigravity Propulsion*, Bear & Company, Rochester, Vermont, 2008, pp. 26–31.
6. Ibid., pp. 54–9.
7. Adamski, George, *Flying Saucers Farewell*, Abelard-Schuman, London, 1961, pp. 36–7.
8. LaViolette, op. cit., p. 70.
9. Ibid., pp. 77–80.
10. Ibid., pp. 106–7.
11. Green, William, *The Observer's World Aircraft Directory*, Frederick Warne & Co., London and New York, 1961, p. 136. For a detailed history of the Avrocar and numerous other such aircraft developed around the world, see *Secret Projects—Flying Saucer Aircraft*, by Bill Rose and Tony Buttler (Midland Publishing, Hinckley, LE10 3EY, U.K., 2006).
12. Good, Timothy, *Above Top Secret: The Worldwide UFO Cover-up*, William Morrow, New York, 1988, pp. 225–6.
13. *Ideal's UFO Magazine*, No. 4, 1978.
14. Personal communications, 2005.
15. Good, Timothy, *Alien Contact: Top-Secret UFO Files Revealed*, William Morrow, New York, 1993, pp. 139–40, citing a letter from Mike Hunt to David Dobbs, April 20, 1980.
16. *Round Robin*, Vol. 23/3, May–June 1967, pp. 7–8. This article was kindly supplied to me by Håkan Blomqvist.
17. Personal communications, December 16, 2010, and May 27, 2011.
18. Personal interview, Mount Palomar, California, August 19, 1976.
19. Dolan, Richard M., *UFOs and the National Security State: The UFO Cover-Up Exposed, 1973–1991*, Keyhole Publishing Co., Rochester, New York, 2009, pp. 457–9.
20. Greer, op. cit., p. 500.
21. Dolan, op. cit., pp. 459–60.
22. Greer, op. cit., p. 504.
23. Adamski, George, *Inside The Space Ships*, Abelard-Schuman, Inc., New York, 1955, p. 47.
24. Personal interview, April 23, 1999.
25. Personal communication, February 3, 1999.
26. Personal interview, April 23, 1999.

27. In 1990, witnesses near Paris observed a giant UFO which carried a "zone of silence" with it (Chapter 16).

28. "The Night We Stumbled Upon An Alien Base," *UFO Universe*, Vol. 1, No. 5, October/November 1991, pp. 52–4. This report was sent to the magazine via Sandra L. Edison, publisher of *Network Newsletter*. Though the author did not want her name associated with the story, Ms. Edison described the witness as "very reliable and trustworthy."

29. Keller, T. L., *The Total Novice's Guide to UFOs*, 2FS (Publishing), LLC, PO Box 5481, Palm Springs, CA 92263-5481, 2010, pp. 139–152.

30. Hamilton III, William F., *Cosmic Top Secret: America's Secret UFO Program*, Inner Light Publications, Box 753, New Brunswick, NJ 08903, 1991, p. 85.

31. Ibid., p. 78.

32. Accessed in 2011 from Youtube.com (Steven Greer/William Pawelec).

33. On June 15, 2006, I was in Washington, D.C. A front-page article in that day's *Washington Post* got my attention: "Hawaiian Marine Reserve to be World's Largest." President George W. Bush had announced plans to designate an island chain covering roughly 1,400 by 100 miles northwest of Hawaii as a national monument—the largest protected marine reserve in the world. The reserve would have been nearly 140,000 square miles, an area nearly the size of Montana, to which access would be strictly controlled. I immediately recalled the alien base allegedly located within that area, and wondered if there was a connection.

34. Corso, Col. Philip J., *The Day After Roswell*, Pocket Books, Simon & Schuster, New York, 1997, pp. 264–5, 268.

35. It will be recalled that Barbara Beavers was told by the aliens on board a craft in Yucca Valley, California, in November 1977 that the propulsion system included a "cloud chamber consisting of plasma and electromagnetism" (Chapter 12). It is also worth mentioning that research by physicists into plasma fields has been ongoing officially for a number of years: "There is a wide range of possible applications of plasma aerodynamics," says Dr. Sergey B. Leonov, a professor at the Laboratory of Experimental Plasma Aerodynamics, Russian Academy of Sciences. "Not all are well-developed, but some are not far from practical realization . . ." (*Aviation Week & Space Technology*, Vol. 173, No. 38, October 24/31, 2011, p. 78.)

36. Personal interview, June 22, 2010.

37. Personal interview, June 24, 2010.

CHAPTER SIXTEEN: LEVIATHANS OF THE SKIES

1. "Memoirs of a Veteran Ufologist (1954–1999)" by Emily Crewe.

2. Dohan, Henry, *UFOs: The Pawn of His Creator*, published posthumously by David R. Kammerer, 2008, p. 49.

3. RAF Northolt currently serves as home to No. 32 (The Royal) Squadron, and to various official visitors, including British and Foreign Royalty, Heads of State and Government Ministers, as well as military personnel of the British and Foreign armed forces, in addition to civilian VIPs and various celebrities.

4. Personal communication, September 29, 2009.
5. *Exmouth Herald*, August 7, 1987.
6. Ibid., August 14, 1987.
7. Personal communications, 1987–89.
8. Stewart, Ian, "UFO experts probe Notts night sights," *Nottingham Evening Post*, December 14, 1987.
9. Personal interviews, Paris, December 12, 2000, and Gretz-Armainvilliers, November 15, 2004.
10. Haines, Dr. Richard and Guénette, Bernard, "A Large Stationary Object Above Montreal," *Alien Update*, ed. Timothy Good, Avon Books, New York, 1995, pp. 95–123.
11. Greco, Dr. Samuel, "The Williamsport Wave," *Alien Update*, ed. Timothy Good, Avon Books, New York, 1995, pp. 124–50.
12. Personal communication, October 20, 1992.
13. Personal communication from Squadron Leader J. A. Bartram RAF, Office of the Commander, Headquarters British Forces Cyprus, November 16, 1992.
14. Letter from Judy Christodoulou, *Flying Saucer Review*, Vol. 37, No. 3, Autumn 1992.
15. Personal communication, November 12, 1992.
16. Personal communication from Squadron Leader A. R. Legg MSc BEng RAF, Office of the Commander British Forces Cyprus, January 22, 2004.
17. Good, Timothy, *Need to Know: UFOs, the Military and Intelligence*, Pegasus Books, New York, 2007, pp. 431–2.
18. Personal communications, July 2008.
19. Personal communication, January 7, 1998.
20. Jasek, Martin, M.Sc., P. Eng., "Twenty-two-plus Witnesses Observe a UFO Larger than a Football Stadium," *UFO*BC Quarterly*, Vol. 4, No. 4, Fall 1999, p. 1; ufobc.ca/yukon/22eventsum.htm.
21. Kitei, Lynne D., MD, *The Phoenix Lights*, Hampton Roads, Charlottesville, VA 22902, 2000/2004, pp. 1–2, 20, 23.
22. Kean, Leslie, "Symington confirms he saw UFO 10 years ago," *Prescott Daily Courier*, March 18, 2007.
23. Kean, Leslie, *UFOs: Generals, Pilots, and Government Officials Go on the Record*, Harmony Books, New York, 2010, p. 262.
24. Personal communication, March 27, 2010.
25. Personal communication, June 11, 2011.
26. Ledger, Don and Styles, Chris, *Dark Object: The World's Only Government-documented UFO Crash*, Dell, Random House, New York, 2001.
27. Ledger, Don, *Flying Triangular UFOs: The Monsters in our Skies*, Halifax UFO International Conference, October 11, 2003. Available via donledger.com.
28. Sirisena, Ananda, "UFO Sighted near British Nuclear Research Establishment," *UFO Matrix*, Vol. 1, Issue 4, 2010.
29. Shaffer, Kim, "Triangle Passes Over Man in Bristol, Tennessee," mufontennessee.org (October 9, 2004).

30. Personal communications, April 29 and May 29, 2005.

31. Located 11 miles southwest of Cambridge, Bassingbourn Barracks served as an RAF station in World War II and as a bomber base of the U.S. Eighth Air Force. Currently it functions as a recruit training base and is home to the Army Training Regiment Bassingbourn and 2484 (Bassingbourn) Squadron Air Training Corps. The B-17 Flying Fortress *Memphis Belle* was based there and Bassingbourn features in the film of that name. The Tower Museum is located in the original control tower.

32. Martin, Andy, "Man About World," *The Independent on Sunday*, December 19, 2004.

33. Murray, Ian, "The End of the Week," *Southern Daily Echo*, December 10, 2004.

34. Kean, op. cit., pp. 73–81.

35. huffingtonpost.com, August 17, 2011.

36. Joiner, Angelia, "Possible UFO sighting," *Stephenville Empire-Tribune*, January 10, 2008.

37. Brown, Angela K., "Small Texas town abuzz over reported UFO sightings," *Seguin Gazette-Enterprise*, January 15, 2008.

38. Erdrich, Ronald W., "Frame by Frame: Unwelcome Visits," ufocasebook.com.

39. Joiner, Angelia, "UFO witness claims harassment," *Stephenville Empire-Tribune*, February 3, 2008.

40. Personal communication, February 22, 2010.

41. "The Truth is Out There: Ghostly UFOs haunting Ross-Monmouth road," *Forest of Dean & Wye Valley Review*, October 10, 2008.

42. Personal communication, February 22, 2010.

43. *Forest of Dean & Wye Valley Review*, October 10, 2008.

44. Ibid., October 24, 2008. What this reader could not have known, since it was not reported in the issue of October 10, is that Finian Handley also saw the craft earlier that evening, in the presence of his passenger.

45. Personal communication from Judith Relf BSc., February 22, 2010.

46. Personal communication, August 4, 2011. Judith Relf contacted me after hearing a broadcast on August 3, in which Mike Sewell, a sports journalist for BBC Radio 5 Live, described his encounter with a flying disc while driving through a village in Hertfordshire (see p. xx). Nicky Campbell later interviewed me on the same show.

CHAPTER SEVENTEEN: EXPLOITATION

1. According to an informed source, the USS *Chicago* is on the ocean floor somewhere near Rennell Island, straight south of Guadalcanal, about 165 miles from Cape Esperance, which is on the north shore of the northwest corner of Guadalcanal. "I don't know exactly where the wreck of the *Chicago* is," said my source, "but its position certainly isn't visible from Cape Esperance."

2. A photograph of a craft similar in some respects to the description given by the Solomon Islanders to Marius Boirayon is reproduced in the plate section. The photograph was taken in Pescara in 1961 on the shores of the Adriatic coast by the science journalist Bruni Ghibaudi, a member of the Amicizia group.

3. Boirayon, Marius, "The Dragon Snake: A Solomon Islands Mystery," *Nexus Magazine*, Vol. 10. No. 5, August–September 2003.

4. La Palma, one of the Canary Islands, has also attracted alien activity. Herr Schaffer, a Swiss engineer, related to me how in 1973 he had observed a fleet of flying saucers landing in the Caldera de Taburiente, once believed to be a huge crater but now known to be an enormous "mountain arch" area in the national park on the island. "First, two machines flew over me, about five or six hundred meters away," he said. "I couldn't move my legs and my skin tingled, after being struck by a greenish-blueish beam of light. I thought I was going to die. The machines landed below me, in the crater, where I noticed another six machines on the ground. They were all about 6.5 meters in diameter, aluminium-metallic, with antennae on top, large transparent domes, and three legs underneath. Later, when I could move again, I saw the impressions in the sand." (Personal interviews, Lausanne, November 24/December 6, 1977.)

5. Willie Durand Urbina and José A. Martínez (Project Argus), *Inexplicata*—The Journal of Hispanic Ufology, September 15, 2005. This account is based on the preliminary investigation.

6. *MUFON UFO Journal*, No. 469, May 2007, p. 17. Based on a report by Lucy Guzman, translated by Scott Corrales.

7. Report sent to me by Maria Rivera, September 5, 2009.

8. Personal communication, September 8, 2009.

9. Personal communication, November 2, 2011.

10. Personal communication, September 8, 2009.

11. Martín, Jorge, "I saw a man being kidnapped by extraterrestrials!," *EVIDENCIA OVNI* No. 1, translated by Gordon Creighton and published in *Flying Saucer Review*, Vol. 42/4, Winter 1991, pp. 10–12.

12. Chalker, Bill, *Hair of the Alien: DNA and Other Forensic Evidence for Alien Abductions*, Paraview Pocket Books, New York, 2005.

13. The story first came to light in the April–June 1962 issue of the Brazilian *SBEDV Bulletin* and was reported by João Martins in *O Cruzeiro*, December 1, 1964.

14. Creighton, Gordon, "The Amazing Case of Antônio Villas Boas," in *The Humanoids*, edited by Charles Bowen, Neville Spearman, London, 1969, pp. 200–38.

15. "Foreign Forum: Brazil—New Light on a Sexual Abduction," *Probe*, September 1980, p. 79.

16. Pablo Villarrubia Mauso, "Antônio Villas Boas: Total Abduction," ufodigest.com 2007.

17. According to Yogi teaching, the solar plexus serves as an abdominal brain and emotional center.

18. Jacobs, David M., Ph.D., *The Threat*, Simon & Schuster, New York, 1998, p. 20.

CHAPTER EIGHTEEN: SPECIAL FORCES

1. Personal communication to CUFOS, November 29, 1999.

2. Jones, William E. and Watson, Eloise G., "Pre-World War II 'Creature' Retrieval?" *International UFO Reporter*, Vol. 26, No. 4, Winter 2001/2002.
3. Wikipedia.
4. Frey, C. E. and Neff, Earl J., "The Rand Corporation UFO Document," *Official UFO*, Vol. 1, No. 4, November 1975, pp. 14–15, 50–1.
5. Good, Timothy, *Need to Know: UFOs, the Military and Intelligence*, Pegasus Books, New York, 2007, pp. 199–200.
6. Fowler, Raymond E., "What about Crashed UFOs?" *Official UFO*, Vol. 1, No. 7, April 1976, pp. 24–5, 54–8.
7. Steinman, William S., with Stevens, Wendelle C., *UFO Crash at Aztec: A Well Kept Secret*, UFO Photo Archives, Tucson, Arizona, 1986, pp. 279–82. Revelatory new material proving the Aztec case is now published in *The Aztec Incident: Recovery at Hart Canyon* by Scott and Suzanne Ramsey. Copies are available from Aztec.48 Productions, Mooresville, NC (see www.theaztecincident.com).
8. ww2.nobelprize.com plus other Internet sources.
9. Good, op. cit., p. 54.
10. "M'Arthur Greets Mayor of Naples," *The New York Times*, October 8, 1955.
11. ww2.nobelprize.com. See also *Secret History: And Why Barack Obama Must End It* by Tony Brunt, Vailima Press, P.O. Box 163072, Lynfield, Auckland 1443, New Zealand, pp. 10–14.
12. Prouty, L. Fletcher, *The Secret Team: The CIA and Its Allies in Control of the United States and the World*, Institute for Historical Review, Costa Mesa, CA 92627, 1973, p. 75.
13. "Classified film of an alien being," *Leicester Mercury*, October 13, 2008.
14. Personal communication, February 10, 2009.
15. Martín, Jorge, "Puerto Rico's Astounding UFO Situation," *The UFO Report 1992*, edited by Timothy Good, Sidgwick & Jackson, London, 1991, p. 105.
16. In Chapter 15, I cited a source who related to a friend of mine that, within five years of working on a certain project at Area 51, six of his buddies had died of cancer.
17. Personal communication, August 28, 2011.
18. Personal communication, July 17, 1995.
19. Personal communication, July 16, 2005.
20. Personal communication, August 1, 2012.
21. Personal communications, January 19, 2009 and October 9, 2011.
22. Komarek, Ed, "ET Shoot-down Over Germany?" posted at www.ufodigest.com/news/1007/shoot-down.html, October 19, 2007.
23. Good, op. cit., pp. 205–6.
24. Prouty, op. cit., pp. vii–viii.
25. Ibid., p. 3.
26. "A Three Star General speaks for the record," *UFO Universe*, October/November 1991, p. 46.
27. I officially assisted Congressman Schiff in his investigations into the Roswell

case in 1994. With a background in law, he had served as a pilot with the rank of lieutenant colonel in the New Mexico Air National Guard. In 1993, when he took up the matter with the General Accounting Office, Colonel Larry Shockley, Deputy Director of Plans and Operations in the Secretary of Defense's Congressional liaison office, warned the GAO investigator, "You've got no business getting into that." Schiff died in office in 1998, after a sudden and virulent bout of skin cancer. (For additional information on the GAO investigation, see *Need to Know*.) I also officially assisted Congressman Solomon P. Ortiz for a considerable time, and in May 2003 supplied him and a number of interested Congressmen with a special briefing document I had prepared: *Exempt from Disclosure: Military Intelligence Perspectives Pertaining to Intrusions of Unidentified Aerial and Submarine Craft*, which I requested to be circulated among those associated with the House Armed Services Committee and relevant Committees and Subcommittees (e.g., Select Intelligence). And many years ago I also assisted Senator Robert C. Byrd (D-WV), via a Counsel to the Senate Appropriations Committee, with an official investigation into the subject. None of these investigations led anywhere. It is my understanding that those members of the Senate and House of Representatives who evince an interest in the problem are seriously "discouraged" from raising the matter officially.

28. Accessed from Youtube.com (Steven Greer/William Pawelec) in 2011.

29. *Public Papers of the Presidents: Dwight D. Eisenhower, 1960*, pp. 1035–1040.

30. Dolan, Richard M., and Zabel, Bryce, *A.D. After Disclosure: The People's Guide to Life After Contact*, Keyhole Publishing Company, Rochester, New York 14692, 2010, pp. 94–5.

31. Richard Sauder's three books are essential reading on these matters: *Hidden in Plain Sight* (Keyhole Publishing Co., 2010); *Underwater and Underground Bases* (Adventures Unlimited Press, 2001); and *Underground Bases and Tunnels* (Adventures Unlimited Press, 1995).

32. Dolan and Zabel, op. cit., pp. 290–1.

CHAPTER NINETEEN: WHAT ON EARTH?

1. Good, Timothy, *Need to Know: UFOs, the Military and Intelligence*, Pegasus Books, New York, 2007, pp. 391–3. Regarding Air Force Office of Special Investigations—founded in 1948 and usually referred to as OSI—the department responsible for evaluating UFO reports allegedly is (or was) the Counterintelligence Division. Classified reports are said to be normally forwarded to the Special Access Division.

2. *The Standard*, London, August 19, 1982.

3. Corso, Col. Philip J., *The Day After Roswell*, Pocket Books, Simon & Schuster, New York, 1997, p. 54.

4. Padula, Richard, "The day UFOs hovered over Fiorentina's Stadio Artemio Franchi," BBC World Service Sport, January 4, 2013.

5. Huneeus, J. Antonio, "A Chilean Overview," *MUFON Journal*, No. 218, June 1986.

6. "A Three Star General speaks for the record," *UFO Universe*, October/November 1991, p. 47.

7. Letter from George Adamski to Emma Martinelli, January 16, 1952.

8. Miley, Michael, "Former U.S. Military Intelligence Officer Suggests Four 'Alien' Bases on Earth," *UFO Magazine*, Vol. 13, No. 3, 1998, p. 7.

9. Miley, Michael, "Room With An Alien View: Part II," *UFO Magazine*, Vol. 13, No. 5, 1998, pp. 37–8.

10. Dennett, Preston, "Project Redlight: Are We Flying The Saucers Too?" *UFO Universe*, May 1990, pp. 40–42, 59.

11. Ronald Drucker (a pseudonym used by Robert F. Dorr), "Alaska's UFO War," *UFO Report*, Vol. 2, No. 6, Winter 1975, pp. 15–17, 52, 54, 56.

12. Alexander, John B., *UFOs: Myths, Conspiracies, and Realities*, Thomas Dunne Books, St. Martin's Press, New York, 2011, pp. 164–5.

13. Breccia, Stefano, *Mass Contacts*, AuthorHouse UK Ltd., 2009, pp. 325–6.

14. Good, Timothy, *Alien Contact: Top-secret UFO Files Revealed*, William Morrow & Company, Inc., New York, 1993, pp. 104–5.

15. Good, Timothy, *Beyond Top Secret: The Worldwide UFO Security Threat*, Pan Books, London, 1997, pp. 534–5.

16. The sighting was first mentioned in *Landslide: The Unmaking of the President*, by Jane Meyer and Doyle McManus, and a follow-up report, based on interviews with Bill Paynter and Norman Miller, appeared in an article by Alan Smith and Ken Potter in the *National Enquirer*, October 11, 1988.

17. openminds.tv/spielberg-confirms-reagan

18. www.presidentialufo.com

19. Speech by President Mikhail Gorbachev at the Grand Kremlin Palace, Moscow, February 16, 1987, published in *Soviet Life* (supplement), May 1987, p. 7A.

20. Interview on Channel RAI TRE, "Che Tempo Che Fa," October 29, 2006.

21. *Daily Mail* (online), September 19, 2012.

22. Neilsen, James (Anthony Kimery), "Gov't. Source Describes UFO Brief," *UFO Magazine*, Vol. 4, No. 2, 1989, p. 10.

23. Letter from Linda Casey Poepsel, Assistant to President Bush, Office of George Bush, Houston, Texas 77024, July 2, 2003.

24. Good, Timothy, *Need to Know: UFOs, the Military and Intelligence*, Pegasus Books, New York, pp. 420–1.

25. Prouty, L. Fletcher, *The CIA, Vietnam and the Plot to Assassinate John F. Kennedy*, Birch Lane Press, 1992, pp. 336–7.

26. Good, Timothy, *Alien Base: The Evidence for the Extraterrestrial Colonization of Earth*, Avon Books, New York, 1999, pp. 138–9.

27. Carlsen, Ragnvald Anders, *Gensing Garden News*, Denmark, November–December 2009, p. 18.

28. thinkquest.org

29. Good, *Alien Base*, p. 139.

30. Crewe, Emily, *Memoirs of a Veteran Ufologist (1954–1999)*, given to me by the author.

31. Dohan, Henry, *UFOs: The Pawn of His Creator*, published posthumously by David R. Kammerer (second, revised edition), 2008, P.O. Box 96701, Las Vegas, Nevada 89193, p. 124.

32. See *The Last Days of Marilyn Monroe* by Donald H. Wolfe, and *Beyond Roswell* by Michael Hesemann & Philip Mantle.

33. Burleson, Donald R., Ph.D, "Marilyn Monroe & UFOs," *MUFON UFO Journal*, No. 397, May 2001, pp. 5–6.

34. "Harvey Jack McGeorge/Jimmy Carter Briefing," supplied to the author in September 2003.

35. Kwek, Glenda, "Out of this world: Russian region leader's alien abduction story shakes officials," May 6, 2010. (Internet)

36. Robbie Graham, silverscreensaucers.blogspot.co.uk—May 17, 2012.

37. Wikipedia.

38. Robbie Graham, op. cit.

39. Madsen, Wayne, "Obama's Deep CIA Connections Revealed," real-agenda.com—May 29, 2011.

40. "Americans favor Obama to defend against space aliens: poll," *Aerospace & Defense News*, June 27, 2012.

41. "Dmitry Medvedev muses on aliens and Vladimir Putin's lateness," *The Telegraph*, London (online), December 8, 2012.

42. *The Moscow Times*, Issue 5032, December 11, 2012.

43. Berliner, Don and Huneeus, Antonio, *Unidentified Flying Objects Briefing Document: The Best Available Evidence*, copyrighted and presented by the UFO Research Coalition, formed by the Center for UFO Studies (CUFOS), Fund for UFO Research (FUFOR) and the Mutual UFO Network (MUFON), November 1995.

44. *Les OVNI et la Défense: A quoi doit-on se préparer?* An independent report by COMETA, published in *VSD* magazine, GS Press-Communications, 1999.

45. Huneeus, Antonio, "The famous Rockefeller UFO Briefing Document," September 3, 2010. openminds.tv/rockefeller-ufo-211

46. Hansen, Terry, *The Missing Times: News Media Complicity in the UFO Cover-up*, Xlibris Corporation, 2000, p. 299.

47. *China Daily*, August 27, 1985, translated for the author by Zhang Laigui, Air Attaché, Embassy of the People's Republic of China, London, January 25, 1986, who commented that he regarded the article as "an official statement and viewpoint of the Chinese government."

48. "China bids for the first world UFO conference," *Asian Times*, London, June 14, 1992.

49. Harris, Paola Leopizzi, *Connecting the Dots: Making Sense of the UFO Phenomenon*, Wild Flower Press, 2003, pp. 42–7.

50. Dolan, Richard M., and Zabel, Bryce, *A.D. After Disclosure: The People's Guide to Life After Contact*, Keyhole Publishing Company, Rochester, New York 14692, 2010, p. 253.

51. Ibid., p. 251, citing "Extraterrestrial Life and Religion: The Alexander UFO Religious Crisis Survey" by Victoria Lacas, in *UFO Religions*, edited by James R. Lewis, Prometheus Books, 2003, pp. 359–370.

52. "Harvey Jack McGeorge/Jimmy Carter Briefing."

53. Pisa, Nick, "There's life on other planets says Pope," *Daily Express*, London, May 12, 2008.

54. Good, *Alien Base*, pp. 136–8.

55. Carlsen, Ragnvald Anders, *Gensing Garden News*, Denmark, November-December 2009, p. 19.

56. Letter from Stan Kelly-Bootle, London N2, *The Sunday Times*, March 2, 2008.

57. Luke 1: 26–35, *The New English Bible: New Testament*, Oxford University Press/ Cambridge University Press, 1961.

58. Luke 2: 9–15.

59. Matthew 2: 9.

60. John 8: 23.

61. Acts 1: 9–11.

62. Acts 22: 6–9.

63. Kersten, Holger, *Jesus Lived in India*, Penguin Books, India, 2001.

64. Petersen, John L., *The Road to 2015: Profiles of the Future*, The Arlington Institute, Arlington, West Virginia, 1994/1998, p. 329. The Institute's current address is: P.O. Box 861, Berkeley Springs, West Virginia 25411.

65. Fry, Dr. Daniel W., *The White Sands Incident*, Best Books Inc., Louisville, Kentucky 40218, 1966, pp. 70–71.

66. Milner, Conan, "White House claims no extraterrestrials," *The Epoch Times*, U.K. edition, November 30–December 6, 2011.

67. Duper, Nikola, "The Story of 'Friendship.'"

68. Article by Mike Wall, SPACE.com senior writer, January 10, 2011.

69. "Little green men, big red face," in "Weird but wonderful," *The Sunday Times*, April 11, 2010.

70. Corso, Col. Philip J. (Ret.) with William J. Birnes, *The Day After Roswell*, Pocket Books, New York, NY 10020, 1997, p. 269.

71. Bekkum, Gary S., "A Disturbing Tale: Why we may never see government UFO disclosure," *American Chronicle*, June 30, 2009.

72. U.S. Government Accounting Office, GAO/NSIAD-96-64, Defense Industrial Security.

73. Bekkum, op. cit.

74. Neilson, James (Anthony Kimery), "Secret US/UFO Structure," *UFO Magazine* (U.S.), Vol. 15, No. 9, 2000, p. 28.

75. Cervé, Wishar S., *Lemuria: The Lost Continent of the Pacific*, Supreme Grand Lodge of AMORC, The Rosicrucian Press, San Jose, California, Sixteenth Edition, 1980, pp. 256–76. Also recommended in this context is *The Problem of Lemuria: The Sunken Continent of the Pacific* by Lewis Spence, Rider & Co., London, 1935.

76. Martin, K., "The Lemurians of Mount Shasta," *Fate*, Vol. 60, No. 11, November 2007, pp. 20–21.

77. Jessup, M.K., *The Case for the UFO*, Citadel Press, New York, 1955; Bantam Books, New York, 1955.

78. Farish, Lucius, "Contact With the Old Ones," *Fate*, Vol. 54, No. 9, September 2001.

79. See *The Comte de St. Germain: The Secret of Kings* by Isobel Cooper-Oakley, Samuel Weiser Inc., New York, 1970. Originally published in Italy in 1912.

80. Not all abductions necessarily have sinister motives. For example, many years ago Lt. Col. Wendelle C. Stevens (USAF, ret.) related to me a case, investigated by Jaime Rodriguez, involving José and his wife Graciola plus more than half a dozen Indian women in Ecuador who in the mid-1990s had been artificially impregnated (consciously, I recall) by aliens. The fetuses were removed after three months. Like the case of Julio Fernández, who in 1978 was taken on board a craft in Spain by humanoids (see *Unearthly Disclosure*), the beings in Ecuador claimed their race was declining due to a decrease of emotions. They explained what they were doing as they conducted the procedures. José and Graciola subsequently became very knowledgeable on many subjects and their psychic perceptions were stimulated. Scientists, psychologists, hypnotherapists, and a polygraph examiner were impressed by the witnesses' testimony.

81. Duper, op. cit.

ACKNOWLEDGMENTS

A
s ever, it would be impracticable to acknowledge all those who have
contributed directly or indirectly to this book, but I would like to
record my thanks in particular to the following (some now deceased):
John Axline and the *Helena Independent Record*; Bexley *News Shopper*;
Birch Lane Press and the Institute for Historical Review; Capt. Ray
Bowyer; Robert Bracken; Edward Bradley; Trevor Brookes and the *Teesdale
Mercury*; Nicky Campbell and BBC Radio Five Live; The Carter Center;
Billy Cox and *Florida Today*; Gaspare De Lama; Paolo Di Girolamo;
Richard M. Dolan; Nikola Duper; the Dwight D. Eisenhower Presiden-
tial Library and Museum; Sandra L. Edison; *Exeter Express & Echo*; *Fate
Magazine*; *Flying Saucer Review*; Becca Gliddon, Simon Horn, and the
Exmouth Journal; Dr. Samuel D. Greco; Dr. Steven Greer; Jean-Gabriel
Greslé; Leonard Griffie; Bill Hamilton; Finian Handley; John Hanson and
Dawn Holloway; Tony Harnden and *The Daily Telegraph*; Mike Hathway,
Victoria Hawkes, and Copyprint Bromley; *Huffington Post*; David M.
Jacobs, Ph.D; Martin Jasek and UFO*BC; Gösta Johansson; Angelia Joiner
and the *Stephenville Empire-Tribune*; William "Bill" Jones and the Center
for UFO Studies (CUFOS); David R. Kammerer; Leslie Kean; Sam Kean
and *Air & Space Smithsonian*; Manuel W. Kirklin; Linda Ladysmithe;
John Lear; Don Ledger; Denny Lombard; Tina Luton; Andy Martin and

The Independent on Sunday; Jorge Martín; Mark McCandlish; Henry W. McElroy, Jr.; Gary McKinnon; The Ministry of Defence; Lt. Col. Gregory Molesworth; MUFON UFO Journal; NASA; James Neff; Amy O'Brien; Darren Perks; Maj. Hans C. Petersen; John L. Petersen; Nick Pope; Judith Relf; Tony Rose and the *Nottingham Evening Post*; Pamela Rossiter; Shane Ryan; *Scottish Daily Record*; Kim Shaffer; Roy Shaw; Ananda Sirisena; Brad Sorensen; Lt. Gen. Thomas P. Stafford; Glenn Steckling and the George Adamski Foundation; William Steinman; the Swiss Directorate of Military Aerodromes; Capt. Bill Uhouse; Willie Durand Urbina and José A. Martínez of Project Argus; U.S. Air Force; Michael Vladeck; Dorothee Walter; Ed Walters; Bruce and Priscilla Wetherill; Brig. Gen. Simon "Pete" Worden; Bryce Zabel.

I am especially indebted to the following: Carl Anderson, for extensive use of material from his rare book and from a public lecture; "Andy," for his impressive account of an enormous craft, accompanied by smaller ones, observed for hours above a hotel in Cyprus; my partner Anne, for helpful advice, acting as interpreter during our two research trips to Italy in 2010, and for her photographs of Stefano Breccia and myself; Shawn Atlanti and Barbara Beavers, for the latter's account of her experience in an alien craft; Håkan Blomqvist, the distinguished Swedish researcher, for kindly allowing me the use of much material from his book and articles on the disturbing encounters of Richard Höglund; Professor Stefano Breccia, for numerous extracts from his book and for unstintingly providing me with so many crucial new revelations relating to the Amicizia saga, during and following my two visits to Italy; Art Campbell, for so magnanimously sending me all his research material pertaining to President Eisenhower's meeting with aliens at Holloman Air Force Base in 1955; Jonathan Caplan, QC, for his foreword; Emily Crewe, for input on new information relating to George Adamski; Leo Dworshak's family for the use of a great deal of material from Leo's book; Margaret Fry, for her friendship and support over the years and for generously sharing her reports on the Bexleyheath flying saucer landings; Col. Charles ("Chuck") Halt, for new information relating to the Rendlesham Forest incident; Claiborne Hancock, editor-in-chief and publisher at Pegasus Books, for his patience and support, as well as Maria Fernandez, book designer and typesetter, and Phil Gaskill, copyeditor, both also at Pegasus, for their exemplary professionalism in checking my manuscript and material relating thereto; Pamela Handford, for her revelations regarding the Apollo 11 landing; Paola Harris, for the manuscript by Lt. Col. Philip J. Corso describing his encounter with an alien being at the White Sands Missile Range; Tom L. Keller, for revelations by Ben Rich, and additional input; Jon "Andy" Kissner, for his many helpful insights; Ed Komarek, for his report on the U.S. Army shoot-down of a UFO in Germany and its subsequent recovery by the U.S. Air Force; Paul LaViolette, Ph.D., for permission to cite some revelatory material from his book; Andrew Lownie, my agent, for all his support over the last twenty-five years; Leonard Mantle, for his detailed report of encounters with an alien in central London; Bobby Mendoza and Josef Wanderka, for their credible tales from the Vienna Woods; Bob Oechsler, for his contribution regarding the Cosmic Journey project; Jim Oglesby, for extensive extracts from his book on encounters with unknown craft near or at Cape Canaveral, Florida, during the early years of the space program; Barry Potter, for much help with my chapter on the Dworshak brothers' encounters; Maria M. Rivera, for her detailed accounts of the numerous intrusions—including abductions—which she and her family have endured for several years in Puerto Rico; Duncan Roads of *Nexus* magazine, for the reports by Marius Boirayon of an alarming alien situation in the Solomon Islands; Margaret Sheppard, for translations from Italian in connection with the Amicizia case; Fred Steckling, for the wealth of insights he gave me; Ian Taylor, for considerable input relating to his observation of a giant UFO seen by thousands in the Aberdeen area, a report of two Territorial Army recruits who encountered an alien being during an exercise, and new insights relating to spacecraft propulsion; "Thomas," for the remarkable account of the year and a half he spent with a small team looking after two aliens at a British military base; Alan G. Tolman, for his accounts of a meeting with intelligence officials while employed by Douglas Aircraft and the dramatic description of a landed craft on George Adamski's property in California; Dr. Milton J. Torres, for his unofficial report of an encounter with a large UFO off the East Anglian coast, released by the Ministry of Defence; Noe Torres and Ruben Uriarte, for extensive material from their book describing Col. Robert B. Willingham's examination of a crashed alien craft and additional related material, also for Ruben's input—together with Steven Reichmuth—on "flying humanoids"; Harold Varnam, for his reports on an indoctrination film relating to Roswell shown to his British Army colleagues plus a detachment of the U.S. Fifth Army in Germany, and an encounter with an unknown, low-level craft during a NATO exercise in Norfolk; Philip and Teresa Waterhouse, for the latter's report on observations of a man-made flying disc and flying triangle during restricted airshows at two U.S. Air Force bases.

As always, my gratitude also extends to those who have helped but must remain anonymous.

ABOUT THE AUTHOR

TIMOTHY GOOD is widely regarded as one of the world's leading civilian authorities on alien phenomena, known for his integrity and determination as a highly skilled researcher. He has lectured at the Royal Canadian Military Institute, Royal Naval Air Station Portland, the House of Lords All-Party UFO Study Group, the Institute of Medical Laboratory Sciences, and the Oxford and Cambridge Union societies. He also lectures frequently at schools. He was invited to discuss his subject at the Defense Airborne Reconnaissance Office at the Pentagon in May 1998, and at the headquarters of the French Air Force in 2002. He has also acted as consultant for several U.S. Congress investigations.

Good's first book, *Above Top Secret* (Sidgwick & Jackson, 1987), became an instant bestseller in the U.K. and Australia and was subsequently published by Morrow in the U.S. and in many other countries. Further books include *Alien Liaison* (Century, 1991), published in the U.S. as *Alien Contact* (Morrow, 1993); *Alien Base* (Century, 1998; Avon, 1999); *Unearthly Disclosure* (Century, 2000); and *Need to Know: UFOs, the Military & Intelligence* (Sidgwick & Jackson, 2006; Pegasus Books, 2007). Several of these titles became *Sunday Times* bestsellers. Four of Good's books have a supportive foreword by Admiral of the Fleet The Lord Hill-Norton, former Chief of the Defence Staff and Chairman of the NATO Military Committee.

A member of the National Union of Journalists, Timothy Good has drawn some of his best evidence from the several thousand intelligence documents—many previously classified Top Secret—as well as compelling photos and inside information he has acquired over the years. As *Sunday Times* defense correspondent James Adams wrote: "The evidence that Good has amassed is too overwhelming to ignore. . . ."

Timothy Good is also a professional violinist. He was a member of the London Symphony Orchestra for fourteen years and has played with all London's major orchestras. For twenty years he was involved mostly with feature films, television dramas and commercials, and recordings with pop musicians, including George Harrison, Elton John, Sir Paul McCartney, and U2. Nowadays he freelances mostly for chamber and symphony orchestras. He is a member of the Royal Society of Musicians.

INDEX